In Memory of

Kelly Hilty

From

The Class of

1999

THE PURINA™
ENCYCLOPEDIA
OF CAT CARE

THE PURINA™
ENCYCLOPEDIA OF CAT CARE

AMY D. SHOJAI

Ballantine Books · New York

A Ballantine Book
Published by The Ballantine Publishing Group

Copyright © 1998 by Amy D. Shojai

Introduction copyright © 1998 by Dr. Jim Humphries

Illustrations copyright © 1998 by Judith Soderquist Cummins

http://www.randomhouse.com

LIBRARY OF CONGRESS CATALOGING-IN-PUBLICATION DATA
Shojai, Amy, 1956–
    The Purina encyclopedia of cat care / Amy Shojai.—1st ed.
       p.   cm.
    Includes index.
    ISBN 0-345-41287-7 (alk. paper)
    1. Cats—Encyclopedias.   I. Ralston Purina Company.   II. Title.
SF442.2.S48   1998
636.8'089—dc21   97-36133

Text design by Holly Johnson

Cover design by Min Choi

Cover photos © Ron Kimball (left), © Robert Dowling/Picture Perfect (right)

Manufactured in the United States of America

First Edition: April 1998
10   9   8   7   6   5   4   3   2   1

For all the furry wonders
who have touched my soul—

Especially for Mahmoud,
who makes it all possible,

for Serendipity,
the new kid on the block,

and for Fafnir, my furry muse.
Still missing you.

Contents

Acknowledgments

This book would not have been written without the help of many people.

I began my love affair with cats and dogs as a child; thank God my parents never thought it strange I preferred stuffed animals to dolls. Mom and Dad, thank you, especially for your sense of humor.

I can't thank my husband, Mahmoud, enough for his unfailing support of my furry obsession, even though at times he finds it hard to understand. And to the Monday night Dream Chasers, the best friends anyone could have. You have been my cheerleaders, confidants, and critics (always in a good way!). I must also thank my colleagues in the Cat Writers' Association, Inc., who have offered technical support and, more important, their friendship along the way. May all your royalty checks have commas.

Countless veterinary teachers and researchers across the nation have given freely of their expertise to answer my questions over the years. In particular, I must thank the veterinary professionals at: Auburn University, Cornell University, Ohio State, Texas A&M, Tufts University, University of California at Davis, University of Florida, University of Minnesota, and University of Pennsylvania. I'd particularly like to thank Dr. Jim Humphries and Dr. Dottie LaFlamme, and especially Dr. James Richards—you know all the reasons why.

Grateful thanks to Kerry Lyman at Purina, who believed in the book before it was ever written; to my editors, Joanne Wyckoff, who had the vision to choose the book and the patience to make it work, and Elizabeth Zack, who pulled everything together and made me look good; and especially to my agent, Meredith Bernstein, who made this writer's dreams come true.

Finally, thanks be to the cats—to those who live in our past, our present, and our future. Without you, this book would never have been written.

—AMY D. SHOJAI

Introduction

After twenty years of veterinary practice, and now as a consultant for the pet-supply industry, I can honestly say that there has never been a single source of concise information that I could confidently recommend to cat lovers who wanted a greater understanding of their pets. Now here it is, from A to Z—or nose to tail! This fine work is an exhaustive reference guide for anyone who loves cats and wants to know more. It's superbly organized and gives the reader just the right amount of background, science, facts, and helpful hints to deliver "just what the doctor ordered!"

This book is not shy about telling you how to correct a problem *at home*—saving you money on visits to the vet's office. But it also makes it clear when *it is time* to seek the expert advice and services of your doctor of veterinary medicine. Knowledge of this kind could make the difference between money-saving and lifesaving decisions.

In today's busy world, things are judged by "how fast" they work for you. The days of wading through page after page of text, searching for golden nuggets hidden in the pages of a book crafted by a skilled wordsmith, are over. Thank goodness! With this book you can, within minutes, read, reference, study, and recall truly useful information, all without cybersurfing through megabytes of useless trivia. This comprehensive work demands a coveted place on your home bookshelf, so that anyone in your home will know where to go for home remedies, first-aid tips, facts for school, and simply solving that age-old hunger to know.

Amy Shojai has culled out the most important in these handy reference blocks of information that outline symptoms, home care, veterinary care, and prevention. I like that.

I especially appreciated the information about cat breeds! Oddly enough, it's something they don't teach in vet school. Also, for a book endorsed by a major pet-food manufacturer, I found the nutrition section unbiased, factual, and complete.

Another unique feature of this book is the underlying gentleness conveyed by the words. Without saying it, practically every page of this book recognizes the special bond between cats and humans. Amy's clear sensitivity to this special relationship is evident without being overly emotive.

I believe this great reference book will set the pace for such material far into the future. This is an invaluable resource for vet clinics, grooming salons, pet shops, cat shows, product development companies, libraries, humane societies, and all those other places where there is a need for quick access to information. I believe its greatest value, however, will be for the people who share their home with a cat or two. My copy will never be far from my desk.

—JIM HUMPHRIES, DVM

Abscess

An abscess is a pocket of infection. When an injury occurs, the body attempts to protect itself by sending specialized cells to attack invading substances, such as bacteria. The body builds a wall to seal off and contain the invader, and in the process also traps dead cells and other liquid debris. Commonly called pus, this liquid material is the end product of the body's fight against infection. The battlefield itself is the abscess, a pocket of tissue that swells as it collects the pus.

Anything that breaks the integrity of the skin can cause an abscess. Foreign bodies—for example, splinters, or even an insect bite—could cause problems. Cats are quite prone to abscesses because feline skin repairs itself so quickly. And when the cat's skin heals, it may actually seal in bacteria.

The vast majority of abscesses are caused by bite wounds. Cats' mouths contain a lot of infectious bacteria, and kitty teeth, though small, can cause serious puncture wounds that plant these organisms deep within the tissues. Scratches can also cause a problem, because cats may pick up bacteria on their feet from the LITTER BOX. Although abscesses can occur anywhere on the body, they appear around the face area most frequently, or on the feet and legs. They almost always occur just beneath the skin.

Abscesses are especially common in outdoor cats and intact felines because of their aggressive encounters with other cats. Elderly cats, very

ABSCESS

SYMPTOMS

Painful skin swelling or draining sore, often on the face or neck; fever; loss of appetite; lethargy

HOME CARE

Moist warm compresses, cleaning with damp cloths, supportive nutrition

VET CARE

Surgical lancing and draining, sometimes antibiotic therapy

PREVENTION

Prevent cat fights by neutering and spaying, and by confining cats indoors

young cats, and cats whose IMMUNE SYSTEMS are compromised tend to have more serious reactions than healthy adult cats.

Diagnosis is usually made from the symptoms, which may at first be very subtle. A bite wound or claw injury is often hidden by fur, but can be painful even before it abscesses. The affected cat may flinch or even vocalize when the owner touches the painful area.

As the infection progresses and pus begins to collect, the area beneath the skin swells. The cat may act lethargic and may not want to eat. Abscesses generally grow outward, causing the surface skin to stretch and become quite thin. Often, the abscess will rupture, expelling a blood-tinged white-to-yellow discharge. While this looks nasty, it actually makes the cat feel much better because the infection has an outlet.

The infection typically results in a fever. A TEMPERATURE over 103 degrees may indicate that the infection has spilled into the bloodstream and spread throughout the system. Only rarely does the abscess rupture inward. If this happens, serious life-threatening problems can develop.

a

Abscesses left too long without treatment can severely damage or even kill surrounding tissue, which sloughs and falls away. The resulting large skin wounds heal very slowly, if at all.

Prompt treatment will prevent such complications. Once you are able to feel a cat's abscesses, most veterinarians recommend opening and draining them surgically.

To drain the abscess, the cat is usually sedated, because abscesses are usually so sore that the cat will not allow treatment otherwise. Once the cat is comfortably sedated, the hair around the swelling is shaved and the skin disinfected with a Betadine or Nolvasan solution. Then the abscess is lanced, usually with a sterile surgical blade or scalpel. The infectious material inside is flushed from the wound with a disinfectant solution like peroxide.

If the wound is extensive, the veterinarian may secure into place a tube to keep the skin from healing too quickly and to allow the pus to continue to drain. Otherwise, the skin will simply close over the infection, and the abscess will return. Drains are left in place for two to four days, and then removed. It may be necessary for the cat to wear an ELIZABETHAN COLLAR to prevent him from undoing the veterinarian's work. The wound may be packed with disinfectant, and often an injectable antibiotic is given, followed by oral antibiotics for the owner to administer at home.

Depending on the extent of the wound and its location, the veterinarian may completely or only partially close the opening with stitches. Sometimes it's left open to allow the body to heal and for the wound to close by itself.

Even when cats have lost large amounts of tissue, surrounding skin may stretch enough to cover the area. Luckily, cats tend to have quite a bit of "extra" or loose skin they can move around in. However, the face, lower legs, and feet have little surplus skin, so abscesses and tissue loss in these areas can cause scarring and disfigurement.

One of the best ways to prevent abscesses is to make sure the cat's skin remains healthy by regular GROOMING and FLEA prevention. But preventing a bite or scratch is even better. Keep your cat inside to stop roaming and contact with strange cats. NEUTERING curbs male aggression—SPAYING may stem female roaming.

a

Acne

This relatively common skin disease of the chin and lower lip is seen in cats of all ages. Acne occurs when the hair follicles become plugged.

Sebaceous glands in the skin secrete a thick, semiliquid fatty material called sebum. It coats and protects a cat's fur, giving it a healthy sheen. When hair follicles become plugged, the sebum is unable to escape, creating clogged pores that are a perfect environment for bacteria to grow.

The exact cause of feline acne remains unclear, but the most common theory is a lack of cleanliness. Most cats are particular about GROOMING themselves, but the chin is difficult to reach. A dampened front paw may not be sufficient to clean away dirt and accumulated oils. Cats with oily skin are more prone to acne, as are cats fed wet food,

ACNE

SYMPTOMS

Blackheads and pimples, red or swollen skin, itchiness or pain on the chin

HOME CARE

Apply damp heat to chin daily, clean twice daily with plain water or use cleansers such as benzoyl peroxide–type solutions

VET CARE

When infected: clip fur and professionally clean with oral or topical antibiotic prescriptions

PREVENTION

Feed cat from nonplastic food bowls, keep chin clean

which may stick to the chin. Cats who sleep with their chins resting on hard surfaces or on dirt also may develop acne.

The first signs are blackheads and pimples that erupt on the chin and lower lip. They may not bother the cat at all, and are often overlooked by owners because they're hidden by fur. But secondary bacterial infections may develop. The area can become reddened, swollen, and either itchy or painful. Severe cases of feline acne result in the chin swelling and the lip thickening. Often referred to as "fat chin," the swelling may make the affected cat look as if he's pouting. Never try to "squeeze out" blackheads or pustules; this can be painful for the cat and may spread infection beneath the skin and cause deeper infections.

In many instances where the cat is not bothered by the condition, the blackheads do not require treatment. But if the area becomes infected, the recommended veterinary treatment includes gently clipping away the fur and cleansing the area with medicated preparations. Infection generally responds to twice-daily cleansing with a 2.5 to 5 percent preparation of benzoyl peroxide (OxyDex), povidone-iodine (Betadine), or chlorhexidine (Nolvasan). Cats with oily skin may benefit from a tar and sulfa shampoo made for cats. However, scrubbing too vigorously, or using medication that is too strong, can make the condition worse. Often, the acne will return once treatment is stopped, and some cats will require maintenance therapy of a topical medication every two to seven days for the rest of their lives.

With stubborn, deep infections, oral and topical antibiotics may be required, or even treatment with certain human preparations like Retin-A, which helps normalize the skin.

Changing bowls to shallower dishes may help keep your cat's chin cleaner and less prone to problems. Metal, ceramic, or glass containers are more easily cleaned than plastic dishes, which seem to cause reactions in some cats. Changing your cat's bed to softer material, such as a blanket that's regularly washed, may also help with cats who habitually prop their chins on hard surfaces. And regularly cleaning your cat's chin will help prevent recurrences of acne.

So, once a day, dip a cloth in warm water, wring it out, and place it against the cat's chin until the cloth cools. Damp heat helps open clogged pores.

Administering of Medication

At some point, every cat owner will need to medicate his or her cat. The procedure is a daunting one, since most cats resist being forced to do anything. The sight of their sharp teeth and claws gives even experienced veterinarians pause.

Yet topical treatments such as lotions and creams, oral preparations such as pills or liquids, and even injectable medication can all be given at home, if the owner knows how. Handled correctly, medicating at home can be far less stressful to the cat than trips to the veterinarian's office.

It's helpful to have two people for any procedure—one to restrain the cat, the other to apply the medicine. Using a cat sack, or wrapping the cat in a towel or blanket first, may also be helpful. For some confident owners who have established a trusting relationship with their cats, such restraints may not be necessary (see RESTRAINT).

Topical Treatments: Cats generally tolerate *skin medications* well without restraints, unless the area is quite tender to the touch. But because cats are such unremitting self-groomers, care must be taken that the medication is not licked off. Follow your veterinarian's instructions regarding application. Some medication may be noxious enough to prevent your cat from licking, but don't depend on that. Distract the cat by playing with him, or hold him for fifteen minutes or so until the medication is dry or absorbed.

Medicating ears can usually be done with minimal restraint, unless the ears are extremely sore. Tip the cat's head so that the affected ear opening is directed at the ceiling, and simply drip in the medication. Let gravity move the medication inside the ear; don't stick anything inside. Typically, after liquids or ointments are applied, you should gently massage the outside base of the ear to spread the medicine. (See also EAR MITES.)

Eye medication should be administered without actually touching the cat's eye. For liquids, tip the cat's head toward the ceiling and drip the prescribed number of drops into the affected eye. For ointments, gently pull down the lower eyelid and squeeze the medication into the

 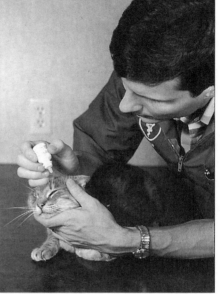

Administering medication to the ears. (*Photo credit: Amy D. Shojai*)

Administering medication to the eyes. (*Photo credit: Amy D. Shojai*)

cupped tissue, or simply apply the ointment into the corner of the eye. Then gently close the cat's eyelid to spread the medicine over the eye's surface.

Oral Treatments: Oral medications come as liquids, pastes, or pills. *Liquids and pastes* are the easiest to use, and often employ squeeze bottles, eyedroppers, or syringe applicators to squirt the medication into the cat's mouth. Insert the tip of the applicator between the cat's lips in the corner of his mouth, tip his head back, and deposit the medicine into his cheek. Watch to make sure he swallows and doesn't spit it out.

You may need to gently hold the cat's mouth closed with one hand and watch his throat until you see him swallow. Licking his nose is often a signal that he has swallowed. Most oral preparations are flavored to appeal to the cat and are readily taken. Some paste medications, particularly those that are specifically for HAIRBALLS, can simply be spread on the cat's paw for him to lick off and swallow through grooming.

Pilling a cat involves opening the cat's mouth, placing the capsule or tablet on the back of his tongue, closing his mouth, and inducing him

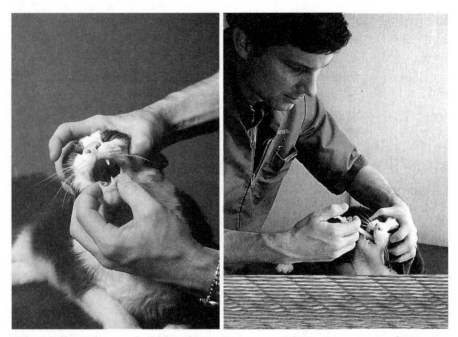

When pilling the cat, hold head as shown. *(Photo credit: Amy D. Shojai)* **Have a vet demonstrate use of a pill syringe first.** *(Photo credit: Amy D. Shojai)*

to swallow. You may want to use a cat bag or other restraint for this maneuver, although sometimes it's easier without. Try kneeling on the floor with the cat between your legs facing out, so he can't squirm away.

Place the palm of your left hand over the cat's head so that your thumb is on one side of the cat's head and your middle finger is on the other and they fit behind the cat's upper canine (long) tooth on each side. Then tilt the cat's head back so he's looking at the ceiling. Gently press the cat's lips against his teeth to encourage him to open his mouth. (*Note:* Pressing one finger against the roof of your cat's mouth will also induce him to open wide. In addition, you can use a finger from your other hand to gently press down on his lower teeth and prop the mouth open.) Then quickly drop the pill as far back on his tongue as possible. Hold his mouth closed and stroke his throat until you see him swallow.

You may choose to use a *pill syringe*, available at most pet-supply stores, rather than risk your fingers when pilling your cat. Ask your veterinarian to demonstrate its use, though, so that you don't risk damaging the back of your cat's throat.

If pills are problematic, you may succeed by hiding the medication in a veterinarian-approved treat. Mixing medicine with food in the bowl isn't a good idea, because the cat won't get the full effect unless every bite is eaten. Hiding a pill in a hunk of cheese doesn't work well either, since most cats will eat the cheese and leave the pill behind.

Unless the medication is a time-release treatment that's supposed to dissolve slowly, the pill can be crushed and mixed into a strong-tasting treat. Powder the pill with the bowl of a spoon, mix into one or two bites of a strong-smelling canned food, and feed to the cat. Offer it before meals to make sure every bit is eaten.

Always give your cat positive attention following successful medication. Praise him, play with him, and if approved by your veterinarian, offer a tasty food reward so the next time will go even more smoothly.

Adoption, of Cat by Human

Adoption describes the act of choosing to have a relationship with another being. A person who adopts a cat accepts responsibility for the life, health, and happiness of that cat.

Finding a cat to adopt is easy. "Free" animals are available through animal welfare organizations, friends, and newspaper advertisements. Often, a cat simply shows up on the back porch. For those seeking a particular feline look and personality, more than forty distinct cat breeds are available. Catteries breed cats to standards defined by various cat associations (see Appendix A, "Cat Associations and Cat Breeds"); these purebred and registered animals are more costly because of the expense involved in producing healthy animals of a particular type.

All cats require routine health care, nutritious food, and the basic comforts of LITTER BOX and SCRATCHING post. Successful adoptions match a cat that has the look, care demands, and personality to fulfill an owner's expectations. For instance, longhaired cats demand more GROOMING than shorthaired varieties; high-energy cats and KITTENS

a

may require greater supervision; adult cats can have bad habits that make them hard to live with; unaltered male or female cats can display obnoxious behaviors (see NEUTERING and SPAYING); and the pets you already have need consideration (see INTRODUCTION).

A number of difficulties can be avoided by adopting a healthy cat. The sickly stray who appears on your doorstep may steal your heart, but it can also run up veterinary bills. It can also expose your other pets to illness (see QUARANTINE).

A healthy cat's coat is clean and shiny. EYES, NOSE, and EARS are free of discharge, and the cat's bottom is clean without any sign of DIARRHEA. A veterinary exam is always advisable to rule out hidden problems. Reputable shelters or catteries may provide preliminary health care prior to adoption, such as basic first VACCINATIONS or discount spaying or neutering. Some offer limited guarantees on the health of the animal. However, regardless of such guarantees, your cat should be taken to your veterinarian for a physical and checkup.

Adoption of a cat—or any pet—is for the life of the animal. We do not give back the human children we adopt when circumstances become difficult; neither should an adopted pet be forsaken when he becomes an inconvenience. At its best, adoption is a joyful yet serious act, undertaken only after careful consideration.

Adoption, of Kittens (or Other Animals) by a Cat

Cats have the capacity to show strong nurturing behavior toward other animals, in addition to their own kittens. Such cats appear to develop relationships and "adopt" other animals. This behavior has often been documented in female cats who are nursing. Such cats are hormonally ready to adopt, nurse, and care for another cat's young. This urge to mother may be so strong that predatory behavior is suppressed. Cats have been known to nurse and raise baby bunnies, puppies, and even rats.

Cats that have experienced motherhood may continue to exhibit such nurturing behavior even after SPAYING. These "aunties" cuddle, wash, and ride herd on their adopted charges, and take baby-sitting duties very seriously. Even male cats sometimes show strong protective behavior and seem to enjoy fostering kittens.

In most instances, cats that adopt other kittens or animals have enjoyed positive interspecies experiences during their impressionable weeks of life (see KITTEN, Socialization).

Affection

Perhaps because people don't readily recognize feline signs of affection, cats have an undeserved reputation as aloof, solitary creatures. Cats communicate their moods, emotions, and desires in a variety of often

Cats that care for one another often cuddle together. *(Photo credit: Lillian Zahrt)*

a

subtle signs. And affection is, after all, a two-way street. The cat who is offered little interaction will return that indifference, while the beloved feline showered with attention blossoms into a loving pet. But as cats are also individuals, they do show distinct personalities.

Cats show affection to other cats—and even to dogs or other pets— by sleeping together and GROOMING each other. They indulge in subtle body contact, like bumping hips as they pass in the room. Affectionate cats share food, and enjoy playing together.

Cats show affection to humans in many of the same ways. They want to sleep on the pillow next to your face, or they groom your hair. Often, cats will solicit owners to play. Affectionate cats twine around ankles; offer head bumps, purrs, and trills; and knead with their paws to express contentment.

Some researchers are reluctant to say that animals experience the same emotions as people. And in fact, there is no way to know exactly what cats are feeling. But from every indication, cats can and do become every bit as fond of us as we are of them.

Aggression

Aggression is the forceful reaction of a cat that feels threatened. It can also be a sign of illness, for cats in pain will often lash out when touched. A cat that suddenly bites for no apparent reason should be examined by a veterinarian.

Whether a shrinking violet shy cat, or boisterous, in-your-face confident cat, any feline may become aggressive given the right circumstances. Growls, hisses, scratches, and even bites are a cat's way to take control of a situation.

Displays of hostility can result from fear or anxiety, overly enthusiastic play, predatory behavior, displaced aggression, or a combination of these or others. Once aggression is a problem, the trigger must be identified and, if possible, prevented from recurring. Physical punishment won't work, and is likely to make the aggressive behavior even worse. An aggressive cat may pose a physical danger to its owner, so diagnosis

a

These felines are behaving aggressively toward each other. *(Photo credit: Ralston Purina Company)*

and treatment of severe aggression in cats is best left to a professional animal behaviorist or therapist.

To reduce the probability of aggression in your cat, be aware of situations that are likely to provoke your cat to unbecoming behavior—for example, some cats will tolerate only limited petting. So know your cat's limits and respect them.

Cats are creatures of habit; they thrive on routine. This means any change at all could trigger fear or anxiety, which, in certain cats, can escalate into aggression. A new baby in the house, a change in your work schedule, or even the addition of new drapes may cause problems. New pets may prompt aggressive behavior in a cat who wants to assert his authority as the dominant feline. So always ease your cat into change slowly, and avoid surprises (see INTRODUCTION).

Cats not properly socialized may strike out at strange people or animals. Each cat has his own "comfort zone," which is the distance strangers can approach without the cat feeling threatened. Invade the cat's space and, if there's not a way to escape, the cat may become aggressive.

When the object of the cat's aggression is out of reach, displacement behavior can occur. Here, instead of attacking the actual culprit, the cat finds a scapegoat. For instance, a cat sitting in the window sees a dog outside invading the cat's territory. Since the cat is unable to get through the window to protect his turf, the aggression has nowhere to go. So instead, the cat redirects the aggression to something within reach—like his owner.

Be aware of the signs of aggression (see COMMUNICATION) so that you can avoid escalating a somewhat miffed cat into an attack animal. Give the cat some space and time to cool down (cats need to be left alone for up to two hours), and if you're able to identify the triggers, avoid them when possible. And remember that the rough handling of kittens encourages them to play rough, bite, and wrestle human hands and feet. So never make a person's hands and feet available as cat toys; use a play mouse or fishing toy to satisfy a cat's stalk-and-pounce urge. What's cute in a tiny kitten becomes painful or even dangerous in an adult cat. Above all, do not hesitate to seek professional help if necessary (see Appendix C, "Resources").

Allergen

See ALLERGIES.

Allergies, Cat

Allergy refers to symptoms that result from the overreaction of the IM-MUNE SYSTEM. Special cells called antibodies protect the body by attacking viruses, bacteria, and other foreign material. Sometimes these cells become overzealous, and attack otherwise harmless substances like house dust, mold, or pollen. The heightened reaction of the immune system to these substances, called allergens, causes the symptoms allergy sufferers experience. Allergies cannot be cured. Avoiding or eliminating the allergen is the only way to control symptoms. That's not easy, because multiple allergies make identification of the culprit(s) very difficult.

a

FLEA ALLERGY

SYMPTOMS

Seasonal itchiness, especially of back and tail area; hair loss; scabby skin

HOME CARE

Treat the cat and home or outside environment for fleas

VET CARE

Sometimes steroids to reduce inflammation or itchiness, veterinary-prescribed flea treatments

PREVENTION

Avoid fleas

Like people, cats may be sensitive to more than one allergen. Whether or not a cat develops symptoms depends on each individual cat's allergy threshold, which is the amount of allergen necessary to produce a reaction. If the cat has a low allergy threshold, a single allergen—say, a flea bite—may be enough to cause itching. Other cats may start itching only with exposure to multiple allergens (i.e., both flea bites and grass pollen). Eliminate enough allergens, and a cat can handle exposure to some allergens without showing any allergic signs.

Like their human companions, cats can be allergic to virtually anything. But while allergic owners often suffer watery eyes, itchy noses, and frequent sneeze attacks, allergic cats most commonly itch and develop skin disorders.

A hypersensitivity to the bite of FLEAS is the most common allergy affecting cats. Sensitive cats react to a protein in flea saliva, and as a result develop skin disease. Just one bite can make the cat itch all over. Signs are usually seasonal, occurring during flea season. A common sign is many tiny red bumps, usually along the back and around the head and neck, that become encrusted (see MILIARY DERMATITIS). Scabs may

INHALANT ALLERGY

SYMPTOMS

All-over itchiness, scabby skin

HOME CARE

Keep cat's coat and environment clean

VET CARE

Skin testing, allergy shots

PREVENTION

Avoid dust, pollens, or whatever causes the problems

be hidden by the fur, but can be felt when you stroke the cat. Other insects like LICE, EAR MITES, and MANGE may cause similar symptoms.

Effective treatment depends on eliminating the allergen. Flea control is essential for such cats, and countless products are available to safely rid the cat and his environment of the intrusive bugs.

Inhalant, or environmental allergy, is the second most common allergy in cats. Also called atopy, the condition in people is often termed *hay fever*. Cats react to the same things people do: pollen, mold, fungi, and even the house dust mite. But what makes people cough, wheeze, and have difficulty breathing causes atopic cats to typically break out in MILIARY DERMATITIS.

Eliminating the allergen means you must first identify it, which can be difficult. Blood tests are not considered reliable by most veterinarians and researchers, but intradermal skin testing can help determine what causes the cat's reaction. In these tests, suspect allergens are injected into the shaved skin of the sedated cat. In five to fifteen minutes, positive reactions result in the skin becoming swollen, red, and elevated.

But even when an owner knows his cat is allergic to grass pollen, it's difficult to eliminate exposure entirely. A cat is like a furry dust

a

FOOD ALLERGY

SYMPTOMS

Itchy face and/or vomiting and diarrhea

HOME CARE

An appropriate diet

VET CARE

Elimination diet to diagnose, sometimes prescription diet

PREVENTION

Avoid problem foods once identified

mop, collecting and holding on to environmental allergens. The best thing is to wash off as much dust, pollen, and other debris on your cat as possible.

A clean environment is key for the atopic cat. Rough surfaces like carpeting and upholstery act as reservoirs that collect and hold dust and dirt particles, while smooth surfaces like linoleum and hardwood floors are easier to clean. Vacuums with water filters are more effective than sweeping, which tends to loft particles into the air. High Efficiency Particulate Air (HEPA) filter systems can be helpful, too.

Eliminating all environmental allergens may be impossible, but other treatments can ease symptoms. Making sure your cat gets essential fatty acids may be helpful, because they promote healthy skin and fur. In the proper balance, Omega 3 and Omega 6 fatty acids are thought to reduce the inflammatory response of the skin that results from some allergies. Your veterinarian can recommend appropriate products.

Another option is immunotherapy, which consists of gradually increasing injections of the allergens to which the cat is sensitive. It's hoped these allergy shots will build your cat's resistance to the allergen and reduce sensitivity. Because improvement from immunotherapy is

a

slow, injections are usually continued for at least a year, and some cats receive maintenance injections for life.

Cats sometimes develop allergies to food ingredients. Food allergies are suspected to affect between 5 and 15 percent of cats, but often may be blamed when they're not really the culprit. A change in diet that coincides with the cat's symptom relief may be attributed to the food when it's actually due to the hay fever or flea season ending.

Signs of feline food allergies can include VOMITING and DIARRHEA, but more often include itching and scratching of the face and ears. Like all allergies, food sensitivities develop from exposure. Animals typically become allergic to proteins like beef, milk, corn, wheat, and eggs—the most common protein ingredients in commercial cat foods. And what's hypoallergenic to one cat may be highly allergenic to another.

Identifying the specific culprit is complicated, because it involves a weeks-long veterinarian-supervised elimination diet. Cats are fed a limited antigen diet containing one unique meat source and one unique carbohydrate source that they have never eaten before, like rabbit and potato or venison and rice. After the symptoms disappear, ingredients from the original diet are reintroduced one by one to see which provoke a reaction. Once the ingredient is identified, the owner finds a food without the offending ingredient and the symptoms should disappear.

The FDA says diets labeled to control specific allergies can only be prescribed and distributed by veterinarians, and there are several kinds that are available. But some owners may balk at these higher-cost prescription diets. While ultimately only a vet can diagnose a food allergy, some food-allergic cats respond well to lamb-and-rice-based commercial diets, if the cat has never been exposed to these main ingredients before. But as these lamb-and-rice-based diets may contain other ingredients to make them complete and balanced, cats can develop allergic reactions to them as well.

Only a veterinarian can diagnose an allergy. But once the offending allergen has been identified, it is up to you to eliminate or reduce exposure. Ultimately, identifying and dealing with feline allergies depends on an owner's dedication coupled with a veterinarian's expertise.

Allergies, of Humans to Cats

It's estimated that nearly 30 percent of cat owners are allergic to their cats. A specialized protein called Fel d 1 found in the saliva and skin of all cats causes the reaction. Some cats produce more of this substance than others, but there's no way to predict which cat is the least allergenic.

Microscopic particles of Fel d 1, often referred to as *dander*, are so light they remain airborne, stick to rough surfaces, and are hard to remove from the environment. Even after the cat has been removed from the home, the substance that remains in the environment can produce symptoms for up to six months.

Symptoms of an allergy to cats can be as simple as a stuffy nose and sneezing, or as complicated as a potentially fatal ASTHMA attack. Itchy eyes, skin rash or hives, runny nose, or even tightness in the chest may develop. A specialist diagnoses the allergy, and may prescribe antihistamines, decongestants, or a class of drug called allergy blockers to manage symptoms.

Immunotherapy (see ALLERGIES, CAT) is another option. In the past, such vaccinations employing components of Fel d 1 protein have not been consistently effective, often requiring months to years of treatment to help, if at all. But a new vaccine, called Allervax-Cat, uses only part of the Fel d 1 protein and promises to reduce the desensitization process to only a few weeks. Clinical trials are under way, and the product may become available in the near future.

Treating the cat is another option. Some experts advocate washing the cat weekly in plain water to dramatically reduce allergic reactions, and several products have been formulated to reduce or neutralize cat antigen. Researchers disagree on how effective these efforts may be, but they may work for you, so try them.

Just as allergic cats have an itch threshold, allergic humans have a sneeze threshold. And if a person is allergic to cats, chances are they're allergic to other allergens as well. Therefore, you can reduce your cat allergy symptoms by avoiding exposure to other allergens.

Avoid heavy odors such as perfumes, cigarette smoke, insecticides,

a

or cleaning fluids that can trigger a reaction. Choose cat LITTER carefully; the dust or deodorant in litter may cause more reactions than the cat. Good ventilation helps lower the concentration of airborne particles, and opening the window a few minutes each day to circulate the air will help. Reduce dander reservoirs; carpet accumulates cat allergen at approximately one hundred times the level of a polished floor. Vacuum daily with water filter machines that trap tiny particles, or use HEPA (High Efficiency Particulate Air) filters or air purifiers.

Cat owners who are allergic also benefit from a "cat-free zone": designate an area in your house—for example, the bedroom—and keep it off-limits to the cat. That provides you with at least eight hours of reduced exposure. Wash your hands after handling the cat, and especially avoid touching your face and eyes until after you've washed. Another family member should provide regular GROOMING of the cat to remove excess dander and hair. And providing your cat with a quality diet lessens SHEDDING and promotes healthy skin.

Aloofness

Cats described as aloof act distant, keep to themselves, and seem to prefer their own company to that of humans. Aloofness may develop as a result of poor kitten socialization, neglect (see STRAY and FERAL), or even outright abuse. But such an attitude may be that cat's normal personality (see AFFECTION).

Remember that every cat is an individual. While some outgoing "people cats" thrive on attention and closeness, others want only limited cuddling or hands-on contact. Simply sharing a room with a human companion may be an intimate encounter for these cats.

To strangers, otherwise affectionate cats may appear aloof and distant. Many cats require time to develop trust before establishing close relationships.

Alopecia

See HAIR LOSS.

Alter

See NEUTERING and SPAYING.

Amputation

Amputation refers to the surgical removal of a limb. Nerve damage from FROSTBITE or FRACTURE, infection, and diseases like CANCER may be beyond human skill to cure. When a leg or tail becomes so badly damaged that it impairs or endangers the cat's health, amputation removes the limb and preserves the integrity of the rest of the body.

Owners tend to notice the loss of the tail or leg more than the cat. Tailless cats rarely slow down at all. Most cats that lose a leg adjust quickly and do well on three legs. They may even flourish, as that which caused the long-standing pain has been removed. Cats with three legs can navigate nearly as well, and may even remain able to jump and climb.

a

Anal Gland

Two pea-size anal glands (also called anal sacs, or scent glands) are located beneath the skin on each side of the cat's rectum. They secrete a liquid or sometimes creamy light gray to brown substance that scents the cat's stool. This signature odor identifies a specific cat in the same way that names identify people, and is used in MARKING territory.

The glands are normally emptied by the pressure of defecation. Cats have few anal gland problems, but if odor is a problem as a result of overactive glands, they can be expressed manually. Impaction is uncommon in cats, but may occur if the sacs become plugged and can't empty normally. Manual emptying of the glands is the treatment, and wearing rubber gloves is recommended.

Raise the cat's tail, and find the openings, located at four o'clock

ANAL GLAND PROBLEMS

SYMPTOMS

Excessive licking of anal area, scooting, strong odor

HOME CARE

Wet warm cloths applied for 15 minutes several times daily

VET CARE

Express contents of glands, apply antibiotic ointment into gland opening; sometimes surgical lancing or removal of infected gland is necessary

PREVENTION

None

a

and eight o'clock on each side of the anus. Place your thumb and forefinger on the skin at each side of the gland, and gently squeeze as you would to express a pimple. Use a damp cloth to wipe away the strong-smelling material that appears as the sac empties.

If the discharge contains blood or pus, if there is swelling on either or both sides of the anus, or if the cat shows pain or "scoots" around on his bottom, your cat may be suffering from an infection. Treatment requires weekly expression of the glands and the application of an antibiotic directly into the sac itself; this should be done only by an experienced veterinarian. You can help the infection resolve itself by applying warm wet packs to the area for fifteen minutes several times a day.

Left untreated, anal gland infections can lead to an ABSCESS. If infections continue to recur, surgical removal of the glands may be recommended.

Anemia

The most common blood disorder in cats is anemia, which is a decrease in the normal number of red blood cells. Signs include depression, increased sleep, weakness, weight loss, rapid pulse or breathing, and pale mucous membranes.

The number of red cells is relatively fixed. Feline red blood cells live about two and a half months and are continually replaced with new ones manufactured by the bone marrow. The constant turnover is like water flowing into a bucket from the top, while flowing out of a hole at the bottom. Anemia occurs when the incoming flow is shut off, or if too much flows out the bottom.

Regenerative anemia occurs when bone marrow still functions and generates new red cells but can't keep up with the number being lost. Blood loss due to trauma or from parasites like FLEAS or the bacteria that causes HAEMOBARTONELLOSIS are the most common reasons for regenerative anemia. Some cat breeds, like Abyssinians and Somalis, may inherit red cell defects that result in regenerative anemia.

In rare instances, immune-mediated hemolytic anemia results

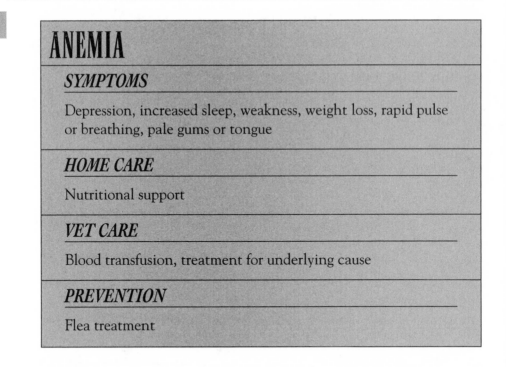

ANEMIA

SYMPTOMS

Depression, increased sleep, weakness, weight loss, rapid pulse or breathing, pale gums or tongue

HOME CARE

Nutritional support

VET CARE

Blood transfusion, treatment for underlying cause

PREVENTION

Flea treatment

when the cat's immune system misidentifies red cells as foreign, and attacks and destroys its own red blood cells. This occasionally happens in cases of haemobartonella infection.

Nonregenerative anemia occurs when the bone marrow stops making enough blood cells. This is usually associated with diseases that affect the bone marrow (see FELINE LEUKEMIA VIRUS, FELINE IMMUNO-DEFICIENCY VIRUS, and FELINE INFECTIOUS PERITONITIS).

However, chronic illness of any kind also may affect the bone marrow's ability to make new red cells, resulting in anemia or chronic disease. KIDNEY DISEASE can also cause anemia, because erythropoietin, a hormone that stimulates red cells to be produced, is made in the kidney. Cats can also have BLEEDING disorders that cause anemia when viral infections, CANCER, or other problems compromise the blood's clotting ability (see also BLOOD).

Treatment of anemia is twofold. First, the lost red cells must be replaced; this is done with blood transfusions. Some veterinary offices keep a supply of blood on hand for such situations, while many others keep an "office cat" who serves as a donor when the need arises. Of

course, the blood from both the donor and recipient cats is cross-matched to ensure compatibility.

Second, the underlying cause of the anemia is addressed. When the anemia results from parasites or trauma, eliminating the fleas or stopping the bleeding resolves the problem. Cats suffering from anemia resulting from bone marrow damage or suppression due to toxins like Tylenol often return to normal on their own. Other times, steroid therapy or anabolic hormones may stimulate the marrow to again begin producing red cells. If this doesn't work, a bone marrow transplant from a donor cat may be effective.

Unfortunately, anemia due to the feline leukemia virus cannot be cured, and the prognosis for such cats is grim. Intermittent blood transfusions along with supportive care for other secondary illnesses may help prolong the cat's life in the short term.

Anemia is best prevented by protecting your cat from exposure to viral infections and parasites.

Anesthetic

A drug used to block the sensation of touch, pressure, or pain, with or without a loss of consciousness, is called an anesthetic. Anesthetics are particularly important in feline medicine, because cats typically refuse to hold still for necessary treatment. Anesthetics can be used to prevent pain, to immobilize the cat for medical treatments, and to prevent further emotional stress to the cat.

Anesthetic drug doses are determined by the weight of the cat. Because of a cat's small size and sensitivity to such medications, the drugs will often be administered in repeated small doses until the desired effect is reached. The drugs are removed from the body by the action of the lungs, kidneys, and liver.

Local anesthetics like Xylocaine are used to block sensation on the skin surface. They may be used to treat problems such as an ABSCESS, but are not appropriate for major procedures such as SPAYING. Locals may be injected into the surrounding tissue, or applied topically as an

a

ointment, spray, or cream. A tranquilizer or sedative may also be given with a local to help make the cat easier to handle.

A general anesthetic leaves the cat unconscious, blocks the pain, and may have amnesiac properties so that a cat does not remember anything traumatic. A variety of both injectable drugs, such as Telazol, and inhalant anesthetics, such as halothane and isoflurane, are available. An inhalant anesthetic is administered either by a tube that carries the gas into the cat's lungs or by a mask that fits over the cat's face. A veterinarian may use general anesthetic alone or in combination with other drugs, depending on the health status of the cat and on the procedure to be done.

Although care is taken with the administration of any anesthetic, complications can occur. Anesthetics affect the way the heart works. Cats suffering from impaired liver, kidney, or heart function are at higher anesthetic risk. Screening tests prior to anesthesia may be recommended to evaluate and reduce possible risks.

Anorexia

Anorexia is an ongoing loss of appetite that results in a refusal to eat. A cat suffering from anorexia may also show signs of weight loss, depression, and sometimes VOMITING. Anorexia is common in cats and may be triggered by a number of things.

Some cats develop strong food preferences. These finicky felines may starve themselves rather than eat anything but their favorite meal (see FOOD). But most often, cats stop eating because they feel bad either physically or emotionally. The STRESS of any change in routine, such as moving to a new home, an absent owner, or a new pet, may prompt an aversion to food.

Pain, fever, and metabolic disorders can also cause a loss of appetite. UPPER RESPIRATORY INFECTIONS, common disorders that result in stuffy nasal passages, can also trigger anorexia. To cats, the smell of food is more important than taste, and nothing spoils their dinner faster than a stopped-up nose.

A refusal to eat can make well cats sick, and sick cats even sicker.

There are few, if any, conditions where withholding food from a cat is necessary; chronic DIARRHEA or VOMITING may be examples. In most instances, appropriate nutrition is important to keep the cat from using his own body tissue for energy.

Kittens should go no more than eighteen to twenty-four hours without eating, and adult cats probably shouldn't exceed forty-eight hours without a meal. Cats that stop eating for several days, especially overweight cats, are at high risk for developing a life-threatening condition commonly called fatty liver disease (see FELINE HEPATIC LIPIDO-SIS). See your veterinarian immediately under these circumstances.

Usually, the physical or psychological condition causing the anorexia must be addressed to solve the problem. Actual treatment is aimed at stimulating the cat's appetite and getting the animal to eat.

At home, an owner may prompt the cat to eat by moistening dry food with warm water or warming canned food. Offering a bit of food to the cat with your fingers, then stroking his head and neck, seems to stimulate some cats to eat. Placing the first bite in his mouth may be all that's needed to get the cat to continue feeding on his own. Or, try smearing a bit on his nose or paw to induce him to lick it off.

Although adding treats to a balanced diet should never be done on a regular basis, all's fair when tempting a sick cat to eat. A drizzle of warm chicken broth, meat baby food, or cottage cheese over the regular diet may do the trick.

Your veterinarian may prescribe drugs such as Valium to stimulate the cat's appetite. The effects of the appetite mechanism are not completely understood, but are in part regulated by certain parts of the brain. Therefore, some drugs (like Valium) that affect the brain may also act on these centers to stimulate appetite. No one knows why.

If the cat still won't eat, force-feeding may be necessary (see ADMINISTERING OF MEDICATION, Oral Treatments). In these instances, a puree of the cat's normal diet and/or a high-calorie special diet prescribed by the veterinarian is fed to the cat. In severe cases, the veterinarian may resort to placing a feeding tube directly into the stomach to force-feed the cat.

Antifreeze

Antifreeze is used in cars to protect them from freezing temperatures. Antifreeze is composed of ethylene glycol, an industrial solvent also used in the removal of rust. It is an odorless, colorless fluid with a sweet taste that appeals to many pets.

Drinking antifreeze is deadly. Less than one teaspoon can kill an average-size cat, and there is an 88 percent mortality rate for antifreeze poisoning in pets.

All cats are at risk, but male cats younger than three years seem to be poisoned most often. Accidental intoxication usually occurs in the fall, winter, and early spring, during peak usage of antifreeze solutions.

Survival of the poisoned cat depends on *prompt treatment*, because antifreeze is rapidly absorbed into the body. The cat's system actually works against itself and turns the relatively harmless ethylene glycol into a more toxic form that poisons the cat.

When the liver breaks down antifreeze, it changes the ethylene glycol into oxalic acid, a substance extremely toxic to the kidneys. Oxalic acid, often used as a bleaching or cleaning agent, is a substance that the cat's body cannot further metabolize. When passed in the urine, oxalic acid can literally eat away parts of the urinary tract. Often, it combines with calcium to form crystals, which clog the kidneys and cause sudden kidney failure (see also KIDNEY DISEASE).

The first symptoms can appear as early as one hour after ingestion. The poison first enters the brain and spinal fluid and produces a narcotic effect. The affected cat acts drunk, and staggers about showing a severe loss of coordination. VOMITING, convulsions, DIARRHEA, loss of appetite, and rapid breathing or panting may also signal antifreeze poisoning.

Ingesting the substance stimulates thirst, so a poisoned cat drinks lots of water, and an early sign may be a temporary increase in urine output. Significant amounts of the poison are passed unchanged in the urine, especially in the first twelve hours.

Animals often survive initial poisoning signs, and may seem to return to near normal in twelve hours. But although a cat may act fine,

a

ANTIFREEZE POISONING

SYMPTOMS

Drunken behavior, excessive thirst, increased urination, diarrhea, vomiting, convulsions, loss of appetite, panting

HOME CARE

EMERGENCY! SEE VETERINARIAN IMMEDIATELY—if help is not available, induce vomiting and/or administer activated charcoal within 2 hours of ingestion

VET CARE

Induce vomiting, pump stomach, treat with intravenous fluids and 100-proof alcohol, provide supportive care

PREVENTION

Use pet-safe antifreeze products, store antifreeze out of cat's reach

even more serious signs return at around twenty-four hours. Symptoms may progress over a week, during which time the cat stops urinating and becomes severely depressed. Vomiting, diarrhea, loss of appetite, DEHYDRATION, weakness, and even seizures may be seen. Ultimately, the cat falls into a coma and dies.

If you know or suspect that your pet has been into the antifreeze, time is of the essence and you should see your veterinarian immediately. If regular office hours are over, most veterinarians have an after-hours emergency service, or you should go to the emergency room of an animal hospital. If help is far away, though, and you've actually seen the cat drinking antifreeze, try to make him vomit if he is still alert. Never attempt to make your pet vomit if he's acting depressed or is not fully conscious. And DO NOT USE SYRUP OF IPECAC, which can cause toxicity in certain pets.

To make your cat vomit, fill a syringe, eye dropper, or squirt bot-

a

tle with hydrogen peroxide (3 percent solution) and give one table-spoon for each ten pounds of pet. If your cat doesn't vomit in the next ten minutes, repeat the dose once. Cats are typically hard to make vomit, even for professionals (see ADMINISTERING OF MEDICATION, Oral Treatments).

Giving the cat activated charcoal also helps improve survival. It's available in drugstores and can be given as tablets or crushed and mixed with water. Charcoal binds the poison to prevent its absorption in the intestinal tract. Whether successful or not with the above-mentioned home treatments, you should still have your cat seen immediately by a veterinarian.

The therapy a vet prescribes is directed at preventing absorption, increasing excretion, and avoiding further metabolism of the poison. Typically, the veterinarian will flush a cat's stomach with a saline/charcoal solution if the antifreeze was ingested within three hours. Subsequent intravenous fluid therapy helps head off dehydration problems, and also encourages the cat to urinate as much antifreeze as possible before it has changed into its more lethal form.

Getting the cat drunk by using 100-proof ethanol alcohol is the recommended treatment for cats. When the cat's blood alcohol content is raised to a high enough level, the liver works overtime on the alcohol instead of changing the antifreeze to oxalic acid. It is hoped that the antifreeze will pass through the cat's system in its original, less toxic form.

If treatment isn't in time, the kidneys will shut down from the poison. Antifreeze-induced kidney disease is sometimes reversible. Humans with kidney failure have the option of machine dialysis, but this is a luxury that is usually unavailable for pets. Instead, peritoneal dialysis may be used. Saline fluid is pumped into the abdominal cavity, where it absorbs the waste the damaged kidneys can't process, and is then withdrawn. Ideally, this procedure gives the kidneys time to start healing so that normal function can return. Even if the kidneys are able to return to normal or near-normal function, it may take three to four weeks for this to occur.

The best prevention is keeping antifreeze safely away from cats. Dispose of drained radiator fluid in a sealed container, and mop up spills immediately. Keep pets away from garages and other areas where antifreeze may be found. Some new antifreeze products contain safer chemicals, such as propylene glycol instead of ethylene glycol. Ask your veterinarian to recommend nontoxic products that address the safety of your pet. (See also POISON.)

a

Arrhythmia

An arrhythmia is defined as any abnormal heartbeat. Electrical impulses control the natural rhythm of the heart. Changes in the impulse may cause the heart to beat too fast (tachycardia), too slow (bradycardia), or irregularly. Turbulence in the blood flow through the heart results in a distinctive sound, referred to as heart murmur.

Drugs, toxins, and electrolyte or a body acid-base imbalance resulting from severe VOMITING or DIARRHEA, urinary blockage, HYPERTHYROIDISM, and CARDIOMYOPATHY are all potential causes of arrhythmias. Drugs are available that help control and regulate the beat of the heart. The underlying cause, however, must be addressed if the problem is to be resolved.

Arsenic

See POISON.

Arthritis

Arthritis is the inflammation of the joint, which results in painful movement. There are several kinds of arthritis.

Cats, usually males, can suffer from chronic progressive polyarthritis (CPP), in which the IMMUNE SYSTEM attacks the joints and causes a

a

ARTHRITIS

SYMPTOMS

Stiff warm joints, difficulty rising, lameness, reluctance to move—particularly in cold weather

HOME CARE

Gentle massage of joints, apply heat to painful areas, keep cat's weight down

VET CARE

Sometimes steroids to reduce pain

PREVENTION

Prompt veterinary treatment of joint or bone injury

condition similar to rheumatoid arthritis in people. CPP in cats is considered rare. The cause isn't known, but the condition may be related to a viral infection like FELINE LEUKEMIA VIRUS.

The typical condition we think about in people, called osteoarthritis or degenerative arthritis, also affects cats. It is a chronic disease of aging that occurs when simple wear and tear slowly destroys the thin layer of cartilage protecting the joint surface.

Arthritis is seen most often in older cats, but it can develop at any age as a result of injury to bone, cartilage, or ligaments. The resulting inflammation of the joint can lead to even more cartilage damage, causing a vicious cycle of degeneration. Arthritis is a progressive disease that, once started, doesn't stop.

Cats mask arthritis quite effectively. Owners may not notice any problems until the arthritis is quite advanced. Typically, arthritic cats have difficulty getting up after they've been resting. Lameness is aggravated by cold, damp weather. Moderate exercise may loosen and warm up the joint and muscles, so that once the cat starts moving the lameness subsides.

Cats are understandably reluctant to move when their joints are painful, but restricting movement over time can cause the muscles and tendons to shorten. Sometimes called muscle tie-down, this limits the cat's movement even further. Rather than limping or holding up a leg the way arthritic dogs do, the arthritic cat typically stops moving around.

Feline arthritis often isn't diagnosed until the cat begins showing obvious signs. The veterinarian can palpate or feel how the joint works by flexing the affected limb. Usually the joint is warm and painful. However, because cats are not always cooperative during examinations, it's not always easy to locate the exact source of the pain. Sometimes they don't want to be touched anywhere, and other times they are so stoic they won't show that something is bothering them.

When an area of soreness or an unusual lump or bump indicates a problem, x-rays are taken. But arthritis is a disease of the cartilage, and changes in cartilage aren't easily seen in X-rays until the damage is severe. In fact, painful arthritis may be present without being apparent on the X-ray at all.

Immune-mediated polyarthritis is treated with drugs, such as steroids, that inhibit the immune system. Treatment of osteoarthritis is aimed at relieving the cat's pain.

Pain-relieving medications such as ASPIRIN *and Tylenol, or other over-the-counter pain medications that are often used for arthritis in people, are highly toxic to cats and should not be used* (see POISON). Human arthritis ointments are not only messy when applied to fur, they can also be poisonous. Menthol products are particularly dangerous. Steroid-type medications that relieve inflammation may be prescribed by the veterinarian as injections, pills, or even skin patches to help relieve discomfort.

In all kinds of arthritis, gentle massage may be helpful to loosen the joint, soothe tight muscles, and relieve the ache. Make circular rubbing motions down both sides of the cat's spine, from head to tail, and gently flex the joints to keep them limber. Don't force the cat to submit; that's counterproductive. Only massage as much as your cat will allow.

Warmth applied to sore joints seems to help as much as anything. Use hot-water bottles, recirculating water blankets, or heating pads, but always buffer them with several layers of towels to prevent burning the skin. Be sure your cat can move off the area if it gets too warm.

There's no way to prevent age-related arthritic changes in cats, and

a

no way to predict which cats will experience problems. But watching for early signs and treating them can help make cats more comfortable.

Extra weight puts stress and strain on bones and joints, so keeping your cat slim may help slow down arthritis (see OBESITY). FRACTURES, sprains, or ligament injuries should receive prompt treatment to minimize the chances of developing arthritis in the future.

Artificial Respiration

Artificial respiration is the means of getting air into an animal that has stopped breathing. In a cat, common causes include ELECTRICAL SHOCK, DROWNING, ASTHMA, and trauma. Smoke inhalation may also cause respiratory distress or stopped breathing. Penetrating chest wounds can damage the lungs, and a blow such as being hit by a car can tear the diaphragm, a muscle separating the abdomen from the chest cavity that expands the lungs.

Signs of respiratory distress in cats include gasping, panting, or slowed breathing. A pale or blue-tinged color to the cat's gums or rims of the eyelids indicates oxygen starvation from poor circulation. Cats in respiratory distress may simply pass out.

If you suspect your cat is choking on a SWALLOWED OBJECT, like a bone or part of a toy, try to remove it with your fingers or tweezers. However, never pull on swallowed string, which may be anchored at the other end by a needle or fishhook; leave that to your veterinarian.

If you're unable to reach the object, lay the cat on her side, place the heel of your hand directly behind her last rib, and gently thrust upward three or four times in quick succession. If the obstruction is not dislodged using this modified Heimlich maneuver, get the cat to a veterinarian immediately.

When respiratory distress isn't due to obstruction, you'll need to help your cat breathe until you can get her to a veterinarian. Remove the cat's collar and place her on a flat surface on her right side. Open her mouth and pull the tongue forward; a piece of gauze or washcloth makes the tongue easier to grasp. Gently close her mouth with her

RESPIRATORY DISTRESS/ARTIFICIAL RESPIRATION

SYMPTOMS

Gasping, panting, slowed or strained breathing, pale or blue-tinged gums or eyelid rims, loss of consciousness, cessation of breathing

HOME CARE

EMERGENCY! Remove any foreign object from mouth, if able to reach (don't pull on string); if unsuccessful, apply Heimlich maneuver by laying cat on side and applying 3 or 4 upward thrusts with heel of hand directly behind cat's last ribs; keep cat breathing until veterinarian is present. If cat is not breathing, remove cat's collar, lay her flat, open her mouth, pull tongue forward, and close her mouth; then give compressions with the flat of your hand to her ribs to express air. If a new breath doesn't result, place lips over cat's nose and blow gently once every 4 or 5 seconds. SEE VET IMMEDIATELY.

VET CARE

Same as home care treatment; also, an endotracheal tube may be placed through cat's mouth directly into lungs, and oxygen given to aid respiration; depending on the cause, specific drugs may be given to stimulate heart or breathing action

PREVENTION

Tape down or eliminate electrical cords to prevent shocks, remain alert to water hazards to prevent drowning, keep cats indoors or safely under your control when outside to prevent car accidents, and if your cat is diagnosed with asthma, remain vigilant to catch respiratory distress early

a

Dislodge obstruction by pressing sharply upward behind the ribs, in a modified Heimlich maneuver.

tongue extended outside. Raise her chin so the neck stretches forward and keeps the airway open. Place one hand flat on her ribs and press sharply to express the old air from her system, then release. If the diaphragm is intact, when you release the pressure an elastic recoil will fill the cat's lungs with air.

When this recoil mechanism doesn't work, you must blow air into

Press gently but firmly, about once every second, then follow with one breath of artificial respiration, until the cat begins breathing on her own.

a

Blow air into your cat's lungs if necessary.

your pet's lungs. Keeping the tongue forward with the mouth loosely closed, place your lips over your cat's nose and blow gently into her nostrils. Watch for the chest to expand, then stop blowing and allow air to escape back out. Blowing too hard can cause lung damage, but excess air should escape through her lips. If the chest doesn't move, blow harder, or try sealing the lips with your hand when you blow. Breathe once every four to five seconds, or twelve to fifteen respirations a minute. Continue as long as the cat's heart beats or until the cat begins breathing again on her own. (See also CARDIOPULMONARY RESUSCITATION.)

a

Ash

The magnesium level in cat food has often been inaccurately referred to as "ash." Ash actually consists of all noncombustible materials in food, only one of which is magnesium (see LOWER URINARY TRACT DISEASE).

Aspirin

Aspirin (acetylsalicylic acid) is a common pain reliever for humans. Although it has a place in home veterinary use for dogs, *aspirin can kill your cat*. Aspirin is broken down more slowly in cats than in people, so the drug stays in the cat's system longer—for days rather than hours. Giving your five-pound cat one adult aspirin tablet is roughly equivalent to a person taking thirty pills. Aspirin dosage in cats may be prescribed by a veterinarian in certain instances, but must be carefully regulated to avoid a fatal overdose.

Signs of aspirin toxicity include DEHYDRATION, loss of appetite, salivation, hyperactivity or depression, incoordination, VOMITING, and DIARRHEA. The vomit and/or diarrhea often contains blood from gastrointestinal bleeding. If you know or suspect your cat has swallowed aspirin, seek prompt veterinary attention. Treatment is aimed at supporting the cat with fluids and administering drugs to help the kidneys get rid of the aspirin.

a

ASPIRIN POISONING

SYMPTOMS

Loss of appetite, drooling, dehydration, hyperactivity or depression, blood in vomit and/or diarrhea, drunken behavior

HOME CARE

Induce vomiting if within 2 hours of ingestion

VET CARE

Fluid therapy, drugs to stimulate elimination of drug, pumping stomach, inducing vomiting

PREVENTION

DON'T GIVE CATS ASPIRIN

Asthma

Feline asthma is breathing distress that results from a sudden narrowing of the airways. The condition is thought to be caused by an allergen, but identifying it is difficult because it can be a single or multiple-component allergen.

Potential triggers include substances that often cause other types of allergic reactions, like inhaled pollens, molds, perfume, smoke, even cat litter dust. Asthmatic cats often seem to suffer from other allergies, but they may also react to air pollution, STRESS, exercise, or simple changes in the temperature. Usually, the trigger remains a mystery, but if it can be identified and avoided, asthmatic attacks can be eliminated.

When the triggering event occurs, an asthmatic will have a reaction within minutes. (Asthmatic cats have the same symptoms as people with asthma.) Muscles and glandular structures surrounding the

a

ASTHMA

SYMPTOMS

Gasping, panting, wheezing, loss of consciousness

HOME CARE

EMERGENCY! SEE VET IMMEDIATELY

VET CARE

Steroids, oxygen therapy, bronchodilating drugs

PREVENTION

Reduce triggers such as dust or stress, use humidifier

lower airways—the bronchials—seem more developed in asthmatics, which means the size of the airways is probably smaller in these cats. The trigger prompts muscles to forcibly contract, which closes down the passageways like a fist.

At the same time, inflammatory cells flood the area to try to neutralize the mysterious trigger. But inflammation causes swelling, which narrows the passageways even further. On top of this, local glands in the lungs release great amounts of mucus to soothe the inflammation, but this acts to clog the little breathing space that remains. The cat is probably left feeling like he's breathing through a straw.

Early signs, like breathing a little fast or showing increased effort in breathing, are so subtle they can easily be missed. Some cats may cough or wheeze, but often the first sign is a full-blown asthma attack. *Gasping, panting, and openmouthed breathing are very dangerous signs in cats; get the cat to a veterinarian immediately.*

The incidence of feline asthma isn't known, but experts agree it's fairly common. Siamese and Burmese cats seem to be affected more often than other cats, and although the condition affects cats of all ages, it's usually seen for the first time in a two- to four-year-old cat.

Asthmatics seem to have a more difficult time during the spring and fall, when pollen and mold counts are high.

Diagnosis is based on signs, clinical tests, and response to treatment. X-RAYS of asthmatic lungs may show thickened bronchials, but sometimes the lungs appear normal. A tracheal wash may offer clues. This procedure takes a sample of the fluid in the airways to look for inflammatory cells. And if treatment for asthma in these cats offers relief, it's presumed that the cat is asthmatic.

Frequently, allergic cats are sensitive to more than one allergen, and each cat has an individual allergy threshold; below the threshold, a cat remains symptom-free. If an asthmatic cat's condition is aggravated by a combination of things, eliminating some of them may help relieve the signs.

Treatment is aimed at reducing inflammation and opening up the lungs with medication so the cat can breathe. Anti-inflammatory drugs like corticosteroids are the mainstay of feline asthma treatment.

Historically, asthmatic cats have been given low doses of steroids only for a couple of days to control immediate problems. Recent studies have shown that these cats often suffer ongoing airway inflammation, even when they aren't showing clear signs of the disease. Some veterinarians now recommend long-term high-dose steroid therapy to manage the disease. Once diagnosed with asthma, cats generally stay on medication for the rest of their lives. Even if the asthma's well controlled, an acute asthma attack can happen at any time and can be fatal.

Inhalers that human asthma sufferers use aren't practical for cats, but pills or injectable brochodilators that open the airways are available. In emergency situations, the cat may require oxygen therapy and other drugs to help relax the muscles so the cat can breathe more easily. Owners may be taught by their veterinarian to give the cat an injectable bronchodilator at home should there be an emergency.

Asthma cannot be cured, but it can be managed. It's helpful to eliminate or reduce anything that might bring on an attack, such as dust or stressful conditions. A humidifier may make breathing for your cat easier.

In most species, including dogs and people, a compound called histamine plays an important role in allergies. Histamine triggers certain inflammatory reactions, and antihistamine drugs help relieve these symptoms. Antihistamines, however, don't seem to work in cats.

a

Many of the symptoms of asthma in cats are instead prompted by a compound called serotonin, which is released by specialized immune cells in response to the presence of the triggering substance. In the same way that antihistamine drugs block the effect of allergy symptoms in people, drugs that block serotonin may reduce or even prevent asthma signs in certain cats. Some veterinarians are now using anti-serotonin drugs such as cyproheptadine as a preventive in feline asthma.

Atopy

See ALLERGIES, CAT.

Bad Breath

Offensive mouth odor, also called halitosis, is not considered normal for a cat. Strong-smelling canned foods may tinge the cat's breath for a short time after eating, but a persistent bad smell more commonly points to a health problem.

BAD BREATH

SYMPTOMS
Mouth odor

HOME CARE
Feed dry crunchy foods, clean teeth

VET CARE
Anesthesia and dentistry

PREVENTION
Routine brushing of cat's teeth

Cats aren't able to brush their own teeth, yet they are subject to some of the same dental risks as people. One of the first signs of gum and tooth infections is bad breath.

Offensive mouth odor can also indicate a sore mouth, like STOMATITIS. Certain types of breath odor can signal disease or poisoning. A strong garlic breath may indicate the cat has been poisoned with arsenic. One sign of late-stage DIABETES MELLITUS is acetone breath; it smells something like nail polish remover. And signs of KIDNEY DISEASE include mouth ulcers and an ammonialike mouth odor.

Halitosis is more than a nuisance and cannot be fixed with a breath mint; medical diagnosis is necessary before treatment can cure the problem. However, bad breath that results from PERIODONTAL DISEASE often can be prevented with routine dental care, given either at home or at the vet's.

Balance

The cat's finely tuned sense of balance is regulated by a specialized organ called the vestibular apparatus found deep inside the EARS. A sense of balance allows a cat to travel great heights and effortlessly leap long distances.

It is the cat's uncanny flexibility and motion control, coupled with an intricate balance sense, that allows the falling cat to land on her feet. She uses a series of spine, shoulder, and flank contractions to twist in midair during a fall, and right herself.

The cat is instantly able to distinguish between up and down, and can determine acceleration as she falls because of her specialized balance organs. Inside the cat's inner ear are three tiny fluid-filled structures called the utricle, saccule, and semicircular canals. Each is lined with millions of microscopic hairs, and the utricle and saccule also contain tiny particles of chalk that float and move with every motion. Whenever the cat's head moves, the fluid moves against the hairs. When the hairs move, they relay information to the brain about body position and speed of movement.

Ear infections can affect the cat's balance (see OTITIS and EAR

b

Cats have a unique and finely honed sense of balance. *(Photo credit: Lillian Zahrt)*

MITES), and falls from short distances may not allow enough time for the righting mechanism to work. Landing on her feet does not prevent a cat from sustaining serious injuries during falls (see HIGH-RISE SYNDROME).

Balding

See HAIR LOSS, SHEDDING, and STRESS.

b # Bathing

See GROOMING.

Behavior

See AFFECTION, AGGRESSION, ALOOFNESS, COMMUNICATION, DOMINANCE, EATING, FEAR, HUNTING BEHAVIOR, KITTEN, KNEADING, MARKING, PLAY, REPRODUCTION, SCRATCHING, SLEEP, and SOILING.

Bleeding

Bleeding is the body's way of cleansing a wound. Injuries to soft tissue that can cause bleeding include cuts, abrasions, and lacerations. Factors in the blood cause it to clot and seal minor wounds, and protect the area while healing takes place. Any deep or gaping wound requires veterinary attention, whether or not the cat is bleeding profusely.

Scratches and abrasions may result in oozing wounds. When an artery has been cut, bright red blood will flow in spurts in time with the cat's heartbeat. Blood from a vein flows evenly, and is a darker red.

In most instances, bleeding can be stopped by applying even, direct pressure. Use a sterile gauze pad or clean cloth to cover the wound, and press firmly for five to seven minutes. Gently lift the pad to see if bleeding has stopped; if not, continue the pressure. *Don't pull the material away from the wound if it sticks;* you risk tearing away the new scab. Instead, place another clean cloth or pad over the first.

If direct pressure doesn't stop the bleeding, as may be the case if an artery has been cut, indirect pressure on the arteries may help. Apply pressure between the heart and the wound. Pressure points are located inside the legs; specifically, try the armpit on the front legs and on the crotch where the hind legs connect. The underside at the tail base is another pressure point. With a cut vein, apply pressure *below* the injury to stop the bleeding. Elevate the wound above the level of the heart; this lets gravity reduce the blood pressure to the wound, which helps slow the bleeding.

If none of these procedures works and the wound is on the leg or tail, then a tourniquet may be used—but only as a last resort. Improper use of a tourniquet may so severely injure the tissue that amputation of the affected limb may be necessary.

Make a tourniquet using a wide strip of cloth, gauze, or other material; the leg from a pair of panty hose works well. The material must be at least one inch wide to prevent cutting into the cat's skin. Wrap the material twice around the limb approximately two inches from the wound, and tie once. Then securely knot a pencil or stick on top of the first tie. Gently twist the pencil, stop immediately when the bleeding slows to a trickle, and fasten the pencil in place. *Release the tourniquet for a brief time every fifteen minutes.* In the meantime, get your cat to the veterinarian immediately.

Internal bleeding is harder to notice and may be caused by a number of critical conditions. Bruises or swollen areas may result from these injuries, but are often hidden beneath the fur (see HEMATOMA). Danger signals indicating possible internal injury include bleeding from the mouth or anus, blood in the stool or vomit, and loss of consciousness. Spontaneous bleeding from the nose or mouth and blood in the urine or stool can also indicate poisoning or advanced LIVER DISEASE. Blood-tinged urine is a sign of CYSTITIS or LOWER URINARY TRACT DISEASE. With the exception of simple abrasions, any cat that is bleeding should see a veterinarian immediately.

Blood

b

In simplest terms, blood is a mass transit system that shuttles the components of life throughout an animal's body. The yellow liquid portion, called plasma, transports waste products, various nutrients, antibodies, and certain clotting proteins. The solid portion is made up of red cells, white cells, and platelets.

Platelets and plasma clotting proteins make clotting possible, so that when a cat tears a claw, the bleeding will stop. White cells are a part of the body's IMMUNE SYSTEM. White cells and antibodies guard against and fight off attacks by foreign invaders, like viruses and bacteria. The red cell's major function is to carry oxygen. The oxygen-carrying pigment (hemoglobin) gives blood its red color.

Not all feline blood is the same. Like their human owners, cats have different blood types. Researchers have identified three feline blood types: A, B, and AB.

Because blood type is inherited, certain cats are more likely to have one kind over another. Most domestic shorthair and domestic longhair cats have type A blood. Siamese and related breeds like Burmese and Tonkinese, along with American Shorthairs, usually also have type A blood.

About 25 to 50 percent of British Shorthair, Exotic Shorthair, Devon Rex, and Cornish Rex cats have type B, and about 15 percent of Persian and Abyssinian cats have type B. Type AB is extremely rare, but has been found in a number of breeds and domestic shorthairs.

Feline blood type matters because type B cats have very strong antibodies against type A, and that's particularly important to know when breeding cats.

Newborn kittens receive antibodies from the colostrum (first milk) they nurse from their mother. If the kittens have type A blood, but the mother cat is type B, the newborns will swallow antibodies that don't like the kittens' red blood cells.

This results in a hemolytic reaction called Neonatal Isoerythrolysis (NI). The antibodies from the queen's colostrum attack and destroy the kitten's red blood cells, causing a condition called fading kitten syndrome. Such kittens start out healthy, but grow weak and usually die within the first week of life.

It's crucial for breeders to identify each cat's blood type before planning any breeding. NI can be prevented by breeding type B females only to type B males.

But for all cats, blood compatibility can be a matter of life and death. Transfusions of whole blood, plasma, or other blood products are used to treat a variety of blood disorders. If a cat is given a transfusion with the wrong blood type, he can have a deadly reaction to the very first transfusion.

When a type B cat receives type A blood, antibodies in the type B blood attack the foreign type A red cells. Called a hemolytic transfusion reaction, the breakage of the red cells causes almost immediate signs of distress in the cat, including reduced heart rate, low blood pressure, slowed breathing, vomiting, defecation, and urination. The affected cat can die within only a few minutes. To avoid such problems, only compatible blood should be given.

If your cat is a breed that has a high prevalence of type B blood, it's important that the cat's blood be typed. Specialized tests are necessary, but only a few places in the United States—veterinary schools and certain commercial labs and animal blood banks—have the capability.

If you don't have access to such a place, cross-matching can be done in your veterinarian's office. This procedure doesn't determine blood type, but will tell if the donor's blood is compatible with the recipient's—in other words, whether a transfusion reaction will occur.

To cross-match blood, a drop of serum or plasma from the recipient cat is mixed with a drop of blood from the prospective donor cat. Clumping indicates that the blood is incompatible.

Many veterinarians keep a clinic cat to serve as a blood donor when necessary. Teaching hospitals at veterinary schools often operate their own animal blood banks, and commercial animal blood banks also have a variety of products available, such as cat-size IV kits, plasma, and whole blood of both types. (See "Pet Services" in Appendix C, "Resources.")

b Body Type

See BREED.

Breed

Breed refers to a particular cat type that has distinct and predictable physical and/or temperament characteristics that are consistently reproduced in the offspring.

A cat of a particular breed has a known, traceable ancestry referred to as the "pedigree." A "purebred" cat is one produced by the mating of a male and female cat of the same breed. To authenticate breed status, kittens must be registered with a cat association (see Appendix A, "Cat Associations and Cat Breeds"). There are over one hundred distinct cat breeds recognized around the world; more than forty are described in this book.

"Natural" cat breeds like the longhaired cobby Persian appeared in nature; selective breeding by cat fanciers has refined the type. "Man-made" breeds like the Bombay are hybrids created by combining existing breeds to form a new one. "Spontaneous mutations" are the third breed type, and they are the inexplicable deviations of nature; examples are the tailless Manx, the folded-ear Scottish Fold, and the bald Sphynx.

Every cat's basic shape is the same, but some are more wiry and others more heavily muscled. Cat body types are described as the extremes of cobby and foreign, with degrees in between. The "cobby" type (i.e., Persian) is a heavy-boned, short-bodied cat with a round head and usually thick tail. "Foreign" body types (i.e., Siamese) have long slender bodies with fine bones and wedge-shaped angular heads. The "Oriental" type takes this foreign look to an extreme. Body types that fall

BREEDS AT A GLANCE

BREEDS	BODY TYPE	COAT TYPE	COAT CARE	ATTITUDE	HEALTH CONCERNS
Abyssinian	semiforeign	short	low	high activity, in-your-face, enjoys kids and other pets	anemia, kidney problems, overgrooming, cardiomyopathy, hyperesthesia syndrome
American Curl	semiforeign	medium-long	medium	average activity, curious, playful, enjoys kids and other pets	no mention of problems
American Shorthair	domestic	short	low	average activity, athletic, affectionate, enjoys kids and other pets	no mention of problems
American Wirehair	domestic	medium	low	average to low activity, quiet, retiring, prefers watching	immune system tends to develop late
Balinese	foreign	medium	low	high activity, talkative, protective, prefers people to pets	no mention of problems
Bengal	semiforeign	short	low	average activity, doglike, very trainable, enjoys kids and other pets	no mention of problems
Birman	domestic	medium to long	medium	low activity, quiet, enjoys kids and other pets	cataracts
Bombay	domestic	short	low	high activity, outgoing, enjoys kids and other pets	no mention of problems
British Shorthair	domestic	short	low	low activity, calm, quiet, independent, can enjoy kids	rare blood type B, cranial deformities, cataracts
Burmese	cobby	short	low	high activity, in-your-face, prefers being only cat	cranial deformities, hyperesthesia syndrome, asthma, cardiomyopathy, wool sucking, overgrooming
Chartreux	domestic	short	low	average activity, quiet, doglike, prefers dogs to other cats	no mention of problems
Colorpoint Shorthair	foreign	short	low	high activity, talkative, devoted, good family pet	no mention of problems
Cornish Rex	foreign	short	low	high activity, athletic, enjoys kids and other pets	may have type B blood, stud tail
Cymric	cobby	medium-long	medium	average activity, affectionate, likes being center of attention	spinal problems, weak hips
Devon Rex	foreign	short	low	high activity, extreme energy, loves people	spasticity, stud tail, may have rare type B blood
Egyptian Mau	semiforeign	short	low	high activity, quiet, affectionate, prefers being only cat	no mention of problems
Exotic Shorthair	cobby	short	medium	average activity, quiet,	may have type B blood

b

BREEDS	BODY TYPE	COAT TYPE	COAT CARE	ATTITUDE	HEALTH CONCERNS
Havana Brown	semiforeign	short	low	undemanding, lap cat, laid back average activity, quiet, affectionate, enjoys kids and other pets	no mention of problems
Himalayan	cobby	long	high	low activity, sweet, laid back, gets along with other cats	cataracts, overgrooming, hyperesthesia syndrome
Japanese Bobtail	semiforeign	short	low	average activity, talkative, active, enjoys kids and other pets	no mention of problems
Javanese	foreign	medium	low	high activity, extremely vocal, curious, wants to be in middle of things	no mention of problems
Korat	domestic	short	low	average activity, gentle, quiet, hates noise, devoted, prefers being only cat	no mention of problems
Maine Coon	domestic	long	medium	average activity, calm, loyal, enjoys kids and other pets	cardiomyopathy
Manx	cobby	short	low	average activity, calm, loves people, likes being center of attention	spinal problems, weak hips
Norwegian Forest Cat	domestic	long	medium	average activity, gentle, loves people, good family pet	no mention of problems
Ocicat	domestic	short	low	average activity, devoted, easy to train, not shy, prefers multipet homes	no mention of problems
Oriental Longhair	foreign	medium-long	low	high activity, talkative, in-your-face, one-person cat	no mention of problems
Oriental Shorthair	foreign	short	low	high activity, talkative, in-your-face, one-person cat	no mention of problems
Persian	cobby	long	high	low activity, serene couch potato, good family pet	glaucoma, stud tail
Ragdoll	domestic	long	high	low activity, sweet, gentle	no mention of problems
Russian Blue	foreign	short	low	high activity, agile, playful, reserved, prefers being only cat	no mention of problems
Scottish Fold	domestic	short	low	average activity, quiet, sweet-tempered, enjoys kids and other pets	inflexible tail, crippled hind limbs
Scottish Fold Longhair	domestic	long	high	average activity, quiet, sweet-tempered, enjoys kids and other pets	inflexible tail, crippled hind legs
Siamese	foreign	short	low	high activity, extremely vocal, very trainable, loves people, great family pet	hyperesthesia syndrome, stud tail, asthma, glaucoma, wool sucking, breast cancer, cardiomyopathy

BREEDS	BODY TYPE	COAT TYPE	COAT CARE	ATTITUDE	HEALTH CONCERNS
Singapura	domestic	short	low	average activity, curious, friendly, enjoys kids and other pets	no mention of problems
Snowshoe	semiforeign	short	low	low activity, affectionate, lap cat, prefers being only cat	no mention of problems
Somali	semiforeign	medium-long	medium	high activity, nonstop action, enjoys kids and other pets	hyperesthesia syndrome, anemia, kidney problems, overgrooming
Sphynx	semiforeign	bald	low	average activity, gregarious, athletic, enjoys kids and other pets	oily skin, sometimes immune system problems
Tonkinese	semiforeign	short	low	high activity, talkative, outgoing, loves people, enjoys kids and other pets	no mention of problems
Turkish Angora	semiforeign	medium-long	low	average activity, intelligent, stubborn, hates noise, one-person cat	no mention of problems
Turkish Van	semiforeign	medium-long	medium	average activity, affectionate, a loner, prefers being only cat	no mention of problems

somewhere between cobby and foreign, like the American Shorthair, may be referred to as "domestic" types.

Cat fur comes in a variety of lengths. Shorthair cats include the peach fuzz coat of the Sphynx, the fine single coat of the Bombay, and the plush double coat of the Chartreux. Most shorthair coats are straight, but the rex coat curls, waves, or ripples (see American Wirehair, Cornish Rex, Devon Rex in Appendix A). Longhair coats vary from two to six inches in length, depending on the breed.

Coat color and pattern are equally diverse. Cats in solid colors are referred to as "self-colored." "Tipped" refers to the hair tip color contrasting with the rest of the cat's hair. When the tip is lighter, it's called chinchilla; when there's a medium contrast it's called shaded; and when there are dark ends with a light undercoat, it's called smoke.

"Tabby" refers to a pattern of darker stripes, spots, or swirls on a lighter background. The classic tabby pattern is a combination of circles and stripes, while the mackerel tabby has more clearly defined stripes. The spotted tabby has various sizes and shapes of spots.

Any solid-color coat with patches of white is referred to as "particolor." "Bi-color" is when the coat's two colors are divided, percentage-wise, two-thirds to one. "Van marking" is a white coat with patches of color on the head and tail, as in the Turkish Van breed. Cats with a solid-color coat with patches of cream or orange are "tortoiseshell" or "tortie"; when white is mixed in, they are called calico.

A "pointed" pattern is a solid-color body with a contrasting darker color on the face, ears, feet, legs, and tail. Kittens typically have their "points" darken as they mature. The most familiar example of pointed pattern cats is the Siamese, which typically sports solid-color points. However, any color or pattern can be restricted to the points, including tabby and lynx (striped). Those point colors or patterns outside the range defined by some associations for the Siamese breed may be referred to as "colorpoint."

"Mitted" cats have dark-colored legs with white on their feet. The most abbreviated white markings (such as only the toes) are referred to as "gloves," and an entirely white foot is called a "mitt" or "mitten." When the white extends up the legs, it's a "gauntlet." The Birman is an example of a mitted cat.

Mixed-breed cats come in a rainbow of colors and types that rival those of any purebred. A mixed-breed cat, also referred to as "random-bred" or "mutt" cats ("moggy" in Great Britain), are the result of un-planned breedings of various purebred or other mixed-breed cats. They have no pedigree, are not often registered, and rarely resemble any purebred standard. It is impossible to predict what the offspring will be like. They make wonderful pets, though, and comprise the majority of household pet cats throughout the world.

Breeding

See REPRODUCTION.

Brushing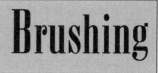

See GROOMING.

Burns

Cats may suffer burns from walking over hot stoves or fresh tar; being
exposed to accidental spills of hot water, cooking oil, or chemicals (see

BURNS

SYMPTOMS

Red skin, blistering, swelling, tender-to-painful area; severe
burns are sometimes charred, with fur easily pulled out

HOME CARE

Soak cloth in cool water, apply to injury, then see vet as soon
as possible

VET CARE

Depending on severity, cold compresses, salves, or ointments;
surgical removal of dead tissue; sometimes fluid therapy or pain
medication

PREVENTION

Confine cat in safe place when hazards are unavoidable;
prevent sunburn with sunscreen; tape down electrical cords;
keep caustic solutions out of reach

POISON); and by chewing electric cords (see ELECTRICAL SHOCK). They also may be burned due to sun overexposure (see SUNBURN) and, rarely, direct contact with fire. FROSTBITE resembles a burn injury.

A minor burn will cause the skin to turn red and sometimes blister or swell, and the area will be tender. Deeper burns turn the tissue white or even char it, and the fur will loosen; severe burns are extremely painful. Severe burns are usually accompanied by excessive loss of fluid and SHOCK, and when 15 percent or more of the body surface is burned, the outlook is grim.

If your cat is burned, soak a towel in cool water and apply to the injured area to alleviate the pain. Then see your veterinarian. Burns should be addressed by your vet, as even minor-appearing injuries may be more serious than you think; the full extent of the damage may be hidden by the hair coat.

To avoid burns, make the stove off-limits to your cat; perhaps confine him in a safe place when you're cooking. When open flame is accessible, such as candles or a fireplace, either confine your cat to a safe place or increase your vigilance to prevent accidents.

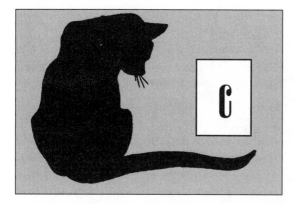

Cancer

Cancer is the abnormal, out-of-control growth of cells that invade and replace normal tissues and interfere with body processes. Such growths are called neoplasms, or tumors. Those that are localized and relatively harmless are benign; more often, feline tumors are malignant.

THE VETERINARY CANCER SOCIETY'S TOP TEN SIGNS OF CANCER IN ANIMALS

1. Abnormal swelling that persists or continues to grow
2. Sores that do not heal
3. Weight loss
4. Loss of appetite
5. Bleeding or discharge from any body opening
6. Offensive odor
7. Difficulty eating or swallowing
8. Hesitation to exercise or loss of stamina
9. Persistent lameness or stiffness
10. Difficulty in breathing, urinating, or defecating

CANCER

SYMPTOMS

See Top Ten Signs of Cancer in Animals

HOME CARE

Maintain good nutrition, nursing care

VET CARE

Surgery, chemotherapy, and/or radiation

PREVENTION

Spay cat before first heat cycle, avoid sun overexposure in light-colored cats, prevent exposure to FeLV, be alert to early lumps and bumps

Malignant tumors may be localized, but more frequently they metastasize, which means tumor cells spread throughout the body. A malignant tumor, commonly referred to as cancer, becomes deadly when it interferes with normal body processes. Approximately 80 percent of the tumors found in cats are malignant.

Cancer is primarily a disease of older cats, and the incidence of tumors in cats also increases with age. According to the American Veterinary Medical Association, cancer accounts for almost half the deaths of pets over ten years of age.

Some cancer-causing agents, referred to as *carcinogens*, have been identified. Cumulative exposure to carcinogens like air pollution and excessive sun over a cat's lifetime may be why cancer is more prevalent in older cats.

Certain diseases are responsible for the development of cancer. One in five cats that are sick with FELINE LEUKEMIA VIRUS (FeLV) suffers from FeLV-related cancer. FeLV causes several kinds of cancers, including cancer of lymphoid tissue (lymphosarcoma) and bone marrow cancers. A mutant form of FeLV called feline sarcoma virus (FeSV) causes cancers of connective tissue called fibrosarcoma. Other feline cancers may be related to the FELINE IMMUNODEFICIENCY VIRUS. Preventing these diseases reduces the chance of a cat developing virus-associated cancers.

Overexposure to sunlight is associated with a skin cancer called squamous cell carcinoma that affects the ears and face, particularly of white-faced or sparsely furred cats. Older outdoor cats that have been exposed over their lifetime are especially susceptible, but even indoor sunbathers can be victims. These tumors are seen more often in the Sunbelt areas of the United States, with the highest incidence in Arizona, New Mexico, California, and Colorado, where elevation makes ultraviolet exposure more intense. Siamese cats are less likely to develop this cancer, possibly because of their dark faces and ears.

Vaccination can also be a culprit. In 1992, researchers first noticed that some cats were developing fibrosarcoma tumors where they'd been vaccinated, between the shoulder blades or in the upper thigh. It's still a mystery why some cats develop vaccine-induced tumors while most do not. Currently, there's no evidence implicating any particular vaccine type or brand over another. The precise frequency of resulting cancerous tumors after vaccination isn't known, but current best estimates are only one to two cats per ten thousand. Therefore, cat owners should continue vaccinating their cats, because the cat's risk of contracting infectious diseases like RABIES is much greater than the possibility of developing these tumors.

Many cancer-related symptoms are confusingly similar to other illnesses or conditions. Most feline cancers are internal, so until they make the cat sick you may not notice anything's wrong. Even external lumps or sores may be hidden by fur. Still, since early detection significantly improves treatment success and chance of survival, cat owners should immediately alert their veterinarians to any physical or behavioral change in their cat.

Cats are subject to the same variety of cancers as people, but three types are more common than any others. The most common type is the *lymph gland cancers*.

Nearly 90 percent of lymph gland cancers in cats are due to FeLV infection. The lymphatic system includes lymph glands throughout the cat's body, as well as blood cell–forming organs, such as bone marrow and spleen.

Skin cancers are the second most frequent type of cancer in cats, and most are malignant. Squamous cell carcinomas are usually found on the head. Initially, these cancers may look like DERMATITIS, or a nonhealing fight wound. Mast cell tumors can be anywhere on the body, and may look like little pimples; they are often benign. Ceruminous gland carcinoma grows in the ear canal; affected cats usually have a smelly brown-to-bloody ear discharge, while the opposite ear appears normal.

Fibrosarcoma is a malignancy of the connective tissue of the body, and is probably the third most common cancer in cats. There is a huge variety of subtypes, but since they often act and are treated the same, they are collectively referred to as soft tissue sarcomas. They can appear anywhere on the body, usually as a solitary lump or mass easily felt beneath the skin. Vaccine-induced fibrosarcomas are multiple tumors that typically appear between the shoulder blades or on the flank where the cat has been vaccinated. Breast cancer is also quite common in cats, with Siamese reported to have a twofold increase in risk over other breeds.

Other common cancers of older cats include digestive tract tumors, mouth tumors, and bone cancers. Cats can get a huge number of other specific cancers as well.

Diagnosis can be made only by microscopic examination and identification of specific tumor cells. The veterinarian may collect a sample by inserting a needle directly into the tumor and withdrawing cells into the syringe. Other times, cancer cells may be identified in the blood, or even in a urine specimen. Most often, diagnosis requires a biopsy, the removal of a piece of tissue for specialized laboratory analysis. The tumor type and its state of progression must be evaluated before a prognosis and treatment can be determined.

The prognosis is defined by how far the cancer has spread; treatment is designed to kill the cancer cells and stop the progression. Cures are possible if tumors are detected and treated during the very early stages. The three major cancer treatments used in cats are the same as those used in people; often, a combination treatment that attacks the cancer from multiple angles works best.

As to treatment, the *surgical removal of tumors* is the primary method of treating cancer in veterinary medicine, and cost varies widely depending on the cancer involved. Surgery may gain the cat an additional six to twelve months, but rarely cures the disease because it's often difficult to remove the entire tumor. Leaving behind even a single cancer cell can result in the tumor growing back. Surgery may be followed by radiation or chemotherapy to address any cells left behind.

Some cancers are impossible to treat with conventional surgery because of the location or invasiveness of the tumor, and the danger of damaging vital tissues and organs. Tumors that can't be surgically removed in their entirety are commonly treated with chemotherapy.

Chemotherapy is a systemic treatment that attacks cancer that has spread throughout the body. With chemotherapy, cell-poisoning drugs are injected into the bloodstream, given as pills, or both.

Chemotherapy is used to destroy as many cancer cells as possible and/or to slow the growth rate of the tumor. Many feline chemotherapeutic drugs are also used in human medicine. Specific treatment and drug choice depends on the type of cancer, but normally a variety of drugs are given to the cat in sequence; initial therapy is quite intense, then becomes less so as the therapy progresses.

These drugs can't be targeted specifically to the cancer, so they also affect healthy tissue. This is what often causes side effects in people. But although prolonged treatment may occasionally cause a loss of whiskers, generally cats don't lose their hair, don't have nausea and vomiting, and don't tend to get sick at all.

Because dosage is based on a cat's body weight, the cost of these drugs is relatively low. But since cats are also commonly affected by other medical problems, expense can quickly mount for the owners.

Fifty to 80 percent of lymph gland cancers treated with chemotherapy shrink in size, or even go away. Still, every case is different, and success depends on the type of lymphoma and how advanced it is when treatment is begun, but generally about 75 percent of treated cats will go into remission for nine months to a year. Although cures are very rare, they do sometimes happen.

Radiation therapy consists of a beam of very intense X-RAY being shot directly into the cancer. It's most effective when used in combination with surgery or chemotherapy. Radiation therapy can reach tumors difficult to remove surgically, such as a growth near the cat's eyes. Cancers involving tissues with rapidly dividing cells, such as bone marrow and skin, respond more readily to radiation therapy. Typically, radiation treatment is repeated twice weekly for six to eight weeks.

Cats must be anesthetized for each radiation treatment, and ANES-THETIC risk may be a concern if the cat is old or ill. Repeated anesthesia increases the cost of an already expensive procedure. But despite the drawbacks, radiation therapy is often quite successful, and as many as 80 percent of certain cancers can be cured this way.

Although surgery, chemotherapy, and radiation therapy alone or in combination represent the most common and successful cancer therapies currently available, veterinary medicine is constantly researching new treatments. *Immunotherapy* enhances immune responses to help the body itself destroy tumor tissue. Immune-boosting drugs like acemannan are being studied and seem promising when used against fibrosarcoma.

Cryosurgery is the selective destruction of cancer tissue using a substance similar to liquid nitrogen to freeze the tumor. This treatment is successfully used on small skin cancers of the face in the same way that warts are removed on people. Depending on the patient, a local anesthetic at the tumor site combined with a mild tranquilizer may be all that's necessary.

Other alternative treatments that largely remain investigational at this point include HYPERTHERMIA, or heat therapy, which is the opposite of cryosurgery, and uses the local application of heat to destroy cancer cells. *Whole-body hyperthermia* is a procedure in which the patient's core body temperature is raised to treat cancer systemically rather than locally. *Phototherapy* involves injecting into the body drugs that target cancer cells. The drugs sensitize the tumor to certain wavelengths of light; the tumor is exposed to the light, which activates the drugs inside the tumor and kills the cancer cells.

The best preventive measure is for owners to pet the cat everywhere. The smaller the lump or bump is when found, the more likely you are to cure it.

A cat's risk of developing breast cancer can be greatly reduced by spaying *before* the first heat cycle. Beware of using a medication called megestrol acetate (Ovaban); it can lead to breast cancer in both male and female cats, whether neutered or intact. (Ovaban is a progesterone-type compound sometimes used as a behavior-modification medicine.) After your cat is vaccinated, monitor the vaccination site for small bumps. Bumps are common, but if they fail to disappear in four to six weeks, your vet should consider surgical removal. And protect your cat, especially light-colored or sparsely furred pets, from the sun (see SUNBURN).

Available cancer therapies may help prolong the cat's quality of life even if a cure isn't possible. Your veterinarian can help you make difficult decisions for your cat when a longer life is no longer necessarily the best choice (see EUTHANASIA).

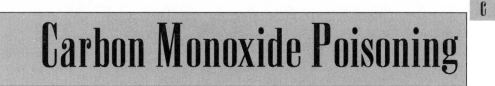

Carbon Monoxide Poisoning

C

Carbon monoxide, a natural by-product of some fuel combustion, is an odorless, colorless, tasteless gas that is deadly to people and their pets. Car exhaust and improperly vented gas furnaces or space heaters are the most common culprits.

The gas affects pets the same way it does people, but because carbon monoxide is lighter than air, pets that are at floor level may not show signs as early as humans, who are inhaling at a slightly higher altitude. However, cats that tend to sleep in high places, such as the top of

CARBON MONOXIDE POISONING

SYMPTOMS

Confusion, disorientation, and difficulty walking; vomiting, lethargy, extreme sleepiness; cherry-red color to gums

HOME CARE

Provide fresh air. EMERGENCY! SEE VETERINARIAN IMMEDIATELY

VET CARE

Oxygen therapy

PREVENTION

Have heating units safety-checked each fall before using them

refrigerators, could be affected earlier. Cats tend to sleep a lot anyway, but if you notice any change in your cat's behavior or your own that coincides with cold weather or the furnace coming on, consult your veterinarian and doctor.

Carbon monoxide poisoning is essentially a kind of chemical suffocation. When inhaled, the gas attaches itself to the oxygen-carrying components of the blood. This prevents the hemoglobin from doing its job of carrying oxygen to the tissues of the body.

In people, the most common symptom of carbon monoxide poisoning is a headache, followed by confusion and disorientation, flulike symptoms with vomiting, and finally coma. We don't know if pets suffer headaches, but they do show signs of confusion, lethargy, difficulty walking, and drunken behavior that are nearly identical to signs of carbon monoxide poisoning in people. In both people and pets, a distinctive sign of carbon monoxide poisoning is that the gums of the mouth turn bright cherry red. If the poisoning takes place while the victim is asleep, chances are they will never wake up.

In minor cases of poisoning, where only a small percentage of the blood is affected, the person or pet will recover on their own as long as no more poison is inhaled. The carbon monoxide stays in the body until the hemoglobin is replaced by the liver and spleen, which occurs naturally every ten to fifteen days. However, when the saturation level of the carbon monoxide in the blood is high, the person or pet will die without emergency therapy. A 25 percent saturation level is considered dangerous for people, but most humans are treated if the saturation level is 10 percent or higher. The same is true for poisoned pets.

The binding of the poison to the hemoglobin is irreversible, and the body can get rid of it only by exhaling. Therefore, administering high concentrations of oxygen increases the amount of poison that is breathed out. Depending on how much carbon monoxide is in the victim's system, hours of oxygen therapy may be required, and ventilation may be necessary.

To protect yourself and your pets, have your heating units inspected each fall before you start using them.

Cardiomyopathy

Cardiomyopathy simply means "heart-muscle disease," and can refer to any disease that affects the heart muscle. Cardiomyopathy represents the majority of feline cardiovascular diseases. But it's hard to know how many cats are truly affected, since no one's ever looked at incidence across the general cat population. But it's seen in cats of every breed or mixture. Based on distinct features of the disease, cardiomyopathies affecting cats are categorized as dilated or congested, hypertrophic, and restrictive. Cardiomyopathies that don't fit into these categories may be classified as intermediate or intergrade.

Dilated cardiomyopathy is a disease of systolic dysfunction, which means the heart muscle isn't able to adequately contract, and has trou-

HEART DISEASE

SYMPTOMS

Labored breathing, lethargy, weakness, loss of appetite, hind limb pain or paralysis

HOME CARE

Nutritional support

VET CARE

Drug therapy to get rid of excess fluid and control heart action, possibly taurine supplements

PREVENTION

Heartworm preventive medication, feed appropriate complete and balanced nutrition

ble pumping blood out of the heart. The heart becomes enlarged and globular like a balloon, and the muscle walls become quite thin.

Hypertrophic cardiomyopathy is a disease of diastolic function, of filling rather than contracting. The muscle wall of the heart thickens and reduces the size of the heart chambers until they cannot fill adequately with blood.

Restrictive cardiomyopathy is a more recently recognized form, with only a few documented cases in the veterinary literature. The heart muscle or the lining of the heart chambers becomes so stiff that the heart cannot fill properly. Affected cats may have a condition where portions of the heart wall don't function well, but other portions appear normal or may just be thicker than normal.

As to what causes cardiomyopathy in cats, between 1987 and 1994, researchers discovered that dilated cardiomyopathy in cats was associated with a dietary deficiency of taurine in genetically susceptible cats. Taurine is an essential amino acid (see NUTRITION). Since cat-food manufacturers started adding more taurine to their cat diets, the incidence of the disease has been reduced by 90 percent in the United States. In fact, if a cat's dilated cardiomyopathy results from taurine deficiency, giving the cat taurine cures the disease.

However, dilated cardiomyopathy in a cat that isn't due to taurine deficiency does still occur. When the cause isn't known, the disease is called idiopathic. Today, at least 50 percent of all heart failure cases diagnosed are still caused by dilated cardiomyopathy, and its cause is primarily still unknown. Research indicates that hypertrophic cardiomyopathy may have a genetic component, and has been identified in one line of related Maine Coons. Any cat diagnosed with cardiomyopathy should not be bred, because the stress of breeding may kill the cat and any surviving offspring may inherit the condition.

Cats can be affected by cardiomyopathy at any age, but hypertrophic cardiomyopathy is most common in young and middle-aged male cats. With dilated cardiomyopathy, all breeds can be affected, but Siamese, Abyssinian, and Burmese seem to be predisposed. The disease has been reported in cats anywhere from five months to sixteen years of age.

The severity of symptoms varies, from cats who appear totally unaffected to those who suffer sudden death. Very mildly affected cats may live a totally normal life with the disease, and only be diagnosed when symptoms suddenly develop due to a stressful event that makes the heart work too hard, such as a flea bath or a teeth cleaning at the vet. STRESS causes an increase in the cat's heart rate, which means there's less time for the heart to fill. If the heart is already difficult to fill, and the time it's allowed to fill is shortened, that may push the cat over the edge.

Affected cats may exhibit labored breathing from fluid-filled lungs, called pulmonary edema, or from fluid in the chest cavity, called pleural effusion, which may be present due to congestive heart failure. Poor cardiac output may result in lethargy, weakness, and/or mental depression. Heart failure that results in poor circulation to the intestines and liver may cause reduced appetite or ANOREXIA.

Another dramatic symptom is hind limb pain or paralysis, which results from blood clots secondary to the cardiomyopathy. The formation of a blood clot, called thrombosis, is common within the cardiac chamber or a vessel in cases of cardiomyopathy. Embolization occurs when the clot breaks off and gets "stuck" in another location and blocks normal blood flow. Such clots usually lodge in the hind legs where the aorta splits. The result is a "saddle thrombus" that causes pain and/or paralysis in one or both rear limbs.

Diagnosis is based on symptoms and diagnostic tests. An electrocardiogram may pick up abnormal heart rhythms. X-RAYS can reveal the presence of fluid in the lungs and chest cavity, as well as the silhouette of the heart itself (the hypertrophic heart is typically shaped like a valentine). Echocardiograms show how thick the wall of the heart is, and how well the blood is being pumped.

When there are obvious clinical signs, this generally indicates the presence of severe disease. In such cases, treatment probably won't prolong the cat's life, but may improve the quality of the time the cat has left. Cats without any symptoms may not require any therapy, but once heart failure is apparent, drug therapy is usually recommended.

Congestion and fluid in the lungs or chest are commonly controlled with a diuretic drug like Lasix (furosemide) that forces the kidneys to get rid of excess salt and water. To make it easier for the cat to breathe, vasodilator drugs open up the constricted blood vessels and help control congestion. In hypertrophic cardiomyopathy, calcium channel blockers and beta-blockers may be used to slow the heart rate, to give the heart more time to fill. Digoxin may help strengthen heart muscles and regulate blood pressure.

About 40 percent of cats with blood clots regain rear limb use

C

within a week *without* treatment. Surgery is rarely an option, because affected cats are high anesthetic risks. Clot-reducing drugs help reduce the "stickiness" of blood platelets and so decrease the chances of clots forming, but their use is controversial. Up to 50 percent of cats that undergo corrective surgery or take anticlotting drugs will suffer another clot.

Cats with dilated cardiomyopathy due to taurine deficiency have a good prognosis if they survive the initial two weeks while taurine is being given. But cats with idiopathic dilated cardiomyopathy have a very poor survival rate, and so do those suffering from restrictive cardiomyopathy. About 50 percent of cats showing signs of hypertrophic cardiomyopathy die within three months of diagnosis, while most cats without clinical signs can be expected to survive more than five years.

Cardiopulmonary Resuscitation (CPR)

CPR is the means of providing mechanical heart action and ARTIFICIAL RESPIRATION for cats whose breathing and heartbeat have stopped. The heartbeat and respiration can be interrupted by traumatic injury, like poisoning or being hit by a car, which leaves the cat lifeless and unconscious. CPR is a short-term method of keeping the cat alive, while stimulating the cat's heart and breathing to resume working on their own.

Use CPR *only* when both the heart and breathing have stopped and the cat is unconscious; you risk injuring your cat further if CPR is administered when the heartbeat or respiration is normal.

Check the breathing by monitoring the rise and fall of the cat's chest. The heartbeat is felt by placing the flat of your palm on the left side of your cat's chest just above and behind her elbow. If the heart is working but respiration is very shallow or nonexistent, then administer only artificial respiration. (Refer to the entry on artificial respiration for instructions in that technique.)

CPR is the application of artificial heart contractions along with artificial breathing, one after the other, in an ongoing rhythm. In the best situation, one person applies heart compression while a second breathes for the cat. It's also advisable to have someone drive you to the veterinary clinic while CPR is administered. External heart massage is accomplished by placing the palm of your left hand beneath the cat's chest, so that your thumb rests on her left side at the point of her elbow, and the other fingers are flat on the cat's right side for compression. Squeeze firmly but gently five times, about once every second, then follow with one breath of artificial respiration. Repeat the sequence until the cat begins breathing on her own. However, if there is no response after fifteen minutes of CPR, revival is unlikely.

Carnivore

A carnivore is an animal that eats other animals. The name comes from its specialized TEETH: Molars in the side of the jaw called carnassial teeth evolved with early meat-eating mammals. These teeth provide a scissorlike action that slices flesh and makes it easier to eat.

Cats are obligate carnivores. That means they have a nutritional requirement for specific amino acids and other nutrients found only in animal products. A cat cannot survive on an exclusively vegetarian diet (see FOOD and NUTRITION).

Car Sickness

Fortunately, cats don't often get sick during car rides. They more frequently become agitated and fearful, and meow a great deal; some actually throw a fit. Introduce your cat to car rides slowly, and always be sure he's contained in a secure carrier to protect him. While he's still a kitten, take him on short trips around the block, and end the ride with

C

CAR SICKNESS

SYMPTOMS

Agitation, crying, screaming, throwing fit

HOME CARE

Situate carrier so cat has a view, or drape carrier to block view

VET CARE

Prescription sedative or Dramamine-type car sickness medication

PREVENTION

Withhold food for 12 hours prior to trip; acclimate cat to car in short trips, use favorite toys/games to make experience more pleasant

a special treat or favorite game so he associates the car with good things. If the only experience in the car your cat ever has ends with unpleasantness at the vet, you can only expect him to protest.

Offering a favorite toy may help calm his nerves. Depending on the cat, seeing where he's going may help calm him down; other cats, though, do better with a towel draped over the carrier. Your veterinarian may prescribe a mild sedative to calm your cat's nerves, or a drug like Dramamine to soothe possible upset stomachs. Never give your cat anything for car sickness without first consulting your veterinarian.

Castration

See NEUTERING.

Cataract

A cataract is cloudiness within the lens of the eye. The lens is inside the eye directly behind the pupil (see EYES). In a normal eye, the lens is clear.

A cataract interferes with sight by partially or completely blocking the clarity of the lens. The cloudiness can vary from a little spot of white to a totally opaque structure that affects the entire lens. If the lens becomes completely masked, the result is blindness.

Fortunately, cataracts in cats are not terribly common. Still, they can affect any age and every breed. While cataracts are extremely common in dogs, cats do not suffer from the diabetes-related or "old-age" cataracts often found in dogs.

Cataracts are reported to be inherited in some breeds of cats. Birman, British Shorthair, and the Himalayan are affected most often. Most feline cataracts are associated with an inflammation inside the eye usually due to systemic disease. Many cats will have chronic inflammation inside the eye as part of FELINE INFECTIOUS PERITONITIS, FELINE IMMUNODEFICIENCY VIRUS, or FELINE LEUKEMIA VIRUS, and as a result may end up developing cataracts.

Injury to the eye or the resulting inflammation from an injury also may cause a cataract, usually in only one eye. Some kittens are simply born with cataracts, probably due to an infection that happened while they were in the uterus.

Cataracts may also result from poor nutrition, but because of modern advances in feline diets, such causes are rare. In some cases, the cataract is idiopathic, which means the cause cannot be identified.

Because a cataract may affect only a tiny part of the lens of one eye, some cats may show no signs of vision loss at all. A cat can have a significant cataract and still not have any meaningful vision loss. Other times, the cataract may cover the entire lens of one or both eyes, causing blindness. And although a vision-impaired cat may do well in familiar surroundings, he may bump into walls when faced with rearranged furniture or a new environment.

Don't make the mistake of confusing a cloudy eye surface with a

C

CATARACT

SYMPTOMS

Cloudiness of lens inside of eye, loss of sight, bumping
into walls

HOME CARE

None

VET CARE

Address underlying cause; sometimes surgery is necessary

PREVENTION

Prevent infectious diseases that may result in cataracts

cataract. A cloudy skin on the eye is more likely a treatable injury to
the cornea, the clear surface of the eyeball. With a cataract you may
notice cloudiness within the pupil space—it looks as if there's a little
white marble inside the eye.

Treatment depends on the severity of the cataract. When trauma or
inflammation is the culprit, the underlying cause is treated. Many
times, when small cataracts cause little vision problems, no treatment is
necessary. As long as only one eye is affected, cats tend to do quite well
with one working eye.

Kittens born with congenital cataracts can have a lot of trouble seeing when they're young, but their vision usually improves with age. The
lens grows as the cat matures, while the area of cloudiness on the lens
remains the same size. By adulthood, most cats born with cataracts
are able to compensate and see "around" the small area of remaining
cloudiness.

In certain instances, surgery is helpful (although it is not indicated
when the cataract is caused by inflammation). When the cat is blind or
going to go blind in both eyes, surgery may be recommended. The same
surgical techniques used on people for cataracts are applied to dogs and

cats. Most veterinary ophthalmologists in private practice or at a university can do the surgery. Done under general anesthesia, the long procedure removes most but not all of the affected lens. The lens itself is contained in a kind of capsule, like an eggshell. Most commonly, surgery removes the front part of the shell and the contents inside, leaving the back half of the capsule/shell intact. In some cases, the whole lens is removed and a new lens is transplanted to replace the damaged lens.

A device called a phako unit is used in the surgery. This unit produces high-frequency sound waves—ultrasound—to break up the lens, which is then removed by suction, or aspiration. Cats that have the surgery usually recover quite nicely.

Cat Associations

See Appendix A.

Catnip

Nepeta cataria, or catnip, is a strong-scented mint that cats find extremely attractive. The plant contains a volatile oil the major component of which is a chemical somewhat like sedatives found in the valerian plant. The chemical may also be similar to one of the substances in tomcat urine, which often triggers the same kind of reaction.

Cats affected by the scent will bite and roll on the plant to release the oil into the air. Cats can detect catnip oil in the air at saturations as low as one part per billion.

Catnip affects the same biochemical pathways in cats that are affected by marijuana and LSD in people. In fact, catnip is a feline hallucinogen; the "high" lasts from five to fifteen minutes and basically causes a loss of inhibition. Catnip-intoxicated cats act like furry fools

A cat's favorite plant: catnip. *(Photo credit: Betsy Stowe)*

who roll and flop about on the floor, drool, and have a wonderful relaxing time. Catnip even builds the confidence of some shy cats.

Not all cats are affected by catnip. Cats rarely respond until they are about six months old, and some cats never do. The trait is an inherited one, with only two out of three domestic cats being affected. Male cats seem to respond to it more strongly than females.

Most scientists agree that catnip provides a harmless recreation for cats, but it can be overused. Overindulgence causes cats to lose their response to the plant. Offering catnip as an occasional treat, perhaps once every two or three weeks, is plenty.

Cat Scratch Disease (CSD)

Formerly called cat scratch fever, CSD is a bacterial infection caused by the tiny bacterium *Bartonella henselae*. The syndrome was first described in 1950, but until recently, researchers couldn't agree on what caused the disease. Much about it still remains unknown.

We do know the bacteria infect the cat's bloodstream without making the cat sick. Cats infected with CSD remain perfectly healthy. Research shows that approximately 41 percent of pet cats actually become infected with the disease.

Problems arise when the organism is transmitted to people, who do become sick. The disease is estimated to affect about 22,000 people each year in the United States. Historically, CSD has been diagnosed most often in children, but recent surveys indicate 43 percent of affected patients were older than twenty years of age, and more than half of these were women.

CAT SCRATCH DISEASE

(HUMAN) SYMPTOMS

Swollen cat scratches, flulike signs, swollen lymph nodes

(HUMAN) HOME CARE

Nutritional support

(HUMAN) DOCTOR CARE

Antibiotics

(HUMAN) PREVENTION

See Preventing CSD in Humans

PREVENTING CSD IN HUMANS

(Particularly important for immune-compromised people)
1. Get rid of your cat's fleas.
2. Avoid rough play that prompts bites and scratches.
3. Wash any bites or scratches immediately with soap and water, and disinfect.
4. Prohibit cat from licking open wounds on your body.

No one really knows just how the bacteria get into the cat, or into people. But for people, the cat connection is a strong one: About 90 percent of those diagnosed with CSD have had contact with a cat, and 80 percent report having been scratched by a cat. The risk of infection is highest among people with a KITTEN.

It's not been established, but it is considered highly likely that the bacteria are spread from the bloodstream of one cat to another by biting FLEAS. Therefore, the risk of the disease goes up if a kitten has fleas. Just how the bug gets on a kitten's claws, which can scratch and spread the disease to people, isn't known. It's theorized that the bacteria may be in an infected cat's saliva, and is transferred to his claws when he grooms himself; or that infected blood contaminates the claws when a cat scratches himself.

However, that doesn't explain the 10 percent of people ill with CSD who never have contact with a cat. Researchers believe, but haven't yet proven, that the fleas may be spreading the disease directly, without the cat's help. That may be why the highest incidence of disease among people is during the summer months of flea season.

Signs in otherwise healthy people are often mild and go away without treatment. A healed cat scratch may again turn red, swollen, and sore, and the lymph node closest to the injury swell. Scratches on a hand or arm tend to affect lymph nodes in the armpit, while those on the ankles and legs affect lymph nodes in the groin region. Vague feelings of fatigue or even flulike symptoms may develop and last up to three months before going away. Ten percent of cases develop conditions affecting the eyes, liver, kidneys, or central nervous system and require hospitalization; with treatment, these rare conditions usually resolve themselves within two weeks.

Diagnosis is based on the signs of the disease, a history of cat exposure, and blood tests. A variety of antibiotics are used to treat the condition.

CSD represents a much greater risk for people with compromised immune systems, such as transplant recipients, people with HIV or AIDS, and patients undergoing anticancer treatments. A suppressed immune system may allow the bacteria to infiltrate the walls of the blood vessels, resulting in a condition called bacillary angiomatosis (BA). The most common sign is raised, red skin lesions, but BA also compromises liver and kidney function, and can cause death. A microscopic examination of affected tissue diagnoses the condition. BA looks quite similar to Kaposi's sarcoma, which commonly affects AIDS patients, but unlike Kaposi's, BA responds extremely well to treatment, and typically infections are cured within a month or so using antibiotic therapy.

Preventing the disease is desirable, particularly for people in the high-risk groups. Yet until we know how the disease is transmitted, testing and treating cats isn't effective or practical. And doing without a beloved cat is rarely something owners are willing or even need to consider.

The emotional and physical benefits of owning a pet have been well documented in medical literature, and most experts agree that high-risk groups should not be denied the joy of cat ownership. The risk of transmission from contact with cats is considered quite low, and can be reduced even further by taking simple precautions. Sensible interaction with adult cats rarely leads to scratches, and DECLAWING isn't generally recommended. Nail covers, though, might help prevent claws from breaking the skin.

If you are in a high-risk group, your physician should know you have a cat. Be aware that adopting an adult cat poses less risk for you than a kitten. Ask a friend to medicate or groom your cat for you to lower the risk of scratches or bites, and always wash your hands after handling your cat.

Getting scratched doesn't automatically result in infection, though. There are 66 million pet cats in the United States, and most owners will never be affected by CSD. (See also ZOONOSIS.)

Cesarean

A cesarean procedure is a surgical delivery performed by the veterinarian when a natural birth is not possible. A healthy QUEEN rarely has a problem with delivery, but those in poor health may need assistance. Trauma or a nutritional deficiency may cause a pelvic deformity that makes natural birth difficult. However, medications may be administered to stimulate uterine contraction, which means surgical intervention is rarely necessary.

When it is necessary, the surgery is performed under general anesthesia by the veterinarian. Generally, the risk to the queen is not great. Prolonged labor, dead kittens, uterine rupture, or toxicity increase the risks for the queen. Usually, within a few hours, the mother is awake and able to nurse her kittens. She may or may not require a cesarean with future pregnancies, depending on the circumstances for the first. (See also REPRODUCTION.)

Chemicals

See POISON.

Chlamydia (Pneumonitis)

See UPPER RESPIRATORY INFECTIONS.

Chocolate

6

Chocolate may appeal to a pet's sweet tooth, but it's toxic to both dogs and cats. Poisonings usually happen around the holidays, when pet owners have candy more readily available.

Chocolate contains a substance called theobromine, which is toxic to pets. Theobromine is related to caffeine, and acts as a stimulant to the cat's nervous system. Essentially, theobromine shifts the cat's nervous system into overdrive.

Milk chocolate found in Hershey Kisses contains about 1.5 milligrams of theobromine per gram. A toxic dose of milk chocolate is five ounces per pound of body weight—meaning nearly two pounds of milk chocolate for a seven-pound cat. But unsweetened baking chocolate

CHOCOLATE POISONING

SYMPTOMS

Drooling, vomiting and/or diarrhea; excessive urination; hyperactivity; muscle tremors; seizures; coma

HOME CARE

EMERGENCY! SEE VETERINARIAN IMMEDIATELY. If ingested in last 2 hours, induce vomiting

VET CARE

Induce vomiting, flush stomach, administer activated charcoal, provide supportive care such as fluid therapy

PREVENTION

Keep chocolate out of cat's reach

contains nearly *ten times as much* theobromine as milk chocolate. A seven-pound cat can become sick by eating as little as 2.5 *ounces* of baking chocolate—about the amount in the frosting of a large cake.

Affected cats show a wide variety of signs. Some cats drool, and most eventually suffer VOMITING and/or DIARRHEA. Occasionally, poisoned cats pass so much urine, they appear to be incontinent. Cats typically become hyperactive, and run around with great energy. The drug not only stimulates the nervous system, but it can also speed up the heart or cause an irregular heartbeat. If cats eat enough of the poison, the signs of toxicity can progress to muscle tremors, seizures, coma, and ultimately death.

There is no specific antidote for theobromine toxicity. Treatment consists of maintaining life support, preventing further absorption of the poison, hastening elimination, and symptomatic treatment of the signs of poisoning.

If a cat ate chocolate within the last two hours, it's generally recommended that the owner make the cat throw up. DO NOT GIVE SYRUP OF IPECAC—IT CAN BE TOXIC IN CERTAIN ANIMALS. Administer one tablespoon of a 3 percent solution of household hydrogen peroxide for every ten pounds of pet (see ADMINISTERING OF MEDICATION, Oral Treatments). Repeat the dose in ten minutes if the first dose doesn't do the trick. If you have difficulty making the cat throw up, bring the cat to the veterinary hospital so it can be done there. And even if the cat *does* throw up, you should still bring him to the vet for examination.

The veterinarian may administer activated charcoal to help prevent additional absorption of the theobromine into the cat's system. Fluid therapy may be needed to counteract signs of SHOCK. Seizures, heart irregularities, vomiting, and diarrhea are each treated specifically with appropriate medications. The treatment is often prolonged, because the half-life of theobromine—the time it takes the body to eliminate it—is 72 hours in dogs, and is thought to be the same or longer in cats.

The best way to deal with chocolate toxicity is to prevent the problem from ever happening. If your cat has a sweet tooth, keep chocolate out of reach (see also POISON).

Choking

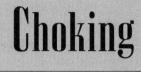

See SWALLOWED OBJECTS.

Claws

Cats have a toenail, or claw, on the end of each toe. Sharply pointed and curved, claws function as grooming tools for combing fur, grappling hooks for climbing and holding prey, and daggers for protection. Cat claws are unique in that they are retractable.

Cats normally have five toes on the front feet and four on the hind feet. The fifth claw on the inside of the front paws that does not reach the ground is called the dewclaw, and is a leftover toe inherited from ancient cats that is no longer truly functional.

Claws are an extension of two small bones found at the end of each toe. The bones rest nearly on top of each other and are "hinged" by tendons. When relaxed, the claws are sheathed inside a skin fold at the end of each toe, and paws look softly furred, smooth, and almost dainty. To extend his claws, a cat flexes the tendon and straightens the folded bones, which pushes the claws down and forward. The action also spreads the paw to nearly twice its former width.

The exterior claw is composed of a hard, nonliving protein or cuticle that is white to clear in most cats. Inside this rigid structure is the living tissue of the nail bed, called the quick, which contains the blood supply and nerve endings. Claws grow out of the quick, and the outer horny layer of claw is periodically shed to expose new growth that is razor sharp.

Cat claws do not wear down during normal activity the way a dog's do, but new claw tips lose their edge. Cats sharpen their front claws by SCRATCHING hard surfaces. Sinking front claws deep into soft surfaces and pulling downward strips away the dead outer layers on their front claws. Nibbling and biting remove outer claw layers on rear paws. Unless this necessary maintenance is attended, claws can overgrow, split, or break off and result in painful infections (see GROOMING, Clipping Your Cat's Nails).

Climbing

Cats seem to prefer high locations that offer the best view of their surroundings. Some breeds tend to climb more than others. Indoor cats

Cats are skilled climbers. *(Photo credit: Amy D. Shojai)*

may leap to the tops of refrigerators or lounge in lofty bookcases. High ledges, fences, and even trees are favorite lookouts for outdoor cats.

The cat was designed with climbing in mind. Strong rear leg muscles enable cats to jump up to seven times their height. A cat's shoulder blades, located on her sides rather than on her back like human shoulder blades, give her greater flexibility. She has no collarbone; her front legs are instead attached to the chest only by muscle. Because they are not connected to a fixed point, the cat's front legs have a superior range of motion. This allows the cat to walk, run, and jump with her front legs close together, which is invaluable when traversing high, narrow areas. The cat also has the ability to "hug" a tree by spreading her front legs wide as she climbs up or down.

Claws curved outward and back help the cat to grasp vertical objects so she can pull herself up. Even cats missing their front claws may be able to climb if the rear claws remain intact (see DECLAWING). Because of the curve of their claws, cats that willingly climb up may be reluctant to descend. Often, they simply yowl for an owner's assistance to avoid the embarrassing necessity of backing down tail first.

Coat Type

See BREED.

Coccidiosis

Coccidiosis is caused by coccidia, a common protozoal parasite that colonizes and attacks the lining of cats' intestines. Adult cats commonly have a few coccidia in their system that cause no problem. However, kittens that are infected may develop a fatal DIARRHEA that's mixed with blood-tinged mucus.

COCCIDIOSIS

SYMPTOMS

Loose stool with mucus and blood that comes and goes

HOME CARE

None

VET CARE

Sulfa-type drugs, sometimes fluid therapy or blood transfusion in severe cases

PREVENTION

Prompt cleaning of litter box

Cats are infected by swallowing the immature parasite. The developing eggs, called oocysts, are passed in an infected animal's stool. These microscopic oocysts require several days in the soil to become infective. Cats contract coccidia by swallowing this infective stage. A cat can become infected by washing himself after walking through contaminated soil, or by eating other animals—such as rodents—that are infected.

Signs of infection in adult cats tend to come and go. Affected cats may pass blood and loose stool with a lot of mucus for two to three days, get better, then a week later have the signs return. Diagnosis is made by finding the oocysts during microscopic examination of a stool sample.

Generally, cats are treated with a sulfa-type drug, and it typically takes a week before improvement is seen. In severe cases, hospitalization may be required to treat DEHYDRATION with fluid therapy or a blood transfusion.

Routine and prompt cleaning of the LITTER BOX helps prevent infection or reinfection. Environmental control includes daily washing of the cat's quarters—his litter box as well as his sleeping area—with boiling water to destroy infective organisms.

Colitis

Colitis is an inflammation of the colon, the large bowel at the very end of the gastrointestinal tract. The colon removes water from the solid waste that's passed. When the intestinal lining becomes inflamed, it interferes with water removal and compromises the way the colon contracts and moves fecal matter along.

Colitis accounts for 15 to 20 percent of diarrhea complaints in cats. Lots of straining is often involved. Cats with colitis produce very frequent (several in an hour) liquid stools that have a great deal of mucus and bright red blood.

In some parts of the country, particularly in outdoor cats in the South, colitis is associated with intestinal parasites (see HOOKWORMS or GIARDIA). When the causative parasites are eliminated through proper

COLITIS

SYMPTOMS

Straining to defecate, frequent liquid stools containing mucus and bright red blood

HOME CARE

None

VET CARE

Address the specific cause, oral medications, high-fiber diets

PREVENTION

Prevent intestinal parasites, keep litter box clean, avoid abrupt diet changes, don't feed milk to cat

C

treatment, the colitis usually goes away. Other times, inflammation may be due to food ALLERGIES, and avoiding the particular food will relieve the situation. Your veterinarian may prescribe oral medications or high-fiber diets to help control the problem (see also DIARRHEA).

The best way to prevent colitis caused by intestinal parasites is to prevent infestation. Do this by keeping the litter box clean and by offering your cat only fresh, clean water. It's not necessary to give your cat bottled water—but if you're concerned about *your* drinking tap water, then maybe the cat should get bottled water, too. Cats should be prevented from drinking standing water like mud puddles, which are an ideal breeding ground for giardia. There's really no way to anticipate a food allergy or prevent an adverse reaction until after it actually occurs. However, milk is a problem for many cats, and should be avoided if your cat suffers colitis after drinking it.

Color Perception

See EYES.

Combing

See GROOMING.

Cats communicate both verbally and nonverbally. *(Photo credit: Betsy Stowe)*

Communication

Cats have often been regarded as mysterious, solitary, unpredictable creatures. This is largely because humans have been unable to understand what a cat is saying. Current research indicates that cats are social creatures; they rely on a distinct feline language to communicate with other cats, other pets, and the humans who make up their world.

But while people rely primarily on speech to communicate, "felinese" is predominantly a silent language. Cats speak by using complex combinations of sign language, vocalization, and scent cues (see MARKING).

Cats have the ability to learn a large human vocabulary, though, especially when words are used with consistency (see TRAINING). But since cats are more highly attuned to body language, they tend to give silent communication more weight. That means when the words repri-

C

Alert/Inquisitive

Fearful

C

Aggressive/Imminent Attack

Submissive

Alert/Inquisitive   **Fearful**

Aggressive/Imminent Attack   **Submissive**

mand but the face smiles, a cat reacts to the person's amusement rather than the aggravation, and acts accordingly.

Cats react even to subtle nonverbal cues that people don't realize they're broadcasting. A cat may seem psychic when in fact she's simply reading a facial expression, posture, or action that she knows indicates a particular emotion or intent. The cat's ability to figure things out proves her to be an excellent observer who pays exquisite attention to the details of our behavior.

Our own limited hearing and scenting ability renders us deaf to many of the nuances of feline language. But an attentive owner can learn to read and translate the more obvious feline signals, and pave the way for smoother interspecies communication.

Verbal expression is a relatively small part of cat communication, although some breeds like the Siamese are more vocal than others. There are as many as sixteen distinct feline vocal patterns, which fall into four generally recognized categories.

Murmur patterns include purrs and trills, which seem to express contentment. Meows are classified as *vowel patterns*, and are almost exclusively directed at humans. Cats have a variety of meows, which are invariably used when the cat wants something from her human (i.e., petting, being fed, to go outdoors or come inside). Usually, the more agitated a cat becomes, the lower the pitch of the meow. *Articulated patterns* are usually recognized as a sign of solicitation or frustration. Cats produce chirping, chattering sounds when they can't reach the squirrel teasing them from the other side of the window. Finally, *strained intensity patterns* are used as warnings to increase the distance between the cat and a perceived threat. These sounds include spits and hisses, growls and screams, and are the feline equivalent to "Back off, buster!" Strained intensity sounds are used in defense, attack, and mating.

Nonverbal signals, on the other hand, offer a number of advantages over verbal ones in the animal kingdom. Vocalizations give away a cat's location to adversaries, while posturing can't be overheard. Nonverbal communication also lasts longer—sign language can be sustained nearly indefinitely with no need to stop and take a breath. The silent semaphore language of cats is accomplished through facial expression and body position, and even the elevation of the cat's fur speaks volumes.

A cat's mood is indicated by the position of the eyelids and the dilation of the pupil (see EYES). Any strong emotional arousal—fear, anger, pleasure, excitement—can result in the sudden contraction of the cat's pupils. Cats open their eyes wide when they are alert. By leaving his eyes open and unprotected, a wide-eyed cat that bumps your face with his cheeks is showing his trust. But a direct unblinking stare from a distance is a sign of dominance and aggression, as are slit-eyed looks. Avoid locking eyes with a cat you don't know. A relaxed, trusting cat has droopy, sleepy-looking eyelids.

The position of a cat's EARS indicates her mood. Forward-facing ears express interest. The ears turn to the sides as the cat feels threatened or uneasy, and flatten tight to the head when fearful or angry.

WHISKERS on a curious cat fan forward, as though to embrace the object of interest. The whiskers of happy, relaxed cats are extended out. Whiskers slicked back and down against the cheeks show a cat is frightened or agitated.

The cat's tail also speaks volumes. KITTENS greet their mothers and confident, happy adult cats greet their owners with tails held straight up, with just the end tipped over—like a finger waving, "hi there." The end of the cat's tail may twitch or flick as an expression of the cat's frustration or irritation, and is a warning to cease and desist. If polite tail flicks are ignored, the tail movement may escalate to lashing or even thumping the ground, which is a final warning to lay off or receive a smack. The relaxed, content cat's tail curves down and up in a gentle U, and goes higher to show interest. A straight tail with bristled fur indicates aggression, but a bristled tail held in an inverted U indicates fear or defensiveness.

Cats use communication to smooth out or establish relationships. A cat who blunders into another's territory must be able to apologize, and the offended cat must understand, or fights would constantly erupt. Cats avoid fights by bluffing with universally understood feline postures. Confident cats face the unknown head-on, their body ready to strike if necessary. Fearful cats turn sideways and arch their backs to bluff their way out of the situation. Cats who are uncertain or afraid puff up their fur to make themselves look larger and more impressive to warn off possible threats. Cats surrender by flattening themselves on the ground, all four feet beneath them, with ears and tail tucked tight. Indeed, cats may posture fifteen minutes or longer without fur ever flying, until one finally backs down. The cat who chases off the less dominant cat wins the confrontation.

Finally, cats place themselves in vulnerable positions to communicate AFFECTION and trust. They groom one another or their owner, solicit PLAY by rolling and presenting their tummies, and may SLEEP, cuddle, or play together. The cat sleeping with his back to you is showing ultimate trust. Other types of body contact, like touching noses or bumping hips when they pass each other, can be signs of affection. And just as human speech is colored by regional dialects, accents, and a variety of languages, cat communication varies somewhat from cat to cat.

Constipation

Constipation is the infrequent elimination of small amounts of dry, hard, dark-colored stool. When feces are not passed for two or three days, the colon removes too much moisture, which makes passing the waste painful.

Cats afflicted with constipation may squat and strain for long periods of time with little result. They may stop eating, and begin to lose weight. Sometimes chronic constipation can cause an inflammation of the bowel lining, which stimulates a release of fluid. In these instances, the fecal matter remains hard and dry, but may be accompanied by dark watery liquid.

A number of conditions, such as HAIRBALLS or SWALLOWED OBJECTS, can cause the cat to become constipated. Diets low in fiber with a high

CONSTIPATION

SYMPTOMS

Straining without passing stool, or hard dry stools accompanied by dark brown liquid

HOME CARE

Hairball medication, nonmedicated Vaseline, Metamucil, or wheat bran added to diet

VET CARE

Suppositories, enemas, or laxatives

PREVENTION

High-fiber diets, grooming to remove shed fur

meat protein concentration may result in stools that are difficult to pass, particularly if the cat drinks little water. The STRESS of new surroundings or a dirty litter pan may induce the cat to delay defecation. Constipation is a common problem in elderly cats, due to a weakness of abdominal muscles, lack of exercise, and improper diet (see GERIATRIC CAT).

Veterinary assistance is often necessary to initially clear the colon; some cats need to be sedated to have hard feces mechanically removed. Veterinary-approved suppositories and enemas may be helpful, but should only be administered by your veterinarian. Over-the-counter products may contain ingredients like phosphates that can be lethal for your cat.

The treatment depends on the actual cause, but in most instances constipated cats are treated the same way people are. High-fiber diets and laxatives prove beneficial. Veterinary-approved stimulant laxatives are available, but can interfere with normal colon function if overused. A usually effective home-remedy laxative is nonmedicated petroleum jelly. Cats often lick Vaseline off their paws like a treat. The nondigestible jelly helps lubricate the stomach and intestinal lining, slick the hairball or dried fecal matter together, and promote movement out of the body.

Bulk-forming laxatives that contain cellulose ingredients attract water and add bulk to the stool. One to three tablespoons of Metamucil a day mixed into the cat's diet will help. Wheat bran works as well, is less expensive, and is a natural product without known side effects. Mix about two tablespoons for each fourteen ounces of the cat's canned diet (canned provides more water than dry) as a maintenance program to help keep your cat regular.

Contraception

See NEUTERING and SPAYING.

Coughing

See ASTHMA and HAIRBALLS.

Cryptorchid

Male kittens are born with their testicles already descended into the scrotal sac. The tiny organs are usually easily felt by about six weeks of age. Testicles that fail to descend and are retained in the abdomen are referred to as cryptorchid; when only one descends, it's called monorchid.

When both testicles are undescended, the cat is rendered sterile. Hormonal therapy administered prior to sexual maturity to affected kittens may sometimes cause the testicles to descend. Cats with one descended testicle may be able to father kittens, but because the condition is thought to be inherited, cryptorchid cats should not be bred.

Retained testicles continue to generate male hormones, so these cats will exhibit the same behavior as any intact male (see REPRODUCTION). But as cryptorchid cats are also at higher risk for testicular cancer, it is recommended that they be neutered. The veterinarian must go into the abdomen to find and remove the organs surgically.

When a cat appears to have been neutered but behaves otherwise, the veterinarian should be able to tell if the cat has a retained testicle. The penis of a mature intact male cat has prominent spines; once neutered, the spines disappear.

Cuterebra

Cuterebra are the larvae of the bot fly, a parasite that usually afflicts rodents. Cats and dogs come in contact with cuterebra from exploring rabbit or mouse habitats. Outdoor cats, particularly hunting felines, seem to be at highest risk, with kittens and younger cats affected most often. Cuterebra infection is seen most often during the summer months.

The eggs of the bot fly are deposited five to fifteen at a time in the soil or vegetation surrounding the animal burrow. The body heat of a nearby host triggers the egg to hatch, and emerging larvae attach themselves to the animal's skin. The larva enters the animal's nose or mouth as it grooms and migrates through the host's body to a location just beneath the skin. This area swells as the parasite matures.

At first, the swelling feels firm. It then becomes fluid-filled and soft, with a central breathing hole for the parasite that leaks blood-tinged

CUTEREBRA INFESTATION

SYMPTOMS

Soft swelling beneath skin, usually of the neck or chest region

HOME CARE

None

VET CARE

Surgical removal

PREVENTION

Keep cat indoors, prevent hunting

fluid. The cuterebra continue to grow and molt, until the CYST beneath the skin that contains the worm is quite noticeable.

A brownish larva covered with quills may reach over an inch in length and a half inch in diameter before breaking free of the host's skin, dropping to the ground, and spending the winter in a pupal stage. Pupae hatch into adult bot flies in the spring, each of which can lay more than two thousand eggs, thus completing the cycle.

In cats, cuterebra usually follow the normal route of migration. Cats are typically affected by only one parasite, but they may have more than one. The swelling often looks like an abscess, and usually appears on the neck or in the chest region. Other than the swelling and draining, cats rarely show distress from the encounter, but the cysts may become infected. The parasite usually remains in the cat's skin for about a month before it emerges.

Never try to remove the parasite at home, and do not try to squeeze or express the cuterebra from the skin. Crushing the parasite may cause a life-threatening anaphylactic reaction in the cat (see INSECT BITES/ STINGS). A veterinarian carefully removes the parasite through the vent hole, enlarging the opening surgically if necessary, then cleans and treats the wound.

In rare instances, cuterebra infestation results in an aberrant migration into the nostrils, spinal column, or scrotum, or even into the brain, which can have life-threatening consequences (see ISCHEMIC ENCEPHA- LOPATHY). Preventing cats from cuterebra exposure by keeping them inside, particularly during the summer months, is probably the best way to avoid infection.

Cyst

A cyst is defined as a thick capsule of tissue containing foreign matter that develops abnormally within the body. Cutaneous cysts (those found in the skin) are uncommon in cats, but they can still appear anywhere on the body.

Cutaneous cysts are usually firm to soft, well-defined round areas. Often bluish in color, they move freely beneath the skin. They may reach an inch or more in diameter and are filled with a greasy, yellow-to-brown cheeselike substance that may drain from a central opening. Cutaneous cysts tend to progress to ulceration and infection, and most should be surgically removed.

Ovarian cysts may develop in females allowed to repeatedly experience heat without being mated (see REPRODUCTION). Called cystadenomas, these tumors are quite common in intact female cats. The ovaries of an affected QUEEN will develop many thin-walled cysts that contain watery fluid, and in time these cysts can completely replace normal ovarian tissue.

Ovarian cysts result in an abnormally high production of the hormone estrogen. This can cause the queen to experience a prolonged or even continuous heat cycle. Affected cats tend to fight with other cats, and will either refuse to mate or will mate frequently but be unable to become pregnant. Surgical removal of the cysts may correct the problem and allow conception to occur. More often, SPAYING the cat surgically removes the ovaries and uterus. Spaying the cat before her first heat cycle prevents the problem from ever occurring.

Cystitis

Cystitis is an inflammation of the membrane lining the urinary bladder. The condition may be caused by viral or bacterial infection, STRESS, or other causes. Diagnosis is made by examination of the cat's urine, called a urinalysis.

Up to 55 percent of cystitis cases are idiopathic, which means a cause cannot be determined. Cystitis in cats is a condition most commonly associated with LOWER URINARY TRACT DISEASE (LUTD). The warning signs for cystitis and LUTD are identical, and are identified on the following chart.

The treatment for cystitis is the same as for LUTD. In addition, the cat's urine is cultured to determine if bacteria have infected the bladder. The first incidence of feline cystitis is rarely due to bacteria; however, catheterization during treatment for LUTD may introduce

CYSTITIS

SYMPTOMS

See Signs of Cystitis

HOME CARE

Prescribed diets

VET CARE

Antibiotics, fluid therapy

PREVENTION

Reduce stress

C

bacteria so that subsequent bouts of bacterial cystitis develop. When bacteria are diagnosed, a specific antibiotic is then given to the cat for up to three weeks.

SIGNS OF CYSTITIS

1. A housebroken cat dribbling urine or urinating in unusual locations
2. Frequent voiding of small amounts of urine
3. Bloody urine
4. Urine with a strong ammonia odor
5. Squatting or straining at the end of urination
6. Listlessness and poor appetite and/or excessive thirst

See a veterinarian *immediately* for any one or combination of these signs.

There's no way to predict which cat will suffer from cystitis, and so there is no easy way to prevent occurrence. But cats that are afflicted once are likely candidates for recurrence. Avoiding stress to the cat is the best way to reduce the incidence of flare-ups.

C

Dander

See ALLERGIES, OF HUMANS TO CATS.

Deafness

See EARS.

Declawing

Declawing is an irreversible surgical procedure that removes a cat's claws. This elective surgery is not necessary or beneficial for feline health but is a means of eliminating normal feline SCRATCHING behavior that an owner may find objectionable.

Declaw operations remain controversial, with some cat experts declaring the procedure unnatural and psychologically damaging to the cat. Certain breed associations will not allow a cat to be shown if declaw surgery has been done. But proponents argue that when the procedure is properly performed, a cat suffers no ill effects, and in fact is more likely to be able to enjoy a permanent home since destructive scratching is eliminated.

Claws are outdoor cats' first line of defense and affect their climbing ability, which means that outdoor cats should not be declawed. When behavior modification techniques have proved unsuccessful for an indoor cat, surgery may be an option.

The procedure is performed under a general ANESTHETIC so the cat feels no discomfort. Because youngsters tend to cope with the loss of claws more quickly than adult cats, veterinarians often recommend that kittens be declawed at three to five months of age. Usually, only the claws from the front paws are removed, since rear claws are not used to scratch furniture. And cats with rear claws still intact are likely to still be able to climb small trees.

There are three bones in each toe, with the claw growing from the end of the last bone. Declawing surgically amputates the end section of this last bone along with the nail to remove the claw and prevent regrowth.

The cat's feet are prepared for surgery by scrubbing and soaking them in an antiseptic surgical solution, such as Betadine and alcohol. The fur is not shaved, but may be clipped if extremely long. A tourniquet is placed to stop the BLEEDING, then each claw is expressed in turn and surgically removed at the joint, leaving only smooth white bone. Each toe is sewn closed with absorbable suture material that will not need to be removed. Once all the claws on a paw are removed, the foot is bandaged snugly to control postoperative bleeding, and the tourniquet is removed.

A day or more of hospitalization is required. Bandages come off in a day or two, but the feet will remain tender for up to a week. Until the toes completely heal, gritty or abrasive litter box fillers should be avoided to prevent introducing dirt into the cat's healing incisions. Shredded newspaper is often recommended to line the litter box.

Cats seem to suffer no more postoperative discomfort than from any other surgical procedure. Most cats are up and walking quite well within forty-eight to seventy-two hours. But if limping or favoring of the paws persists, or the incisions begin to bleed or appear swollen, bring your cat back to the veterinarian for further evaluation. If the claw bed has not been completely or properly removed, the claw may regrow or produce a misshapen claw, and a repeat of the surgery will be necessary.

Cats without front claws may still go through the motions of scratching furniture. Even without toenails, a cat feels impelled to scratch, which leaves invisible scent marks on the upholstery (see MARKING).

A newer, supposedly less stressful surgical procedure called a flexor tendonectomy is another option. This procedure leaves the cat his claws but prevents him from extending them.

A tendon connects the second and third bones of the cat's toes and controls the extension of the claws. The cat is anesthetized, then each tendon is cut and a tiny portion removed; in this way the cat cannot flex and extend the claws. The incisions are closed with skin glue, and the cat, after spending the night at the veterinary hospital for observation, usually goes home the next morning. Following this procedure, the claw base tends to thicken and nails may become more blunt, probably because of a limited ability of the cat to shed and sharpen the claws. Owners need to monitor the cat's toenails and clip them as necessary (see GROOMING).

Dehydration

Dehydration is the excessive loss of body water. Normal water loss occurs in the cat's litter box deposits, through moisture exhaled with the breath, and through sweat. These fluids are replaced when the cat eats and drinks.

Any illness may prompt the cat to stop eating and drinking, and prolonged fever increases the loss of body fluid. Specific disease conditions or injuries may result in excessive urination (see DIABETES MELLITUS and KIDNEY DISEASE), and VOMITING, DIARRHEA, and BLEEDING are all common causes of dehydration.

A normal adult cat's total body water is approximately 60 percent of his body weight. Signs of dehydration become apparent when the cat loses as little as 5 percent of normal body water. A 12 to 15 percent loss of total body water results in SHOCK and imminent death.

d

DEHYDRATION

SYMPTOMS

Loss of skin elasticity, dry mouth, stringy saliva, delayed capillary refill time, sunken eyeballs, muscle twitches, cold paw pads

HOME CARE

Give lots of water, and/or solutions like Pedialyte as directed by veterinarian

VET CARE

Fluid therapy, supportive care, sometimes blood transfusion

PREVENTION

Provide lots of fresh water at all times, offer shelter from the heat

---

The earliest noticeable sign of dehydration is the loss of skin elasticity. When the loose skin at the cat's shoulder blades is gently grasped and lifted, it should quickly spring back into place upon release. When slightly dehydrated, the cat's skin retracts slowly; more serious dehydration causes retracted skin to remain in a ridge, and spring back little, if any.

Dry mucous membranes are another sign of dehydration. The cat's mouth is dry, the gums are tacky instead of wet, and saliva may be stringy and thick.

Also, capillary refill time—the time it takes for blood to return to tissue after pressure is applied—is delayed. Gently press one finger to the side of your cat's gums; this will briefly block blood flow, and turn normally pink tissue white when the pressure is quickly released. Normally it takes less than two seconds for the white to return to pink. At 7 to 8 percent dehydration, capillary refill time is delayed by another two to three seconds. Longer than four or five seconds indicates severe dehydration. Such cats may also have sunken eyeballs, involuntary muscle twitches, and paw pads that feel cold to the touch.

A cat with noticeable dehydration needs immediate veterinary attention. Fluid and electrolyte (mineral) loss must be replaced, and steps need to be taken to prevent further loss. Intravenous fluid therapy may be necessary.

In mild cases in which the cat is not vomiting, oral hydration with plain water may be sufficient (see ADMINISTERING OF MEDICATION, Oral Treatments). Or your veterinarian may prescribe a balanced electrolyte solution, such as Ringer's solution with 5 percent dextrose in water. Fluids for treating dehydration in children, such as Pedialyte, are also suitable for cats. They should be given as directed by your veterinarian.

Make sure plenty of clean drinking water is always available to your cat to help prevent this condition.

Dermatitis

Dermatitis is inflammation of the skin. It can be generalized and involve the entire body, or confined in isolated areas. Dermatitis in cats is most often associated with allergies, but may be induced by sunburn, and very rarely is a psychological disorder related to stress. Signs and treatment vary depending on the cause (see ALLERGIES, CAT; MILIARY DERMATITIS; STRESS; and SUNBURN).

Destructive Behavior

See AGGRESSION, SCRATCHING, and SOILING.

Dewclaw

See CLAWS.

Diabetes Mellitus

Diabetes mellitus is a common disorder of the endocrine system and results from a malfunction of the pancreas. The pancreas produces insulin, a hormone that stimulates the movement of glucose (sugar) from the blood into the cells where it is used. When the pancreas fails to produce enough insulin, diabetes mellitus results.

DIABETES MELLITUS

SYMPTOMS

Increased eating with weight loss, increased drinking and urination, possible breaks in litter box training

HOME CARE

Administer insulin injections as instructed by veterinarian

VET CARE

Stabilize cat with fluids and other medications, regulate diet and monitor urine and blood, determine proper insulin dosage

PREVENTION

Prevent obesity

The onset of disease is so slow that the condition often goes undiagnosed until it becomes quite advanced. The incidence of the disease is reported to be only about one percent of the pet cat population. Male cats are diagnosed more often than females, and most cats are seven to nine years of age when diagnosed.

Warning signs of diabetes mellitus include excessive drinking, increased urination, and/or an increase of the appetite along with weight loss. These symptoms occur because the cat's body can't metabolize food; he becomes very hungry and weak, eating more and more, trying to compensate.

The level of glucose in the cat's blood continues to increase because it's not being used, with the excess excreted in large volumes in the urine. The sugar in the urine actually pulls more water out of the cat's system in a process called osmotic diuresis.

As a cat's need to urinate greater quantities more frequently continues, he may have "accidents" outside the litter box. This excessive loss of water through urination tends to make the cat thirsty, so he drinks more water to compensate. The result is a vicious cycle; drinking more water increases the need to urinate, which causes more thirst and drinking, and on and on.

There are two types of diabetes mellitus. Fifty to 70 percent of feline cases are *insulin dependent,* or *Type I,* in which the body produces little or no insulin, and insulin injections are necessary. Idiopathic amyloidosis is the most common cause of Type I feline diabetes mellitus; it is a deposit of a waxy protein/carbohydrate substance that inhibits function of the pancreas. Other causes include PANCREATITIS or even reactions to drugs like Ovaban.

Non–insulin dependent diabetes, or *Type II,* occurs when insulin is present in the body but other factors suppress its use. OBESITY is thought to be a major player in Type II diabetes mellitus because fat cells may become resistant to insulin when exposed to it. Diet and weight loss may help control certain cases of non–insulin dependent diabetes mellitus.

Diagnosis is based on the signs of disease, along with evaluation of the blood and urine. Without treatment, the diabetic cat develops life-threatening ketoacidosis. When the body isn't able to metabolize glucose for energy, eventually it switches to catabolism, which means the body burns its own fat and muscle tissue. This condition results in an excess of ketone bodies in the blood and urine. Ketone bodies are a normal part of fat metabolism, but too many result in a diabetic coma and death. Treatment for ketoacidosis may include fluid and electrolyte replacement, along with bicarbonate to restore the balance.

Diabetes mellitus cannot be cured, but in many cases it can be managed. Treatment is aimed at supportive therapy for any complications of the disease, and replacing insulin that the body is no longer able to produce.

A small percentage of cats suffering from Type II diabetes mellitus seem to benefit from high-fiber diets, which appear to reduce the need for insulin and promote weight loss, both of which make the patient much easier to regulate. Higher-fiber diets also tend to help relieve the surge of glucose that increases insulin requirements shortly after eating certain foods. Most cats suffering from diabetes mellitus, though, require insulin injections.

Commercial insulin is made from a variety of species, including pork, beef, beef/pork combinations, and even human derivatives. All are effective in cats, but some may work better than others. There are various types of insulin categorized by how quickly they work, how long they work, and the intensity of the effect. Mixtures of short-, moderate-, and long-acting insulins are available. Determining the appropriate therapy for an individual cat typically requires several days of hospitalization, during which time the cat's blood and urine glucose levels are monitored. Even after the cat returns home, adjustments will need to be made, with veterinary reevaluation necessary every month.

Most owners become quite adept at giving insulin injections to their cats. Diet and exercise influence insulin requirements, and should be kept constant. Unauthorized snacks or an exuberant chase around the room can be devastating to the diabetic cat.

Too much insulin can cause insulin reaction, referred to as hypoglycemia. Symptoms include disorientation, weakness and hunger, lethargy, shaking, or head tilt. Without treatment, the cat's symptoms progress to convulsions, coma, then death. Giving the cat a glucose source, such as Karo syrup or honey, should reverse signs within five to fifteen minutes. Then get your cat to the veterinarian immediately.

Insulin coma occurs when not enough insulin is given, and may result from a variance in diet or exercise, or if the insulin has expired and isn't effective. This is an emergency that your veterinarian must address.

A new treatment that is experimental is an oral medication called

Glucotrol, which appears to stimulate the secretion of insulin from the pancreas in a certain percentage of diabetic cats.

In the majority of cases, diabetes mellitus cannot be prevented, only controlled once diagnosed. However, keeping your cat slim and preventing obesity will lower his risk of developing the disease.

d

Diarrhea

Diarrhea refers to more-frequent-than-normal bowel movements that are abnormally soft or fluid. Diarrhea is not a disease but rather a symptom of ill health. Gastrointestinal upsets occur fairly frequently in cats, and diarrhea is one of the most common signs. Any prolonged change of bowel habits should be addressed by the veterinarian.

The condition is generally classified as either acute, which happens suddenly, or chronic, which is an ongoing condition.

Diarrhea can result from a number of things. Common causes include intestinal parasites or viruses. Eating too much, or an abrupt change in diet, may bring on diarrhea. Unhealthy FOOD SUPPLEMENTS like table scraps can upset a cat's stomach. MILK causes problems for many cats, because they may lack the dietary enzyme that allows them to digest it properly. Outdoor cats are more likely to suffer diarrhea when they capture and eat rodents or birds, or ingest toxic substances (see POISON). Some cats can develop allergies to their food (see ALLERGIES, CAT). And swallowing foreign material may also result in diarrhea (see HAIRBALLS and SWALLOWED OBJECTS).

Diarrhea is treated in three ways. *Symptomatic therapy* treats the signs. For example, an antidiarrheal medication would be given to control diarrhea. *Supportive treatment* is given when the cat has become debilitated by the disease; a DEHYDRATED cat would be given fluid therapy. *Specific therapy* treats the underlying disease when a specific diagnosis has been made. If the diarrhea is caused by parasites, worm medicine would be given.

With acute disease, treating the symptoms often works. Start by withholding food for at least twenty-four hours to rest the gastrointestinal tract. Offer only small amounts of water, or ice cubes for licking,

d

during this period. When you again offer food, make the first meal bland and divide it into several small servings rather than offering it all at once. Try a mixture of one part skinless white chicken meat or chicken baby food with two parts cooked white rice. The second day, mix the chicken half and half with your cat's normal diet. Reduce the mixture until, by the fourth day, your cat is back to eating a normal ration. Sometimes mixing in a tablespoon of a fiber supplement helps firm the stool; try natural wheat bran or Metamucil.

In addition, your veterinarian may suggest that you treat the cat

DIARRHEA

SYMPTOMS

More-frequent-than-normal bowel movements that are soft or fluid

HOME CARE

Withhold food for 24 hours, offering only minimal water or ice cubes to lick; offer bland first meal (1 part white chicken and 2 parts rice) in several small servings, then mix with regular diet, equal-size portions of each; gradually increase ratio of normal diet over 4-day period. Add 1 tbsp. natural wheat bran or Metamucil to food

VET CARE

If intestinal parasites diagnosed, specific medications prescribed; antidiarrheal medication; sometimes fluid therapy, or other medications depending on diagnosis

PREVENTION

Vaccinate cat against viral illnesses; keep cat indoors to prevent him from eating vermin; avoid sudden diet changes, table scraps, and milk treats

with antidiarrheal medication. Ask for an expert's recommendation; it could be dangerous to give your cat over-the-counter medication without your veterinarian's direction.

In cats with chronic disease, simply treating the diarrhea usually doesn't work. If you suspect your cat has ingested something dangerous that's causing the problem, or if the stool contains blood, SEE A VETERINARIAN IMMEDIATELY. Your cat also should see a doctor when diarrhea doesn't resolve with the above steps and persists for more than twenty-four hours. A further diagnosis is necessary to understand what's causing the problem before it can be appropriately treated. (See also COLITIS, ENTERITIS, and INFLAMMATORY BOWEL DISEASE.)

Most episodes of diarrhea can be prevented by protecting your cat with vaccinations against viral illnesses and intestinal parasites. Keeping your cat indoors curbs his opportunities for rodent snacks, which can cause diarrheal episodes. Don't feed your cat table scraps or milk, and avoid any abrupt change in the diet.

Diet

See FOOD and NUTRITION.

Discipline

See TRAINING.

Distemper

See FELINE PANLEUKOPENIA VIRUS.

Dominance

Dominance is behavior used to achieve a desired result. Most cats aren't satisfied with anything less than being King Cat and getting their own way. That's because the feline social system is not a hierarchy with one ruler and lesser-ranking individuals in a stairstep order below. Rather, feline ranking is described as despotic, which basically means that each cat considers himself *the* cat that counts, with other cats/ people below and having no particular ranking whatsoever.

A confident cat may exhibit dominant behavior toward family members, using anything from aggression to trickery to get his way. Cats that meow constantly for more food, attention, and to go inside or out, are asserting their dominance. To turn off this behavior and establish yourself as King Cat, don't let your cat push your buttons. If he meows for you to pet him, then pet him only when he's quiet and ignore him when he's noisy. If he meows to be fed, feed him before he turns up the noise, and don't give in to pleas at any other time. Consistency is key; owners reinforce the cat's identity as despot by giving in *just one time*. Cats know that if it worked once, it will likely work in the future.

A cat's sense of self has a great deal to do with the territory each "owns." Dominant cats defend their territory against interlopers. Your cat may identify the entire house, a portion of the house, or even individual furniture as his territory. His sense of possession may extend to the front yard visible from the window, even if he's never been allowed outdoors. And his territory most certainly extends to you, his owner.

If he feels his territory is threatened—a strange dog crosses the yard, a new boyfriend is taking up your time and attention, another cat sits in his chair—the dominant cat may react with aggressive behavior (see AGGRESSION) or some other action to reestablish who is King Cat.

For instance, some cats need only stare intently at a subordinate cat to induce it to move. Others make their point by hissing or posturing. And some devious cats even use subtle aggravation—grooming the other cat until he can't stand it and moves away, or simply leaning against him to make him leave. Your cat may simply get between you and the new boyfriend when you sit on the sofa.

Most cats sort out their own social order with compromises that avoid face-offs. As long as each cat has enough "territory" to satisfy his or her sense of ownership, the chance of feuds is lessened. Cat One may rule the first floor, and makes way for Cat Two on the second floor, and vice versa; Cat Two "owns" the sofa, while Cat One claims the top of the television.

In multicat households, dominance struggles increase in direct proportion to the decrease in available territory. An apartment that was adequate for one or two cats to share may be insufferable for five dominant felines. And when there's not enough territory to go around, dominant cats will constantly jockey for position and ownership and be in constant turmoil. They may resort to MARKING behavior and/or fighting. A good rule of thumb is to have no more cats than there are bedrooms in your house; that gives everybody a room of his own, and proves handy if temporary separation becomes necessary.

Dreaming

Cats, like other animals with highly developed brains, dream during the phase of deep sleep. Cats spend up to three hours each day enjoying dreams, while people only dream one and a half to two hours each day.

The exact purpose of dreams, for either people or animals, isn't known, but cats seem to relive the activities of everyday life in their dreams just like humans do. The dreaming cat's muscles relax, and his eyes move rapidly beneath his eyelids (REM, or rapid eye movement phase, sleep). During dream sleep, a cat is hard to awaken. A trusted owner whose scent and touch are familiar may even be able to move the cat without waking him. During dreams, the cat's paws may twitch and his tail switch; he may purr or growl; and his whiskers may bristle with excitement as he pounces on dream mice.

Drinking

See EATING.

Drowning

Drowning is suffocation caused by submersion in water. Drowning is an infrequent occurrence with cats, as they are natural swimmers. Although some breeds, like the Turkish Van, relish swimming, many cats dislike getting wet and avoid water hazards. Cats that drown are typically youngsters that fall into water and are unable to climb out. With very small kittens, even a water bowl may be dangerous, but outdoor hazards like swimming pools, ponds, rivers, and streams are more often involved.

Treatment consists of removing water from the lungs and getting air back into the cat. Position the cat head down, holding her with both hands around the lower abdomen, and swing her back and forth for twenty to thirty seconds. This should remove most of the water.

Then begin resuscitation to get the cat breathing again. If the water was cold, the cat's body will need to be warmed as quickly as possible. Seek veterinary attention immediately. Such cats are frequently at risk for PNEUMONIA. (See also CARDIOPULMONARY RESUSCITATION and HYPOTHERMIA.)

Prevent accidental drowning by keeping your cat indoors, away from dangerous waterways, such as rivers, ponds, swimming pools, and hot tubs. And be alert to potential indoor hazards, such as toilet bowls or deep water bowls.

DROWNING

SYMPTOMS

Loss of consciousness, no breathing apparent, cat found in or near water

HOME CARE

Grasp cat's lower abdomen and swing cat downward to express water; begin resuscitation; once cat is breathing, keep warm and get to a veterinarian

VET CARE

Oxygen therapy, possible rewarming therapy, precautions against pneumonia

PREVENTION

Bar the cat from exploring dangerous waterways, supervise young kittens and cats around water bowls, whirlpools, rivers, etc.

d

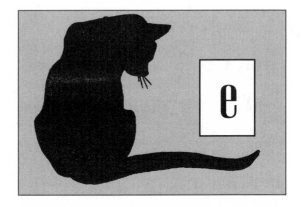

Ear Mites

These tiny parasites, common in cats, cause otodectic mange, more commonly known as ear mite infestation. Ear mites are a kind of arthropod that are actually related to and look something like spiders. The first four legs in all stages of development have unjointed short stalks and suckers; adult males also have suckers on the rear legs.

The mites live on the surface of the skin of the ear and ear canal. Adult females lay eggs with a cement that sticks them in place. After incubating four days, the eggs hatch into six-legged larvae. Larvae feed for three to ten days, consuming the debris of the ear canal and piercing the skin to suck lymph. Each larva hatches into an eight-legged protonymph, which then molts into a deutonymph. The deutonymph becomes attached to an adult male end-to-end by the suckers on each of their rear legs. If a female adult emerges from the deutonymph, fertilization occurs and the female becomes egg-bearing. The life cycle from egg to adult lasts three weeks.

Ear mites are the most common cause of ear inflammation, referred to as OTITIS. Symptoms of ear mite infestation include a brown, waxy debris in the ear canal and/or crust formation. The crawling mites inside the ear canal produce intense itching and discomfort in the cat. Infested cats will shake their heads, dig at their ears, and show a variety of restless behaviors.

EAR MITES

SYMPTOMS

Black to brown tarry or crumbly debris in ears, itchy ears, scratching or rubbing ears

HOME CARE

After diagnosis by vet, clean ears with prescribed medication

VET CARE

Sedation of cat to flush ears clean, sometimes medication to reduce inflammation or itching, mite-killing medication

PREVENTION

None; monitor ears, prevent contact with other possibly infected animals; keep environment controlled

e

Excessive head shaking or scratching at the ears caused by ear mites can result in secondary trauma to the pinna, the external portion of the cat's ear. This can cause a kind of blood blister, called a HEMATOMA.

Ear mites are extremely contagious, and kittens often acquire them from their mother. These parasites aren't selective; they infest many species, including cats, dogs, rabbits, ferrets, and other pets. Outdoor cats are most commonly affected.

If one pet is diagnosed with ear mites, all the animals in a multipet household must be treated to prevent reinfestation. When left untreated, ear mites can cause severe problems of the middle and inner ear, which may affect the cat's hearing and BALANCE.

Diagnosis is made by actually seeing the mite. The parasite is tiny, white, and nearly impossible to see with the naked eye. Generally, the veterinarian will make a slide of a sample of the ear debris and examine it under the microscope to identify the parasite.

Treatment consists of flushing out the debris and applying insecticide to kill the mites. Bland oil, like mineral oil, squirted into the ear canal followed by gentle massage helps flush out the crumbly material. Because of the three-week lifespan of the mites, more than one treatment may be necessary to kill the mites as they hatch.

A number of ear-drop medications are available for treating ear mites in cats. Many of them contain insecticides such as carbaryl or pyrethrins in a mineral oil solution. Sometimes steroids are necessary to help the inflammation subside, and an antibiotic ointment may be indicated to treat bacterial infections.

Not all of the mites are in the ear at any one time, so whole-body treatments are ideal. Sores may be limited to the external ear canal but are commonly found on other parts of the body, especially the cat's neck, rump, and tail. Some of these cases look very much like a flea bite allergy (see ALLERGIES, CAT). In severe cases, the body of the animal may need to be treated weekly for four weeks to kill the mites not in the ear canal. Products that kill fleas will also eliminate ear mites.

Just as fleas infest the environment, ear mites may live in the premises for months. Control is especially difficult in homes with many pets. The same procedures for premise control of FLEAS work for eliminating ear mites in the environment. Repeat premise treatments weekly for four weeks at a minimum; experts suggest treating the environment two weeks *beyond* the pet's apparent cure.

When the cat's ears are very sore, sedation may be necessary to properly clean the ears. Even when ear drops are effective, some cats object to having their ears cleaned and treated, and unless the entire course of treatment is completed, the problem will recur. In addition, some cats are resistant to certain medications, or are hard for owners to handle and medicate at home.

For these stubborn cases, an injectable medication may be the answer. One or two beneath-the-skin injections of an insecticide called ivermectin have been reported to cure the problem, with preliminary tests suggesting the treatment is very safe. However, because this protocol has not yet been approved in the United States, veterinarians may use the drug "off label"—not according to the label's suggested purpose—with the informed consent of their clients.

Ears

The ear is a sensory organ that provides cats with both the ability to hear and their sense of equilibrium, or balance.

The cat's sense of hearing is extraordinarily acute, and she relies on it for protection from danger, for enhanced hunting skills, and for everyday living.

Nineteen separate muscles allow the large external ear that you see, called the pinna, to swivel 180 degrees. The pinna is triangular cartilage covered by skin on both sides. It functions as a funnel, to collect and direct sound waves to the tympanic membrane, or eardrum, situated inside the ear canal. Sound waves cause the sensitive membrane of the eardrum to vibrate.

That sound is amplified by a chain of three tiny bones, called ossicles, located on the other side of the cat's eardrum. The first bone, the hammer, is attached to the eardrum. The middle bone, the anvil, and the third, the stirrup, lie against the hammer.

The greater the ratio between the length of the hammer compared to the length of the anvil, the better the cat will hear low-intensity sounds. This measure is nearly tripled in the cat's ears compared to that of humans, explaining why we are deaf to many of the interesting sounds cats detect. Together, the bones augment and transmit sound deep into the inner ear.

The inner ear contains fluid-filled structures called the semicircular canals, the utricle, and the saccule. These organs dictate equilibrium, and define what is up and down for the cat (see BALANCE).

The utricle and saccule carry the sound vibration on to the tiny organ responsible for hearing. Called the cochlea, this fluid-filled tube is coiled like a snail shell and is lined with a membrane called the cochlear duct that spirals its length. The "organ of Corti," a specialized area of this lining, is where hearing actually takes place.

The organ of Corti is covered with minute hair cells sensitive to sound vibrations. These vibrations are transmitted as signals to the brain via the auditory nerve, and there the sound is interpreted.

This complex system enables cats to hear high frequencies beyond

e

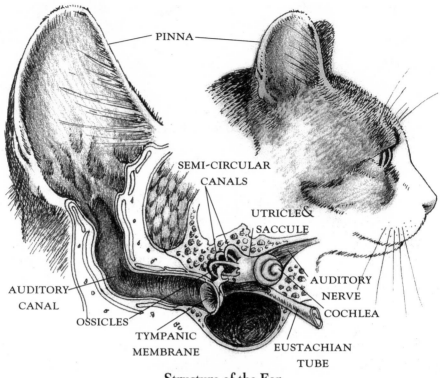

PINNA

SEMI-CIRCULAR
CANALS

UTRICLE&
SACCULE

AUDITORY
CANAL

AUDITORY
NERVE

OSSICLES

COCHLEA

TYMPANIC
MEMBRANE

EUSTACHIAN
TUBE

Structure of the Ear

the detection of human hearing. Young cats hear better than old cats, and in her prime a cat can detect the high-frequency squeaks of mice that are 50 to 60 kilohertz (people can only hear as high as 20). However, cats can't hear sounds as low and deep as people can. Cats are able to pinpoint sounds that are only three inches apart at a distance of three feet away.

Hearing loss may develop due to inner ear infection (see EAR MITES and OTITIS). Sometimes white cats, especially those with blue eyes, are born with a condition that causes the cochlea to degenerate, which results in deafness. Deafness can also develop due to age, because the bones of the middle ear lose their mobility and the nerves of the cochlea degenerate with time.

It's difficult to test a cat's hearing, but if your cat fails to respond to the sound of kibble clattering into the bowl, there may be a problem. Some veterinary universities can evaluate a cat's hearing using electrodiagnostic procedures. Most cats with a hearing loss compensate and do well as long as they remain in familiar, safe surroundings. Routine ear cleaning is important to stay ahead of possible health problems (see GROOMING).

Eating

There is no doubt that eating is one of the cat's dearest pleasures. Every cat has individual eating styles and food preferences, but owners should cater to the cat's taste buds only after ensuring that the diet is appropriate.

The cat who must hunt for his food typically catches small game like mice, rats, birds, or rabbits. Crouching over the kill, he swallows small prey headfirst—fur, feathers, and all. Larger birds—for example, blackbirds—may be plucked first to remove tail feathers. Rabbit-size prey are eaten more slowly.

Eating is one of the cat's dearest pleasures. *(Photo credit: Ralston Purina Company)*

The cat's TEETH are designed for a carnivorous lifestyle. The dagger-shaped canine teeth are used to kill, while the tiny incisors across the front of the jaw pluck feathers or skin from the prey. Rather than chewing, cats shear off manageable portions of food with their molars, then swallow these chunks. As these specialized teeth are located in the side of the cat's mouth, a cat typically tilts his head to the side while eating. To rasp off small pieces, a cat nibbles with his incisors and licks with his rough TONGUE.

To drink, the cat curls his water-absorbent tongue into a spoon shape. He scoops up any liquid by lapping, and swallows every four to five laps. A bowl of clean water should be available to a cat at all times.

Cats appreciate routine, so establish a dinner habit early. Feed the cat in the same place and at the same time every day. A low-traffic area is best so the cat isn't disturbed during meals—a corner of the kitchen or the laundry room is often appropriate. Be sure the feeding station is some distance away from the LITTER BOX, or the cat may refuse to eat in that location.

Cats relish food that is at body or room temperature. Food cooler than this may be refused—or even VOMITED up when eaten cold—so always allow refrigerated foods to warm before serving. A few seconds in the microwave often helps, but don't overheat.

When you have more than one cat, feed them in separate bowls some distance apart to help avoid confrontations. Some cats share food bowls with no problem, but dinnertime is less stressful when everyone has his own place.

Several bowl choices are available. Consider what the cat likes before making your choice.

Longhair and flat-faced cats prefer shallow bowls that allow them to eat to the bottom without bending their whiskers or getting their face dirty.

Plastic bowls tend to hold odors, are hardest to keep clean, and have a light weight that allows them to slide around the floor. Generally, cats dislike chasing a lightweight bowl over the floor, and are turned off by a dirty or smelly dish. Some cats may suffer skin problems like ACNE as a result of eating from plastic food bowls.

U.S.-made ceramic bowls are better choices because of their solid weight and ease in cleaning. The glazes in ceramic bowls manufactured in some foreign countries may contain lead.

Heavy, nonbreakable glass bowls are also good choices, and cats may drink more water from glass containers because they like the taste. But care must be taken if the glass is breakable.

Stainless-steel bowls are the choice of veterinary clinics because they are easily sterilized and nonbreakable. Some cats object to the taste of water or food offered in such containers, though. You may need to experiment before finding a safe, practical alternative for your cat.

By the age of *six to seven weeks*, kittens should be completely weaned and eating an appropriate commercial kitten ration. Moisten dry foods to soften the kibble and make it easier for a youngster to eat. Use three parts dry food to one part water (not MILK) to soften the food.

Offer a kitten food three times a day. A kitten's tummy is too small to allow him to eat the amount needed for proper nutrition all at one time. Instead, kittens tend to eat several small meals—perhaps only having three or four bites at a time, leaving, and then returning later to nibble again. Give the kitten about an hour to eat his fill, then throw out the uneaten portion. Wet food spoils if left out longer.

Soft diets may be fed for the cat's lifetime but may contribute to dental plaque or tartar. Kittens are able to eat plain dry food by about *three months of age*. To get a kitten used to dry food, gradually decrease the amount of water over a week's time until the kitten ration is completely dry.

Once the kitten is *six months old*, his meals can be reduced to twice a day. He should continue to eat kitten ration, though, as long as he continues to grow, until at least a year old.

After one year of age, the cat should be fed an adult maintenance ration. Never change the diet abruptly—this can cause upset stomachs and result in DIARRHEA. Instead, introduce the new food over a week's time by mixing it with the familiar food. Gradually increase the proportion of new food while reducing the amount of old until the cat is eating only the new diet.

The amount of food the cat needs depends on the cat and the individual food. Outdoor cats and those that are more active require more food than indoor couch potato felines. But an average cat that weighs seven to nine pounds and has normal activity will require six to eight ounces of canned food, or about two to three ounces (one half to one eight-ounce measuring cup) of dry food each day. Cats that eat nutrient-dense super premium foods can eat less than cats that eat other category diets.

Since commercial cat food products offer feeding suggestions on the packaging as a guideline only, you may wish to consult with your veterinarian as well.

Adult cats tend to be "occasional" feeders. They like to come and go from the food bowl, and nibble rather than eat an entire meal all at one time. For this reason, cats should have access to their food for several hours at a time. Canned food, however, tends to spoil if left out for long periods, and should be meal-fed two to three times a day.

Free feeding of a dry-food ration is a popular option for both owners and their cats. Dry food can be left in the bowl all day without spoiling, so the cat can nibble at his leisure. (See also FOOD and NUTRITION.)

A cat's appetite may vary from day to day, but a loss of appetite over several days may indicate illness, so see your veterinarian.

Eclampsia

Also called milk fever, this condition is caused by a low calcium level. Eclampsia is associated with the birth of a large litter of KITTENS that deplete the QUEEN's calcium stores from nursing. But it is much more common in dogs than in cats.

At first, the mother cat will simply appear restless and anxious. She leaves her kittens and paces, breathing rapidly, with a stiff-legged uncoordinated gait. Her TEMPERATURE may soar as high as 106 degrees. Her facial muscles tighten, which may expose her teeth, and her gums and lips appear pale. Finally she collapses, exhibits muscle spasms, and drools. Left untreated, eclampsia can be fatal within a few hours. *This is an emergency that must be immediately addressed by a veterinarian.*

The antidote is an intravenous organic calcium solution, such as calcium gluconate. Given in time, treatment results in a rapid, dramatic improvement within fifteen minutes of administration. When the cat's temperature exceeds 104 degrees, she should also be treated for heatstroke (see HYPERTHERMIA).

Kittens from the litter should be bottle-fed and not allowed to nurse from the stricken queen for at least twenty-four hours. Your veterinarian can best advise you whether it's safe for Mom to return to

ECLAMPSIA (MILK FEVER)

SYMPTOMS

Restlessness, pacing, ignoring kittens, stiff-legged gait, drunkenness, rapid breathing, high fever, grimacing expression, pale lips and gums, drooling, collapse with muscle spasms

HOME CARE

EMERGENCY! SEE VETERINARIAN IMMEDIATELY

VET CARE

Intravenous calcium treatment, therapy to counter high fever

PREVENTION

Calcium supplements in pregnant and nursing cats previously affected by the condition—or don't breed the cat

e

nursing at all. Cats afflicted once with eclampsia are at higher risk for a recurrence, and such cats may benefit from calcium supplements during subsequent pregnancies.

Electrical Shock

Injury and death from high-voltage electricity may be caused by lightning, contact with fallen electrical cables, or faulty circuits. Most often, however, kittens suffer electrical shocks when they chew through an electric cord. The current may cause muscle contractions that make a cat involuntarily bite down even harder and prevent her from releasing it.

Should you find your cat in contact with an electrical wire, *shut*

*off the current and disconnect the plug before attempting to touch the cat
or you may be shocked as well.* If the cat has stopped breathing, begin
resuscitation.

The seriousness of this injury varies depending on the degree of
voltage and the pathway taken by the current. Death is usually instan-
taneous if lightning is involved, but an accident of this kind more typically affects farm animals than cats. The exception might be a tree hit
by lightning in which a cat is perched.

The most common signs of electrocution are burns in the mouth
area and water in the lungs (which often develops within twelve hours
after the incident). This pulmonary edema is caused by damage to the
tiny capillaries in the lungs, which then leak fluid and make breathing
difficult.

The current can also cause an irregular heartbeat and circulatory

ELECTRICAL SHOCK

SYMPTOMS

Mouth burns, difficulty breathing, convulsions, loss of
consciousness, shock

HOME CARE

Shut off current first, then administer resuscitation if cat isn't
breathing; SEE VETERINARIAN IMMEDIATELY;
nutritional support during convalescence

VET CARE

Oxygen therapy, drugs to rid fluid from lungs, surgical removal
of burned tissue, antibiotics, possible placement of feeding tube
and prescription nutrition

PREVENTION

Supervise cats and kittens around electrical cords

collapse, and may affect breathing and other bodily functions. Without treatment, the pet may fall into a coma, suffer convulsions, and finally die; those who survive may have permanent nerve damage.

Treating the burns resulting from electrical shock may require surgical removal of damaged tissue, antibiotics, and possibly use of a feeding tube passed through the nose to bypass the damaged oral cavity. Heartbeat irregularities are usually addressed with drugs to stabilize the rhythm and with fluid therapy to prevent circulation problems. The edema may be treated with diuretic drugs like furosemide, which help rid the body of excess water, along with bronchodilating drugs and oxygen therapy, which help the cat breathe. Some cats may need mechanical help breathing until their lungs can compensate. Cats that go into SHOCK from the trauma should be treated accordingly, and any cat suffering electrical shock should be seen by a veterinarian as soon as possible.

Electrical shock is better prevented than treated after the fact. Kitty-proof your home, particularly when young cats are present. Unplug appliances that aren't in use, tape down cords to keep them from being tempting playthings, and WATCH your kitten at all times when he has access to electrical cords.

Elizabethan Collar

The Elizabethan collar is used to prevent a cat from further injuring herself by licking or biting her healing wounds, suture lines, itchy skin, or other problem areas.

The collar is named for the elaborate, wide stand-up dress collars (usually ruffled) worn during the Elizabethan period. The stiff material, which typically is plastic or cardboard, fits snugly around the cat's neck and extends outward approximately one foot in a cone shape. Pet-supply stores and veterinarians offer the collars in various sizes.

Owners can also make their own collars using stiff cardboard. Cut out a twelve-inch circle of cardboard, and at the center cut an opening the size of your cat's neck (plus one inch or so). Measure the cat's collar to get the right length. Remove a piece the size of a wedge of pie from one part of the circle—about one-fourth of the diameter. Put tape around the inside opening to buffer the edges, since they will fit about the cat's neck. Then punch three small holes into the inside border to accept a string. Place the collar around your cat's neck and tape the cut sides together to form a cone. Use the three strings to secure the Elizabethan collar to your cat's existing collar.

Some cats refuse to eat or drink while wearing the collar; if that's the case, remove it for dining. Cats aren't able to navigate as well wearing the collar, and should not be allowed outdoors when wearing one.

Enteritis

Enteritis refers to an inflammation of the stomach and small intestine, and can be a sign of several diseases. The cat with enteritis may suffer from a simple loss of appetite to intermittent VOMITING and/or DIARRHEA.

Inflammation of the gastrointestinal tract can result from a variety of things. Parasites are a common cause of tummy upset, but most often, the upset occurs when a cat eats something he shouldn't. Cats who gorge themselves and overeat commonly suffer from vomiting; this can be controlled by offering smaller portions. Viruses may also result in enteritis.

Although cats are considered fastidious creatures, some are not above swiping a slice of bacon from their owner's plate or raiding the garbage. Any food item unfamiliar to the cat, even a change in commercial diet, may cause enteritis. Cats that hunt and eat their prey are also prone to digestive upset. Acute signs usually resolve themselves simply by resting the gastrointestinal tract (through the withholding of food) and treating the symptoms. In most instances, when the problem is dietary in origin, withholding food for twelve to twenty-four hours may be all that's required. An antidiarrheal medication prescribed by the veterinarian may be given to control diarrhea. Supportive treatment, such as fluid therapy for a cat DEHYDRATED by diarrhea, may also be required.

ENTERITIS (UPSET STOMACH)

SYMPTOMS

Loss of appetite, vomiting, watery diarrhea

HOME CARE

Withhold food and offer only ice cubes to lick for 12 to 24 hours to rest the system; if symptoms continue longer or are severe, see a veterinarian

VET CARE

Fluid therapy, diagnostic tests, treatment specific to cause

PREVENTION

Feed feline gluttons smaller portions to slow down eating; cut out table scraps or other inappropriate supplements; when diet change is necessary, do so gradually

Cats with chronic disease won't respond to symptomatic therapy, and the veterinarian must play detective to discover what's causing the problem so that specific treatment can begin. Eating nonedible objects can also be life-threatening (see SWALLOWED OBJECTS). Should you see your cat swallow something he shouldn't, call your veterinarian immediately. Depending on the object, you may be asked to simply monitor the litter box for a day or two to see that the object passes without further incident. Other times, your cat may need to be seen immediately. And anytime you see signs of distress following ingestion of foreign material, get your cat veterinary help.

Most cases of enteritis are preventable. Protect your cat with vaccinations against viral illnesses, and prevent exposure to intestinal parasites. Keep him from hunting and eating vermin and from swiping unauthorized snacks from your plate or the trash. Feed feline gluttons in smaller portions several times a day to slow down their gulping. (See also FELINE PANLEUKOPENIA VIRUS, GIARDIA, and HOOKWORMS.)

Eosinophilic Granuloma Complex

e

Formerly called lick granulomas, eosinophilic granulomas are skin diseases that result in three kinds of skin sores. *Eosinophilic plaque* affects young to middle-aged cats most often, and is thought to be associated with CAT ALLERGIES. It's an extremely itchy area of elevated skin that's bright red and oozing. It can appear anywhere on the body, but usually is located on the inside of the cat's thighs or on the abdomen. Diagnosis is made by skin biopsy, and allergy treatment often cures the problem.

Eosinophilic granulomas are also believed to be allergy-related, and most commonly affect kittens and cats less than a year old. These are yellow to yellow-pink raised sores that form straight lines, and are usually found on the back of both hind legs. Like the plaques, eosinophilic granulomas are diagnosed by biopsy, and usually go away when the allergy is treated.

The *rodent ulcer* (also called indolent ulcer) is a nonitchy, nonpainful red-to-brown thickened, glistening area usually found on the cat's upper lip. Female cats are affected three times more often than male cats. Because rodent ulcers may evolve into cancer, there's a need for aggressive therapy. Cortisone given either orally or by injection is administered until the ulcer disappears. Ulcers that have become cancerous should be addressed with appropriate cancer therapies (see CANCER).

Epilepsy

Epilepsy is a generic term used to describe a condition characterized by recurrent seizures. Also called convulsions or fits, seizures result from the misfiring of electrical impulses inside the brain.

The neurons of the brain normally discharge electrical impulses that function as "messengers"; they travel the highways of the nervous system to direct bodily functions. When neurons misfire, they generate a kind of power surge that literally blows out the breakers of normal processes, so the brain temporarily shuts down; the result is seizures.

Seizures are caused by injury to the brain, toxicity, or metabolic dis-

EPILEPSY

SYMPTOMS

Seizures usually characterized by falling down with involuntary jerky or paddling motions of legs, grinding of teeth, loss of bladder and bowel control

HOME CARE

None; see veterinarian for diagnosis; do not interfere with seizuring cat; *seizures lasting longer than three minutes are a medical emergency*; SEE VETERINARIAN IMMEDIATELY

VET CARE

Medications like Valium to control seizure episodes

PREVENTION

Once diagnosed, medication may reduce the frequency; there is no prevention

ease. In cats, most seizures result from poisoning. Head trauma from being hit by a car may also cause seizures, with the onset often delayed until several weeks after the injury. Severe KIDNEY or LIVER DISEASE, tumors, or organic or infectious disease like FELINE LEUKEMIA VIRUS or FELINE INFECTIOUS PERITONITIS may cause seizures. There is evidence that even a food allergy may be the culprit in certain instances (see ALLERGIES, CAT). When the cause is identified and successfully treated, seizures are usually eliminated.

Unfortunately, the condition is often considered idiopathic, which means the cause cannot be determined. Such cats may have been born with a brain disorder that causes convulsions. Idiopathic epilepsy tends to appear at age six months to three years (cats that acquire the disease for some other reason are more likely to be affected for the first time later in life).

The most common seizure activity seen in cats is the major motor seizure, also called the grand mal. This type of convulsion affects the entire body. A partial motor seizure affects only specific groups of muscles; for instance, a leg may twitch or one side of the cat's face may spasm. Psychomotor seizures affect behavior; the cat may suddenly become aggressive or fearful, or perhaps attack invisible objects or even himself (see HYPERESTHESIA SYNDROME).

Typically, there is an altered period of behavior that occurs immediately prior to the seizure, called the aura. Cat owners may be alerted by the cat acting disoriented or staring into space. During the first ten to thirty seconds of the convulsion itself, the cat loses consciousness and falls over, the legs extend rigidly, and breathing stops. This rigid phase is followed by the agitated phase in which a cat exhibits jerky running or paddling leg movements, chews and grinds his teeth, and drools. Cats often lose control of their bowels or bladder, their eyes dilate, and their fur stands on end.

Do not interfere with your cat during a seizure. As a cat's muscle contractions are involuntary, you may be severely bitten while the cat remains unaware you are even there. Move the cat only when he is in danger of falling or injuring himself further, then cover with a towel and stand back. In some epileptic cats, light or noise may prompt the continuation of the seizure, so shielding your cat with a towel may help shorten the duration of the episode. Most episodes last no longer than three minutes. When the seizure stops, take the cat to the veterinarian.

Recovery time varies. Some cats act normal within a few seconds or minutes. Others suffer from restlessness or lethargy following seizures, and may act confused or even blind for hours.

Seizures lasting longer than three minutes are dangerous. Wrap the cat in a towel or blanket and get him to your vet's emergency room immediately. Status epilepticus is the name given to rapidly recurring convulsions without recovery in between, or of prolonged, ongoing seizure activity. Convulsions burn many calories, which can cause body temperature to rise and blood sugar levels to drop. Either of these conditions can stimulate seizures to continue. And uncontrolled, ongoing seizures may cause severe metabolic abnormalities, irreversible brain injury, and even death. Typically, Valium is administered intravenously to bring the cat out of ongoing convulsions.

A single seizure does not usually warrant anticonvulsant medication, and cats that suffer infrequent seizures may not require medication at all. Epilepsy cannot be cured, so treatment is aimed at reducing the frequency, shortening the duration, and/or reducing severity with a minimum of side effects. Realistically, limiting episodes to one or two seizures per month is considered a success.

Veterinarians prescribe some of the same medications for controlling seizures in cats that are used for humans. Oral phenobarbital is commonly prescribed, and sometimes oral Valium. Side effects such as sedation and increased thirst, appetite, or urine output are seen in some patients. Extreme care must be taken regarding dosage, since these drugs can be toxic if misused. For instance, Dilantin works well in humans but is toxic to cats, and Primidone is often used in dogs but doesn't seem to help cats. Researchers at Ohio State University are investigating a potentially promising anticonvulsant treatment for cats that combines potassium bromide (an easily metabolized salt) with Tranxene (a long-acting anticonvulsant) in combination with phenobarbital. Ask your veterinarian about the latest drug therapies.

Regulation of the medication requires veterinary supervision and strict owner compliance to be successful. Missing a dose can actually cause a seizure. Most patients improve with therapy, but 20 to 30 percent need intensive medical attention. Generally, even cats with idiopathic epilepsy can, with treatment, enjoy a quality life.

Estrus

See REPRODUCTION.

Euthanasia

As it applies to veterinary medicine, euthanasia is the act of causing merciful death when the pet is ill, injured, and/or suffering with no reasonable hope of recovery. Choosing euthanasia—putting your cat "to sleep"—is not an easy decision, and should be made with the understanding and guidance of a compassionate veterinarian.

When we take a cat into our hearts, we must inevitably face the loss of that pet. That's the deal we make when we love and care for these unique creatures. Elderly cats can continue to enjoy a quality of life with special care, and even chronically ill or injured felines benefit from modern veterinary medicine, but eventually age and illness will take their toll.

As your cat's best friend, you will know when a longer life for your cat doesn't necessarily mean a better life. You will know when awakening is no longer a feline delight, when pain outstrips pleasure, and when your cat yearns for life beyond your lap. When that time comes, you have it in your power to grant your cat the greatest gift of all—a merciful death.

Your veterinarian will administer an injection of an anesthetic agent in a large enough dosage that will allow your cat to fall immediately and painlessly asleep and stop her heart. Some veterinarians allow you to hold your cat as she passes from this life. Her final moments are difficult for your veterinarian and staff as well as for you. Many practitioners recommend or offer counseling and emotional support (see "Pet Services" in Appendix C, "Resources").

Eyes

Two eyes grace the front of the cat's face and provide the cat not only with the sense of sight but also with an important means of silent feline COMMUNICATION. These highly specialized organs are quite similar to human eyes but are designed with the night-hunter in mind. Their shape and function have evolved to make the most use of light, along with the ability to detect the slightest movement. Vision brings the cat a finely tuned understanding of spatial relationships, and that, coupled with superb motor skills—as well as hearing and scent sense—make the cat an exceptional hunter.

The eye records images that are carried by light to the brain; the brain then translates the images into meaning. The eyeball is cushioned in fat and situated deep inside a bony socket in the skull. The eyelids support the front of the eye, and ride over the surface of the eyeball on a thin layer of tears. Cats also have a third eyelid, called the NICTITATING MEMBRANE or HAW, that normally is invisible and originates at the inside corner of the eye. This membrane lubricates and protects the eye by sliding across and wiping the surface clean.

The clear front surface of the cat's eye is called the cornea. The outer edge is the sclera, the "white of the eye" that's more apparent in people than in cats. A thin layer of tissue called the conjunctiva covers the sclera, the inner eyelid, and the sides of the nictitating membrane. Tears produced in glands found in these structures not only lubricate and clean the eye but contain immune substances that help fight bacterial infection. Directly behind the cornea is the anterior chamber filled with aqueous fluid.

At the center of the eye is a dark opening, called the pupil, through which light passes. The pupil is surrounded by the colored portion of the cat's eye, called the iris. The iris is a figure-eight muscle that opens and closes the pupil to regulate the amount of light that passes into the eye. In very low light, the iris opens the pupil wide, in a circle, to capture as much light as possible; in very high light, the iris closes the pupil to a vertical slit. Squinting also further reduces the amount of light and helps to focus images for the cat.

Light passes through the pupil and is focused by the lens onto the retina at the back of the eye—somewhat like a movie projector shining an image onto a screen. The area between the lens and retina contains a gel-like substance called vitreous, which helps hold the retina in place. Millions of light-receptor cells on the retina called rods and cones gather the information on the patterns of light. Other cells then send signals through the optic nerve to the brain's visual center, where the impulses are translated into meaningful images.

The rods allow the cat to see shades of white, black, and gray, while the cones provide color sense. Although a cat has the ability to detect differences between certain reds, greens, blues, and yellows, it is not known how important colors are to cats. Perhaps a cat sees color, but does he care? We don't know.

Human eyes aren't nearly as light efficient as cat eyes. Compared to people, cats require only one-sixth the illumination level to see. They can use twice as much available light as people, because their rod-to-cone ratio is much higher than ours. They also benefit from a layer of highly reflective cells, called the tapetum lucidum, that is located behind the retina. The tapetum lucidum captures and reflects back any light the eye captures, in effect making use of the light a second time around. It's this eerie glow that you see at night when light shines in your cat's eyes.

Proportionally, the cat has the largest eyes of any carnivore; a simi-

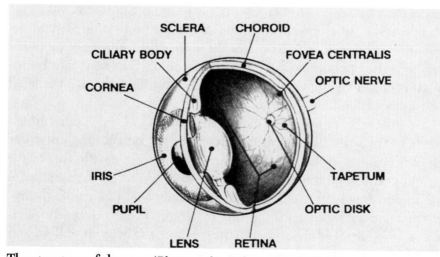

The structure of the eye. (*Photo credit: Ralston Purina Company*)

lar eye-to-face ratio in people would result in human eyes being *eight inches across*! When facing forward, the cat's field of vision overlaps and gives her three-dimensional sight, which is critical when judging distance. This provides her with 130 degrees of binocular vision, compared to our own 120 degrees. In addition, cats have 155 degrees of peripheral vision (compared to 90 degrees in humans), and are experts at detecting motion from the corners of their eyes.

Their near vision isn't as sharp as ours, however, because the muscles that focus their lenses are rather weak. A cat must focus long and hard on stationary objects, whether near or far. Typically, a cat relies on movement to locate and identify objects.

The eye is prone to conditions that can be extremely painful to the cat and require immediate veterinary attention. Signs of a painful eye include squinting, tearing, avoidance of light, and sensitivity to touch. A visible nictitating membrane is often a sign of pain. Flat-faced breeds that have more prominent eyes, like the Persian, may require routine cleaning of the eyes. Signs of injury and/or disease may include any kind of eye discharge, redness, crusting, cloudiness to the eye, or a hard or soft eye. (See also CATARACT, GLAUCOMA, and UVEITIS.)

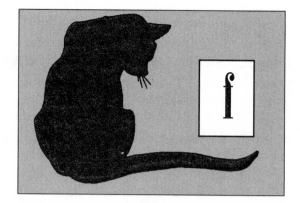

Falling

See BALANCE and HIGH-RISE SYNDROME.

False Pregnancy

This is exactly what it sounds like: The cat shows signs of pregnancy when in fact she is not expecting KITTENS.

False pregnancy occurs when ovulation takes place but the eggs that are released are not fertilized. Following ovulation, hormones like progesterone prepare the cat's body for nurturing kittens. This may result in a cat eating more and gaining weight, or even in nesting behavior. Rarely, cats suffering a false pregnancy will produce milk.

Treatment is not necessary for this condition, which will resolve by itself within about forty days following the heat cycle. However, cats are prone to repeated false pregnancies. When kittens are not desired, the cat should be spayed to prevent future occurrences. (See also REPRODUCTION and SPAYING.)

Fatty Liver Disease

See FELINE HEPATIC LIPIDOSIS.

Fear

Our feline friends come by the term *scaredy-cat* honestly. Cats are creatures of habit who dislike change, and the unknown can be frightening to them. A new house, a new pet, or a new person in your life may seem threatening, and such cats typically run away and hide if they can. When escape isn't possible and the cat feels cornered, a fearful cat can become hostile (see AGGRESSION). Your cat communicates his fear using hisses, fluffed fur, and/or flattened ears.

The best way to prevent fear in cats is to build confidence at an early age by exposing them to novel experiences (see KITTEN). Mature cats need to be introduced slowly to new experiences, so plan ahead before throwing something new in your cat's face. With older cats, it's often necessary to identify the cause of the fear before addressing the problem.

Soothing music, particularly classical pieces, seems to calm frightened cats. Play the music on a low volume. Offer a cat some easy escape routes, like elevated perches or a cat bag on a dresser. Often, cats feel more secure when they have an unobstructed view. And playing with the cat is a great confidence-builder. Some of the best toys are fishing-pole style. Nothing makes a cat forget her fears like attacking—and capturing!—that fierce toy mouse on the end of the string.

An extremely fearful cat, particularly one that becomes aggressive, may need more help than you can offer. Consult a professional animal behaviorist for advice (see Appendix C, "Resources").

Feeding

See EATING and NUTRITION.

f

Feline AIDS

See FELINE IMMUNODEFICIENCY VIRUS.

Feline Calicivirus (FCV)

See UPPER RESPIRATORY INFECTIONS.

Feline Enteric Coronavirus

See FELINE INFECTIOUS PERITONITIS.

Feline Hepatic Lipidosis (FHL)

Feline hepatic lipidosis, commonly called fatty liver disease, is the most common liver ailment affecting cats. The condition refers to the accumulation of fat cells within the liver that interferes with normal function.

Although cats of all breeds and any age are at risk, those most often afflicted with FHL are middle-aged obese felines. The major trigger of the condition is ANOREXIA; the cat stops eating.

If an adult cat refuses to eat for forty-eight hours, consult a veteri-

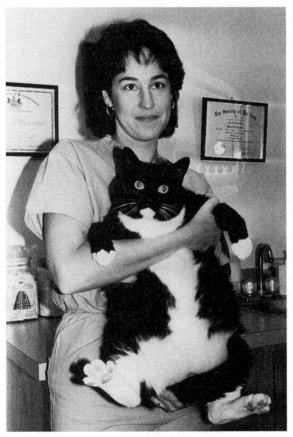

Middle-aged, obese felines are the most at risk for FHL. (*Photo credit: Fran Pennock Shaw*)

FELINE HEPATIC LIPIDOSIS

SYMPTOMS

Refusal to eat for more than 48 hours, particularly in obese or overweight cats

HOME CARE

EMERGENCY! SEE VETERINARIAN IMMEDIATELY; nutritional support once diagnosed and stabilized by veterinarian

VET CARE

Supportive care, placement of feeding tube, and force feeding

PREVENTION

Keep cat trim, don't allow obesity to develop

narian. Monitor the amount your cat eats as well; cats that drastically reduce their caloric intake over several weeks also run the risk of developing FHL.

The reason why cats develop FHL is not known, but researchers speculate that it may have something to do with the cat's unique metabolism as a meat eater. Fasting triggers the cat's body to find new energy sources normally supplied by food; fat stores are moved into the liver in response, and become trapped. Once cells throughout the liver are packed with fat globules, the liver can't work properly. That makes a cat feel sicker and sicker, so she continues to refuse food, creating a vicious cycle that, if left untreated, will result in death.

The treatment of choice for FHL is simply getting the cat to eat. In such cases, tempting the cat with special treats rarely works. An extremely aggressive feeding program that forces the cat to eat offers the best hope of success, and veterinarians report up to a 90 percent recovery rate when a feeding tube is used.

A gastrostomy tube is surgically placed in the stomach through the body wall. The tube extends about eight inches outside the cat's side, and is kept clean with a bandage covering. Other options are a smaller nasogastric tube, which runs through the nose into the stomach, or an esophagostomy tube, which is placed down the cat's throat through the esophagus and into the stomach. The look of the apparatus typically bothers owners more than their pets; cats tolerate feeding tubes quite well.

A high-calorie soft food is then given to the cat through the tube three to four times a day. Calorie-dense prescription formulas are available, but even good-quality kitten rations are appropriate; canned food forms are easier to use. Mix the food in the blender with water to the proper consistency, and warm in the microwave to about 100 degrees to prevent upsetting tummies.

LIVER DISEASE typically requires other supportive care as well. Fluid therapy helps replace lost nutrients and liquids, and antibiotics may be administered to help fight infection. Special medication may be necessary to help reduce toxins the liver is unable to handle. Cats with liver disease typically have trouble moving food from their stomach into the intestinal tract where it can be processed, and often suffer from VOMITING; medication addresses these problems.

Once stabilized, the cat can go home, with the owner continuing to feed the cat through the tube as instructed by the veterinarian. The recovery time depends on how far the disease had progressed. A majority of cats feel better soon after tube feeding begins. Most begin eating within the first month, but it can take anywhere from two to eighteen weeks before the cat begins eating on her own. Aside from the tube, these cats live an otherwise normal life during their convalescence.

The best way to prevent this devastating condition is to keep your cats trim to reduce the risk of FHL. To slim down tubby tabbies, always consult with your veterinarian before implementing a safe, gradual weight-loss program (see OBESITY).

Feline Immunodeficiency Virus (FIV)

Sometimes referred to as feline AIDS, FIV is a lentivirus similar to simian and human HIV that was first identified in 1986. FIV actually turns the cat's body against itself by changing healthy cells into factories that manufacture more virus. Just like in monkeys and people, the virus suppresses the immune system and makes the cat susceptible to other kinds of illnesses. However, people cannot be infected with the

FELINE IMMUNODEFICIENCY VIRUS (FIV)

SYMPTOMS

Nonspecific signs include fever that comes and goes, swollen lymph nodes, weight loss, dehydration, trouble breathing, anorexia, vomiting, claw or mouth sores, chronic skin infections

HOME CARE

Supportive care, good nutrition

VET CARE

Supportive care, good nutrition, treatment to relieve individual symptoms

PREVENTION

Reduce exposure to this fatal disease by keeping cats inside, avoiding contact with other cats

cat virus, and cats cannot be infected with the human virus; although similar, they are species specific.

FIV is found in both domestic and wild feline populations throughout the world. Unlike some other feline viruses, FIV is relatively difficult to catch. Mutual grooming, shared food bowls and litter boxes, and sexual contact are considered unlikely methods of infection, and the virus is not transmitted from the mother cat to kittens.

FIV is thought to be primarily spread through cat bites that transmit infective saliva. For that reason, intact male cats allowed to roam and fight tend to be at highest risk for the disease. And because FIV generally incubates three to six years before signs develop, most reported cases occur in cats five years old or older. Cats positive for FE-LINE LEUKEMIA VIRUS (FeLV) are up to twice as likely to also suffer from FIV. The reported incidence of FIV varies, but it is thought to be 1 to 3 percent of the pet cat population.

Cats are diagnosed using an ELISA (enzyme-linked immunosorbent assay) test, which evaluates a blood sample to detect the presence of antibodies. When the test is positive, a follow-up test using an IFA (immunofluorescence assay) or Western Blot Immunoassay is recommended in a few months to confirm the diagnosis.

The earliest signs appear four to six weeks after infection and include a transient fever, swollen lymph nodes, and a low white blood cell count. Cats may act lethargic, suffer diarrhea, or simply have a poor coat condition. These signs often go unnoticed by the owner, and most cats recover from the first stage of disease. FIV-infected cats may stay healthy for five to ten years, yet all the while be potential carriers of the disease.

Once true immunodeficiency develops, cats suffer chronic infections throughout their body. Signs include any one or a combination of: weight loss; DEHYDRATION; trouble breathing; loss of appetite; VOMITING; claw or mouth sores; or chronic infections of the skin, intestines, bladder, or respiratory tract. Many of these signs are similar to those exhibited by FeLV-infected cats. Some cats also suffer from neurological signs, which vary from strange behavioral changes to epileptic convulsions (see EPILEPSY).

Cats remain infected for life; there is no cure, nor at this time is a specific preventive available. Treatment is aimed at soothing specific symptoms and making the cat as comfortable as possible. Infected cats may lead happy lives for many years when owners are attentive and promptly and aggressively treat each illness.

FIV-infected cats are currently being used as models for developing effective treatments for human AIDS patients. As research continues, it is anticipated that more effective treatments for cats will also become available.

FIV-positive cats in multicat homes should be isolated and kept indoors. This protects them from exposure to diseases, and prevents them from spreading FIV to healthy cats. High-quality NUTRITION is particularly important in immune-compromised cats, and regular veterinary exams are essential.

Ultimately, FIV-positive cats no longer rally with treatment, and usually die of secondary illnesses. EUTHANASIA is the humane choice for cats that can no longer be made comfortable.

The best protection against FIV is to prevent exposure. Cats that are kept indoors and not allowed contact with free-roaming cats are at low risk for becoming infected.

Feline Infectious Anemia (FIA)

See HAEMOBARTONELLOSIS.

Feline Infectious Enteritis

See FELINE PANLEUKOPENIA VIRUS.

Feline Infectious Peritonitis (FIP)

f

FIP is a deadly viral disease of cats caused by a coronavirus first described in the early 1960s. The FIP virus acts on the tiny blood vessels throughout a cat's body, particularly those in the abdomen, lymph nodes, and internal organs. Virtually all cats that contract the disease will die.

Nobody knows exactly how the virus is transmitted, but scientists believe cats breathe or swallow the virus after contact with infected cats. The virus is fragile outside the body, and can be killed by most household detergents. Four ounces of bleach diluted in a gallon of water is an effective disinfectant.

Cats are also susceptible to several viruses related to FIP, which include feline enteric coronavirus (FECV), canine coronavirus (CCV), and a virus that normally affects swine called transmissible gastroenteritis virus (TGEV). While some of these agents, like FECV, produce only mild digestive tract disturbances and affect primarily very young kittens, others produce FIP.

Outdoor cats; cats raised in multicat households; cats stressed from infection, malnutrition, or overcrowding; and cats treated with high doses of immune-suppressing drugs like steroids are at the highest risk for FIP. Most cases occur in cats less than four years old, and those infected with FELINE LEUKEMIA VIRUS are also at high risk. Yet FIP is relatively uncommon and is thought to affect fewer than 1 percent of cats.

FIP is an immune-mediated disease, which means the cat's own body actually speeds the progress of disease. The virus first infects lymph glands; then, within a week after exposure, it infects blood cells, which transmit the virus throughout the body, particularly to the liver, spleen, and lymph nodes. The virus infects the walls of the blood vessels and produces an intense, destructive inflammation that allows fluid to escape, which eventually accumulates in body cavities.

f

FELINE INFECTIOUS PERITONITIS (FIP)

SYMPTOMS

Nonspecific signs include anorexia, weight loss, depression, persistent fever, progressive painless swelling of the abdomen

HOME CARE

Supportive care, good nutrition

VET CARE

Supportive care, good nutrition, treatment to relieve individual symptoms

PREVENTION

Reduce exposure to this fatal disease by keeping cats inside and avoiding contact with other cats; high-risk cats may benefit from protective vaccinations

Clinical signs may occur suddenly, or progress slowly over time. Periodic loss of appetite, weight loss, and depression are general signs, along with a persistent fever. In addition, there are two major forms of FIP distinguished by the accumulation of fluid, or its absence, within the body.

The *effusive*, or *wet*, form of the disease has the most dramatic symptom, consisting of a progressive, painless swelling of the abdomen with fluid. Fluid may also accumulate in the chest cavity and make breathing difficult. Yellowing of the pale areas of the skin, called jaundice, and a mild ANEMIA may develop. Cats typically survive only two to three months after the onset of these clinical signs.

The *noneffusive*, or *dry*, form of the disease is hardest to diagnose and is the more prolonged form of FIP. Anemia, fever, weight loss, and depression are typical signs. Cats also may show signs of specific organ failures, such as KIDNEY or LIVER DISEASE. The most common signs of the dry form include incoordination, partial or complete paralysis of hind legs, convulsions, personality changes, and eye disease. Some of these cats may survive a year or more after clinical signs first appear.

Diagnosis is based on symptoms and laboratory tests. Antibody tests may indicate exposure to a coronavirus, but cannot determine whether exposure was due to the deadly virus or to its more innocuous relatives. An FIP-negative, perfectly healthy cat may have a positive antibody test, while a clinically infected cat may test negative. So definitive diagnosis can be made only by microscopic evaluation of a tissue sample.

There is no cure for FIP. High levels of steroids along with antibiotics may be given in an effort to slow the inflammation and infections. The goal is not to cure the disease but to make the cat comfortable for as long as humanely possible. Providing good nursing care and feeding a well-balanced, nutritional diet makes the cat more comfortable in the terminal stages of disease.

Vaccines are currently available that are administered as nose drops; the nasal passages are vaccinated to try to block the virus from ever getting into the cat's body. However, this vaccine has received mixed reviews from researchers, who report that experiments to date have not shown consistent results regarding protection. Because the effectiveness of the vaccine remains under investigation, the FIP vaccine is not routinely recommended. If your cat is in a high-risk group, consult your veterinarian on how best to protect your cat.

Feline Ischemic Encephalopathy

This mysterious condition is caused by a disruption of blood supply to part of the brain and results in sudden signs of nerve damage. The syndrome has been around for years, but was only first described in the veterinary literature in the late 1960s. Feline ischemic encephalopathy is like a stroke in humans.

The problem rarely affects kittens, and is seen most often in outdoor cats. It usually occurs during the hot summer months. No studies have been done to determine the frequency of the condition, but experts believe the syndrome is common in cats.

The onset of symptoms is typically abrupt—cats are normal one

FELINE ISCHEMIC ENCEPHALOPATHY

SYMPTOMS

Sudden behavior changes, mild depression with fever and/or obsessive pacing, circling, seizures, blindness

HOME CARE

Keep cat quiet, administer prescribed seizure medication when seizures are ongoing

VET CARE

Little can be done; sometimes, parasite medication, seizure-controlling drugs, and/or behavior modification medications; often, euthanasia is the final option

PREVENTION

Prevent cat's exposure to cuterebra infestation by keeping cat indoors and curtailing hunting

moment, and stricken the next. However, signs vary greatly depending on the severity of the brain damage. Some cats suffer only a mildly depressed state, sometimes with fever. More dramatic symptoms include obsessive pacing and circling, blindness, and/or seizures (see EPILEPSY). Following the initial onset, cats tend to recover significantly over the first several days, but oftentimes, weakness on one side of the body or seizure episodes may continue. In many cases, the attack leaves the cat with a permanent personality change for the worse; typically, the cat becomes hostile and is no longer a suitable pet, in which case owners may choose to euthanize the cat.

The exact cause of feline ischemic encephalopathy remains a mystery. Atherosclerosis, a narrowing and hardening of the arteries from deposits of fatty substances, like cholesterol, is commonly associated with stroke in people. However, cats don't suffer from problems with cholesterol. Certain features of the feline disease suggest the syndrome may be due to the parasite CUTEREBRA, because the time frame during which cats are most commonly affected parallels the parasite's life cycle. Also, the syndrome has never been reported in New Zealand or Australia—where cuterebra is not found—but is common in the continental United States, where the parasite is native. Some researchers speculate that aberrant migration of the parasite into the cat's brain causes this vascular disease, possibly due to a toxicity released by the cuterebra that may cause a spasm or stricture of the vessel that blocks the blood supply.

Once the cat suffers brain damage, there's little treatment available. Some veterinarians may prescribe a medication called ivermectin that is used to kill other parasites, but it is not clear whether this experimental therapy helps or not. Some seizures can be controlled with anticonvulsant medications, but behavior changes due to brain disorder rarely can be modified.

Because a definitive cause of the syndrome has not been determined, it's difficult to suggest how best to prevent the condition in your cat. Preventing exposure to cuterebra by keeping your cat indoors and curtailing hunting activity is probably the best way to reduce the risk of Feline Ischemic Encephalopathy.

Feline Leukemia Virus (FeLV)

Feline leukemia virus was first identified in 1964 and is considered one of the leading causes of pet cat deaths. This retrovirus has the ability to insert its genetic code into healthy cells, which turns these cells into virus factories; in effect, FeLV programs the cat at the cellular level to self-destruct. The disease does not simply cause leukemia (cancer of the blood); instead, it gives rise to a complex of infectious diseases that are either directly or indirectly caused by the virus.

FeLV causes lymphosarcoma, a variety of bone marrow cancers, ANEMIA, and certain reproductive disorders. The virus also results in suppression of the cat's IMMUNE SYSTEM, which makes the cat susceptible to a wide array of illnesses.

A great many cats who suffer from severe bacterial infections,

FELINE LEUKEMIA VIRUS (FeLV)

SYMPTOMS

Wasting away, sluggishness, loss of appetite, weight loss, chronic upper respiratory infections, periodontal disease, sores around the claws

HOME CARE

Supportive care, good nutrition, stress reduction

VET CARE

Supportive care, good nutrition, treat specific symptoms

PREVENTION

Reduce exposure to this fatal disease by keeping cats inside and avoiding contact with other cats; high-risk cats may benefit from preventive vaccinations

HAEMOBARTONELLOSIS, or TOXOPLASMOSIS are also infected with FeLV. Cats with FELINE INFECTIOUS PERITONITIS or FELINE IMMUNODEFICIENCY VIRUS are also often positive for FeLV.

Symptoms of the many associated diseases are extremely varied, but the affected cat frequently undergoes a chronic wasting disease marked by anemia, sluggishness, and poor appetite. Anytime a cat loses weight and has recurring colds, bloody stool, DIARRHEA, swollen glands, trouble breathing, excessive urination, PERIODONTAL DISEASE, or sores around the claws, FeLV should be considered.

The virus is extremely contagious and is spread through contact with an infected cat's saliva, feces, and urine. FeLV can also be passed from the QUEEN to her KITTENS either through the placenta before they are born or through her milk when they nurse. All cats are susceptible, but outdoor cats and those in multicat households are at highest risk for the disease. Those cats who are very young, very old, or already ill are more vulnerable to infection.

Shared food bowls and litter pans, cats grooming each other, or bite wounds are ideal transmission opportunities. However, the virus cannot survive for long outside the cat's body, and is easily killed by alcohol and most household detergents.

The virus enters the membranes of the eyes, nose, or respiratory tract and infects nearby lymph nodes. From there, the virus infects the bloodstream and is distributed throughout the body within two weeks of initial infection. About 30 percent of cats are able to fight off the infection and develop immunity to the virus. Another 30 percent or so develop latent infections, which means they harbor the virus in their bodies but do not become sick; while they are not infective to other cats, nursing kittens may become infected through their milk.

The remaining 40 percent of exposed cats become sick. It appears that repeated or continuous exposure is necessary for successful disease transmission. About 50 percent of persistently viremic cats die within six months of infection, and more than 80 percent die within three years.

The virus is diagnosed using the ELISA (enzyme-linked immunosorbent assay) or IFA (immunofluorescence assay) test, which identifies components of the virus in the infected cat's blood. Because the virus is present only during certain stages of the disease, and because incubation takes time, more than one test may be needed for accurate diagnosis. The IFA, which is performed by outside laboratories, identifies the virus in white blood cells, which indicates that the bone marrow is infected and the cat is probably infective to other cats. ELISA test kits, which are available for clinic or home use, detect the virus in whole blood, saliva, and tears. ELISA more easily detects transient or early infections. However, cats with latent infections will not be detected by either test.

There is no cure for FeLV. Some treatments, though, may provide remissions of certain cancers. Diseases such as leukemia (too many white blood cells), anemia (too few red blood cells), and leukopenia (too few white blood cells) generally respond poorly to therapy. STRESS often brings on illness in FeLV-infected cats. Some cats may temporarily respond to blood transfusions and supportive care. For the most part, treatment is aimed at preventing the spread of the disease to healthy cats while keeping the infected cat comfortable as long as humanely possible. Survival rates vary, and may be enhanced by supportive care and/or aggressive treatment.

Indoor confinement and isolation from other cats help reduce exposure to bacterial, viral, and fungal infections. Stressful situations should be avoided.

Preventing exposure to infected cats is the best way to safeguard your pet. QUARANTINE and test any new cat you plan to bring into your home. Should a cat in your care succumb to the virus, enforce a minimum thirty-day waiting period after the cat has died before introducing a new cat to your home.

Should one of your cats be diagnosed with FeLV, consult with your veterinarian on how best to safeguard your other cats. Isolation of the infected cat coupled with daily disinfection of all feline items (food bowl, litter box, bedding) will help, but not ensure, safety.

Several vaccinations are currently available to help prevent the disease, but none offers 100 percent effectiveness and each has its limitations. And a cat must test negative for FeLV before being vaccinated. It's best to consult with your veterinarian for the best way to protect your cat.

Feline Panleukopenia Virus (FPV)

FPV, also called feline distemper or feline infectious enteritis, is a highly contagious viral disease that affects all members of the cat family, both wild and domestic. A cat of any age is at risk, but kittens are at highest risk. Outbreaks of the disease appear to be seasonal and coincide with the birth of kittens.

This parvovirus causes, among other things, an overall drop in the numbers of circulating white blood cells, which is what "panleukopenia" actually means. FPV is closely related to canine parvovirus type 2.

Infected cats shed the virus in all their body secretions—saliva, urine, vomit, feces—and infection usually results from direct cat-to-cat contact. Cats typically are infected by swallowing the virus during self-grooming or other oral contact. However, during some stages of the disease, fleas may carry the virus from an infected cat to susceptible cats. A virus may survive for years in the environment and can be spread from contact with contaminated litter boxes, food bowls, bedding, or the hands and clothing of owners. Most cats allowed to roam outside are exposed to the virus during their first year of life. FPV is highly resistant to most disinfectants, but can be killed by using a mixture of one part bleach to 32 parts water.

Incubation is two to ten days after exposure. The virus multiplies in the most quickly reproducing cells of the cat's body; in very young kittens, that's the brain. If a kitten survives, the brain damage results in permanent incoordination that includes tumbling or rolling when walking, shaking, or swaying and twitching of the head or body. In older cats, the lymphoid tissue, bone marrow, and intestinal lining are most seriously affected.

Signs vary from cat to cat, with some showing none to few signs at all. But generally, the condition is characterized by the sudden onset of fever of over 104 degrees, refusal to eat, and depression, followed by VOMITING and DIARRHEA that leads to severe DEHYDRATION. Sick cats may crouch with their head between their front paws, crying with pain,

FELINE PANLEUKOPENIA VIRUS (FELINE INFECTIOUS ENTERITIS)

SYMPTOMS

Sudden high fever, anorexia, depression, vomiting, diarrhea, painful abdomen (hunching posture)

HOME CARE

EMERGENCY! SEE VETERINARIAN IMMEDIATELY

VET CARE

Supportive care including fluid therapy, blood transfusions, drugs to control vomiting and diarrhea

PREVENTION

Vaccinate your cat

and vomit immediately upon swallowing water or food. Late in the disease, a profoundly low body TEMPERATURE often develops, generally followed by coma and death within a few hours.

The actual illness rarely lasts more than five to seven days, and the mortality rate is high. In acute cases, kittens die within twelve hours of onset of signs. Diagnosis is generally based on clinical signs. Laboratory tests to measure the white blood cell count may be required to confirm diagnosis.

There is no specific treatment once a cat is infected. The disease must run its course until the cat's system mounts a defense and circulating white blood cells are replaced. Antibodies generally appear three to four days after first signs of illness (see IMMUNE SYSTEM). Therapy is aimed at supportive nursing care, which includes rehydration using fluid therapy, possible blood transfusions, and medications to help control vomiting and diarrhea. Sick cats are at higher risk for contracting concurrent UPPER RESPIRATORY INFECTIONS.

Food and water are withheld until vomiting subsides, and then frequent, small amounts of water and bland, easily digestible foods are offered. Cats that survive five to seven days will probably recover; however, cats may continue to shed virus for up to six weeks following recovery, and should be isolated from other cats during convalescence.

VACCINATIONS to prevent this disease are available. They are highly effective and provide long-term immunity. *FPV is a devastating disease that is highly preventable, and all cats should be protected with appropriate vaccinations.*

Feline Pneumonitis (Chlamydiosis)

See UPPER RESPIRATORY INFECTIONS.

Feline Rhinotracheitis

See UPPER RESPIRATORY INFECTIONS.

Feline Urologic Syndrome (FUS)

See LOWER URINARY TRACT DISEASE.

Feral

The term *feral* as it applies to cats refers to a domesticated feline that has reverted to the wild state. In contrast to abandoned or lost cats, which may relish human contact but are forced to live on their own (see STRAY), the feral feline usually has been reared without benefit of human contact.

Feral cats are extremely shy of people and are often unapproachable. They behave as any wild animal would. Ferals can and do live anywhere in the country, but colonies are often found living in cities near food sources like restaurant Dumpsters, where scraps and vermin for hunting are available.

The typical feral cat's lifespan is short—three to five years—due to injury, disease, and malnutrition. Well-meaning individuals who feed feral populations without addressing the other issues may perpetuate the problem. Feral colonies are not only a nuisance, but they also pose a health risk to pets and people because they may spread diseases like FELINE LEUKEMIA VIRUS, FELINE INFECTIOUS PERITONITIS, and RABIES; and uncontrolled breeding creates more and more feral kittens destined for short, sad lives. Local health departments may resort to trap-and-kill programs to control the problem.

As a rule, feral cats do not make good pets. With great effort, some can learn to tolerate or even appreciate attention from one or two individuals. Most, however, lead a tortured existence if forced to live indoors when "rescued" by concerned cat lovers.

Informed individuals, animal welfare organizations, and citizens groups support feral cat programs that address multiple issues. Trap/neuter/release is the preferred method for population control, and cats should also be given a three-year rabies vaccination before release. Feeding stations help keep colonies from roaming, which also aids in monitoring populations.

Feral cats being cared for in such programs should be distinguished in some way from nonmonitored populations, to protect them from indiscriminate trap-and-kill programs. Ear tipping—removing the top one-quarter inch of the left ear—is used as an international designation for feral cats who have caretakers. (For the address of Alley Cat Allies, see "Animal Welfare and Information Sources" in Appendix C, "Resources.")

A feral cat. (*Photo credit: Amy D. Shojai*)

Fever

See TEMPERATURE.

Fighting

See AGGRESSION.

Fit

See EPILEPSY.

Flatulence

Flatulence, or passing gas, can prove highly offensive and even embarrassing to a cat owner. Intestinal gas is a natural part of digestion, and in most cases is more a nasty nuisance than a danger. Some cats simply produce more gas than others; however, flatulence can be the sign of a health problem.

Eating highly fermentable substances, drinking milk, or gulping air when eating or drinking is usually the cause. High-fiber or carbohydrate diets may make the condition worse, and so can inappropriate FOOD SUPPLEMENTS. Any sudden diet change, from treats to raiding the

FLATULENCE

SYMPTOMS

Passing gas, offensive odor

HOME CARE

Provide a more digestible diet, cut out table scraps, feed activated charcoal as directed by veterinarian, or add yogurt to the diet

VET CARE

Prescription for gas-control medication such as Flatulex or CurTail

PREVENTION

Slow down gulping of food (and air) by feeding free choice, or in smaller quantities several times a day, or away from other pet competition

garbage, may result in a tummy upset with predictable results. Eliminating these culprits from a cat's diet often solves the problem.

Providing a more highly digestible diet also helps. Check the ingredients list on a food package (see READING FOOD LABELS) or ask your veterinarian to recommend an appropriate choice. Make food changes gradually over a week's time. Start by mixing two-thirds of the old diet with one-third new, then progress to half and half, then one-third to two-thirds, and finally the new diet entirely.

A too-full tummy gives food extra time to ferment. Slow down gluttons by feeding your cats at different times, or in separate bowls at opposite ends of the room to reduce food competition. Free-feeding— leaving dry food available at all times—may allow your cat to eat more leisurely, rather than gulping everything down at once. Or try feeding smaller portions several times a day.

Plain yogurt contains bacteria that help digestion and reduce flatulence, and many cats relish the flavor. Try adding a teaspoonful as a food topping. As a last resort, your veterinarian may prescribe a human medication like Flatulex that contains simethicone and activated charcoal to control the gas. There is also an antigas veterinary product called CurTail that contains an enzyme that aids food digestion and reduces flatulence.

Fleas

These are insect parasites that feed on blood. Fleas are the most common complaint of cat owners. All cats are at risk for flea infestation, except for those living in mountainous areas above five thousand feet or in extremely dry environments that are inhospitable to fleas. Although fleas tend to be more prominent during warmer summer months, indoor cats can harbor fleas all year round.

Flea bites cause everything from mild skin irritation and itchiness to severe allergic reactions. But more than mere itchy aggravations, fleas are potential carriers of other parasites and diseases such as PLAGUE and TAPEWORMS. In large enough numbers they can cause severe ANEMIA and even death from blood loss.

Fleas belong to the insect order *Siphonaptera*, which means "wingless siphon." They have six legs equipped with hooks that are used to snag a host as the animal walks by. An elasticlike protein called resilin is compressed in the flea's abdomen by leg and thorax muscles; when released, it catapults the flea upward. That's why fleas are able to jump eight inches vertically and sixteen inches horizontally. Piercing-sucking mouth parts then allow the flea to actually cut into a host's skin and insert a sucking tube to feed.

The flea body is flat from side to side and covered in protective cuticle plates that make it nearly impossible to crush. Its narrow profile allows rapid movement through the thickest forest of cat hair. Fleas remain on the cat unless physically removed, and typically live for about thirty days. But the adult flea represents only about 5 percent of the total bug count; 95 percent of the flea population is found in the "invisible" life stages of egg, larva, and cocoon.

FLEA INFESTATION

SYMPTOMS

Presence of fleas, black pepper-like residue on skin, itchiness particularly of back of neck and head or above the tail, scabby skin, tapeworm segments; extreme cases show lethargy with pale lips and gums from anemia

HOME CARE

Treat cat and environment with appropriate cat-safe insecticides

VET CARE

For anemia cases: fluid therapy and/or blood transfusions, then appropriate flea treatment, sometimes steroid therapy to relieve itching

PREVENTION

Routine flea control, keep cats indoors

After mating, the female flea stores sperm for use as needed. A blood meal stimulates egg-laying. A mama flea can lay fifty eggs a day, and about two thousand eggs in her lifetime. Most eggs fall off the cat into the environment, where they may remain dormant for six months or longer. More typically, eggs hatch into tiny, maggotlike larvae within two to three weeks. They feed on the undigested blood passed by adult fleas (sometimes referred to as flea dirt) and other organic material.

In another three weeks, the larvae spin cocoons, where they undergo further development. Once mature, the flea uses antennae and bristles sensitive to body heat and odor, changes in light, touch, and moisture, and even traces of carbon dioxide exhalation to detect when a host is nearby, and only then leaves the cocoon and mounts a furry host. The cycle from egg to adult takes about thirty days.

Cats are diagnosed by finding the fleas themselves, or evidence of

Fleas cause cats to itch and scratch. *(Photo credit: Lillian Zahrt)*

f

flea presence such as the dark brown specks of digested blood excreted by the flea. The adult flea is visible, but moves so fast it's hard to detect in thick cat hair. Cats also tend to groom away many of the nasty nuisances, so they may not be seen.

Fleas seem to prefer a cat's hindquarters, and flea dirt can be found on the skin near the base of the tail. Simply part the fur and look, or comb your cat after standing her on a light-colored towel (flea dirt will pepper the towel as you groom the cat). When the specks are placed on a damp cloth, they dissolve and turn red. Evidence of tapeworms, which are usually contracted from swallowing fleas, also points to flea infestation. Look for dried ricelike grains in the litter box, or in the fur below the cat's tail.

There is a wide array of flea products available for controlling the problem. However, flea control is complicated by both flea biology and feline sensitivity—meaning there is no quick fix for controlling fleas.

Traditional flea control relies on various classes of chemical insecticides available in various forms. However, cats are very sensitive to a number of chemicals, and what kills a flea may also make the cat sick—or even dead. Flea products for dogs are often toxic to cats, and even products that are safe for cats may prove deadly if applied inappropriately or in the wrong combinations. The first rule when treating your cat for fleas is to read, understand, and follow product directions for use.

Products that use the class of chemicals *cholinesterase inhibitors should be used on cats only with extreme caution.* Their effects can be cumulative; using an environmental spray that contains these chemicals when the cat has been dipped with a similar product can result in toxic levels for the cat. This group includes organophosphates such as chlorpyrifos (Dursban), malathion, Diazinon, cythioate, and fenthion; and carbamates like carbaryl and propoxur. Also beware of products containing chlorinated hydrocarbons, which include DDT, lindane, and methoxychlor; they are poisonous to cats (see POISON).

Pyrethrins, made from a relative of the chrysanthemum flower, *are one of the safest insecticides for cats available.* Synthetic pyrethrins called pyrethroids include permethrin and provide a broader and longer flea-killing action than natural pyrethrins. Products may be combined with compounds like piperonyl butoxide (PBO) that are synergistic; these increase the effectiveness of insecticides and allow lower, safer concentrations of the chemical to be used. However, PBO makes some cats drool. Some products use microencapsulation; this reduces toxicity to the pet while enhancing the product's long-term effect by delivering small amounts of insecticide inside permeable microcapsules that release the product over a longer period of time.

A relatively new class of flea products are insect growth regulators (IGRs). These products are extremely safe for cats because they're formulated specifically to affect insects, not mammals. Methoprene and phenoxycarb are two of these hormonelike compounds that work by turning an insect's own natural metabolic process against itself. Adult fleas aren't killed, but immature fleas are prevented from maturing, which breaks the life cycle.

New chemistry has developed insecticides that are safer for the cat and the environment, while providing better and longer-lasting flea control. A relatively new product is the IGR lufenuron (Program), which is mixed in a cat's food once a month. Fleas that bite a cat treated with lufenuron won't produce eggs that hatch. However, fleas that bite can still cause itchy skin disease, so this product isn't appropriate for flea-allergic cats. Lufenuron is available only through veterinarians.

There are two new insecticides that affect only the insect's nervous system, not the cat's. They are imidacloprid (Advantage Flea Adulticide), which kills adult fleas, and fipronil (Frontline Top Spot), which kills both adult fleas and ticks. Both products are waterproof. Applied once a month as drops to the skin of the cat's shoulder blades, they spread from there over the cat's entire body. Fipronil actually spreads to the hair follicles, where it coats each hair as it grows. These products are currently available only through veterinarians.

Flea products are usually applied topically, but some forms are more effective and/or easier to use than others. Traditional delivery systems include collars, shampoos, dips, powders, and sprays. (For specifics on shampooing your cat, see Bathing Your Cat under GROOMING.) Flea collars seem easiest to use but in the past have been the least effective; recent products are better able to spread their "cargo" over the entire pet. Unless they are equipped with safety breakaway catches, collars can be dangerous, for they can catch on something and strangle the cat. Shampoos kill fleas only as long as the shampoo is on the cat. Powders and dust last longer, but are messy to apply and can be drying to a cat's skin. Sprays offer a good initial flea kill, and offer residual protection as well, but cats may object to sprays. Alcohol-based sprays also can be drying. Dips are applied wet and allowed to dry; they penetrate the hair coat and have some lasting effect, but extra care must be taken with these stronger products so that toxicity doesn't occur.

Concerned cat owners may seek out "natural" means to control parasites, and some do work. Rotenone and d-limonene are considered botanicals; they are insecticides made from roots and citrus fruit extracts. Desiccants are drying agents that cause fleas to dehydrate and die; some commercial pest control companies use derivatives of borax on carpets to kill flea larvae, which helps break the life cycle. Desiccant diatomaceous earth (DE or Diatom Dust) also has a drying effect against a certain percentage of fleas and larvae, but is messy to apply. Certain kinds of nematodes (worms) that eat immature fleas are sold in pet stores and garden shops, which are mixed with water and sprayed in the yard.

A host of "natural" products flood the market each year; *please be aware that compounds claiming to have activity against parasites must pass*

EPA guidelines for safety and effectiveness claims, and will have an EPA registration number on the label. Avoiding insecticidal claims and calling themselves "natural" allows some products to avoid expensive safety and efficacy tests. Just because a product is natural doesn't necessarily mean it's safe—or that it works.

A flea comb with tines very close together is the safest "natural" way to rid a cat of fleas. Comb the cat from head to tail, and after each stroke, drown the fleas captured in the comb in a bowl of soapy water. A flea comb, though, won't do a thorough job if your cat has a substantial problem.

The most effective way to approach treatment on your cat is to use an IGR-containing product to break the flea life cycle, along with a cat-safe adulticide product to kill adult fleas. Consult your veterinarian for a recommendation.

To stay ahead of fleas, it's essential to treat the cat, other pets in contact with the affected cat, and the environment. When the cat is an inside pet, "environment" means the house. Outside cats pose a dilemma, since it's nearly impossible to control reinfestation if a cat's allowed to roam the great outdoors.

If your cat spends any time outdoors, you must treat the yard for fleas. Fleas prefer a moist, cool habitat and shun the sun, so letting the sun shine in will go far toward chasing the bugs away. Treat only the shaded areas; keep grass clipped close and brush cleaned up. Check with your local county extension agent to learn what environmental insecticides are approved for use in your area. Some products containing IGRs can control fleas for up to twelve months, but be aware that some IGRs may also affect beneficial insects, like bees or butterflies, so choose your weapons wisely.

For inside premises, vacuum carpet several times to lift the flea eggs and larvae to the surface of the pile so flea products can reach them. Change the vacuum bag frequently to keep surviving bugs from reinfecting the house. Follow product directions to treat the house and yard, and don't allow pets or people access until these areas are completely dry.

Flehmen

See JACOBSON'S ORGANS.

Food

f

Food is organic material used by the body to sustain growth, repair tissue, maintain vital bodily processes, and provide energy. Historically, cats viewed small mammals and insects as food and, given their choice, modern felines may still relish the occasional grasshopper or mousy morsel. But pet cats can't be depended on to choose proper foods, and owners must take responsibility for providing them with a balanced and complete diet.

An appropriate food must address the individual cat. The age, the lifestyle, and even health status influence the optimal formulation. Growing kittens have higher energy needs than adult cats, and GERIATRIC CATS or those with special health problems may require specific diets. Designing cat foods is extremely difficult, even for professional feline nutritionists. With rare exceptions, homemade diets aren't a good choice for your cat.

The best nutritional choices for your cat can be found in a variety of commercial products that provide an appropriate food for every cat and condition imaginable. Reputable pet-food companies invest years in ongoing research to ensure that the diets they produce fulfill the various needs of pet cats.

Pet-food companies design cat food to please owners as well. The product must be appealing to you because unless the food is purchased, the cat will never eat it. Some components, like the color of the food, are aimed specifically at getting owners to open their pocketbooks. Your cat couldn't care less what a food looks like. To make the best choices, consider the cat's requirements ahead of anything else.

Cats need complete and balanced diets. *(Photo credit: Ralston Purina Company)*

Commercial cat-food products can be divided into three broad categories: super-premium products, premium products, and low-cost products. The category that is best for your cat depends on his age, body condition, and activity level.

Super-premium foods are typically higher in nutrient density and digestibility than the other categories of cat foods. They are more expensive because the higher-quality ingredients that are used cost more. A higher fat content makes this category extremely palatable; in other words, the food tastes very good to cats. Nutrient density means the cat doesn't need to eat as much volume as in other categories to get the same nutritional benefits. And high digestibility means the cat's body is able to use a high percentage of the food's nutrients, which results in less waste; consequently, the amount that ends up in the litter box is reduced. Super-premium foods are typically available at specialty pet stores or veterinary clinics. Some can be purchased at the grocery store.

Premium name-brand products are usually sold through grocery stores, large pet stores, and some department stores. These nationally distributed brands are considered a more economical choice than super-premium cat foods. The average cat tends to do quite well eating these diets, but because they are not as nutrient dense, the cat must eat more of these foods to obtain the same calories. In this category, look for products made by reputable manufacturers that have been tested through feeding trials; this ensures a diet of consistent quality that offers complete and balanced nutrition.

Low-cost products are typically the cheapest category of food, and may be sold in the grocery store, sometimes as the "store brand." This category uses the least expensive ingredients, and the products may not be as tasty or digestible as more expensive ones. Low digestibility can increase the stool volume in the litter box. And a cat may need to eat much more of these foods to obtain adequate nutrition. Store-brand products claim nutritional value equal to national name-brand products but at a lower cost, and to be sure, some cats may do well on these foods. However, the quality of such low-cost products is extremely difficult to predict and can be inconsistent from batch to batch. Try your best to avoid generic cat foods. Choose quality over cost to ensure that your cat receives the best possible nutrition.

Your veterinarian can advise you as to whether a super-premium, premium, or other product is most appropriate for your cat. The form of the food should also be considered.

There are three basic forms of cat food: semimoist, canned, and dry. High-quality semimoist foods are quite palatable, are easy to serve, and can be stored without refrigeration. Ingredients like corn syrup are added to keep the food moist and prevent it from drying out, but these ingredients may also make the cat thirsty. Semimoist forms are convenient when traveling with your cat, because they're packaged in individual servings. Usually they're more expensive than dry forms. Semimoist foods on average contain 16 to 25 percent protein, 5 to 10 percent fat, 25 to 35 percent carbohydrate, and 25 to 34 percent water.

Canned cat food is processed in the same way as human canned products. After the formulation, or recipe, is determined, the grain and meat ingredients are ground together and the mixture is delivered into the cans at high-speed filling lines run by computers. The food inside the cans is then cooked and sterilized in giant pressure cookers, then sealed, labeled, and shipped. Canning preserves food without adding chemicals. As long as it's not opened, a canned product stays fresh nearly indefinitely. Canned foods contain 10 to 20 percent protein, between 2 and 10 percent fat, and 72 to 78 percent water.

Dry-food ingredients are mixed into a dough or batter, cooked under extreme pressure for a short time, then pushed through a die plate to give the food its characteristic shape. Called extrusion, this process dries the kibble and gelatinizes the starches in the grain ingredients to make them more digestible. Dry cat foods generally contain 28 to 36 percent protein, 8 to 22 percent fat, and less than 12 percent water.

The quality of the food—whether name brand, premium, or super-premium—depends much more on the ingredients and proper processing than on the form of the food. All three forms are capable of providing complete and balanced nutrition, but there are certain misconceptions as well as advantages associated with each.

Canned cat foods tend to consist of more protein and fat than dry forms. Carbohydrates aren't as usable in the canning process, so it's more difficult to create lower-calorie foods in canned than in dry forms. Some canned cat foods are composed entirely of meat and fat, with necessary vitamins and minerals added to balance the diet. And while meat meal (dehydrated and ground meat products) is used in dry foods, canned products often contain fresh meats cited on the label as beef, fish, chicken, and meat by-products.

But some canned products don't contain any fresh meat at all. These products may incorporate an extruded soy product that is less expensive but looks like meat. It is typically identified on the label as textured vegetable protein, soy protein, or soy protein isolate. When formulated correctly, this product is perfectly fine for the cat.

Some cats produce a softer stool when fed canned products as compared to dry forms. That may be because canned food rarely includes a fiber source, which helps form fecal material, and because carbohydrates, which help food retain its form, are incorporated in smaller quantities in canned than in dry-food forms. To compensate for their lower quantities of carbohydrates, canned foods may include gum arabic, xanthan gums, and vegetable gums as viscosity enhancers to help the food set up. This is what makes the "gravy" that owners (not necessarily cats!) are so fond of in canned products. Color enhancers like iron oxide and caramel may be added to make cat food look more like something the owner would want to eat. Some cat foods are even designed to look like humans' luncheon meat!

Canned cat foods do tend to rate higher on palatability because water releases odor and odor stimulates the cat's appetite. Liquid is required for the canning process, and raw meat is also approximately

83 percent water. This is why canned foods typically are so high in moisture.

Added moisture is a benefit for those cats who don't drink enough water, and soft foods are easier for some cats to eat. However, canned and semimoist foods tend to stick to the cat's teeth and may affect the cat's dental status (see PERIODONTAL DISEASE).

Canned foods are also attractive to cat owners who don't want their cat to become bored with one food. Dry foods typically are sold in larger quantities, while canned products can be purchased in single servings. This makes offering one's cat a smorgasbord easier for the owner—even though the cat does not require variety in the diet.

The biggest drawback to canned cat foods compared to dry forms is the cost. Ounce for ounce, both forms may cost the same, but cats need to eat three times as much canned food as dry to compensate for the bulk added by water. Also, canned diets spoil quickly once opened and cannot be fed free-choice, and leftovers must be refrigerated.

The greatest advantage to dry cat foods is convenience for the owner. Dry diets are easier to store and do not require refrigeration. They can be fed free-choice. Some nutritionists believe multiple small feedings are better and more efficient for the cat than one or two feedings a day. The cat's bowl can be filled to allow a cat to nibble at her convenience, which is more consistent with the cat's preferred style of eating.

Dry diets typically are only 8 to 10 percent moisture, which means the food is more energy dense—the cat can eat less of the food while getting the same amount of energy. Because of the packaging, dry diets are more economical to purchase in bulk than canned products.

Some cats do prefer crunchy foods over soft ones. Palatability is influenced not only by flavor and smell but also by the way the food feels in the cat's mouth. Mouth appeal preferences probably have a great deal to do with what the cat experienced as a kitten, and what she saw her mother accept as food.

Crunchy kibble won't stick to teeth as much as canned diets, and may in certain instances slow down the development of tartar or even help reduce dental plaque. But a dry diet alone will not prevent dental disease in cats. Only proper dental care, including brushing the cat's teeth, will get rid of tartar.

Fat makes foods taste good, but if unprotected, it begins to break down and deteriorate within hours of a dry food's manufacture. To prevent the fat from turning rancid, preservatives added to dry food keep it fresh for up to a year after manufacture, so optimum nutrition is delivered when the food is eaten. Antioxidants like BHA, BHT, ethoxyquin, vitamin E, and vitamin C are often used to help maintain freshness. (See also FOOD ADDITIVES, NUTRITION, and READING FOOD LABELS.)

Food Additives

A food additive is an ingredient incorporated in a diet formulation that provides desirable characteristics to the food. Pet-food regulations require that additives in pet foods be proven harmless to pets. Many currently in use are also approved for use in human foods.

Additives can be divided into those that are nutritional and those that are nonnutritional. Vitamins, minerals, fats, and amino acids like taurine are nutritional additives that may be incorporated in the diet formulation to ensure that it is nutritionally complete and balanced. Flavorings, texture enhancers, colors, and preservatives are nonnutritional supplements.

Additives are used to enhance the taste and appearance of food. Natural colors like caramel or carotene and artificial dyes like iron oxide provide a consistent appearance or distinguish between various particles in multiparticle foods. Texturizers like guar gum, gum arabic, xanthan gum, carrageenan, and cellulose flour are sugar-type substances. The jelly in canned foods, its aspic appearance, or pseudogravy is created using these additives, and are designed to "feel good" in the cat's mouth when eaten. They also make cat food look more like human food, which appeals to owners who must choose to buy a particular product.

Flavor enhancers are often added to increase palatability. Enzymatically degraded (predigested) fish or animal organs are called animal digest, and this flavor enhancer is sprayed on dry foods to make them taste good to the cat. Palatability is extremely important, because even the best food provides no benefit unless the cat actually eats it.

Preservatives protect food from degrading and guard the nutritional quality of the product. Canned diets are preserved by the canning process, but dry and semimoist forms of food require preservatives to prevent the breakdown (oxidation) of the nutrients. Oxidation is a kind of biological rust, and is the reaction between oxygen and other compounds, especially fats. Antioxidants prevent fat from turning rancid, preserve the flavor of foods, and keep essential fatty acids and fat-soluble vitamins at optimal nutrient value (see YELLOW FAT DISEASE).

A variety of synthetic and natural antioxidants are used by commercial pet-food companies. Chemical preservatives such as sorbic acid or potassium sorbate are humectins that hold water and help keep semimoist products moist, and also protect these foods from mold and bacterial growth. WARNING: In the past, propylene glycol was used for these purposes in semimoist foods, but recent studies show high levels of propylene glycol can damage a cat's red blood cells. Most reputable pet-food companies have suspended the use of this chemical; avoid any cat food that lists propylene glycol on the label (see READING FOOD LABELS).

Synthetic antioxidants used most widely in dry pet foods include ethoxyquin, BHT (butylated hydroxytoluene), and BHA (butylated hydroxyanisole). Ethoxyquin has been used in pet foods since the mid-1950s, when five-year efficacy and safety studies were done. Many pet-food nutritionists consider ethoxyquin to be the most effective preservative on the market, with BHA and BHT fairly close behind. Recently, however, the safety of ethoxyquin has been questioned. Although the FDA currently endorses it as safe, and there is no scientific data to suggest it is not safe at levels found in cat foods, many pet-food companies have suspended its use pending further studies.

Natural antioxidants are preservatives found in nature. They include ascorbic acid (vitamin C) and tocopherols, which are chemical compounds collectively referred to as vitamin E. Natural antioxidants used in combinations with each other usually provide good preservation, but typically do not last as long as synthetic forms. Foods preserved with mixed tocopherols should usually be used within three to six months of manufacture, or by the product's expiration date.

Food Supplements

Food supplements are defined as anything fed in addition to an otherwise complete and balanced diet. Cats requiring homemade diets, cats who refuse to eat, and cats with specific medical problems may benefit from dietary supplementation. Your veterinarian's recommendation is imperative in these instances.

Food supplements can be anything from vitamin and mineral mixes, to treats and table scraps. Unauthorized supplementation of an otherwise nutritionally adequate diet throws the nutrition level out of balance.

Cats require nutrients in the proper amounts and combinations, and too much can sometimes be as bad as too little. Supplements are not only unnecessary when feeding a balanced and complete diet, but giving your cat a vitamin or mineral supplement or other food item when it's not needed can be downright dangerous.

For instance, adding raw eggs to the diet can cause a vitamin deficiency. A protein called avidin is found in raw egg whites; avidin destroys biotin, one of the B vitamins, and can result in poor growth and hair loss in the biotin-deficient cat.

Vitamins D and E are found in wheat germ and cod liver oils, and cats may relish these treats. But too much can cause toxicities that can result in skeletal deformity, reproductive problems, and even calcification of soft tissues.

Raw food may be the natural choice in the wild, but it's not smart for house cats. Raw meat carries parasites and bacteria like salmonella and TOXOPLASMOSIS. Regular consumption of raw liver can cause vitamin A toxicity that results in deformed bones, weight loss, ANOREXIA, and even death.

Table scraps place your cat at risk for OBESITY, gastrointestinal problems that result in upset tummies with signs like VOMITING or DIARRHEA, or even metabolic problems such as PANCREATITIS. Table scraps should make up no more than 5 percent of the total amount of food your cat eats, but no table scraps are the best choice of all.

Highly palatable food treats like tuna or meat baby foods may create food addictions that can result in a variety of problems. Unlike humans, who need variety in their diet to achieve nutrient balance, your cat is perfectly content to eat the same food day in and day out—unless he is taught otherwise. Offering tasty treats or switching back and forth to different highly palatable foods tends to create finicky eaters and "train" the cat to be picky. Find a complete and balanced diet your cat accepts, and stick to it. To find such a diet for your cat, learn to read pet-food labels.

There are few regulations that apply to products marketed as "natural" supplements, so pet owner beware. *Approach such products cautiously; just because something is natural does not necessarily mean it's harmless.* After all, poisonous mushrooms are natural, too. Ask questions of the manufacturer, and if you don't like the answers—or can't get any answers—avoid the product to protect your cat. Rely on the reputation of well-known pet-food companies that have been around for a while and have the nutritional research to back up their claims.

An occasional treat probably won't hurt your cat. In fact, there are some commercial cat treats on the market that claim to be complete and balanced. For those who simply feel they must treat their cat, try reserving a bit of your cat's regular ration for special tidbit feedings throughout the day. That way, you don't risk unbalancing the nutrition, but both you and the cat will feel special.

If you feel your cat would benefit from eating more, add a teaspoon of warm chicken broth to his food; this usually increases the calorie intake of dry food by about 10 percent. An even better choice would be finding a more nutrient-dense ration that provides the cat with more calories even if he doesn't eat a great deal. (See also FOOD, NUTRITION, and READING FOOD LABELS.)

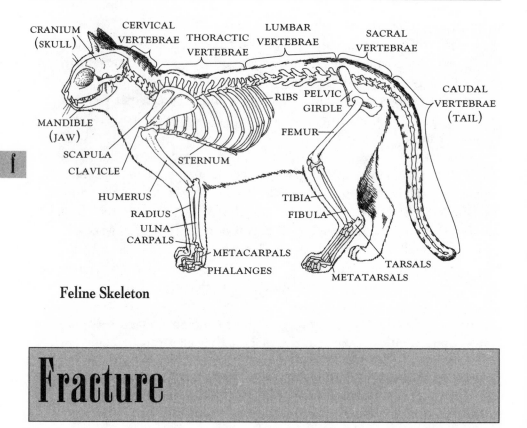

Feline Skeleton

Fracture

A fracture is the breaking of a bone. Bones are the solid support of the body that gives the cat his shape. The feline skeleton is composed of approximately 244 separate bones—about 40 more than people have. (The "extras" are located mostly in the spine and tail.) Individual bones can withstand only small amounts of stress without fracturing.

Fractures are categorized into three broad classifications: fatigue fractures, pathologic fractures, and traumatic fractures. Repeated stress to a bone results in fatigue fractures, which are rare in cats. Pathologic fractures are caused by systemic conditions like malnutrition or cancer that weaken individual bones or the entire skeleton and make them more susceptible to being broken. In these cases, the underlying problem as well as the fracture must be treated. In cats, most fractures are the result of trauma, with injuries due to falls or car accidents leading the way.

Cats suffering broken bones due to trauma may also suffer other injuries. Conditions such as BLEEDING and SHOCK take precedence over

FRACTURES

SYMPTOMS

Floppy "unhinged" legs or tail, limping, swelling, exposed bones, reluctance to move

HOME CARE

Immobilize with temporary splint if possible, then get cat to the vet

VET CARE

Diagnosis with X-ray; application of casts, surgical plating, wire, or pinning; sometimes antibiotic therapy; occasionally amputation

PREVENTION

Keep cats indoors away from cars, secure windows to prevent falls

fractures, and should be addressed before anything else. A veterinarian should be seen as soon as possible.

In young kittens, bones tend to crack or split rather than break; these are called greenstick fractures. Complete breaks are classified according to whether or not the skin is broken. They are called closed fractures when the skin is not broken, and open or compound fractures when bone protrudes from the skin. Open fractures put cats at higher risk for tissue or bone infections, which are painful and can be fatal.

Although every bone in the cat's body can be broken, the cat's femur (thigh bone) is fractured most often, accounting for nearly 30 percent of all feline fractures seen. Pelvic fractures, also very common, make up about 22 percent of feline fractures.

Head injuries can result in skull fractures, and a broken palate or jaw often happens as a result of a fall. Although the cat may try to land on his feet, the speed of the fall usually causes a cat's chin to smack the ground. Other common fracture sites include the cat's tail, the rear leg (tibia/fibula), the lower foreleg (radius/ulna), and the upper foreleg (humerus).

Signs of fracture include the affected limb moving or flopping loosely. The cat may hold his injured leg at an odd angle, or his tail may hang limp. A cat with a pelvic fracture isn't able to stand and support his weight. Bleeding and the white bone itself are visible in compound fractures. With greenstick or other closed fractures, the cat may exhibit pain by refusing to move, limping, or holding up the affected limb, which may be swollen.

Cats suffering fractures should be moved as little as possible. Do not try to feel or manipulate the injury; broken bone is sharp and can damage the tissue and nerves. Movement may turn a closed fracture into an open one or damage internal organs. Handle your cat with care so that you don't injure him further or injure yourself (see RESTRAINT).

If the fracture is above the elbow, wrap a towel about your cat to hold the limb snug against the body. Fractures of the leg below the elbow or knee are best immobilized using a temporary splint. The splint must extend both above and below the injury to be effective. Cover open wounds with sterile gauze or a clean cloth before splinting to help prevent infection.

Nearly any long, stiff material will work as a temporary splint. A rolled newspaper placed about the leg or a cylinder of cardboard from the core of a roll of paper towels may work. (Split cardboard tubes up the center so that the injured limb can be laid inside.) A pair of wooden spoons also work well; use one on the inside and one on the outside of the leg, and wrap with gauze, a towel, or even panty hose or a necktie. You should be able to insert one finger between the leg and bandage, so it's not wrapped too tight. Use tape over the gauze, towel, or cardboard to hold it in place. A simple hand towel by itself, wrapped about the limb, also may be sufficient. Then place the stricken cat on a towel in a box or carrier, and get him veterinary attention as soon as possible.

Veterinarians palpate (feel) the injury and use X-RAYS to learn the extent of the injury and determine the best treatment. Setting fractures is called reduction, and various techniques are used to hold bone in the proper position for healing to take place.

Splints and casts are generally used with fractures in the mid-portion of legs below the elbow. These work best when the bone fragments fit back together easily. But the closer the fracture is to a joint, and the more pieces there are, the more difficult it is to fix. Internal surgical fixation with wire, metal plates, or pins may be necessary.

Wire helps broken jaws heal; metal plates replace missing sections of bones and hold multiple breaks in correct alignment; and metal pins thread the breaks in long bones together like beads on a string. The hardware may become a permanent part of the cat, or may be removed after the fracture heals.

Feline bones heal relatively quickly and easily, especially those of growing kittens. Some types of feline fractures, particularly minor breaks in the pelvis, heal by themselves even when multiple fractures are present. If the cat is kept from moving, new bone called callus forms across the fracture site and helps stabilize it. Hard-bone formation follows shortly, with an eventual return to normal function.

Cats suffering fractures in the ball-and-socket formation of the hip often regain most limb function within three to five weeks simply by resting the affected leg. Other times, the damaged femoral head and/or neck are surgically removed, and the body creates a new false joint out of tissue that functions like the original.

When the fracture won't heal properly—typical of broken tails or toes—AMPUTATION may be necessary. Cats typically adjust quite well to missing toes, tails, or even legs, should that happen.

Outdoor cats are at highest risk for broken bones when they encounter vehicles; indoor cats suffer more often from falls. Prevent injury by staying alert to rocking chairs that can crush legs or tails, slippery perches that a cat may misjudge, and open windows (see HIGH-RISE SYNDROME).

Frostbite

Frostbite is the partial or complete freezing of specific parts of the body, usually the extremities. In cats, frostbite most often affects the ears, toes, scrotum, and tail.

Because our bodies contain more than 90 percent water, freezing can cause great damage. Just as an overfilled ice cube tray expands over

f

FROSTBITE

SYMPTOMS

Initially very pale to white flesh on affected areas, commonly ear tips, nose, testicles, tail, and toes; areas then swell, turn red, and may blister; finally tissue peels, and may fall off

HOME CARE

SEE VETERINARIAN IMMEDIATELY; if vet help isn't available, soak affected white areas in 104-degree water 15 to 20 minutes until tissue is flushed, then apply antiseptic ointment like Neomycin—see a vet as soon as possible

VET CARE

Antibiotics, pain medication, possible amputation of affected tissue

PREVENTION

Confine cats indoors during cold weather; provide shelter from wind, wet, and cold

the top as it freezes, living cells also expand when frozen. But the frozen matter has nowhere to go, and when the integrity of the cell ruptures, tissue is destroyed. Severe cases of frostbite can lead to infection and a loss of affected body parts.

Initially, a mildly affected area looks white and pale; as blood circulation returns, the area turns red and may swell. Severe cases result in blisters that actually look like burns. In these cases, tissue may peel, and dead skin eventually sloughs off.

Treating frostbite involves rewarming the frozen area, and first aid at home is extremely important. To thaw the area, soak in water warmed to 104 to 108 degrees for 15 to 20 minutes or until the skin becomes flushed. *Don't apply snow or ice, and don't rub or massage the injury; that will cause further damage to the tissues and compromise recovery.*

After thawing, apply an antiseptic ointment like Neomycin to the af- fected area.

Your cat's injury should then be evaluated by a veterinarian. It may require several days to determine the full extent of the damage. Anti- biotics, pain medication, or even surgery to remove damaged or dead tissue may be necessary in severe cases. Healing may take several weeks. Cats that have suffered frostbite in the past are prone to recurrence in the formerly afflicted area.

Frostbite can be prevented by confining cats indoors during cold weather. Outdoor cats should have access to warm, dry shelter away from the wind. (See also HYPOTHERMIA.)

f

Fungus

See RINGWORM.

Geriatric Cat

The term *geriatric* refers to the aged. A cat may be considered geriatric when she reaches eight to ten years of age. A cat ages much more quickly than people; each year added to an adult cat's life is roughly equivalent to four human years. However, just as in people, the signs of aging are extremely individual and vary from cat to cat.

The feral cat that lives on her own has a relatively short life span, and can expect to live only about six years before succumbing to disease or accident. Pet cats live much longer because of better nutrition, medical care, and a more protected lifestyle. Today, the average house cat typically lives to age fifteen or more. It's not unusual for well-cared-for felines to enjoy healthy lives into their late teens or even twenties.

Feline longevity means caretakers must deal with more age-related issues of their pet cat. Many of these do not impact the cat's quality of life, and parallel the infirmities people can expect as they age. Older cats become more sedentary and sleep more. Athletic cats may lose muscle tone and start to appear wobbly on their feet. Joint pain from ARTHRITIS can make cats reluctant to move and may cause irritability.

As cats age, their senses become less sharp, and this can be distressing for the cat. Many older cats suffer from painful dental problems, including PERIODONTAL DISEASE. Weight loss may be due to pain when eating or other problems and is an indication that something is wrong. Elderly cats often have problems GROOMING themselves, and an owner's

This elderly feline is twenty-three years old. *(Photo credit: Ralston Purina Company)*

help in this area is particularly important to keep a cat feeling like herself. Irregularity may plague geriatric felines (see CONSTIPATION). Very old cats (seventeen and older) can suffer from senility and may wander and cry with bewilderment and need comforting. Senile cats may lose litter box training, but medications are available that may help.

The effectiveness of the IMMUNE SYSTEM also tends to fade with age, making an elderly cat's health more fragile than that of a robust youngster. Geriatric felines get sicker more quickly and take longer to recover than healthy young cats. Prompt veterinary attention is vital to keep older pets healthy.

Health checks should be performed more frequently—annually at the least—as the cat ages. Care is aimed at reducing physical discomfort and emotional stress while slowing the signs of aging as much as possible.

A number of diseases and conditions typically affect geriatric felines. Renal failure is probably the most common cause of death in aged cats (see KIDNEY DISEASE). Kidneys just seem to wear out more quickly than other organs. Although it also affects cats of all ages, HYPER-THYROIDISM is also quite common in geriatric felines, and if left untreated, it can lead to heart failure (see CARDIOMYOPATHY). The risk of DIABETES MELLITUS is greater in older cats, and the chances for CANCER increase as the cat ages. And because of a compromised immune system, geriatric cats may suffer a wide range of opportunistic infections.

AGE COMPARISON

Each cat ages differently. The rate at which a cat ages depends on his lifestyle, health status, the care he receives early on and throughout his life, and even his genetics. Certain breeds of cat mature more slowly, while others may be longer lived. A cat's maturity at one year old is roughly equivalent to that of a young human adolescent. Emotional and physical maturity quickly follow. After age five or so, each year of a cat's life is roughly equivalent to four human years.

CAT'S AGE	HUMAN YEARS
1	15
2	18
3	24
4	29
5	34
6	38
7	42
8	46
9	50
10	54
11	58
12	62
13	66
14	70
15	74
16	78
17	82
18	86

Old cats do not tolerate hospitalizations well, though, and prescribed treatments are often most successful when done by owners at home.

Good NUTRITION is important to maintain the geriatric cat's health. Commercial diets are now available that are formulated for the special needs of older cats. For most animals, energy requirements decrease with age. Although this hasn't been proven specifically to be the case with cats, most geriatric diets are reduced-calorie rations. Older cats benefit most from food that's easily digested and/or chewed.

To make the quality of life as enjoyable as possible for your older pet cat, modify the cat's living quarters to make her more comfortable. If she can no longer leap to a favorite window perch, providing her with a ramp that allows her access will do wonders for her self-esteem. Grooming her daily not only makes her feel good but provides an opportunity for you to check for problems. Make the LITTER BOX more accessible, and provide her with cozy warm spots to sleep near her favorite thing—you.

g

Gestation

See REPRODUCTION.

Giardia

Giardia is a protozoan, a single-cell organism that inhabits the small intestine. The parasite interferes with the cat's ability to properly process food. Consequently, cats infected with giardia may have soft to normal-appearing stools, poor haircoats, a swollen tummy from gas, and trouble gaining or maintaining weight.

Cats catch the parasite from contact with infected soil or water—the infective cyst stage of the organism lives in the environment. A

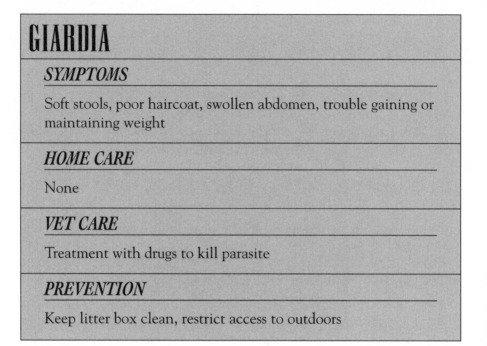

GIARDIA

SYMPTOMS

Soft stools, poor haircoat, swollen abdomen, trouble gaining or maintaining weight

HOME CARE

None

VET CARE

Treatment with drugs to kill parasite

PREVENTION

Keep litter box clean, restrict access to outdoors

g

mud puddle is a perfect giardia environment. Cats can transmit giardia to one another through contact with feces.

Diagnosis is difficult; because the organism is so small, it's hard to find in stool samples, even using a microscope. To complicate matters further, giardia may not be present in the stool all the time, so repeated microscopic examination of fresh stool may be necessary to detect the parasite.

Giardia can be treated with a drug called Flagyl (metronidazole) to kill the parasite. Keeping the LITTER BOX clean and restricting the cat's access to the outdoors helps prevent the chance of infection.

Gingivitis

Gingivitis is the inflammation of the gums that surround the teeth. The tissue will appear red rather than light pink, and may be tender or bleed when the cat chews hard food. Gingivitis is an early sign of dental disease (see PERIODONTAL DISEASE).

Glaucoma

Glaucoma is a disease characterized by increased pressure inside the eyeball that damages the retina and optic nerve (see EYES). Glaucoma is considered uncommon in cats.

The sphere of the eye is filled with a specialized fluid that holds the structures of vision in place. But the liquid is not static; it's constantly replaced with fresh as the old drains out into the rest of the body.

The front portion of the eye directly behind the cornea contains watery fluid called aqueous humor (the rear chamber of the eye holds a

g

GLAUCOMA

SYMPTOMS

Painful eye with squinting, pawing at the eye, tearing, bloodshot or cloudy-looking eye; swelling of the eyeball; nonresponsive pupil

HOME CARE

None

VET CARE

Medications to control pressure, pain medications, possibly surgery, sometimes removal of affected eye

PREVENTION

Prevent exposure to predisposing viral diseases

clear, gel-like material called vitreous humor). A membrane called the ciliary epithelium constantly produces the aqueous fluid, which normally drains through the iridocorneal angle where the cornea and iris meet. If the normal input/output balance is disrupted, the increased pressure from this liquid inside the globe of the eye results in glaucoma. The eyeball keeps filling, and the fluid has nowhere to go.

The increased pressure is extremely painful for the cat. The pressure also pushes the internal structure of the eye into abnormal positions until the cat's vision is destroyed.

The condition is categorized as either primary or secondary glaucoma. The primary form, in which the condition occurs without any preceding disease, is rare in cats and may result from congenital defects in the eye. This form of the disease is thought to be genetic, and is seen most often in Siamese and Persian cats.

Cats suffer more commonly from secondary glaucoma, which results from underlying injury or disease. Inflammation of the eye, called UVEITIS, can cause glaucoma, and most often it results from infectious diseases like FELINE IMMUNODEFICIENCY VIRUS, FELINE INFECTIOUS PERITONITIS, FELINE LEUKEMIA VIRUS, or TOXOPLASMOSIS. Tumors or injuries can also cause glaucoma.

Signs of pain may be hard to detect, and often involve behavior changes. The cat with a painful eye may squint or paw at the eye, or the eye may tear. The cat's eye may become bloodshot or appear cloudy. By the time signs are more obvious, it may be too late to save the cat's vision. Late signs include swelling of the eyeball and a dilated pupil that doesn't respond to light.

Diagnosis is made using a tonometer, an instrument that measures pressure inside the eye. The veterinarian administers eyedrops so the cat will feel no discomfort, then gently balances the instrument on the cat's cornea. A mercury level on the tonometer measures the pressure within the eye. Sometimes a special examination of the interior of the eye is done using a special contact lens placed on the cat's eye.

Glaucoma may be reversible when inflammation is caught early and is not too severe. Many times, only one eye is affected, but usually both are treated to prevent involvement of the second eye. Drugs are given that help transfer water and decrease the production of fluid. Other medications help contract the pupil and control the pressure by inhibiting nerve impulses, while steroids may reduce the inflammation.

If the glaucoma is severe, the cat may lose an eye. (*Photo credit: Amy D. Shojai*)

Surgery may even be necessary to remove the membrane that produces the fluid.

When inflammation is severe, or the cause cannot be successfully treated, glaucoma may not get better even with treatment. When blindness is inevitable and medication doesn't relieve the cat's pain, removing the eye (enucleation) is necessary. Usually, the eyelid is sewn closed over the empty socket. Sometimes, a prosthesis is placed for cosmetic reasons.

Cats do quite well with only one eye. Once the pain is gone, they start to feel and act better almost immediately. Cats that become blind also do very well in familiar surroundings by relying on scent and sound.

There is really nothing that can be done to prevent glaucoma, other than preventing viral infections that may lead to it.

Grass, Eating

Cats are obligate carnivores, which means they do not rely on vegetables or fruits in their diet, but require meat to survive. In the wild, the only vegetable matter a cat eats is found in the stomach and intestines of his prey.

Yet for unknown reasons, most cats occasionally eat grass. Usually, they carefully choose and eat the tips of only a few blades at a time. The grass may be used as a natural emetic to stimulate VOMITING of HAIRBALLS. Or, cats may simply like the flavor and enjoy grazing from time to time. There is some speculation that eating grass may provide trace elements of vitamins in the cat's diet.

Whatever the reason, cats seem to enjoy chewing grass. Indoor cats may nibble houseplants when they feel the urge to graze; depending on the plant, this can be dangerous (see POISON). Pet-supply stores offer planting kits that contain wheat grass or other appropriate greens for grass-craving felines.

Griseofulvin

See RINGWORM.

Grooming

Grooming is the act of cleaning and conditioning the body, and in cats refers specifically to the proper maintenance of the haircoat (although it also involves proper attention being given to EARS, EYES, CLAWS, and

TEETH). Grooming can help meet a cat's physical and social needs, and just plain feels good to the cat (see TOUCH).

Grooming is directly responsible for maintaining healthy skin. Sebaceous glands in the skin at the base of each hair release an oily secretion, called sebum, when the cat's grooming tugs at the fur. Sebum is spread by the cat's tongue during grooming, and lubricates and waterproofs the hair coat. Grooming also combs out loose hair, which if left in place can cause painful tangles or mats. As they clean themselves, cats also search their skin and fur for parasites (see FLEAS, LICE, and TICKS).

A healthy coat does more than look good; it's insurance against injury. HAIR normally falls in loose layers that help protect the cat's body from injury and insulates her from temperature extremes. Cats do not have the same cooling system of SWEAT GLANDS people do, and instead rely on grooming to maintain their body temperature. A well-groomed coat free of mats can be fluffed and allows air to pass between the hairs and cool the skin. Cats also pant to cool themselves when they are very hot, but licking the skin and hair is even more effective. The evaporation of saliva spread by grooming provides an extremely effective method of keeping a cat cool.

Self-grooming is learned early. Some cats are neatness freaks and seem to be constantly washing themselves; others allow themselves to become quite shabby before cleaning up. Cats learn grooming technique from their mothers; consequently, if a Mom-cat was less than meticulous about grooming, her kittens won't be as particular about their appearance either. Kittens learn to lick themselves by two weeks of age, and are washing themselves by the time they are weaned. As adults, they'll spend up to 50 percent of their awake time in some form of grooming.

The teeth and TONGUE are used for much of a cat's self-grooming, and cats often assume odd positions to wash hard-to-reach areas. The specialized structure of the tongue makes it a perfect fur comb, while teeth nibble and gnaw at any tangles, dirt, and burrs caught in the fur.

Typically, a cat licks his mouth, chin, and whiskers clean first, followed by each shoulder and foreleg. He then proceeds to wash both flanks and hind legs, the genitals, and then the tail from end to end. He uses his dampened forepaws to scrub his face, head, and ears. He redampens his paw by licking after every few swipes, and switches paws depending on what side he is washing. Using his rear claws, he grooms

g

A cat grooming himself with dampened forepaw. *(Photo credit: Betsy Stowe)*

This calico cat grooms her back. *(Photo credit: Amy D. Shojai)*

the neck and ears by SCRATCHING them. He keeps his rear claws in shape by nibbling on them, and grooms his front claws by scratching objects.

Grooming of Others: Cats groom each other as a way to express their friendly relationship. Mutual grooming also helps cats take care of hard-to-reach areas, and usually focuses on the head and neck areas.

But the activity is usually more of a social gesture than a hygienic one. It can be a form of communication—an expression of comfort, of companionship, even of love. A cat that grooms an owner's hair or accepts the owner's petting is expressing affection by indulging in mutual grooming with that owner.

Displacement Behavior: It's also thought that cats use grooming to make themselves feel better emotionally. Behavior that appears to be inappropriate to the situation is called displacement behavior, and cats employ grooming for this purpose more often than any other. Cats may groom themselves when fearful, to relieve tension, or when uncertain how to react to situations.

A cat confronted with an aggressive animal may, instead of running or attacking, suddenly begin to furiously groom. The same behavior is seen when the cat does something stupid—perhaps misjudges a leap and falls on his furry fanny. Such behavior usually prompts an intense session of self-grooming. Other times, cats use displacement grooming when other behaviors aren't allowed; perhaps you've put the cat on a diet, or are trying to convince an outdoor cat he should stay inside.

Animal behaviorists speculate that self-grooming is a way for a cat to deal with conflict. It's unknown whether grooming has a direct effect on the neurologic impulses in the brain, or simply is a way for the cat to distract himself. Some animal behaviorists suggest that strong emotion (fear? embarrassment?) results in a rise of body temperature that the cat cools by grooming. But with the benefits of massage and touch well documented, it appears that the mere physical action of massage could help calm feline anxiety.

Some displacement grooming is normal for a cat. Only if your cat becomes obsessive about grooming, and begins to lose fur or damage the skin, should you seek veterinary assistance.

And always remember that grooming is a barometer of feline health: an UNTHRIFTY appearance often signals illness in the cat. Emotional and/or physical conditions may trigger grooming behavior that is inappropriate or excessive, or may cause the cat to stop self-grooming altogether (see HAIR LOSS, HYPERESTHESIA SYNDROME, and STRESS).

Grooming Your Cat: Even the most fastidious cat benefits from grooming by the owner. Grooming a cat helps tone a feline's muscles, and removes loose dirt, dander, and fur that can contribute to ALLERGIES. Removing dead hair also helps prevent hairballs. A grooming routine doubles as an at-home exam for detecting problems with a cat's eyes, ears, claws, or skin.

A thorough weekly brushing may be all that's required for short-haired coats, but longhaired felines require more help.

Cats groomed daily as kittens will learn to relish and expect the attention. For reluctant cats, keep grooming sessions brief so the cat won't lose interest, or patience. It's no fun to groom an unhappy cat, and forcing the issue makes a feline dread future grooming sessions.

Make the event as pleasurable for both of you as possible. Cats appreciate an established routine, so always try to groom at the same time and place. Plan ahead by having equipment handy, stop before your cat demands it, and finish with a favorite game or toy. You can always finish where you left off later.

The proper tools include a small table or countertop without a lot of distractions. This should be a place identified with grooming in which you can confine the cat's activity, like the top of the dryer in the laundry room. Some cats do better with one person lightly holding them while a second person uses the comb or brush. Other cats go into ecstasy when groomed, and will delight in the attention anytime, anyplace.

Grooming brushes and combs are available at pet stores, veterinary offices, and mail-order supply companies. They come in a variety of styles, and your cat's haircoat defines the type you need. Longhaired cats may require an assortment of brushes, while shorthaired cats can often get by with one.

A rubber curry brush works well on shorthaired cats. The slicker brush, with fine wire bristles in a rubber pad, tends to reach best through thick, long hair. The pin-and-bristle brush has metal pins on one side for removing shed hair, and natural bristles on the other for smoothing the coat.

Combs come in fine, medium, and coarse teeth—this defines the amount of space between the tines. As a rule of thumb, cats with thick, long fur should be combed with coarse combs where the tines are far apart, while shorthaired cats benefit from medium to fine combs. The ends of the teeth on any comb should be smooth and rounded. Teflon-coated combs reduce the amount of static electricity and reduce tearing or the breaking of the hair. Cats also enjoy being groomed with "cat gloves," special gloves with inset rubber nubs on the palm that smooth the hair coat and collect loose fur as you pet the cat.

Allow cats that have never been groomed before to sniff and investigate the equipment well ahead of time to familiarize themselves with the tools. And always begin a session with petting—this helps you learn the contours of the cat's body and alerts you to any mats or other problems ahead of time.

Cats with long heavy double coats—Persians and Himalayans—develop painful mats very quickly when dead hair tangles with live hair. These knots of fur tend to develop in the armpits of all four legs, behind the ears, and beneath the tail—places the cat just can't reach. A badly matted coat is probably best left to the attention of a reputable feline groomer.

Minor problems, however, may be teased out by using a coarse-toothed comb. Rub cornstarch into the mat to help separate the hairs,

Care for your cat by combing or brushing his fur. *(Photo credit: Ralston Purina Company)*

then thread the comb through the mat—to protect the cat from painful pulling—and brush over the comb with a slicker brush. Begin at the tips of the hairs and gradually work deeper into the mat. Don't use scissors; cat skin is quite thin and very tender, and you're liable to cut a wiggling cat as well as his fur. If gentle combing or brushing doesn't work, you may need to use an electric razor to break up the mat or shave out the area.

For routine grooming, run your fingers over the cat's body and through his fur until he is relaxed, then begin with light, short strokes with a brush in the direction the fur grows. Longhaired cats benefit from using the slicker brush first, followed by the comb. Begin and end at a cat's "sweet spots"—the areas beneath his chin, cheeks, or throat that make him close his eyes and purr with delight. Talk soothingly to your cat throughout the session to help calm him, and keep him connected to you.

Progress from the face area to each side, taking care not to be too rough against the spine or nipples. Don't forget the flanks both inside and out, the area beneath the tail, and the tail itself. Cats tend to resist attention to their underside, so be alert to the cat's mood and back off before he becomes too aggravated. Try lifting one hind foot off the table while you attend to the other rear leg; that gives the cat less balance and something else to think about, while allowing you access to the area.

Think of it as scratching the cat's skin rather than brushing. The cat will tell you by arching his back into the brush when he wants a heavier stroke. For longhaired cats, follow the brushing with a comb. Again, begin with a light touch and short strokes until you've reached through the haircoat to the skin. Finish with cat gloves to polish the coat. A pair of panty hose slipped over your hand also works well.

Clipping Your Cat's Nails: Most cats attend to their nails themselves, but claws can overgrow, tear, and split, causing painful infections. Trimming your cat's nails regularly reduces the chances of these problems—and tempers his urge to claw furniture. On average, a monthly trim should be adequate. Older cats may need trims more often.

Human nail clippers work well on some cats, particularly kittens with tiny claws. Commercial cat toenail clippers are available from your veterinarian, pet-supply store, or mail-order catalogs. These are designed to cut kitty claws at the proper angle without the risk of splitting or crushing the nail. There are trimmers designed like scissors as

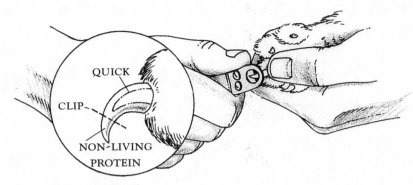

QUICK

CLIP

NON-LIVING
PROTEIN

Clipping Your Cat's Nails

well as guillotine-type clippers. The best clipper has very sharp blades and is one you're comfortable handling.

Get your cat used to having his paws handled while still a kitten. A good time to clip nails is when your cat is relaxed, perhaps after a nap. Often, it's easiest to have two sets of hands available during nail clipping—one pair to hold and calm your cat, the other to trim (see RE-STRAINT). Trimming nails single-handedly works well with trusting cats who have confident owners.

Grasp the paw and gently press it between your fingers and thumb to express the claws, using your other hand to clip the nails. Don't forget the dewclaw, located in the "thumb" position inside the lower legs. And don't forget that cats can have extra toes—referred to as polydactylism—that will need to be clipped, with some cats having as many as seven toes on each foot. Trim only the end of each nail, which is usually white, and avoid the pink quick, which will bleed. If you cut too closely, use a styptic pencil or cornstarch on the nail, or rake the claw through a bar of soap to stop the bleeding.

Work quickly, and if your cat begins to fret too much, let him go even if only one or two paws are done. You can finish later. Reward the cat with a play session or special treat, so he'll associate nail trimming with good things. And always trim your cat's nails before bathing him. (See also CLAWS.)

Bathing Your Cat: Although they are intrinsically clean creatures, all cats benefit from an occasional bath. Illness, poor grooming habits, parasite infestation, or simply getting themselves dingy may require more help than a brush can handle.

A bath stimulates the skin and removes excess oil, dander, and shed hair. But bathing a cat too often can dry the skin. A good rule of thumb is to bathe shorthaired cats no oftener than every six weeks; two to three times a year during shedding season should suffice unless your cat gets really grubby or is a show cat. Longhaired cats benefit from more frequent baths.

Kittens should not be bathed until they are at least four weeks old. Elderly cats or extremely ill cats may be stressed by bathing. Babies and geriatric cats have difficulty regulating their body temperature, and can become chilled and develop PNEUMONIA very easily. Follow your veterinarian's recommendation in these instances.

Just as with brushing, assemble your equipment beforehand. The cat should be thoroughly brushed and/or combed ahead of time. All hair mats must be removed before bathing, because water will just cement these mats into place.

Assemble your shampoo, several towels, and washcloth near the sink or tub, and run warm water (about 102 degrees, or cat body temperature) before you bring in the cat. Some cats, like the Turkish Van, actually enjoy water, but no cat wants to be forced to do something. Don't create undue stress by making your cat watch your preparations. Instead, make bath time a (hopefully) pleasant surprise.

The bath area should be warm and draft-free. The bathtub will do, but a waist-high sink is easier on your knees. Move all breakables out of reach, and push drapes or shower curtains that can spook your cat out of the way.

One reason cats dislike bathing is that they feel insecure on slippery surfaces. Placing a towel or rubber mat in the bottom of your tub or sink to give a cat a foothold will do wonders for his confidence. Or try standing the cat on a plastic milk crate, which gives him something to clutch with his paws, while allowing you to rinse him top to bottom without turning him upside down.

If you're debugging the cat, be sure your shampoo contains a cat-safe insecticide that will only affect the FLEAS. For routine cleaning, a simple grooming shampoo labeled specifically for cats is sufficient. *Never use human products, dishwashing soap, or laundry detergent on your cat.* At best, they can be harsh and dry out the skin; at worst, they can be toxic and kill your cat.

Before you begin soaking the cat, place half a cotton ball inside each ear to keep them from filling with water. Some veterinarians recommend putting a drop of mineral oil in each eye before bathing, to protect them from soap.

For small cats or kittens, the bucket method of bathing often works best. Use the double sink in the kitchen, two or more large roasting pans, or a couple of buckets or wastebaskets set in the bathtub. Fill each with warm water, then gently lower your cat (one hand supporting his bottom, the other beneath the chest) into the first container to get him wet.

Don't dunk his face or splash water on him—that's what gets cats upset. Let him stand on his hind legs and clutch the edge of the container as you thoroughly wet him. Then lift him out onto one of your towels and apply the shampoo, using the washcloth to clean his face. Once he's thoroughly soapy, dip the cat back into the first container to be rinsed. Get as much soap off as possible before removing him, and sluice off excess water before rinsing him in subsequent containers of clean water. Rinse his face with the washcloth.

Adult cats may object to being dunked like this, and find running water scary. Another bathing method works better with large cats. Again, fill a couple of buckets or wastebaskets with water ahead of time, but use a ladle to dip water over him instead. If you have a spray nozzle from the sink, use a *low* force, starting at his feet to get him used to the idea. Keep the nozzle close to the fur so he doesn't see the spray. *Never spray in the face; use the washcloth to wet that area.* Keep one hand on the cat at all times to prevent escapes; it's doubly hard to catch a wet, soapy cat. Professional groomers often use a figure-eight cat harness to tether the cat in place, which leaves the bather's hands free.

If flea shampoo is used, suds the neck area first to create a barrier the fleas won't cross. Lather from the neck down the body, to legs, feet, and tail; use the washcloth on his face. For flea treatment, the shampoo must soak for up to ten minutes. Wrapping the soapy cat in a towel and holding him for the duration may be easier than keeping an unfettered foamy feline in the tub. Rinse the cat's face with the washcloth, taking care to avoid getting soap or water in his eyes or ears. Then rinse beginning at the neck and down his back; don't neglect beneath his tail or under his tummy.

When the water finally runs clear and you know he's clean, rinse him once more just to be sure. Don't forget to remove the cotton from his ears.

Wrap the squeaky-clean cat in a dry towel. Shorthaired cats dry quickly, but longhaired felines may need two or more towels to blot away most of the water. Some cats enjoy the blow dryer, but use only the lowest setting to avoid burning the cat. Combing long fur as you blow-dry will give an added "oomph" to the longhaired coat.

Caring for Your Cat's Eyes: Flat-faced cats like Persians have large prominent eyes that tend to water. Tears may stain the fur beneath the eyes, particularly of light-colored cats. Normal eye secretions are clear and liquid, just like human tears; see your veterinarian if the discharge is cloudy or dark.

But even normal tears may turn crusty on the fur and irritate the skin, which can lead to infection. Daily maintenance prevents these problems. Use saline-soaked cotton balls to soften the secretions at the corners of your cat's eyes and clean them away. There are also commercial preparations available from pet stores that help remove the stain from fur.

Caring for Your Cat's Ears: The inside of a healthy cat's ear is pink and free of discharge. Small amounts of light yellow wax are normal,

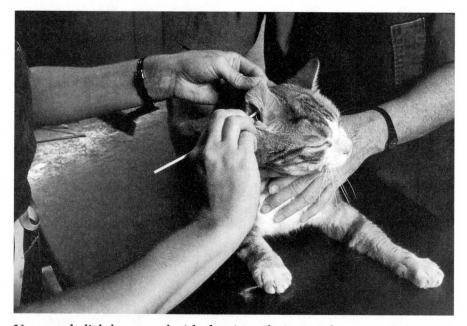

Use a swab, lightly covered with cleaning solution, to clean your cat's ears.
(Photo credit: Ralston Purina Company)

but dark or crumbly material is not and may indicate the presence of EAR MITES. Check your cat's ears at least once a week during routine grooming sessions.

For routine maintenance, use mineral oil or baby oil or obtain a cleaning solution suitable for cats from your veterinarian or pet store. Place a few drops of it on a cotton ball or swab, and gently wipe out the easily visible areas. *Don't place drops of anything into the ear unless your veterinarian tells you to.* When using a cotton swab to clean the tiny indentations, never go down into the ear farther than you can see, or you may damage the cat's hearing.

Caring for Your Cat's Teeth: See PERIODONTAL DISEASE.

g

Haemobartonellosis

Haemobartonellosis is a disease caused by specialized bacteria that live on the surface of red blood cells. The parasite, called *Haemobartonella felis*, affects domestic cats around the world and was first recognized in the United States in 1953. Formerly, this condition was called feline infectious anemia, or FIA, because the most obvious sign of the disease is ANEMIA.

Cats with acute disease often suffer a sudden high fever of 103 to 106 degrees, act depressed or weak, lose their appetite, and have pale gums. Some cats also become jaundiced from the rapid destruction of blood cells; the light areas of their skin take on a yellowish cast. But cats can have such minor symptoms that the owner may never realize the cat is infected.

The primary form of the disease develops without other disease being present. About one-third of cats infected with haemobartonellosis will die from severe anemia if not treated.

The more common secondary form occurs when other illnesses like FELINE INFECTIOUS PERITONITIS or FELINE LEUKEMIA VIRUS have compromised the cat's immune system. Fewer cats survive this secondary form of the disease.

Infectious blood must be introduced into a healthy cat to transfer the disease, but nobody is quite certain how this happens. In experiments, blood transfusions have been shown to transmit the disease, and kittens can become infected before they are born when the mother has the disease. It's not been proven but is highly likely that haemobartonellosis is transmitted through the bite of bloodsucking parasites, most likely FLEAS.

Anemia is caused a couple of different ways. Parasites that colonize the surface of the cat's red blood cells may cause the cells to rupture and die. Also, the body's IMMUNE SYSTEM marks the infested cells for the spleen to filter them out of circulation. These blood cells are then either destroyed by the spleen or cleansed and returned to circulation. But these cleansed cells remain damaged, and they die more quickly than normal cells. The bone marrow usually remains active—making new blood cells to replace those being lost—but when production can't keep up with demand, anemia occurs.

The disease can affect all cats of any age or breed, but occurs most often in male cats between four and eight years of age. The true incidence is difficult to know, because current tests do not always detect the bacteria.

Diagnosis is based on actually finding the parasite on the blood cell, so blood samples are examined with a microscope to find the tiny bugs.

h

HAEMOBARTONELLOSIS

SYMPTOMS

Sudden high fever, depression, weakness, anorexia, pale lips or gums, sometimes yellow cast to tissue (inside of ears)

HOME CARE

None

VET CARE

Tetracyclinelike antibiotic

PREVENTION

Flea control

But since the spleen sequesters infected cells, the parasites may be hidden away during much of the illness. Testing the blood for up to six consecutive days is recommended to find the bacteria.

The parasite is most likely to be found in the tiny capillaries where the blood doesn't move quite so quickly. A drop of this so-called sludged blood is collected by piercing the cat's ear with a needle and collecting the tiny drop that appears. Cats typically don't mind this type of sample collection nearly as much as drawing blood from a larger vein in the leg or neck.

Cats with suspicious signs are treated whether the parasite is found or not. The disease is primarily treated for ten days to two weeks with oral tetracycline, an antibiotic that kills the parasite.

It is suspected that infected cats are never completely cleared of the parasite, and stress or illness may prompt flare-ups of the disease for the rest of their lives. Cats diagnosed or suspected of having been infected with this bacteria should never be used in blood donor programs. Ongoing studies are trying to determine the exact route of infection, as well as develop more accurate tests to identify infection in cats.

There is no known way to prevent haemobartonellosis, since the means of transmission remains unclear.

Hair

Hair is the outgrowth from the skin of multiple threadlike colored filaments composed of keratin. These in combination make up the haircoat that covers the cat's skin.

Fur serves as a protective barrier between the cat's skin and the elements. All cats have fur, although the amount and type of haircoat varies from cat to cat and from breed to breed. Even "hairless" cats like the Sphynx breed typically sport a peach fuzz dusting of velvety fur.

Each hair is made up of the root, seated within the skin itself, and the shaft, which is the visible portion of the hair. Most cats have three types of hairs. Guard hairs are the coarse, long, straight hairs found in the outer coat; awn hairs are of medium length and make up the intermediate coat; and soft, short downy fur that's curly or crimped composes the undercoat. Sinus hairs, also called WHISKERS, are found on the face and legs and offer specialized sensory input.

Hair production is cyclic, growing from the root outward in a pattern of rapid growth, slower growth, and a resting period. Each cat hair grows about a third of an inch each month. That means a cat generates about sixty feet worth—total—of hair each day. Old hairs are pushed out by the new hair (see SHEDDING). The length of an individual hair varies by breed; a longhaired cat has hair that grows up to four inches long, while a Sphynx's fuzz grows to about one-eighth of an inch.

Proper nutrition is essential for a healthy coat. Hair is 95 percent protein, and gains its sheen and healthy "glow" from the proper balance of fats and other nutrients. Poor nutrition is often reflected in a cat's skin and haircoat first. GROOMING is beneficial for all cats, and especially important for longhaired cats, to keep their haircoat healthy.

h

Hairballs

Hairballs are hotdog- or cigar-shaped masses of compressed fur that are vomited by the cat. Cats spend a great deal of their time licking and cleaning themselves during self-grooming, and swallow fur as a part of this process.

Most swallowed hair passes through a cat's digestive system, is expelled during bowel movements, and causes the cat no problems. Hair that doesn't pass collects in the stomach in a dense ball and is expelled by throwing up. It is normal for cats to occasionally experience hairballs. Owner-grooming reduces the amount of fur cats swallow and helps prevent hairballs, which in some instances can become dangerous.

Large amounts of swallowed fur may block the digestive tract, and become impossible for the cat to vomit or excrete. Impaction is the most common cause of feline CONSTIPATION, with 50 percent of cases due to hairballs. Cats have been known to suffer hairballs as big as baseballs that require surgical removal. Frequent vomiting is the most common sign of intestinal blockage (see also SWALLOWED OBJECTS). A problem hairball may also result in DIARRHEA, loss of appetite, a wheezing cough or dry retching, or a swollen abdomen. See your veterinarian

When grooming themselves, cats often swallow fur. *(Photo credit: Lillian Zahrt)*

immediately if your cat exhibits any one or more of these signs.

Commercial products are available to help the hairball pass more readily, and usually are composed of a nondigestible fat-type ingredient. Take care to follow label instructions or your veterinarian's advice, because such products can interfere with the cat's use of fat-soluble vitamins if overused.

Occasional use of home products may also work well. Avoid digestible fats like butter, which tend to cause diarrhea or are absorbed before they can move the problem out. One of the most effective home treatments is nonmedicated petroleum jelly, which many cats consider a treat. Spread the jelly on the cat's forepaw for him to lick off.

High-fiber diets and fiber supplements may be a better choice for chronic problems. The extra bulk helps carry the hairs naturally through the system so they're eliminated in the litter box. Commercial veterinary products also are available. Plain bran, flavor-free varieties of Metamucil, or a teaspoon of canned pumpkin (a favorite with some cats) added to the diet also provides the necessary bulk.

HAIRBALLS

SYMPTOMS

Throwing up wads of hair; when hairballs are too large to expel in this way, diarrhea, loss of appetite, dry retching, or swollen abdomen

HOME CARE

Feed cat hairball medication following product instructions or offer nonmedicated petroleum jelly

VET CARE

Surgery occasionally required to remove blockages

PREVENTION

Routine grooming; add fiber like Metamucil or pumpkin to diet; switch to higher-fiber rations

Hair Loss

It is normal for cats to lose hair as new growth replaces old dead hair (see SHEDDING). Longhaired cats normally shed their heavy undercoat in clumps, leaving a moth-eaten appearance that can look alarming to the owner. Most cats, particularly shorthaired cats, have areas of thinning hair at the temples.

Hair loss in isolated areas may be a sign of parasite infestation or skin disease such as ALLERGIES, FLEAS, or RINGWORM. In these instances, the skin is often inflamed with scabs or sores. A veterinary diagnosis is necessary before the proper treatment can begin.

Occasionally, cats suffering STRESS react by overgrooming themselves, which can result in hair loss. Displacement grooming can become a habit if the stressful conditions are not addressed (see GROOMING, Displacement Grooming; see also HYPERESTHESIA SYNDROME).

Hair Mats

See GROOMING.

Haw

See EYES.

Heartbeat

See PULSE.

Heart Disease

See CARDIOMYOPATHY and HEARTWORM DISEASE.

Heartworm Disease

Feline heartworm disease (FHD) is caused by a type of roundworm that belongs to a group of parasites called filarids. Although FHD was first reported in 1922, dogs are the natural host and are much more commonly affected. Until relatively recently, it was believed that cats were not at risk for the disease.

In fact, cats do get heartworms. But because the resulting disease and its symptoms, diagnosis, and treatment are quite different from those of dogs, FHD has remained an invisible killer.

To become infected, a cat must live in an area that has infected dogs, and with mosquitoes that have a taste for both dog blood and cat blood. The mosquito ingests baby heartworms, called microfilariae, when it bites an already infected dog. The heartworm spends about three weeks developing inside the mosquito, molting and growing until the larvae migrate to the mouth parts of the insect. It is this stage that is infective to the cat or dog. When the mosquito again takes a blood meal, larvae are deposited upon the skin and gain entrance to the host's body through the bite wound.

During the next several months, the immature parasites undergo a number of further molts and development stages inside the animal's body, ultimately migrating to the heart and pulmonary arteries, where they mature. In dogs, adult worms mate and shed microfilariae into the animal's bloodstream, completing the life cycle, but cats are known as "dead-end hosts" because their small bodies are rarely able to sustain enough mature worms for the parasite to be able to reproduce. Consequently, cats almost never show the presence of microfilariae. Also, some cats appear to mount an immune defense against the parasite that kills the baby worms and effectively cures the cat. Still, an unknown number of cats die of the disease without ever being diagnosed.

All cats exposed to mosquitoes are at risk, but indoor cats may be at highest risk because their natural resistance may not have been primed by past unsuccessful exposure (see IMMUNE SYSTEM). Current studies estimate the incidence of FHD to be about 10 percent that of the disease in dogs in any given geographic location, which can range from up to

FELINE HEARTWORM DISEASE

SYMPTOMS

Difficulty breathing, weight loss, sudden collapse, coughing, asthmalike signs of wheezing, chronic vomiting not associated with hairballs or food

HOME CARE

Supportive care, reduce stress, limit activity

VET CARE

Supportive care, treat specific symptoms

PREVENTION

Use feline preventive medication as directed by veterinarian

85 percent of dogs in some areas to 8 percent of dogs in others. The American Heartworm Society has identified FHD cases in thirty-eight states, including the District of Columbia and Puerto Rico; about 70 percent of cats are at risk in areas where there are heartworm-infected dogs.

The majority of infected cats probably don't develop symptoms, and may recover without anyone knowing they were infected. However, the acute form of the disease occurs in cats more frequently than in dogs; such cats appear normal one moment and then suffer sudden respiratory failure and die within minutes. Because of their larger size, dogs typically can live with a relatively heavy worm load without ill effects. But in cats, one worm can cause severe distress; two worms can kill.

Chronic FHD has vague signs different from the canine version of the disease. Dogs often develop signs of heart failure, which is rare in cats. Instead, cats suffer from diseases of the arteries of the lungs, have difficulty breathing, lose weight, become weak, and may suddenly collapse. FHD can cause breathing problems similar to ASTHMA, or even

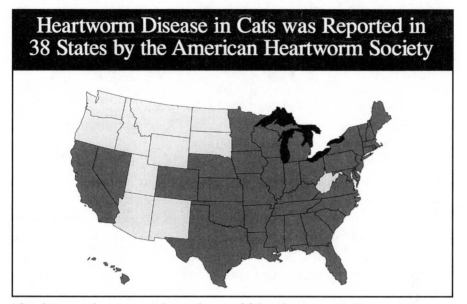

Heartworm Disease in Cats was Reported in 38 States by the American Heartworm Society

The thirty-eight states with incidence of feline heartworm disease. *(Photo credit: Heartgard for Cats)*

coughing, which is rare in cats. Many cats suffer vomiting that isn't associated with eating.

Diagnosis is based on signs of disease, blood screening techniques, X-rays, and echocardiography. There is no definitive blood test for cats. Traditional tests look for microfilariae, but this isn't helpful in cats, which rarely have immature worms.

A better test for cats detects the antigen that the worms release into the bloodstream. A positive test is considered diagnostic, but the worms must be female, at least five months old, and in sufficient numbers to be detected. Cats usually host only two to three worms, which typically die before becoming old enough to be identified by this test. That means a negative test can't be trusted.

Another test screens for antibodies made by the cat's immune system in defense against the worms. A positive test means exposure has taken place, but a negative test is inconclusive. Using the antibody and antigen tests together, though, can be helpful.

The only heartworm drug approved by the FDA to kill heartworms is thiacetarsamide sodium, which is a derivative of arsenic. *It is not ap-*

proved for use in cats. Treatment in dogs consists of killing the worms in the heart and allowing the body to slowly absorb the debris. But in cats, worms more typically are in the pulmonary arteries of the lungs. Worm debris can block the blood flow in the lungs, and this embolization can kill the cat.

For that reason, heartworm disease in cats is usually treated only with supportive care aimed at relieving the cat's symptoms of distress. It is hoped the cat will survive the infection.

Preventive medication has been available for dogs for many years; only *recently has a feline preventive been approved by the FDA.* Heartgard (ivermectin) for Cats is a chewable once-monthly tablet that kills the tissue stage of the larvae; it also prevents HOOKWORMS. The medication is recommended for cats six weeks of age or older and is considered safe for pregnant or breeding cats. It's recommended that cats be tested for FHD first, but the preventive is safe to give to cats already infected with FHD.

Heat (Estrus)

See REPRODUCTION.

Heatstroke

See HYPERTHERMIA.

Hematoma

Hematoma refers to a swelling beneath the skin that contains blood. Hematomas are generally caused by a blow or bruise, and usually resolve by themselves. Large hematomas may require surgical drainage.

Aural hematomas, those occurring in the skin of the ear flap, often appear as a result of parasites or an ear infection. The parasite or the infection causes a shaking or scratching of the ears, which results in a bruising. When the bruising separates the ear cartilage from the skin and the pocket between fills with blood and fluid, the pinna swells suddenly, causing a hematoma. The soft swelling is usually on the inside but can be on the outside surface of the ear flap. The condition is much more common in dogs, particularly breeds with floppy ears. The underlying cause for the injury must be treated as well as the hematoma (see EAR MITES and OTITIS).

HEMATOMA

SYMPTOMS

Soft swelling of (usually) the inside or sometimes the outside of the ear flap

HOME CARE

None

VET CARE

Surgical drainage and repair

PREVENTION

Routine ear cleaning to prevent self-trauma from scratching at parasites (e.g., ear mites)

Unless the trapped blood is removed, the ear cartilage may scar and shrivel. Small hematomas may be treated by drawing out the blood with a syringe, followed by firm bandaging for seven to ten days. But often, the ear simply reinflates in a day or two with new blood and serum.

Surgery provides the best results. The cat is anesthetized and a small incision is made to the inside surface of the cat's ear. Collected blood and other debris is removed and the separated flaps of tissue stitched together, leaving a narrow opening at the incision line. This allows fluid to drain as the incision heals, and prevents the wound from reballooning with fluid.

In severe cases, a soft padding or bandage may be used to minimize deformity and help the ear retain normal shape as it heals. Typically, cats that undergo this surgery are fitted with an ELIZABETHAN COLLAR to prevent them from scratching at the wound.

Hematomas cannot be prevented, but it is helpful to treat ear mites promptly.

Scratching of the ears can cause aural hematomas. (*Photo credit: Betsy Stowe*)

Hemorrhage

See BLEEDING.

High-Rise Syndrome (HRS)

h

The term *high-rise syndrome* was coined to describe cats who fall from tall buildings. The syndrome is most common during warmer summer months, when apartment windows are left open or loosely screened, or cats are allowed access to high terraces and balconies. All cats are at risk, but young cats seem to fall most often.

The incidence of HRS increased as cats became ever more popular big-city apartment pets. And whether the cat rolls off a windowsill in his sleep, misjudges a leap, or simply loses his BALANCE and falls, the end result is severe injury at best, and often death.

Survival rate and the extent of injuries depend on the height from which the cat falls. Terminal velocity—the highest speed a cat will reach when falling—is sixty miles per hour and is achieved from falls greater than five stories.

Falls from the fifth through ninth floors are the most dangerous and result in the worst injuries. The cat's sense of balance prompts him to turn in the air and land on his feet. The cat falls with his legs braced in front of him, and lands rigid. His legs hit first, then his head, and both can suffer terrible bone-shattering injury.

Surprisingly, cats survive falls from higher than nine stories with fewer injuries. Falls from these heights apparently allow the cat time to relax and "parachute" the legs outward so that the wind catches the loose skin in the thighs and armpits and slows the fall. Landing spread-eagle allows the chest and abdomen to absorb most of the shock, rather than the head and legs. Falls from the first through fourth floor aren't as

h

Windows and screens should be kept locked and secure to avoid injuries to your feline. *(Photo credit: Amy D. Shojai)*

likely to cause serious injuries, perhaps because the cat doesn't have time to reach tremendous speeds.

Injuries from falls can include any combination of FRACTURES of the legs, pelvis, ribs, back (with resulting spinal cord implications), jaw, teeth, and palate. Internal injuries that aren't necessarily visible are common. A cat that suffers a fall and lands wrong, or falls from any height over six feet, needs immediate veterinary evaluation. Protect your cat by keeping windows closed, screens secure, and access to balconies or terraces restricted.

Hookworms

Hookworms (*Ancylostoma* and *Uncinaria*) are intestinal parasites common to dogs and less common in cats. These tiny, thin worms are less than a half inch long, take bites out of the wall of the small intestine, and live on the host's blood. Several kinds of hookworms affect pets.

The parasite is found more often in southern states where higher humidity and temperature make the parasite feel more at home. The adult females lay eggs, which are passed with the stool. When conditions are right, these eggs hatch and develop into infective larvae.

Hookworms prefer sandy soil, but may crawl onto vegetation seeking a host. Cats get hookworms by eating an infected mouse or cockroach, by swallowing larvae found in the soil or feces, or when larvae simply penetrate the skin, usually of the footpads. The immature worms

HOOKWORMS

SYMPTOMS

Diarrhea and anemia, sometimes blood in the stool, weight loss, low energy

HOME CARE

None

VET CARE

Hookworm medication, supportive care such as fluid therapy or blood transfusion if cat is anemic or dehydrated

PREVENTION

Keep litter box clean, avoid outdoor exposure

migrate through the body until they reach the intestines, where they mature. Although puppies can become infected before they are born or through ingesting infected milk from their mother, this has not been definitively proven with cats.

Note: Infective hookworm larvae are capable of penetrating human skin and causing a condition called cutaneous larva migrans, in which migrating larvae in the skin cause small, red itchy trails.

Hookworms cause blood loss. Typical signs of hookworms are DIARRHEA and ANEMIA. A large amount of blood in the stool may turn the feces black and tarry, but this is uncommon in cats. Adult cats with chronic infections typically suffer weight loss, diarrhea, anemia, and a general lack of energy. In young kittens and weak or malnourished cats, hookworms can cause sudden collapse and death. Hospitalization to address the anemia and SHOCK may be necessary in severe infections.

Diagnosis is made by identifying eggs during microscopic examination of the stool. The standard treatment to kill the adult worms in the intestinal tract is a liquid oral medication (pyrantel pamoate, or febantel and praziquantel) given in two doses two weeks apart. However, immature forms of the parasite may be retained in the cat's body, and may cause a new outbreak when they migrate to the intestines during times of STRESS.

Preventing hookworm infection can be difficult. The best way is to practice good hygiene by keeping the litter box immaculate. HEARTWORM preventive also prevents hookworms. Outdoor exposure poses the greatest risk, so confining the cat indoors also helps.

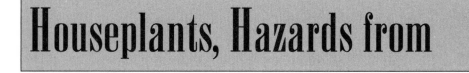

Houseplants, Hazards from

See POISON.

Hunting Behavior

The cat is by nature a predator, and is born with innate behaviors specific to hunting prey. This applies whether the cat is a free-living FERAL animal who relies on these behaviors to eat, or a pampered house cat that never wants for food. Many play behaviors use the same techniques as those used for hunting.

However, instinct alone does not make every cat a successful hunter. Although all cats have the ability to hunt, skill and technique are learned only through practice. KITTENS hone technical skills through play with their littermates and by their mother's example. But even cats never exposed to prey as youngsters can learn to become successful hunters as adults.

Hunger does not necessarily trigger hunting behavior; sound and sight of moving prey are what provide the stimulus. Even well-fed house cats react to a fluttering moth, a leaping cricket, or a scampering

h

An alert feline about to go on the hunt. (*Photo credit: Amy D. Shojai*)

mouse. The reaction of chase-and-capture is as natural to the cat as purring.

Feline hunting behavior relies heavily on sight and hearing to locate prey. Cats then use a couple of hunting strategies, depending on the prey they seek. Sometimes a feline prefers ambush, and will crouch in a likely spot—perhaps with eyes glued to the mouse hole—and wait with infinite patience for prey to appear. Cats may return time after time to areas where their hunts have been successful.

Fishing requires patience, too. Typically, the cat waits in a likely spot on the bank for a suitable candidate to appear, then uses a paw to scoop and flip the fish from the water. In shallow water, a cat may wade in and use both paws by pouncing and grasping the fish. Not all cats are

h

Here a cat crouches over a hole in search of rodents. (*Photo credit: Amy D. Shojai*)

able to perfect fishing technique, probably because of visual perception difficulty regarding the water.

The stalk-and-pounce method is often favored. The cat walks slowly, pausing to stare about until prey is located. When the target is some distance away, a cat quickly moves closer while staying low to the ground and using ground cover to shield her presence. When the distance is judged to be right, the cat abruptly stops and assumes the classic lying-in-wait pose: head and neck extended forward, body crouched close to the ground, rear legs primed to spring forward. The cat may freeze in this position for endless minutes, patiently watching her prey. If the target moves farther away, the cat adjusts by ever-so-slowly creeping forward one paw-step at a time, even freezing with a foot in mid-air to avoid revealing herself. Again, she'll pose in the lying-in-wait stance, then readies herself for the grand finale.

The cat gathers her rear legs beneath her, preparing for a forward thrusting takeoff, and without warning springs toward the target. It may take several darting leaps before she's near enough for the final pounce.

Rarely is the quarry dispatched right away. Often, it escapes and the cat must attempt to chase it down for recapture. Cats often indulge in a great deal of pouncing and tossing of prey into the air, allowing escape only to recapture small game.

But the action of playing with live prey is not intentionally cruel. It's a way for the cat to practice her skills, and also tests just how dangerous that rat or snake might be. Properly socialized felines have learned to inhibit their bite through play with owners and other cats, and toying with the quarry helps them build up the necessary excitement for the coup de grâce.

Cats kill by biting the neck where the skull joins the spine, severing the vertebrae with the daggerlike canine teeth. They grasp the neck and use a "chattering" movement to position their bite accurately. In fact, cats frustrated in the hunt (i.e., watching from a window as squirrels play outside) often exhibit this chattering behavior—which is actually the killing bite—in reaction to seeing out-of-reach prey.

Once the prize is dead and stops moving, the cat typically seems to lose interest for a short time. After the thrill of the hunt, the chase, and the kill, the cat needs time to return to an emotional equilibrium, and may begin GROOMING herself before claiming the prize. Then she'll carry the prey to a well-sheltered area to eat.

For house cats, it's natural to bring prey home. Some behaviorists theorize that cats may look on humans as inept cat-children unable to hunt for themselves, so cats present food gifts with seeming pride to the chief caregiver in the home. More likely, the cat returns the prize to her nest—the house—with every intention of eating it later.

Eating wild game exposes cats to the risk of parasites like TAPE-WORMS or HOOKWORMS, as well as becoming nuisance bird-killers. Cats often learn to stalk without ringing the preventive warning bells attached to their collars. The only way to prevent unacceptable hunting is by keeping the cat indoors. To keep the cat happy, provide alternative outlets for hunting behavior (see PLAY).

h

Hyperesthesia Syndrome

Hyperesthesia is defined as excessive sensitivity to touch. First described in the 1970s, the syndrome in cats refers to several specific obsessive/compulsive behaviors that have no recognizable stimulus.

All cats can be affected at any time in their life, but it typically first appears in cats one to four years old. Hyperesthesia syndrome has been reported more frequently in Siamese, Burmese, Himalayans, and Abyssinians.

The true incidence isn't known, perhaps because not all cases are being properly identified or diagnosed. Some feline practitioners who specialize in problem behaviors estimate that about 4 percent of the cats they see suffer from this syndrome. However, the incidence in the general cat population would probably be much lower.

Hyperesthesia syndrome has three primary behavior patterns. The most common is called hypermotor activity, characterized by excessive GROOMING. Typically, the pupils of the cat's EYES dilate, followed by rippling of the skin on the back. It seems as if an increasingly intense sensation is felt by the cat on his tail and lower back. When a cat can't stand the feeling any longer, he begins frantically licking and grooming the area over his spine and down to his tail. Some cats become so aroused they actually attack and mutilate themselves.

Inexplicable AGGRESSION is the second pattern of behavior. Cats

HYPERESTHESIA SYNDROME

SYMPTOMS

Rippling skin on the back, excessive self-licking or self-mutilation of tail, inexplicable aggression toward owner, seizures

HOME CARE

Interrupting behavior with hand claps, loud noises, or spraying water

VET CARE

Anticonvulsive, antianxiety, or antidepressant drugs like Prozac may be helpful

PREVENTION

None

h

seem friendly, and even beg for attention, then furiously attack when the owner attempts to pet them. The final behavior pattern reported by the veterinary literature is seizure.

Experts disagree on how to characterize the syndrome. The condition has been considered a type of EPILEPSY, and some behaviorists believe the strange behaviors are caused by psychomotor seizures triggered by STRESS. Other researchers believe the syndrome parallels human panic attacks and obsessive/compulsive disorders that occur due to the individual cat's personality in combination with the pressures of his environment, frustrations, and stress levels.

Diagnosis involves eliminating other conditions that could prompt similar behavior, such as itchy skin, back pain, or simply high-energy play. A behavior specialist is probably the best choice to make a definitive diagnosis (see Appendix C, "Resources").

Special equipment such as MRI or a SPECT scan may be used to take pictures of the cat's brain. If the stress factors that seem to trigger incidents can be identified, it's hoped the syndrome can be eliminated. But even when problems can be identified, they often can't be fixed.

Some cats can be distracted from the behavior by an unexpected spritz of water from a squirt gun, or a sudden noise like clapping your hands or slapping a newspaper against a table. Cats also respond to human antianxiety drugs and antidepressants. Drugs like Prozac and others that act on the brain to put a brake on the behavior are helpful in certain cases. Hyperesthesia syndrome currently cannot be prevented, as so much is unknown.

h

Hyperthermia

Hyperthermia, also referred to as heatstroke, is body TEMPERATURE elevated above normal. Hyperthermia results when the body's cooling mechanism is unable to adequately relieve excessive body temperature. Poor ventilation, direct sunlight, and high humidity are predisposing factors. The condition most commonly affects cats during warm summer months.

Cats are not well equipped to deal with the heat and do not tolerate high temperatures well. What is warm to you may be unbearable to your cat. Whenever the environment reaches cat body temperature or above, unless steps are taken to protect the cat, hyperthermia will occur.

Most cases of heatstroke in pets are due to their being left in a poorly ventilated car parked in the hot sun. Cats also suffer the condition when confined to cat carriers without adequate drinking water, or if unable to escape direct sunlight. Hot rooms or apartments that have poor circulation can be dangerous for cats. Curious felines that seek the warmth of the clothes dryer may suffer hyperthermia—not to mention a possibly lethal battering. And cats may develop problems after extremes of exercise, even if the environmental temperature is comfortable. Cats with respiratory problems like ASTHMA, obese cats, and short-nose cats like Persians and Himalayans are highly susceptible to the condition.

A rectal temperature over 106 degrees is diagnostic, but anything

HYPERTHERMIA (HEATSTROKE)

SYMPTOMS

Panting, drooling, vomiting, temperature to 106 degrees, rapid pulse, staring, diarrhea, bright red gums, bloody nose, severe weakness, coma

HOME CARE

Wrap cat in cool wet towel or immerse cat in cool water until temperature drops to 103; SEE VETERINARIAN ASAP

VET CARE

Cool water enemas, oxygen therapy, fluid therapy to fight dehydration

PREVENTION

Keep cool water available at all times, provide good ventilation, never shut cat in closed car, keep cat's fur well-groomed, restrict cat's exercise during hottest times of the day

h

above normal should be addressed. Your cat needs help if she suddenly begins panting or breathing quickly, drooling, or VOMITING. The cat suffering heatstroke has a rapid pulse and staring or glazed eyes, and may develop DIARRHEA. In severe cases, the cat's gums become bright red and she may develop a bloody nose. In the final stages, panting turns to gasping, and the cat becomes comatose and ultimately dies.

Treatment involves rapidly cooling the cat. Either wrap the cat in a towel soaked with cold water or immerse the cat in a cool bath. Check your cat's temperature every ten minutes, and continue cooling her until her temperature drops to at least 103 degrees.

Cats that show signs of severe weakness or that lose consciousness require immediate veterinary attention. Cool water enemas may be necessary to rapidly reduce the cat's internal temperature. Cats suffering severe hyperthermia may need treatment for SHOCK, including fluid therapy to combat DEHYDRATION. Oxygen therapy helps prevent brain damage.

Prevent heatstroke by providing your cat with fresh drinking water at all times, along with proper ventilation and access to adequate shade. Avoid leaving any pet in closed, parked cars; even in the shade, the temperature in a closed car can reach 120 degrees in less than ten minutes.

A matted coat keeps heat from escaping, so keep your longhaired cats properly groomed and mat-free, or clip their coat short during the summer months. Restrict exercise during the hottest times of the day, particularly in high-risk cats.

h

Hyperthyroidism

The term *hyperthyroidism* refers to overactivity of the thyroid gland. The condition is common in middle-aged and older cats, particularly those twelve years or older (see GERIATRIC CAT). Hyperthyroidism is considered the most commonly diagnosed disease of the endocrine system in cats.

The thyroid gland has two lobes and is located at the base of the cat's neck. It secretes hormones that help regulate a body's metabolism—the rate at which food and oxygen are turned into energy by the body. In elderly cats, for unknown reasons, one or both lobes of the thyroid often enlarge, producing a toxic nodular goiter seen as a swelling in the neck. This results in an overproduction of hormones, and this excess shifts the cat's metabolism into overdrive.

The affected cat typically develops a ravenous appetite. He is always hungry, but no matter how much he eats, he loses weight. He may act irritable or agitated, even hyperactive, and pace a great deal. Some cats have upset stomachs and vomit, and often the stool and urine volume increases, with the stool usually being soft. Cats suffering from hyperthyroidism may develop an oily coat, and typically exhibit very rapid growth of CLAWS. A veterinarian may be able to feel the enlargement of the thyroid gland in the neck, or detect an increased heart rate.

Because these signs may occur singly or in any combination, and

HYPERTHYROIDISM

SYMPTOMS

Ravenous appetite with weight loss, increased drinking and urination, seeks cool places to rest, hair loss, diarrhea, vomiting, hyperactivity, oily coat, rapid claw growth

HOME CARE

None

VET CARE

Drug therapy, surgery, or radioactive iodine therapy

PREVENTION

None

because they can also point to a number of other problem conditions, diagnosis often requires blood evaluation, microscopic examination of thyroid tissue, and/or other screening tests. Treatment depends on the individual cat's age, anesthetic risk, health status, and other factors.

Surgical removal of the diseased thyroid will cure the cat. If both lobes must be removed, a daily thyroid supplement provides the necessary hormone.

An antithyroid drug called Tapazole is available that helps control, but doesn't cure, the signs of hyperthyroidism. The cat must stay on the medication religiously for the rest of his life.

The third treatment option is the use of radioactive iodine, which selectively destroys thyroid tissue. This treatment has a 98 percent cure rate but is limited to specialized referral hospitals like university teaching hospitals. The use of radioactive iodine is regulated by the government, and a treated cat must be kept under QUARANTINE for one to four weeks, and his urine and feces monitored for radioactivity, before he is released.

Hypothermia

Hypothermia is body TEMPERATURE that falls below normal. Cats have several built-in protective mechanisms to keep warm. Insulating fur traps a layer of warm air next to the skin; heat is conserved further when a cat curls up in protected, sheltered areas. The action of shivering generates heat, and in cold weather cats keep themselves warm by burning more calories at the cellular level. In extremes of cold, the cat's body diverts circulation from the ears, toes, and tail and shunts blood to the trunk. (This action, which protects vital internal organs from

HYPOTHERMIA

SYMPTOMS

Lethargy, shivering, loss of shivering impulse, body temperature less than 98 degrees, loss of consciousness, slowed body function, cat appears dead

HOME CARE

If still shivering, wrap in blanket or give warm bath when already wet; when cat stops shivering and/or has subnormal temperature, it's an EMERGENCY! SEE VETERINARIAN ASAP

VET CARE

Aggressive rewarming with heating pads, water bottles, warm-water enemas, heated oxygen, and/or heated intravenous fluids

PREVENTION

Confine cats indoors during cold weather, provide shelter from wind, wet, and cold

the cold, actually promotes damage to the extremities [see FROSTBITE].) Failure of these protective mechanisms can result in hypothermia.

Outdoor cats are in the high-risk category for hypothermia. Very young kittens unable to regulate their own body temperature are prone to hypothermia. Internal heat production relies on muscle and fat reserves; these are less available in the young KITTEN and GERIATRIC CAT, and makes them more vulnerable to the cold. But any cat that is exposed to extreme cold, becomes wet, or suffers SHOCK or other injuries risks hypothermia.

The condition is designated as mild, moderate, or severe, according to the cat's body temperature. The cat suffering from mild hypothermia will act lethargic and shiver, and perhaps suffer muscle tremors. The body temperature will be 90 to 99 degrees F. If the cat is wet, a warm bath will help rewarm him. Dry him thoroughly with towels but avoid using hair blowers, which can burn him. Simply wrapping him in a warm blanket allows the cat's own body to rewarm itself, and in mild cases it is all that's necessary.

Cats experience moderate hypothermia when their body temperature falls between 82 and 90 degrees; at this stage, the shivering response will stop. Severe hypothermia occurs at body temperatures below 82 degrees and is characterized by the cat losing consciousness with a severe slowing of heart and breathing rate. The cat may actually look dead.

Veterinarians have special thermometers able to record these low body temperatures, but standard rectal thermometers only measure as low as 93 degrees. *If the cat has stopped shivering, and/or loses consciousness, veterinary attention is necessary if the cat is to survive.*

Treatment is aimed at rewarming the cat, preventing further heat loss, and keeping vital organs working. Passive warming—wrapping in a blanket—is not sufficient in moderate and severe hypothermia.

Moderate hypothermia requires active external rewarming, which is the use of hot water bottles, electric blankets, recirculating water blankets, heating pads, or other heat sources. Heat is applied only to the body, keeping the extremities cool to prevent shock, which may kill the cat. The cat must be protected from direct contact with the actual heat source; hypothermia prevents the body from conducting excessive heat away, so cats can be easily burned.

Severe hypothermia requires core warming, which basically is heating the cat from the inside out. This can involve warm water enemas, warm intravenous fluid therapy, airway rewarming with oxygen, and even heart/lung bypass machines that warm the blood. Fluids may be repeatedly flushed into the abdomen to warm the organs and tissues, then drawn back out until body temperature returns to normal. The prognosis for full recovery from severe hypothermia is guarded; organs and tissues are often damaged beyond repair.

If you believe your cat is suffering from moderate to severe hypothermia but are unable to reach veterinary help, treat the cat yourself using the external warming techniques just described. The temperature of water bottles should be about 100 degrees—warm to the touch but not burning. Buffer the bottles with towels or blankets, and place them on the cat's chest and abdomen, and in the armpit areas beneath the cat's legs. Take the cat's temperature every ten minutes until it reaches 100 degrees. When your cat begins to revive and move, give her one to two tablespoons of honey or Karo syrup. Take her for veterinary evaluation as soon as possible.

Hypothermia can and should be prevented. Most cases of hypothermia occur in severe weather, but even moderately cold temperatures can be dangerous when the windchill is factored in. Wet fur compounds the effects of cold, and wind strips away the protective warm air layer caught in the cat's fur.

Outdoor cats must have access to shelter from the wet, wind, and cold. Loose bedding like straw or several blankets helps trap and hold pockets of warmer air when the cat builds a nest or burrows into it. An infrared lamp or warming pad is also helpful, but should be positioned so the cat can escape direct warmth to avoid burns.

Feed outdoor cats a higher energy-dense food during cold temperatures. The body must use more energy to maintain optimum temperature, so increase the frequency and the amount fed. Check with your veterinarian for a recommendation; a super-premium adult ration or a high-calorie kitten food is appropriate. The best way to prevent hypothermia in cats is to keep the animal indoors.

Ibuprofen

See POISON.

Identification

Outdoor cats in particular but also indoor pets should wear some form of easily recognizable identification to protect them from being stolen, and to ensure their safe return if they stray from home. Seventy percent of animals that arrive at shelters have no identification, and a great percentage of these are humanely destroyed (see EUTHANASIA).

One of the best precautions an owner can take to protect a cat is to record the cat's appearance with photographs. These should include a close-up of the face, as well as full-body shots from both sides and the back. Document any distinguishing marks; there are many gray and white cats, but yours may be the only one with three gray freckles in a triangular pattern on a white tummy. Should the worst happen and your cat becomes lost, take these photos from your file or photo album, make posters advertising your cat being lost, and post them at strategic spots in your community. Even leave copies at area shelters to alert them.

**Make sure your cat is
properly identified.**
*(Photo credit:
Amy D. Shojai)*

Other kinds of identification are even more crucial. A number of
pet identification systems are available, the most common and simplest
being a metal or plastic tag that attaches to the cat's collar and contains
the owner's contact information. RABIES tags documenting vaccination
that are attached to collars are also a form of identification. They usually include the contact information of the veterinary clinic, and a se-
rial number that identifies the cat and its owner. Cats may lose collars,
though, and strays often are wearing no easily visible identification.

Tattoos are used more often in pet dogs than in cats, and provide a
permanent identification on the animal's body. The owner's social secu-
rity number or the animal's registration number is commonly tattooed
onto the skin, often on the inside of the thigh. The tattoo number can
then be registered in a local or national database that can retrieve the

owner's contact information should that animal become lost. The drawback of tattoos is that whoever finds the cat must know to look for the telltale mark, as well as know what to do with that information. Also, tattoos may be obscured by fur or fade over time.

The newest form of identification is the microchip. A tiny silicon chip similar to those used in computer technology is programmed with an identification code, encased in surgical glass the size of a grain of rice, and implanted beneath the cat's skin between his shoulders. Special scanning equipment is designed to read the microchip information in much the same way that food-item prices are scanned at the grocery store. A database keeps track of the owner and pet information, and matches the identifying code to the animal so the owner can be contacted. Many veterinary clinics and animal shelters are now equipped with microchip technology (see Appendix C, "Resources").

Immune System

The immune system is a complex defense mechanism that protects the cat from invading substances capable of causing injury or disease. The immune system targets foreign invaders, called antigens, and attempts to either neutralize or destroy them. Antigens include viruses, bacteria, toxins, and abnormal cells like CANCER.

The primary immune system is composed of organs like the bone marrow and thymus, which produce protective disease-fighting cells and molecules. These components of the immune system patrol the blood and lymphatic system for anything that doesn't belong. The secondary immune system's lymph nodes and spleen are a part of an intricate body-wide filter that removes antigens from circulation.

The immune system manufactures a kind of protein called an antibody in response to the presence of an antigen; this mechanism is referred to as a humoral immune response. Each antibody is a custom creation that reacts to only one specific kind of antigen. Antibodies are not killers; they don't destroy the antigen directly. They simply attach themselves to the antigen, marking it as foreign material so that other specialized cells can destroy it.

Sometimes specialized cells like macrophages and lymphocytes attack and destroy virus-infected cells or tumor cells without the aid of antibodies. This is called a cell-mediated immune response.

The combination of a humoral and a cell-mediated immune response doubles the body's protection. It's a type of insurance policy; what one system fails to neutralize, the other kills.

In addition, the body has a built-in memory for immunity. Even after the antigen has been destroyed, antibodies that "remember" the disease continue to circulate. They immediately recognize and react to the disease should it ever return, and this provides a kind of early-warning system that prompts an immune response before damage can be done. This memory for danger is referred to as active immunity.

Active immunity lasts for a variable length of time, depending on the particular antigen involved. Active immunity can be artificially created by stimulating the cat's immune system to protect him from disease by using VACCINATIONS. Kittens receive what is called passive immunity from their mother when they nurse her antibody-rich first milk, called colostrum. A kitten's passive immunity lasts about four months at most, and provides the same protection from disease that the mother cat has.

Your cat can become sick when she is exposed to disease and her immune system fails to destroy the antigen. This can happen because there has been no previous exposure through vaccinations, and so there are no existing antibodies to mount an attack. It can also happen when a particularly virulent antigen, such as a virus, overwhelms the immune system. Sometimes the immune system misrecognizes an antigen like pollen as deadly, and mounts an immune response that results in an allergic reaction. In relatively rare instances, the system goes haywire and misrecognizes components of the cat's own body as foreign, and attacks itself.

Incontinence

See SOILING.

Inflammatory Bowel Disease

Inflammatory bowel disease (IBD) refers to the chronic inflammation of the small intestine and occasionally the stomach. The cause isn't known, but it's suspected that something prompts the IMMUNE SYSTEM to misfire and attack its own cells. The resulting inflammatory response plugs up the tiny microscopic filaments that line the surface of the intestinal tract and transfer nutrients into the bloodstream.

Chronic VOMITING is the most common sign of IBD. Episodes may be sporadic and occur during times of STRESS, or the vomiting can be continuous. The cat may also frequently strain to defecate but pass only small amounts of feces that may be blood-streaked.

Diagnosis usually is made only after ruling out other causes for vomiting, such as GIARDIA, HEARTWORMS, or a SWALLOWED OBJECT. Conclusive evidence requires a biopsy of the intestine in which a sample of

i

INFLAMMATORY BOWEL DISEASE (IBD)

SYMPTOMS

Chronic vomiting, straining to defecate with minimal results

HOME CARE

As prescribed by your veterinarian

VET CARE

Treating underlying cause, if it can be determined; sometimes antibiotics or immune-suppressing drugs

PREVENTION

None

tissue is removed surgically from the anesthetized cat for microscopic evaluation. Sometimes a special instrument called a colonoscope is inserted into the cat's rectum to view the tissue. But because only portions of the tissue may exhibit inflammation, diagnosis still may not be definitive. The disease over the long term can result in scarring of the intestine, which further compromises food utilization and bowel function.

Some research supports the notion that food ALLERGIES may be at fault, and in some cases a limited antigen diet may help the cat. Drugs to treat bacterial overgrowth or GIARDIA infection may be prescribed. Immune-suppressing drugs may also be beneficial.

There is no known prevention for IBD.

i

Inoculations

See VACCINATIONS.

Insect Bites/Stings

Cats are bugged by the same insects that afflict their owners. Insect bites cause allergic reactions and spread disease. Stinging insects more often cause local irritations, but they can cause life-threatening reactions as well.

Cats are often tempted to chase and pounce upon fluttering insects. While moths or grasshoppers are harmless, catching a wasp or bee can have severe consequences. Fur protects the cat from body injuries, but stings often occur on the lips or inside the mouth when a feline tries to catch the bug. Fire ants most often affect kittens that inadvertently stumble into their mound; they typically bite in swarms on the kitten's tender tummy and inside the flanks.

Stings and bites are painful and usually result in swelling and some-

BUG BITES AND STINGS

SYMPTOMS

Local irritation, swelling or itching at site, drooling or difficulty eating when stung in the mouth; anaphylactic shock happens nearly immediately and is an EMERGENCY—signs are drooling, difficulty breathing, swelling of face, drunken behavior, collapse

HOME CARE

Apply ice packs or dab ammonia on spots to relieve burn; apply baking soda paste or flush with baking soda and water to soothe; anytime cat has trouble breathing, see a vet ASAP

VET CARE

An injection of epinephrine (adrenaline) counteracts life-threatening reactions

PREVENTION

Avoid contact with dangerous insects by keeping cat indoors

i

times itching. A sore mouth can cause drooling and difficulty in eating. Bees leave behind stingers, which are visible; if the stinger can be seen, remove it with tweezers or scrape it free with a credit card.

Sparsely furred areas like the belly and inside the thighs can be treated with a paste of baking soda and water, but this is messy to apply when the sting is surrounded by fur. Dabbing ammonia directly on the bites with a cotton ball or cotton swab helps soothe the pain, and ice packs will reduce the swelling of stings.

Stings inside the mouth are more difficult to treat. If your cat will allow it, flush the area with a teaspoon of baking soda mixed in a pint of water. Use a turkey baster to squirt the fluid onto the area, but take care the cat doesn't inhale the liquid. Called aspiration, this will choke the cat and could result in pneumonia from fluid in the lungs.

While one or two stings can be painful, they are rarely dangerous. However, should the cat stumble into a hive or nest and receive multiple stings or bites, the situation can become lethal. Bring your cat to a vet immediately if your pet has been stung repeatedly.

When swelling in the mouth, nose, or throat area is severe, breathing is difficult. Cats occasionally suffer an allergic reaction called anaphylactic shock in which the airways become so constricted that the cat cannot breathe. The cat will also drool, become uncoordinated, and collapse. These signs appear almost immediately following the bite or sting. *Anaphylactic shock is an emergency that must be immediately addressed by a veterinarian if the cat's life is to be saved.*

Be vigilant in preventing your cat from playing with stinging insects.

Insecticides

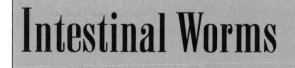

See FLEAS and POISON.

Intestinal Worms

See PARASITES.

Introduction of New Pet into Household

It has long been thought that lions were the only truly social cats that voluntarily lived together. More recent studies have uncovered a parallel in our domestic cats. When food is abundant, FERAL cats do tend to live in close proximity and get along well together in extended social groups. In pet cats, this acceptance includes nonfeline family members.

i

A nose-to-nose meeting between new cats. (*Photo credit: Amy D. Shojai*)

Cats, however, prefer the status quo, and for a cat, the unexpected is cause for alarm. Therefore, the introduction of a new pet into the household must be done gradually, with attention to the resident cat's sensibilities.

Some cats are more accepting than others. How well the cat adapts to other cats, dogs, or family members depends a great deal on the cat's own personality and sense of self, and on the finesse of initial introductions. Dominant cats may turn aggressive, while fearful cats become stressed and depressed if the proper preparations are not made.

Kittens generally accept new family members more readily, and usually adult cats are more accepting of kittens or puppies, which aren't a threat to the resident cat's status. Introducing an adult resident cat to a new adult cat or dog can be done, but expect that the pair must sort out who is to be head honcho.

If possible, introduce the scent of the new pet to your resident cat before a true nose-to-nose meeting. This can be done by petting the new animal with a sock or handkerchief, then leaving the scented item in your house for the Resident Cat (R.C.) to find, sniff, and investigate.

Make one room of your house temporarily off-limits to R.C. and make this the new pet's home base. If you can manage, have a friend bring the new pet to your home and set her up in the room, while you play or feed R.C. to distract him. That way, R.C. doesn't immediately feel the entire house has been invaded by the interloper, and the new pet has some privacy to become acquainted with the new surroundings.

R.C. and the new pet should first get to know each other by sniffing under the door. Some cats will posture, hiss, and growl; others will ignore the entire venture until they think you're not watching. Either behavior is normal. Be encouraged if the pair begin poking and playing with each other's paws under the door.

Try not to make a big deal over the new pet; it should be business as usual. Be sure to continue to make time for R.C. If he's a shy, retiring cat, he may feel threatened and begin to withdraw if he feels he's losing your attention.

After two or three days—whenever R.C. stops growling at the door—have the pair switch places for half an hour or so. That offers each pet a chance to investigate the other critter's smells up close, and allows the new pet an opportunity to become comfortable with the rest of the house.

For introducing a new cat to an R.C., you simply open the door and allow them to meet at their own speed, on their own terms. Perhaps they'll ignore each other, or they may immediately become fast friends. Every case is different. Typically, cats begin introductions by sniffing each other's necks, then the anal regions. They may turn circles trying to sniff the other while preventing themselves from being sniffed.

The resident cat usually has the upper "paw," but that's not always the case. There may be some hissing or growling, and unless the situation escalates to imminent attack, let the cats sort things out (see AG-GRESSION). Interrupting too soon may actually delay the determination of who's to be top cat, and force a replay of the display at a later date.

There should be an escape route handy—a tabletop, or cat carrier—for either pet to get away when they've had enough. Until the pair have accepted each other, keep them separated when you are not there to supervise.

If the new pet is a puppy or older dog, he should be introduced in a carrier or on a leash, and under your direct control. Most adult cats can deal with a puppy, who will soon learn what a hiss and claw mean. Use caution when introducing your cat to an adult dog that has never met cats. Dogs typically want to please their owner, so if the dog knows you want him to like your cat, you'll be on the right track. Obedience-training the dog is a big help.

A dog gate will keep the new arrival in one part of the house, while allowing R.C. to get to know him through the grillwork. Once you are satisfied that the dog understands the cat is a part of his family, put him on a leash and take down the gate. If the dog is well behaved, remove the leash; still, the cat should always have a safe retreat the dog cannot reach. *Don't leave them alone together until you are convinced that the dog knows the cat is off-limits.* Often, the dog is quite content to let the cat be the boss.

Many of the same principles apply when introducing new human family members to your resident cat. If you have a kitten, do yourself and your pet a favor by introducing him as a youngster to a variety of people of all ages. An adult cat who has never been around men can exhibit behavior problems when his single female owner decides to marry. And a new baby in the house can turn the most complacent cat into a jittery ball of furry nerves.

Allow R.C. to familiarize himself with the scent of the new family member(s) ahead of time by bringing home a scented sock—just the same as with a new pet. Record the voice of your fiancé (or whomever) and play it while you pet your cat; have your fiancé bring over special treats or new toys if possible. The new family member's presence should be associated with only good things for your cat.

When you are expecting a baby, tape the sound of a baby crying and let R.C. listen. As you prepare the nursery, let the cat investigate the new scents (you should wear baby powder) and sights in the room. Make changes gradually; you've got nine months to paint, change wallpaper, put up the bed and mobile, so don't do it all at once; the change could throw your pet into a tizzy.

Don't shut out the cat. Set up a baby gate if you don't want R.C. in the room; that way he can at least watch and understand what's happening. Excluding your cat from this happy occasion in your life only makes the cat feel left out, confused, and even scared.

Cats are typically very good with babies and children. When you bring home your new baby, act like it's no big deal, even though it is. Remember, you want R.C. to react as if this were an expected part of cat life. Don't force an introduction, but if your cat is interested and calm, let him sniff the baby's foot or hand. Let the cat see what smells so different and sounds so interesting, so he knows it's nothing to fear.

And praise the cat when he behaves. When R.C. knows that treating the new baby like one of the family is to his advantage, there should be no problem. If you like, R.C. can be allowed in the nursery when you are there to supervise. Letting the cat be a part of things takes away the mystery and the threat, so that the cat associates your baby with good things for himself.

As your baby grows, be sure that she understands R.C. is not a toy. Cats learn to put up with a lot from young children, yet it's the cat's home, too. Children can and should be taught to respect pets from an early age. Teach your baby how to pet and hold the cat, and how to care for R.C. In that way, a mutual respect will grow into love that can last a lifetime for them both.

Amy D. Shojai

Abyssinian, rudy

Amy D. Shojai

American Curl,
tortoiseshell

Amy D. Shojai

American Shorthair,
silver tabby

American Wirehair, calico

Mark McCullough

Balinese, blue point

Amy D. Shojai

Mark McCullough

*Bengal,
brown tabby*

Amy D. Shojai

*Birman,
blue point*

Amy D. Shojai

Bombay

British Shorthair, blue

Mark McCullough

Burmese

Amy D. Shojai

Chartreux

Colorpoint Shorthair, seal lynx point

Cornish Rex,
red mackerel tabby
and white

Cymric,
black

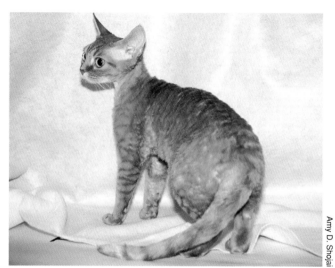

Devon Rex,
red mackerel tabby

Mark McCullough

Egyptian Mau,
silver

Amy D. Shojai

Exotic Shorthair,
tortoiseshell

Mark McCullough

Havana Brown

Amy D. Shojai

Himalayan,
seal point

Amy D. Shojai

Japanese Bobtail,
red and white

Javanese,
blue lynx point

Korat

Maine Coon,
brown tabby

Mark McCullough

Amy D. Shojai

Amy D. Shojai

Manx,
white

Amy D. Shojai

Norwegian Forest
Cat, brown mackerel
tabby and white

Amy D. Shojai

Ocicat,
cinnamon spotted

Amy D. Shojai

*Oriental Longhair,
ebony ticked tabby*

*Oriental Shorthair,
lavender*

*Persian,
blue/white and
red/white bicolor*

Ragdoll

Russian Blue

Scottish Fold,
red tabby and
white

Amy D. Shojai

Scottish Fold Longhair,
red and white van

Amy D. Shojai

Siamese,
blue point

Singapura

Mark McCullough

Snowshoe

Vickie Jackson

Somali,
red

Amy D. Shojai

Vicki Jackson

Sphynx,
brown and white

Amy D. Shojai

Tonkinese,
platinum mink

Turkish Angora,
white

Turkish Van,
red and white van

Jacobson's Organs

Cats have a second scenting mechanism called Jacobson's organs, or vomeronasal organs. The organs are located between the hard palate of the mouth and the septum of the nose. Each connects to one of the incisive ducts, tiny conduits that open behind the cat's upper incisor TEETH in the mouth and pass up into the nasal cavity. The ducts allow air to travel from the mouth into the nasal cavity.

The cat's tongue traps scent particles, then transfers them to the ducts behind these upper teeth using a flicking action. Cats displaying this behavior, called by the German term *flehmen*, seem to grimace with distaste, with their lips curled back and mouth open.

Although all cats have and use these specialized scent organs, it appears that intact male cats exhibit *flehmen* behavior most often. The behavior occurs primarily when a male cat of breeding age contacts the urine of a female cat that's in heat.

The vomeronasal organs are linked to the hypothalamus, an area of the brain that acts as a kind of switchboard to direct information to higher centers. The hypothalamus integrates taste and smell, motivates appetite, and triggers certain sexual and aggressive behavior patterns. It's believed that vomeronasal organs mostly detect chemical substances, called pheromones, that are produced by animals to stimulate specific behavioral responses, especially sexual activities.

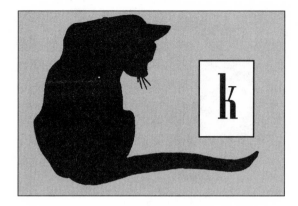

Kidney Disease

Kidney disease refers to a number of conditions that damage the organs and result in impaired kidney function. Normally, the kidneys work as an organic filtering system that screens waste products from the bloodstream and excretes them into the urine. Kidneys also regulate the body's fluid composition and the nutrient content of the blood, and produce hormones that control red blood cell production and blood pressure. Kidney disease is characterized as acute (of recent origination) or chronic (of long duration).

The acute form can affect any cat at any age, and results from disease or poison that damages the kidney. The most common causes of acute kidney disease are periods of inadequate blood flow to the kidneys; toxicity from chemical agents such as ANTIFREEZE, Tylenol, or certain antibiotics; and infectious agents. Some lines of Abyssinian cats suffer from inherited amyloidosis, a rare condition in which protein is deposited in the kidneys, leading ultimately to organ failure.

Dialysis, which provides cleansing of the blood, may be used to treat acute kidney failure as an interim measure in the hope that once the poison or infection has passed, the kidneys will begin working again. But cleansing the blood by using a machine—as in human medicine—isn't an option, because the machines are expensive and rarely available.

More commonly, peritoneal dialysis is used. This procedure pumps

KIDNEY DISEASE

SYMPTOMS

Increased thirst and urination, loss of appetite, weight loss, depression and weakness, dehydration, brown-colored tongue, sores in the mouth, ammonia breath

HOME CARE

Supportive care, good nutrition

VET CARE

Supportive care, drugs to normalize blood, prescription diets, sometimes kidney transplant

PREVENTION

Provide adequate water at all times, avoid dehydration

k

fluid into the cat's abdominal cavity using a large syringe. The fluid absorbs waste products and is then drawn back out.

Chronic kidney disease is considered a common condition of GERIATRIC CATS. Studies estimate that 15 to 30 percent of cats over fifteen years of age have some degree of kidney disease. However, the cause is rarely diagnosed. It isn't known why elderly cats suffer kidney damage, but it's thought to be the result of the lifetime of work that the kidneys engage in.

Signs of acute disease are severe and appear all at once, while signs of chronic kidney disease develop very slowly over time. The kidneys are still able to work quite well even when severely damaged, and cats typically show few symptoms until 70 percent of their kidney function is gone. Consequently, owners rarely notice anything is wrong until the disease is quite advanced. Untreated kidney failure results in death.

One of the earliest signs is increased thirst and urination. This happens because when the kidneys lose their ability to concentrate urine, the cat must drink more and more water to compensate for excessive water loss. Cats in kidney failure may seek water in unusual locations, like the toilet bowl, fish tank, or sink. Owners often notice a refusal to eat, weight loss, depression and weakness, or even DEHYDRATION.

As kidney disease progresses, the cat may develop a brownish discoloration on the tongue and sores in the mouth. The breath may smell like ammonia. Finally, the cat falls into a coma and dies.

Diagnosis is based on signs of disease as well as blood tests and urine analysis. X-RAYS, ULTRASOUND, or other specialized examinations of the kidneys may be required. The prognosis depends on how far the disease has advanced. Some cats live with kidney disease for several years if the condition is mild to moderate.

Compromised kidney function in extremely advanced kidney failure makes it difficult for the cat to filter the waste produced from protein metabolism. For that reason, traditional therapy includes changing the cat's diet to a high-quality but lower-protein ration.

Cats with kidney failure are also unable to get rid of extra phosphorus, and the excess can result in a number of secondary problems. Special diets for kidney disease typically reduce phosphorus levels. Some diets also adjust the amount of dietary salt. Your veterinarian can recommend an appropriate diet for your individual cat's needs.

Drugs like sodium bicarbonate help normalize the blood if it becomes too acidic, and potassium supplementation can help even out the blood potassium level. Lots of fresh water should be available to the cat at all times.

Depending on the specific case, kidney transplant may be an option. The best candidates are cats in the earliest stages of the disease that don't have other health problems. Currently, the procedure is available only at major veterinary referral centers, among them the University of California at Davis (where the procedure was pioneered), Angell Memorial Hospital in Boston, the Animal Medical Center in New York City, and Michigan State University. Only a handful of private practices are performing feline kidney transplants as of this writing. But for certain candidates, the donated organ provides a new lease on life.

Transplant involves not only the surgery itself but also immune-suppressant drugs to address possible rejection of the transplanted organ, and intensive follow-up monitoring and care. The cost is several thousands of dollars. Most feline kidney transplant programs require that you adopt or find a home for the cat who gives up his kidney so your cat can live.

Early detection is the single best way to identify kidney problems before they become severe. A blood test may catch the disease in your older cat before signs become apparent. All middle-aged and older cats should undergo periodic examinations. There is no known means of preventing kidney disease.

Kitten

A kitten is an immature cat. Generally speaking, a cat is designated a kitten from birth to about one year of age.

Every cat develops differently, and some breeds of cats do not reach full maturity before they are two or even three years old. However, in the show ring, the kitten class encompasses purebred kittens between the ages of four and eight months. More generally, a cat should be considered a kitten as long as he continues to grow.

Newborn kittens are about four to six inches long and two to four ounces in weight. They are born flat-faced, blind, deaf, and toothless, and are totally dependent on their mother. Unable to regulate body temperature, or even urinate or defecate on their own, kittens will die without prompt attention from the QUEEN.

A kitten's first impulse is to find warmth. Blunt kitten faces act as heat-seeking sensors that direct the babies toward the queen's warm breasts. Kittens depend on the queen and their littermates for warmth. Littermates nest together in furry piles to warm each other. A kitten that is separated from his siblings or mother is in grave danger of dying from the cold. Whenever a kitten finds itself alone or starts to feel cold, he begins to cry loudly for his mother to rescue him.

One of the first sensations the newborn kitten feels is being washed by his mother. The queen grooms her babies not only to keep them and the nest clean but also to stimulate them to defecate and urinate. The vibration of her contented PURR is a beacon that tells the babies where she is and calls them to her.

From the beginning, scent helps identify life for the kitten. Kittens

k

Newborn kittens use their littermates for body warmth. (*Photo credit: Ralston Purina Company*)

leave their own personal smell upon the queen's breast when they first nurse, and from that time forward preferentially seek that particular nipple. The kittens push against the mother's breasts rhythmically with their forepaws, KNEADING to stimulate the flow of milk. The first milk the kittens drink, called colostrum, is rich in maternal antibodies that provide passive immunity and help protect the babies from disease during these early weeks of life.

The first week is spent eating, sleeping, and growing. Birth weight doubles by the end of the first week. Weak legs provide only limited locomotion, and so the newborns drag themselves on their bellies using their front legs. Soon the young kittens exercise their muscles by crawling over and around each other.

Great changes take place during the second week of life. Eyelids that have been sealed shut since birth begin to open between the ninth and twelfth day, and the kittens begin to see their world for the first time. It is at this point that the babies learn specifically what their mother looks like. This optical imprinting helps define for the kittens what they and other cats should look like. All kittens' eyes are blue at this point; their adult eye color usually develops by the age of twelve weeks.

About the same time, kittens' ears unseal, and sound sense begins to develop. Kitten teeth also begin to erupt until all the baby teeth are in by about seven to eight weeks of age. Kittens are also standing for the first time on wobbly legs, and trying to imitate their mother by walking.

By the third week, they're beginning to PLAY with their littermates. The kittens follow the queen to the LITTER BOX, and are soon imitating her bathroom etiquette. They learn how to retract their claws, which to this point have been continually extended. And they begin grooming themselves.

By four weeks of age, kittens will have doubled their weight again. When kittens are between four and six weeks of age, the queen's milk production slows down just as the babies' energy needs increase. The mother begins weaning the kittens from nursing, and they start sampling solid food. They'll be able to do without their mother's milk by the time they're eight weeks old.

Kittens spend a great deal of time playing with one another. Play is

Kittens often play with each other. *(Photo credit: Lillian Zahrt)*

fun for the babies, but it's also great exercise that helps kittens learn how to use their bodies properly to do important cat activities, like leaping, pouncing, running, and climbing. Social skills are learned by interacting with littermates and the mother. The kittens learn to inhibit the use of their claws and teeth when they are bitten or clawed by each other. By playing with a variety of objects, like leaves, bugs, or string, kittens learn what can and cannot be done with that object. A nine-week-old kitten spends up to an hour playing each day. Everything is filed away in the feline memory and applied to life.

It's during this time that the babies learn to identify friend and foe. Kittens exposed to friendly people, whether babies, children, or adults, and other animals like cats and dogs during this impressionable period, will more readily recognize them as safe and accept them as family members later in life. Kittens that are not introduced to people and other animals during this socialization period will be fearful of these encounters and have a more difficult time adjusting. In fact, it appears that kittens handled daily by people during the first month of their life have an improved learning ability.

Kittens are ready to go to new homes by the time they are twelve weeks old. By waiting until this age, the babies receive full benefit of playing and learning from their siblings, which helps them be better adjusted to other cats as adults.

A healthy kitten has bright, clear eyes and clean, soft fur. He has clean, clear ears, nose, and anus with no discharge. Well-socialized kittens are curious and friendly, and are easily engaged in a game. Proper health care includes preventive vaccinations, screening for intestinal parasites, and a nutritionally complete and balanced kitten diet.

Kneading

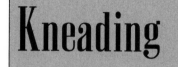

The term refers to the cat's habit of treading with her front paws as though "kneading" dough. Cats flex each of their front paws rhythmically in turn against usually soft surfaces like carpet or an owner's lap. Kneading can be performed with or without claws extended.

The action is used by kittens against their mother's breast to prompt the flow of her milk. The behavior in adult cats is thought to hearken back to kittenhood, and appears to be an expression of contentment.

k

Labor

See REPRODUCTION.

Lice

Lice are parasites that live on the skin. The tiny insects are flat, wing-less creatures equipped with either sucking or biting mouth parts. There are a number of types that affect animals, and each type prefers a specific host. Cats are parasitized by *Felicola subrostrata*, a biting louse that feeds on sloughed skin debris.

Louse infestation, called pediculosis, is not common in cats, but all cats are at risk. The condition is often associated with poor sanitary conditions or neglect, and usually affects malnourished, debilitated cats unable to groom themselves. Cats are generally infected by direct contact with an infested animal.

Lice seem to thrive during cold winter months. Seeing the parasite or the eggs glued to the individual hairs of the fur coat is diagnostic. Signs vary from cat to cat, but may include scaling skin, itchiness, or scabby skin (see MILIARY DERMATITIS).

LICE

SYMPTOMS

Scaling or scabby skin, itchiness, visible bugs or eggs stuck to hairs

HOME CARE

Treat weekly with a cat-safe topical flea product, destroy infected bedding, thoroughly vacuum premises

VET CARE

Rarely necessary

PREVENTION

Keep cat well groomed, avoid contact with other cats

Treatment consists of a weekly topical treatment of a cat-safe flea product applied either as powder, shampoo, or dip for up to five weeks. Lice can't survive for long when off the host. Destroying the cat's infected bedding and thorough vacuuming of carpets is usually sufficient to eliminate the parasite from the environment.

To prevent your cat from contracting lice, keep him from contact with strange animals. Cleanliness of his sleeping quarters, bedding, and litter box is key. And most important, keep your cat healthy by providing good-quality nutrition. Grooming your cat is particularly important when the cat has trouble keeping himself clean (see GROOMING).

Lick Granulomas

See EOSINOPHILIC GRANULOMA COMPLEX.

Life Span

See GERIATRIC CAT.

Litter

When a multiple birth occurs in animals, the offspring are collectively called a litter. A mother cat's babies are referred to as a litter of kittens.

Litter also describes the absorbent substance, often clay, that owners provide for their cat's indoor toilet. Commercial litter products are a relatively new innovation, and have changed the lives of cats for the better. The convenience of the first dried ground clay product, introduced as Kitty Litter in 1947, paved the way for cats to move permanently indoors.

The best litters are absorbent products that help control odor and are acceptable to cats. A wide variety of innovative products are available, made of everything from recycled newspaper to cedar shavings or processed grass.

However, clay-based litters remain the most popular choice for cats and owners alike. Clays that clump—the "scoopable" innovation introduced in the late 1980s—are a favorite with some owners because they make cleanup easier. These products absorb urine into a ball, which can be easily removed while leaving the rest of the litter clean so the cat's toilet doesn't need to be changed as often. Such products often incorporate sodium bentonite, a kind of swelling clay, to enhance clumpability. Because it also clogs plumbing pipes, it's not recommended that litters containing sodium bentonite be flushed.

Litter Box

A litter box is a shallow pan, usually plastic, that holds absorbent litter material and is designed to serve as the cat's toilet. A wide variety of commercial litter boxes are available, from fancy to plain.

The basic box should be large enough so that the cat has no trouble maneuvering inside. Most are about five inches deep, which is adequate for holding the preferred depth of two inches of litter without spilling when a cat begins serious digging.

Standard pans are about twelve inches by eighteen inches but are available in larger dimensions for big cats, or for multicat use. Covered boxes are available that help contain odor, offer the cat privacy, and keep litter in the box.

Kittens begin to mimic their mother's litter box habits as soon as they're able to follow her from the nest. Bathroom etiquette varies

Litter boxes are usually plastic, and should be big enough so the cat can maneuver. *(Photo credit: Amy D. Shojai)*

slightly from cat to cat, but most cover over their waste, which means the litter should be good for digging.

Cats may be enthusiastic diggers who end up showering litter out of the box, or they may simply go through the motions and leave most of their bathroom deposit visible. Big cats, particularly males, may need larger boxes to keep from hanging over the edge of the box and missing the target when they eliminate. Some cats consent to share toilet facilities, but if you have more than two cats, multiple facilities are better. One box per cat is ideal.

Many cats have distinct preferences regarding their litter boxes, but a few simple guidelines should keep the cat happy.

First of all, locate the toilet away from sleeping and eating areas. Once the toilet location is determined, don't move the box.

After finding litter your cat likes, don't change it. Switching brands can confuse the cat and may cause elimination problems.

Most important, keep the box clean. Feces and wet spots should be removed daily, and the entire box emptied and disinfected weekly. Proper hygiene not only reduces the risk of health problems for your cat but also prevents many potential behavior problems. Plus, cats often refuse to use a dirty box (see SOILING).

Liver Disease

Liver disease is any condition that impairs the liver's normal function. The liver is the body's metabolic headquarters. It serves a dual role, both as a kind of factory and as a filter.

Food absorbed by the intestines is carried by the BLOOD directly to the liver. There, the liver processes sugars and fats, stores vitamins and minerals, and makes necessary proteins and enzymes. The liver also manufactures hormones and important blood-clotting substances, as well as the bile that's necessary for the absorption of fats. The processed material is either stored or delivered throughout the body as needed by the blood.

Blood is also filtered as it passes through the liver. Drugs and other substances that are carried by the blood are metabolized, or altered,

LIVER DISEASE

SYMPTOMS

Refusal to eat for more than 48 hours, particularly in obese or overweight cats; vomiting; diarrhea; weight loss; lethargy; sometimes yellow tinge (jaundice) to inside of ears or to whites of the eyes or gums

HOME CARE

EMERGENCY! SEE VETERINARIAN IMMEDIATELY; once diagnosed, supportive nutrition

VET CARE

Supportive care, sometimes placement of feeding tube and force feeding

PREVENTION

Keep cats trim, don't allow obesity to develop, keep poisons out of reach of the cat

into other forms. Bacteria, toxins, even viruses are shifted out of the blood system by the liver. Consequently, the liver is exposed to infection and injury more than any other part of the cat's body. Parasites, birth defects, and cancer may interfere with normal liver function. Liver disease is serious and often life-threatening to the cat, and it is estimated to affect 3 to 5 percent of sick cats seen by veterinarians.

The signs of various kinds of liver disease are remarkably similar, and typically include loss of appetite, VOMITING, DIARRHEA, weight loss, and lethargy. Some conditions will cause the pale areas of the cat's skin to turn yellow, or jaundiced. This is most often apparent on the inside of the ears, the whites of the eyes, or the gums. Because the signs are so vague and resemble other feline health problems, the cat owner may not realize the cat's in trouble until the disease is quite advanced.

Treatment depends on the specific cause of the disease. The veterinarian first runs diagnostic blood tests looking for changes in liver enzymes. An ultrasound evaluation is also helpful, but a definitive diagnosis often requires a microscopic examination or culture of the liver tissue. This biopsy generally is done by anesthetizing the cat. Cells may be collected using a fine needle inserted into the liver through the abdominal wall, or the procedure may require surgery.

FELINE HEPATIC LIPIDOSIS (FHL), also called fatty liver disease, is the most common liver ailment in cats. Overweight cats are at highest risk for this condition, and the definitive sign is when an obese cat suddenly stops eating. For reasons not completely understood, fat is moved into the liver and becomes trapped, resulting in compromised liver function.

An inflammatory condition of the bile tract that interferes with the excretion of bile is called cholangiohepatitis, and is considered the second most common feline liver disease. Cure is rare; therapy is designed only to control the disease. When the problem is caused by bacteria, long-term antibacterial therapy is prescribed. Conditions that result from overreaction of the IMMUNE SYSTEM require immune-suppressing drugs like corticosteroids.

Hepatitis, or inflammation of the liver, is the usual result of exposure to a toxin like chemical insecticides, or drugs like ASPIRIN or Tylenol. Treatment consists primarily of supportive care and removal of the POISON. In certain toxicity cases, early intervention allows the liver to recover with little or no damage to the organ.

There is no way to prevent congenital liver problems, or to anticipate some immune or bacterial conditions that affect the liver. However, you can greatly reduce the risk of FHL by keeping your cat slim. Also, be vigilant in the medications you give your cat to avoid toxicities that can damage the liver.

Lower Urinary Tract Disease (LUTD)

Lower urinary tract disease, in the past called feline urologic syndrome or FUS, refers to a complex of disease conditions that affect the urethra, urinary bladder, and/or ureters. Cats are prone to urological disorders because many normally urinate only once a day, and some only once every two or three days, and this provides a good environment for urine to crystallize.

LUTD is associated with a wide range of conditions, including the formation of urinary stones, the obstruction of the urethra, and CYSTITIS. The syndrome affects male and female cats equally, although the

SIGNS OF LUTD

1. Crying during urination
2. Excessive licking of genitals
3. Straining at the end of urination
4. Bloody urine
5. Strong ammonia odor arising from the urine
6. A break in house training or dribbling urine in unusual locations
7. Frequent visits to the litter box with little or no result
8. Listlessness, loss of appetite, excessive thirst

Straining with only tiny amounts of urine expressed may indicate life-threatening blockage. COMA AND DEATH OCCUR WITHIN 72 HOURS AFTER COMPLETE OBSTRUCTION OF URINARY TRACT. See a veterinarian immediately for any one or combination of these signs.

LOWER URINARY TRACT DISEASE (LUTD)

SYMPTOMS

See signs of LUTD

HOME CARE

Provide fresh clean water to assure adequate hydration; keep litter box clean; sometimes administer medication or feed special diet, but only as prescribed by veterinarian

VET CARE

Hospitalization, fluid therapy, possibly catheterization, sometimes surgery

PREVENTION

None

narrow structure of the male cat urethra makes them more prone to suffer from blockage.

The true incidence of LUTD is not known, but the condition is estimated to affect about 10 percent of pet cats seen by veterinarians, with new cases each year reported to be less than 1 percent of the total cat population.

A variety of conditions, alone or working in combination, appear to be responsible for LUTD. However, the majority of cases are idiopathic, which means nobody knows why the cat has problems. A major contributing factor appears to be STRESS. Treatment depends on the specific symptoms, and the cause (when it can be determined).

Inflammation of the urinary bladder affects some cats and results in cystitis. Bacteria may be involved in recurring cases, but often the initial cause is unknown. When infection is present, it can spread up the ureters into the kidneys. Without treatment, the kidneys may be damaged.

New research points to striking similarities between interstitial cystitis in women and idiopathic LUTD in cats. The symptoms seem to be identical. Both feline and human sufferers can go for long periods without problems, and then experience painful flare-ups. Stress appears to trigger the condition and/or make it worse.

The formation of mineral crystals in the cat's urinary tract is called urolithiasis. These crystals or stones were once thought to be the major cause of LUTD, but more recent findings suggest that urinary tract stones account for only a small percentage of cases.

These mineral deposits range from microscopic to sand-size or even golf ball–size stones. Crystals irritate the lining of the lower urinary tract and cause life-threatening problems if they block the flow of urine and cannot be passed through the system.

Blockage of the urinary tract usually results from the formation of soft, pastelike urethral plugs that may contain a combination of minerals and a mucuslike substance referred to as matrix. No one is certain exactly what causes the development of these plugs; however, because some urethral plugs are composed of blood protein components, there is speculation that they may result from the leakage of blood from inflamed bladder walls, which is commonly found in idiopathic LUTD.

The blockage of urine flow may develop slowly, over a period of weeks, or quite suddenly. In either case, the condition is extremely painful—imagine the bladder filling and expanding like a balloon with no outlet. Urine may be forced up into the ureters, in which case the kidneys stop working and poisons build up in the blood. Reversible damage may occur within twenty-four hours, and irreversible kidney damage within five days. Coma followed by death occurs within seventy-two hours following complete obstruction.

Blockage is a veterinary emergency. Plugs often lodge near the urethral opening, and may be moved by massaging the cat's penis. Other times, the cat must be anesthetized and a catheter passed into the urethra. Gentle pressure with fluids moves the plug, then flushes the crystal-laden urine from the cat's system. Fluid therapy increases urine output and rehydrates the cat. If a catheter is unable to unblock the cat, a needle is passed through the cat's abdomen directly into the bladder to empty the urine.

Cats suffering an episode of LUTD often require hospitalization for up to a week. Upon the cat's return home, a management program designed to eliminate existing crystals and keep them from recurring must be instituted. Up to 70 percent of cats with LUTD relapse one or more times.

The mineral content of the cat's urine and the urine's acid-base balance have an influence over whether crystals will form. Infrequent urination concentrates minerals in the cat's urine; reduced exercise and reduced water intake also contribute. The content of the cat's diet, however, may be the deciding factor. One common type of crystal, called struvite, is composed of a combination of minerals including magnesium. This led to the belief that dietary magnesium caused struvite formation, but further research has shown that it's not that simple.

Cats normally produce an acidic urine, but the composition of the diet can affect urine acidity. Some kinds of magnesium, like magnesium oxide, may foster struvite formation by decreasing the acidity of the urine, while types like magnesium chloride help to acidify the urine and don't contribute to struvite formation. Neither of these magnesium sources are used in commercial cat foods; adequate amounts are obtained naturally from other ingredients. Today's cat foods are typically formulated to promote a cat's natural urine pH, or to help produce an acidic urine. These commercial diets are usually considered appropriate for cats that have never before suffered an episode of LUTD.

There's also been speculation that dry foods cause LUTD, but research has been unable to show a consistent connection.

Because the causes of LUTD are multifactoral and often idiopathic, preventing the condition in cats that have never before suffered from LUTD isn't possible. When a cat has previously experienced problems, your veterinarian may prescribe special diets as a treatment or management, depending on the problems.

Cat owners should also be aware that a small but growing percentage of LUTD cats are developing another type of crystal formation, composed of calcium oxalate. The signs are the same, but the treatment is different.

It's thought that the increase in calcium oxalate may be due to the fact that urinary pH levels that inhibit the development of struvite actually promote the formation of calcium oxalate crystals. The acid urine that dissolves struvite, and reduced magnesium levels that help prevent struvite formation, increase the acid level of the cat's blood. An increased blood-acid level tends to leach calcium from the bones, which is then spilled into the urine where it can form calcium oxalate stones.

Unlike struvite crystals, which can be dissolved by feeding the cat a special diet, calcium oxalate stones that can't pass out of the body when the cat urinates must be removed surgically. After removal, there is a 30 to 40 percent chance of recurrence.

Increasing the cat's water intake helps keep calcium oxalate stones from re-forming. Some researchers recommend feeding the cat an alkalinizing diet—such as the prescription diets designed for those cats with kidney failure—to help reduce the chance of calcium oxalate stone recurrence.

Lungworms

Lungworms are slender, hairlike worms (*Aelurostrongylus abstrusus*) that parasitize the cat's lungs. Cats contract the worm by eating rodents, birds, or frogs that harbor the parasite.

Adult worms live in the lung tissue. The eggs they lay hatch into larvae that migrate up the windpipe to the throat, and then are swallowed and reach the digestive tract. Immature worms are then excreted with the feces. Finding larvae in a stool sample is diagnostic.

The larvae must be eaten by and then spend developmental time in a snail or slug to become infective. When a bird, frog, or rodent eats this infective snail or slug, the cycle is complete.

Most cats infected with lungworms exhibit respiratory signs so mild that they often aren't even noticed. Others may suffer from a dry, hacking cough as a result of secondary infections like bronchitis or PNEUMONIA. In severe cases, the cat's breathing is noticeably labored, sometimes to the point of death.

Bronchitis and pneumonia are treated with antibiotics and require a veterinarian's care. Worm medications such as fenbendazole and levamisole, though not approved for use in cats, are generally effective against lungworms, and may be used off-label. The possibility of lungworm infection can be avoided if the cat is prevented from hunting and eating small game.

LUNGWORMS

SYMPTOMS

Dry cough, labored breathing

HOME CARE

None

VET CARE

Medication to kill the parasite

PREVENTION

Prevent the cat from hunting and eating infested prey

Lymphosarcoma

See CANCER.

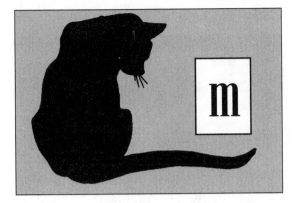

Magnesium

See LOWER URINARY TRACT DISEASE.

Mammary Glands

The mammary glands are modified sebaceous glands that in female mammals secrete milk through the nipples. Both male and female cats usually have eight breasts, located in four pairs along the abdomen.

In male cats and in female cats that are not producing milk, the breasts are relatively flush with the abdomen, and are apparent only by slightly elevated, light pink nipples. When milk is produced, the breasts swell slightly, the nipples darken, and the fur on the abdomen surrounding the nipples may thin. The breasts nearest the flanks tend to be most favored by kittens because they produce the most milk.

A lump, bump, or swelling of the breast not associated with nursing kittens should be seen immediately by a veterinarian to rule out CANCER. The mother cat exhibiting a high fever during nursing can also be an indication of trouble; stop the kittens from nursing and see a veterinarian (see ECLAMPSIA and MASTITIS).

Mange

Mange refers to a skin condition caused by microscopic parasites, called mites, that burrow into the skin. Mites are similar to insects but are actually more closely related to spiders. Mange is not common in cats, but there are several kinds that can potentially cause problems.

The most common mite affecting cats is *Otodectes cynotis*, the EAR MITE. Otodectic mange, which infects the skin, is uncommon. The mite more frequently affects only the skin of the ears.

Notoedric mange, also called head mange or feline scabies, is caused by the mite *Notoedres cati*, which deposits eggs in burrows it makes in the outer surface of the cat's skin. The mite completes its life cycle in a two-week period spent entirely on the cat, and can't survive long in the environment alone.

Notoedric mange is extremely contagious. It is considered uncommon but can appear more often in certain geographic regions. Diagnosis is made by scraping the cat's skin, to collect mites that are present, and examining the material microscopically.

Signs of mange are intense itching of the head, face, and neck. The cat typically scratches and shakes his head, trying to get relief. Red scaly sores develop with yellowish thick crusting on the skin surface; as the hair thins, the skin thickens and becomes leathery and wrinkled. The affected skin smells musty or mousy.

Cats and dogs in contact with the infected animal should also be considered infected and treated. Gentle soaking with warm water and mild soaps helps loosen the crust, while antibiotics and steroid therapy treat secondary infections and relieve itchy skin. A 2.5 percent lime sulfur dip used weekly will kill the mites. Pets showing signs should be dipped two weeks beyond apparent cure, while exposed pets should be dipped at least twice. Also, thoroughly wash the cat's bedding, clean all surfaces, and vacuum carpeted areas and throw away the bag.

Sarcoptic mange and demodectic mange, both common afflictions in dogs, are extremely rare in cats. The signs, diagnosis, and treatment of sarcoptic mange in cats are similar to those of feline scabies. Itchiness

MANGE

SYMPTOMS

Intense itching of face, head, and neck; red scaly sores; yellowish crusting on skin; thinning hair and thickening skin; mousy odor

HOME CARE

Warm water soaks to loosen crusts, mild grooming shampoos to cleanse; once diagnosed by vet, lime sulfur dip to kill otoedric mange mites, or benzoyl peroxide topical products for localized demodex mites; wash bedding, vacuum carpet and throw away bag

VET CARE

Skin scraping to diagnose, sometimes antibiotics or anti-inflammatory medication, prescription shampoos or dips

PREVENTION

Avoid contact with infected animals; if cat is exposed, consult with veterinarian before initiating treatment

m

and red scaly sores with hair loss are the signs of sarcoptic mange. Demodectic mange may not itch, but results in patchy hair loss or overall thinning of the haircoat, with or without pus-filled lesions and crusty sores.

The demodex mite isn't contagious, and is a normal inhabitant of cat skin. It occasionally causes problems in immune-suppressed cats that have other health problems. Most often, cats that are affected are youngsters.

Initial signs include localized areas of HAIR LOSS, usually on the face and especially surrounding the eyes and ears. Such areas eventually develop itchy, crusty sores that can become infected. A generalized form of demodectic mange can affect the whole body. The mite can also in-fest the ears.

A skin scraping is used to diagnose the condition, but often the mite is hard to find. For unknown reasons, the condition often goes away without treatment.

The localized form may be treated topically with benzoyl peroxide–containing products that exfoliate, or strip away, layers of the skin along with the mite. For generalized demodectic mange, aggressive veterinary treatment is necessary.

Marking

Marking is a behavior that cats use to identify territory. Cats spray urine and defecate, scratch, and rub against objects to leave visual and olfac-tory cues. These signals not only indicate ownership but also tell other cats who has been there before them, how long ago the mark was left, the sexual status of that cat, and other important information. Because the pungent scent tends to fade as soon as it contacts the air, markings must be constantly freshened with new markings on top of or near the original. As a result, cats can avoid confrontations by recognizing how fresh or old the mark is, and adjusting their paths accordingly.

Cats, both males and females, normally urinate in a crouching posi-tion, releasing the urine over a flat surface such as the litter in a litter box. Marking with urine, called territorial spraying, is done by using a slightly different technique. Rather than releasing urine downward while squatting, the cat stands erect and sprays the urine outward against vertical surfaces such as walls or trees. The cat backs up to the target, tail held straight up with the tip quivering, and releases short bursts against the item.

Territorial spraying is a sign of dominance and is a normal behavior for sexually intact cats, particularly males. Spraying marks the bounda-ries of the cat's territory, and works toward suppressing the sexual be-havior of less dominant cats that venture into that territory. Intact female cats who spray do so more often during breeding season to an-nounce their availability to potential partners.

Scratching is one kind of marking behavior. *(Photo credit: Betsy Stowe)*

m

Normal spraying behavior is a nuisance to humans, particularly when the cat is an indoor pet. The unaltered male cat's urine has a particularly strong odor that is difficult to eliminate from household furnishings. NEUTERING the cat stops territorial spraying in 80 to 90 percent of cases.

Altered cats of either sex that spray are usually experiencing STRESS. When feeling insecure, a cat attempts to assert control over his or her environment by aggressively marking territory with the comforting familiarity of personal scent.

While cats normally cover their waste, aggressive cats tend to leave their droppings uncovered and prominently displayed as a sign of their dominance and ownership of a particular territory (see AGGRESSION). Cats less self-assured or those who are "trespassing" in another cat's "owned" territory cover their waste to avoid detection and, perhaps, as a sign of deference to the cat in control. It's probable that house cats cover their waste in deference to living within a territory "owned" by a more dominant, potent creature—the human owner. In general, the cat's habit of covering waste is often attributed to instinctive behavior left over from a wild existence that was designed to protect cats living in the wild from a predator's detection.

Cats that leave their waste uncovered may be signaling that the territory belongs to them—but they may also be expressing dissatisfaction with a situation. However, inappropriate elimination can also be caused by health problems and should never be ignored (see SOILING).

Marking behavior also includes a combination of visual and olfactory cues left by scratching an object. Proper care of the CLAWS requires that the cat scratch objects to shed old growth and keep new nails healthy. Scratching also scars the object with visible claw marks and leaves behind scent from special glands located in the cat's paw pads. Scratching is a normal behavior for the cat and cannot and should not be eliminated. Objectionable scratching can usually be addressed by redirecting the behavior to more acceptable objects (see SCRATCHING).

Bunting refers to the cat's habit of bumping and rubbing her head and body against people, other animals, or objects. Cat owners typically consider the action to be a sign of affection, but it is even more than that. Special glands in the skin of the chin, lips, forehead, and tail secrete the cat's identifying scent. Other cats, objects, and people are paid the highest compliment when they are bunted by a cat, or the cat rubs and twines about them. The scent that's transferred identifies that person or other animal as "family," a sharing of scent that is comforting and familiar to the cat. Social grooming is also thought to figure in this mechanism of sharing scent. In effect, an owner so marked becomes a part of the cat's territory—perhaps the most important part of all.

Mastitis

Mastitis refers to an inflammation of one or more of the glands of the breast. The infection usually is caused by bacteria that are introduced through a scratch or puncture wound.

Cats suffering from mastitis typically have a high fever and refuse to eat. The affected breast appears swollen, pink-to-blue in color, and is usually extremely tender to the touch. The milk may appear normal but is often tinged with blood or a yellowish cast, or is thick or stringy.

Get an infected QUEEN to a veterinarian immediately. The infected milk will be cultured to determine the type of bacteria involved, so the

MASTITIS

SYMPTOMS

Mother cat with high fever, anorexia, swollen tender breasts that are bluish in color, yellow or blood-streaked milk, or milk that's stringy or thick

HOME CARE

EMERGENCY! Remove kittens and hand-feed; once diagnosed, massage affected breast several times daily and apply warm wet compresses; have vet check kittens for toxicity

VET CARE

Culture milk to diagnose, administer appropriate antibiotics, sometimes surgical drainage is required

PREVENTION

Clip kittens' claws

m

appropriate antibiotic can be administered. If an abscess has developed, treatment may involve surgical drainage of infected glands. Gentle massage of the affected breasts several times a day, and application of moist warm towels, may be helpful.

Both the tissue and the milk a breast produces are affected; kittens that drink this toxic milk become ill and can die. Signs of toxic-milk syndrome in kittens may include depression and lethargy, diarrhea, fever, and bloating. Get your queen and litter to a vet immediately if you suspect infected milk. Kittens who have not been infected, but have no healthy mother's milk available, should be bottle-fed using a canned commercial kitten milk replacer, available from your veterinarian (see MILK, AS FOOD).

To help prevent mastitis in a queen, keep the nails of all the kittens in the litter clipped.

Mating

See REPRODUCTION.

Mega Colon

Mega colon describes a greatly enlarged and flaccid colon that has lost the ability to move fecal material out of the body. The cause of the condition remains a mystery. It is suspected that a poor nerve supply to the organ results in the inability to properly contract.

The condition creates a vicious cycle. When feces aren't moved out regularly, the lining of the colon continues to pull more and more moisture from the material. As the fecal material dries, it becomes harder and even more difficult to move. The colon soon fills up with dry fecal balls, and the colon expands as more and more feces are added.

If the fecal ball becomes so large it can't pass through the cat's

MEGA COLON

SYMPTOMS

Constipation

HOME CARE

Veterinary prescribed laxatives, enemas, special diets

VET CARE

Anesthetize cat to clean out impacted colon, drugs to promote colon motility, sometimes surgical removal of diseased colon

PREVENTION

None

m

pelvis, veterinary assistance is needed. Treatment may require an ANES-THETIC so the colon can be cleaned out.

Most cats can be managed with a variety of therapies, including laxatives, enemas, and special diets that are also used in less serious cases of CONSTIPATION. Drugs like cisapride (Propulsid) that help the colon to contract are beneficial to some cats. But if dietary management and drug therapy aren't helpful, the colon may be beyond help.

In these cases, surgery seeks to correct the cat's "plumbing" by removing the sick portion of the large intestine. The rectum is left intact, and reattached to the small intestine to create a functional bowel. The surgery is complicated and used mostly as a last resort.

Microfilaria

See HEARTWORM DISEASE.

Miliary Dermatitis

Miliary dermatitis, also called scabby cat disease, is a skin reaction that is a symptom of disease rather than a separate disease in itself. The condition is quite common, and cats develop it in response to a number of things.

Miliary dermatitis is characterized by rashlike scabby bumps. The crusty sores are easily felt beneath the fur when the cat is stroked. The condition may have been named "miliary" because the bumps feel similar to millet seeds. Miliary dermatitis may be concentrated in a single, isolated area or scattered over the entire body.

Cats develop the rash in response to allergic reactions to any number of things, most typically flea hypersensitivity, atopy, and food allergies. Symptoms also may arise from RINGWORM or skin parasites like LICE or MANGE. Bacteria, immune-mediated conditions, drug reactions, and NUTRITION problems can also cause this condition.

m

MILIARY DERMATITIS

SYMPTOMS

Scabby rash beneath the fur

HOME CARE

Flea control

VET CARE

Treat underlying cause

PREVENTION

Avoid allergy component such as fleas, pollens, ringworm, lice, or mites

Successful treatment requires diagnosing the underlying cause and addressing it specifically. For instance, if miliary dermatitis is due to an allergic reaction to FLEAS, then when the bugs are eliminated the rash should go away. Unfortunately, about one in six cases of miliary dermatitis is idiopathic, which means a cause cannot be determined. Cortisone may help control severe itching associated with some cases, and antibiotics may be prescribed to control secondary infections.

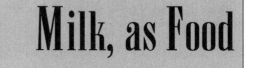

Milk, as Food

From birth, kittens thrive on their mother's milk. If a kitten loses her mother or the mother is unable to feed the baby, cow's milk seems an obvious nutritional substitute.

However, the composition of cat's milk and cow's milk is quite different. Among other things, the calcium and phosphorus levels in cow's milk are much higher than in a QUEEN's milk, which makes it an inappropriate substitute for kittens. Human baby formula—similar in composition to cow's milk—provides less than half the protein and fat a kitten needs. It can be used in a short-term emergency situation only, by mixing it at twice the recommended concentration.

A better choice for long-term supplemental or replacement feeding of kittens is a *commercial feline formula*. These are formulated to closely resemble the nutrient composition of a queen's milk. Just Born, KMR, and other brands are available from your veterinarian and pet store.

Although a number of adult cats may relish cow's milk, remember that it should never replace water in your cat's dish, nor be considered a complete food. Many cats and kittens aren't able to properly digest lactose, the sugar found in cow's milk.

Lactase is the enzyme required to break down lactose. If the cat's intestinal tract doesn't contain the right amounts of this enzyme, then drinking milk will most likely result in a nasty bout of DIARRHEA. A few commercial lactose-free milk drinks made for cats are available for owners who want to treat their cat without risking upset tummies.

m

Milk Fever

See ECLAMPSIA.

Mismating

Mismating refers to a drug that can be administered to a female cat that has "accidentally" been bred. An estrogen compound called estradiol cypionate (ECP) is injected by the veterinarian within forty hours after the mating. This interferes with the normal implantation of the fertilized egg into the wall of the uterus, and thus interrupts the pregnancy.

However, a number of side effects have been reported with use of the drug, including a prolonged heat cycle, bone marrow suppression, and uterine infections. ECP has not been approved for use in cats in the United States.

For cats who have bred accidentally, clinical abortion can be induced for up to forty days into gestation using injections of prostaglandin, which causes the uterus to contract. Hospitalization is required, and some cats suffer severely after the treatment, experiencing vomiting, diarrhea, increased heart rate, or even death.

A much better and safer alternative is permanently preventing unwanted breedings and kittens by surgically sterilizing your pet cats (see NEUTERING and SPAYING). Spaying can be done within thirty days after breeding without added risk to the cat.

Molting

See SHEDDING.

Monorchid

See CRYPTORCHID.

Nail Clipping

See GROOMING.

Navigation

Navigation, in terms of felines, refers to a cat's seemingly innate ability to find his way home. Free-roaming cats often frequent territory of half a square mile or more. The homing mechanism for both FERAL and free-roaming cats is a necessary survival skill if the cat is to successfully range farther away to hunt and return home to feed offspring.

Cats note, or leave behind, visual landmarks, scented signposts, and familiar sounds along the way. These signals essentially map the cat's territory so that he can easily retrace his steps.

Cats that move beyond familiar territory seem to somehow "know" the direction they should head in to reach their homes. There is some speculation that, like birds, cats may use the position of the sun or setting stars to point them in the right direction to get them within scent—or hearing range—of their own or a neighboring animal's territory. From there, they can find their way directly.

Microscopic deposits of iron have been found in the front part of the brain of cats and some other animals, like homing pigeons. Scientists believe this iron acts as a kind of neurological compass, one that partially relies on geomagnetic sensitivity to the earth's magnetic field. This seems the best explanation for the extraordinary homing ability of the rare cat able to travel dozens or even hundreds of miles to get home.

Nephritis

See KIDNEY DISEASE.

Nesting

See REPRODUCTION.

Neutering

Neutering, also called altering or sterilizing, is the surgical removal of an animal's reproductive organs. In pets, neutering commonly refers to the male, while SPAYING refers to the female.

Neutering not only prevents the birth of unwanted kittens, it reduces and in some cases eliminates certain health and behavioral problems. Excessive AGGRESSION that can result in an ABSCESS and MARKING behavior like urine spraying are greatly reduced in neutered cats, making the cat a better domestic pet.

The greatest benefits are obtained when cats are altered before reaching sexual maturity. The exact timing varies from cat to cat and from breed to breed, but most male cats are able to reproduce by five to six months of age. While healthy males may be castrated at any time, the American Veterinary Medical Association now endorses four months of age as the ideal time for surgery.

Neutering is done while the cat is under general anesthesia. A gonadectomy, also called castration, is the surgical procedure that removes the male cat's testicles. Because the procedure is done quickly, often a relatively short-acting injectable drug is used. Other times, inhalant anesthetics may be used, or a combination of drugs (see ANESTHETIC). Depending on the cat, preanesthetic blood work may determine which anesthetic is best for the animal.

As with humans, it's important that the cat's stomach be empty during the procedure so that if the cat vomits while asleep, the danger of inhaling the material into the lungs is reduced. Called aspiration, inhaling foreign material can cause life-threatening complications, including PNEUMONIA. Generally, the cat should not eat or drink food or water for a period of time prior to the surgery. If the cat sneaks an unauthorized snack, tell the veterinarian so that appropriate precautions can be taken or the surgery can be delayed.

Once the cat is comfortably anesthetized, the surgical site is prepared by removing the hair and disinfecting the area with solutions like betadine and alcohol, or chlorhexidine and alcohol. The cat is placed on a towel or heating pad positioned on the surgical table to keep the cat's TEMPERATURE constant. The surgeon wears sterile gloves and uses sterile surgical instruments, and the cat is draped with sterile cloth or towels to keep the site clean.

The two fur-covered spheres seen between the male cat's rear legs are the scrotum, skin sacs that contain the sperm-producing testicles. Each testicle is joined to a spermatic cord that contains an artery and the spermatic duct.

Testicles are expressed, one after another, through incisions made in each scrotal sac. The attached spermatic cords are tied with suture material to prevent bleeding, then the testicles are cut free. The stub of the spermatic cord recedes back into the surgical opening, leaving the scrotal sac empty. An antibiotic may be sprayed into the cavity, but scrotal incisions are usually left open to heal without benefit of stitches. Feline castrations rarely take longer than a few minutes to perform.

In rare cases, there's a failure of one or both testicles to descend into the scrotal sac as the cat matures. However, both testicles must be

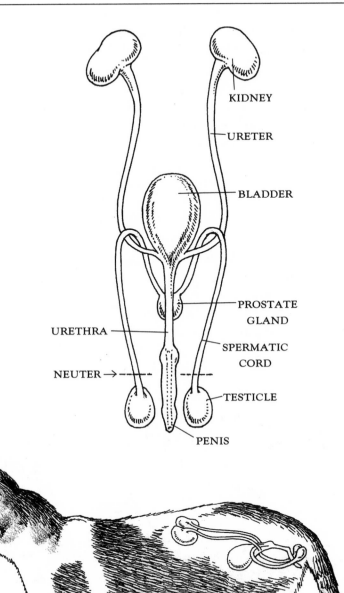

KIDNEY

URETER

BLADDER

PROSTATE
GLAND

URETHRA

SPERMATIC
CORD

NEUTER →

TESTICLE

PENIS

n

Male Urogenital Tract

removed to prevent objectionable sexual behaviors. So, in castrating a CRYPTORCHID cat, the abdomen must be opened to find the hidden testicle. Your veterinarian can determine if your neutered cat has a retained testicle—besides behavioral differences, the intact male cat's penis has prominent spines that disappear once the cat is neutered.

Following surgery, the cat may be held overnight and monitored by the veterinarian. Cats often act a bit disoriented or even drunk for a short time after anesthesia, depending on the type of agent used. Cats typically are up and about within an hour or so of the anesthetic wearing off.

Limit your cat's exercise for two or three days following the surgery, and monitor the incision site. The neutered cat doesn't need to see the veterinarian again unless there's a problem.

Postneutering difficulties are rare, but see the veterinarian if there is a discharge or puffiness at the surgery site. Most problems are minor and involve the cat licking the incision. This can be prevented by using an ELIZABETHAN COLLAR to keep your cat away from the incisions until they heal.

n

Nictitating Membrane

See EYES.

Nose

The nose is a sensory organ that provides the cat with olfaction, or sense of smell. Scent cues give the cat her sense of place in the world. Smells identify friend from foe, communicate sexual information, and even prompt feline hunger. In many ways, scent rules the cat's life.

The cat's external nose varies in size and shape from breed to breed. Oriental breeds like Siamese have long, straight "Roman" noses and wedge-shaped muzzles, while Persians, with their flat-faced profiles, have broad snub noses and an indentation (break) between the eyes. The length of feline noses can vary as much as two inches from one type to the other.

In fact, the short skulls of certain snub-nosed breed cats can distort and narrow the nasal passages and airways. Called brachycephalic airway syndrome, this can make affected cats work so hard to inhale that they may develop breathing problems. Physical activity, excessive heat, or stress prompts wheezing and noisy breathing. In some cases, surgery to increase the size of air passages may be necessary.

In domestic cats, the hairless point of the nose is called the leather, and comes in a variety of colors that, in purebred cats, typically matches or coordinates with the coat color. The nose leather is ridged with a unique pattern that is like a feline fingerprint; no two are alike.

The nostrils, or nares, are situated in the leather. They are the outside opening to the internal nasal cavity that runs the length of the cat's muzzle and ends when it opens into the cat's throat behind the soft palate. The nasal cavity is enclosed in bone and cartilage. Open spaces in the bone, called sinuses, connect to the nasal cavity. Sinuses help shape the sounds the cat makes, and are why "meows" sound the way they do. These openings may also function to reduce the weight of the skull. Sinuses in kittens are small and grow larger as the animal matures.

The nasal septum is a vertical plate made of bone and cartilage that divides the nasal cavity into two passages, one for each nostril. A series of rolled, bony plates called turbinates are located inside the nasal cavity. They are covered by a spongy thick membrane, called the olfactory mucosa, which contains the scent-detecting nerves and cells. How well the cat smells depends on how many of these cells the cat has, which in turn is decided by the size and shape of her muzzle. Longer-nosed cats have more scent-sensing equipment than flat-nosed cats.

However, despite the cat's small size, she still has many more of these cells than people do. Humans typically have from 5 to 20 million scent-analyzing cells, compared to the cat's 67 million. The king of scenting animals, the bloodhound, has 300 million.

Odor particles are carried in the air and captured and dissolved by a coating of mucus that keeps the nasal cavity moist. Millions of microscopic hairlike receptors set in the olfactory cells extend into this thin layer of moisture and make contact with the odor particles. It is be-

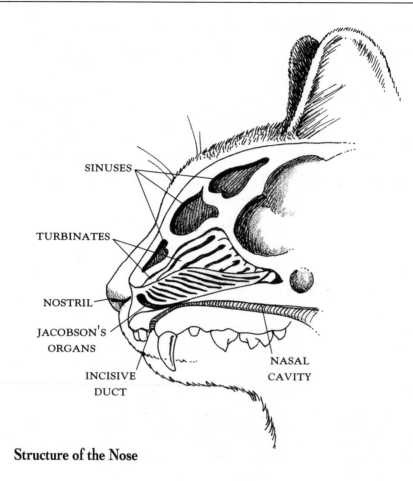

SINUSES

TURBINATES

NOSTRIL

JACOBSON'S
ORGANS

INCISIVE
DUCT

NASAL
CAVITY

Structure of the Nose

lieved that each different odor has a specific molecular "shape" that decides how much stimulation the nerve cell receives. The stimulated nerves signal the olfactory bulbs, which send the information directly to the brain, where the smell is interpreted as a mouse or whatever. A second, more specialized scenting mechanism is thought to be used primarily in sexually related odors (see JACOBSON'S ORGANS).

The cat's nose is not only a scenting organ but it also helps protect the respiratory tract by warming and humidifying air as it's inhaled. A protective layer of moisture is produced by serous glands and mucus glands throughout the nasal cavity. This mucociliary blanket is composed of microscopic cells covered with hairlike filaments called cilia that move the moisture toward the nostrils and throat. This mucus coating protects the body against infection by trapping foreign material.

However, because cats typically sense their world by sniffing, they are often exposed to illnesses and infected through inhaled bacteria or viruses. Nasal disorders such as discharge, sneezing, or bleeding from the nose can indicate a number of different conditions, such as an UP-PER RESPIRATORY INFECTION.

A cat may tilt her head to one side, or squint her eye on one side when a foreign body lodges in the nasal passages. Or she may violently sneeze and paw at one side of the nose. Foreign matter like grass, an insect, or dust may work its way out by itself; other times, a veterinarian's help is advisable. Don't try removing foreign bodies yourself, or you could injure the delicate structures of the cat's nose.

The biggest problem in nasal disorders is that the cat loses her appetite. The smell of food prompts hunger, and when a stopped-up nose interferes with scent detection, the cat just won't get hungry, and stops eating. Illness typically becomes even worse when the cat loses her appetite (see ANOREXIA).

Nutrition

Nutrition, in this case, refers to the food your cat eats. Cats require a nutritionally complete and balanced diet to maintain optimal health. "Complete" means all necessary components are in the diet, while "balanced" means the components are in the proper ratios to one another.

Nutrients are the components of food that provide nourishment. They must be supplied not only in the correct amounts but also in the proper balance, because they benefit the cat both individually and by interacting with one another. Cats need a combination of six different classes of nutrients for good health. These are: water, protein, carbohydrates, fats, minerals, and vitamins.

Water is the most important nutrient. Eighty-four percent of a kitten's body weight is water, and up to 60 percent of an adult cat's body

Felines need complete and nutritionally balanced diets. *(Photo credit: Ralston Purina Company)*

n

weight is water. Water lubricates the tissue and helps distribute electrolytes like salt throughout the body. Moisture is used in digestion and elimination, and helps regulate body temperature. Even a 15 percent loss of body water, referred to as DEHYDRATION, results in death.

Protein helps build and maintain bone, blood, tissue, and even the IMMUNE SYSTEM. Proteins are composed of twenty-three different chemical compounds called amino acids. Some amino acids cannot be produced by the body in sufficient amounts, and are called essential because they must be supplied by the diet. Cats require dietary histidine, isoleucine, leucine, arginine, methionine, phenylalanine, threonine, tryptophan, valine, and lysine. Unlike dogs, cats also require dietary taurine. A deficiency of taurine in the cat may result in blindness or heart disease (see CARDIOMYOPATHY).

Cats require much higher levels of dietary protein than do dogs, and should never be allowed to eat dog food. Cats are carnivores and must have animal source nutrients—or synthetic replacements—in their diet. Neither meat alone, nor a totally vegetarian diet, provides balanced nutrition for the cat. Signs of a protein deficiency may include loss of appetite, weight loss, poor haircoat, poor growth, and impaired reproductive performance.

Carbohydrates provide energy, and are obtained from starches and grains. Fiber gives minimal energy but helps regulate the bowels, assists other nutrient absorption, and may give a full feeling for obese cats that are dieting.

Fats provide two and a quarter times the available energy per unit of weight than carbohydrates or proteins, and are particularly important for cats with high energy requirements, like pregnant or nursing QUEENS. Fat also helps make food taste good to the cat. Fats are the only source of essential fatty acids and are necessary for fat-soluble vitamins to be used. Fatty acids and fats promote healthy skin and fur, and signs of a deficiency include greasy fur, dandruff, weight loss, and poor healing of wounds.

Minerals are needed in relatively tiny amounts but are essential for nerve conduction, muscle contraction, acid-base balance, fluid stability inside the cells, and many other things. The term *ash* is used to describe the total mineral content of a particular food. The measure is obtained by burning the food, and measuring the unburned ASH portion (mineral) that is left.

Necessary minerals include calcium, phosphorus, magnesium, potassium, sodium, chloride, and the trace minerals cobalt, copper, iodine, iron, manganese, selenium, and zinc. Minerals work together, and the balance is as important as the amount. Too much can be as dangerous as too little. An imbalance can cause bone deformities, ANEMIA, muscle weakness, heart or KIDNEY DISEASE, and countless other problems.

Vitamins are used in biochemical processes inside the cells. Very small amounts of them are required for a cat's good health. Vitamins are divided into two groups: B-complex vitamins, which are water soluble, are not stored in the body, and must be replaced every day; and vitamins A, D, E, and K, which are fat-soluble and stored in the body. If vitamins are not in proper combinations and amounts, severe problems can result. Oversupplementation can be toxic to the cat, while insufficiency can cause dangerous diseases. Too much or too little of certain vitamins may result in problems such as lameness, skin problems like YELLOW FAT DISEASE, rickets, anemia, BLEEDING, and even neurological disorders.

Nutrient requirements for cats vary depending on several factors, including the animal's age, health status, activity level, and living conditions. Every cat has different requirements, but most are able to obtain optimum nutrition by eating commercial cat foods that have been properly formulated for their life stage (this is known as "staged feeding").

Always choose a food that is appropriate to your cat's life stage. For example, pregnant cats, mothers nursing kittens, and growing kittens require much higher levels of energy than do adult cats. Among other things, kittens need more protein, fat, and calcium than mature felines. Adult cats may gain too much weight if fed a high-calorie kitten ration. High-quality commercial pet foods clearly label their products for growth and reproduction (pregnant or nursing mothers and kittens), maintenance (adult cats), or all life stages (from kittenhood to motherhood and adult maintenance). Feed only products that have been tested and are proven to be complete and balanced. Choose appropriate diets by READING FOOD LABELS.

Specialty diets are also available that address a number of nutrition-related concerns. Those that help control health problems generally are available only through a veterinarian, and should be used only as prescribed. Many are designed to relieve specific clinical signs of disease by manipulating nutrient profiles, and are not appropriate for routine maintenance in healthy cats.

Obesity

Obesity is an excessive amount of body fat that compromises health or body function. Obesity is of growing concern—25 to 30 percent of pet cats seen by veterinarians are overweight.

The condition seems more common today than it was twenty years ago, primarily because of differences in feline lifestyle and feeding. A large number of cats are exclusively indoor pets with limited opportunities for exercise. Palatable commercial foods prompt more feline attention to food when a cat is bored and left with little else to do. And the higher the fat and calorie content of the food, the greater becomes the risk for obesity.

All cats have the potential for becoming overweight, but the problem appears to be more prevalent in mixed-breed cats. The highest incidence appears in neutered, middle-aged six- to eleven-year-old male cats.

There are a number of theories why neutered cats are more prone to obesity than intact ones. The removal of reproductive organs alters the hormonal balance and causes metabolic changes. Also, cats are usually neutered in late kittenhood or early adulthood—a time when energy requirements are declining but owners may fail to make appropriate dietary adjustments. Finally, neutering tends to curb certain cat behaviors, such as roaming and fighting; the resulting decline in activity

Twenty-five to 30 percent of pet cats are overweight. *(Photo credit: Ralston Purina Company)*

contributes to weight gain when the diet isn't adjusted (see NEUTERING and SPAYING).

In fact, surveys of overweight cats show they tend to be very inactive and SLEEP up to eighteen hours a day. Overweight and obese cats are more likely to be fed high-fat, nutrient-dense rations such as certain super-premium or prescription diets.

Few studies have been done that document health problems specifically associated with obesity in pet cats. In humans, excessive weight raises the risk for a number of conditions, including atherosclerosis, which cats almost never develop.

Preliminary feline studies indicate that overweight cats are more likely to develop DIABETES MELLITUS, skin problems, lameness due to ARTHRITIS, and FELINE HEPATIC LIPIDOSIS. Severely overweight cats may be at greater risk for surgical complications from BLEEDING or from the ANESTHETIC, heat or exercise intolerance, and complications from cardiovascular diseases.

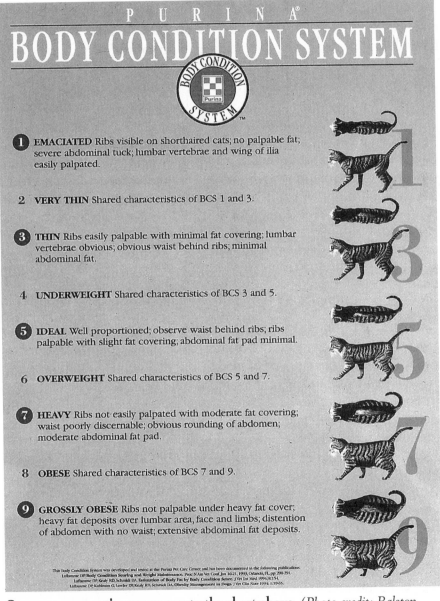

P U R I N A®
BODY CONDITION SYSTEM

1 EMACIATED Ribs visible on shorthaired cats; no palpable fat; severe abdominal tuck; lumbar vertebrae and wing of ilia easily palpated.

2 VERY THIN Shared characteristics of BCS 1 and 3.

3 THIN Ribs easily palpable with minimal fat covering; lumbar vertebrae obvious; obvious waist behind ribs; minimal abdominal fat.

4 UNDERWEIGHT Shared characteristics of BCS 3 and 5.

5 IDEAL Well proportioned; observe waist behind ribs; ribs palpable with slight fat covering; abdominal fat pad minimal.

6 OVERWEIGHT Shared characteristics of BCS 5 and 7.

7 HEAVY Ribs not easily palpated with moderate fat covering; waist poorly discernable; obvious rounding of abdomen; moderate abdominal fat pad.

8 OBESE Shared characteristics of BCS 7 and 9.

9 GROSSLY OBESE Ribs not palpable under heavy fat cover; heavy fat deposits over lumbar area, face and limbs; distention of abdomen with no waist; extensive abdominal fat deposits.

This Body Condition System was developed and tested at the Purina Pet Care Center, and has been documented in the following publications:
Laflamme DP, Body Condition Scoring and Weight Maintenance. Proc N Am Vet Conf. Jan 16-21, 1993, Orlando, FL, pp 290-291.
Laflamme DP, Kealy RD, Schmidt DA. Estimation of Body Fat by Body Condition Score. J Vet Int Med. 1994;8:154.
Laflamme DP, Kuhlman G, Lawler DF, Kealy RD, Schmidt DA, Obesity Management in Dogs. J Vet Clin Nutr. 1994; 1:59-65.

Compare your cat's appearance to the chart above. *(Photo credit: Ralston Purina Company)*

Obesity is typically defined as 20 to 25 percent over the cat's "ideal" body weight. But determining this ideal isn't easy, and weight alone isn't a good measure of the percentage of body fat compared to muscle-bone mass. A better method of evaluating a cat's condition is to look at his profile and feel his body.

You should be able to feel your cat's ribs but not see them. The ideal body condition viewed from above reveals an hourglass figure. The cat has a slight indentation at the waist beginning at the back of the ribs to just before the hips. In profile, a cat should have a slight tummy tuck beginning just behind the last ribs and going up into the hind legs. To evaluate your cat's condition, compare his appearance to the illustrations in the "Body Condition System."

Always consult a veterinarian before placing your cat on a diet. An expert should help you evaluate how much weight your cat needs to lose, and advise you on the best way to proceed. Weight loss should be done slowly and with great care, or your pet's health may be jeopardized. Most diets target losing about 1 to 1.5 percent of the cat's starting weight per week.

With some cats, simply eliminating the treats (see FOOD SUPPLEMENTS) and slightly reducing the amount of their regular ration is adequate. Canned food is less calorie dense than dry foods, so rather than free-feeding dry food, success may be obtained by feeding your cat canned food. Divide the canned food into four or even five small meals a day to help keep your cat from feeling deprived. Multiple small meals also tend to increase the body's metabolic rate, which can help the tubby tabby slim down.

In other cases, switching the cat to a lower-calorie, lower-fat diet is a better option. Special "lite" diets are designed to provide complete and balanced nutrition in a reduced-calorie, reduced-fat formulation that also satisfies the cat's need to feel full. These diets typically replace fat with indigestible fiber, dilute calories with water, or "puff up" the product with air. But some feline nutritionists believe cats are metabolically programmed to eat a set amount of calories, and eat until this point is reached. If this is true, special reducing diets may not work when offered free-choice, because the cat simply eats more of the reduced-calorie food to get the same number of calories he'd get from a more concentrated food.

The definition of "reducing-type" food products for pets has varied historically among pet-food companies, so that one company's "lite" product might actually have more calories than the next company's "regular" food. Pet-food regulators have proposed defining the term to establish an industry-wide standard. The new standard, accepted but not yet fully implemented, requires cat foods labeled "lite" to be 10 percent reduced in fat and calories compared to the industry's average cat food.

In extremely obese cats, veterinary-prescribed reducing diets in conjunction with a therapeutic weight-loss program supervised by the veterinarian are the safest option. In all cases, increasing the cat's exercise through the use of interactive toys is encouraged.

To keep your feline in prime condition, offer her a quality complete and balanced diet. Monitor the cat's body condition and adjust the amount of food offered as needed. Don't feed her table scraps and severely limit treats. And play interactive games with your cat to promote healthy exercise. (See also FOOD and NUTRITION.)

Olfactory

O

See NOSE.

Otitis

Otitis is an inflammation of the EAR that may either happen suddenly or be ongoing. It is generally categorized as otitis externa, otitis media, or otitis interna. These categories refer to the area of the ear affected by the inflammation.

Cats suffering from immune disorders or diseases like FELINE LEUKEMIA VIRUS or FELINE IMMUNODEFICIENCY VIRUS are more prone to developing otitis. Normal ear secretions being thrown out of balance predispose the cat to otitis, which can be caused by something as simple as getting water in the ears during a bath.

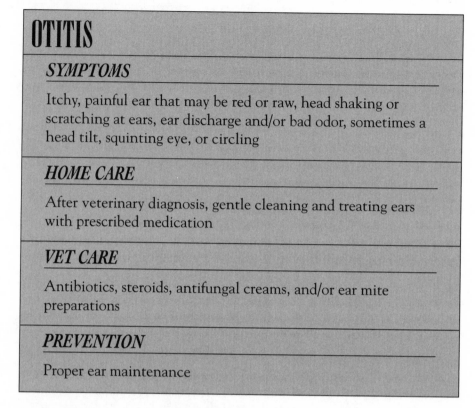

OTITIS

SYMPTOMS

Itchy, painful ear that may be red or raw, head shaking or scratching at ears, ear discharge and/or bad odor, sometimes a head tilt, squinting eye, or circling

HOME CARE

After veterinary diagnosis, gentle cleaning and treating ears with prescribed medication

VET CARE

Antibiotics, steroids, antifungal creams, and/or ear mite preparations

PREVENTION

Proper ear maintenance

O

Cats most commonly suffer from otitis externa, which is confined to the external portion of the ear canal and/or the ear flap. Otitis externa occasionally advances into the middle ear (otitis media), and even more rarely into the inner ear (otitis interna).

EAR MITES are the number one cause of otitis externa in cats. ALLERGIES or foreign bodies like grass seeds can cause ear inflammation; yeast or bacterial infections are also common causes of otitis externa. Otitis media is usually due to the progression of infection from the external ear canal, or from penetration of the eardrum by a foreign object. From there, the problem can progress into otitis interna, where the condition becomes really serious.

Signs of otitis include itchy or painful ears that may be red, raw, or even bloody if the cat has scratched them. Excessive shaking or scratching may result in a HEMATOMA. A bad odor emanating from the ear indicates infection, as does any sort of discharge. Normal ear wax is light amber in color; an abnormal discharge can vary from clear and thin to waxy and crumbly, or even thick and cloudy yellow or green.

When the middle or inner ear is affected, the cat can show signs of nerve involvement. Symptoms include a head tilt, droopy eyelids, or facial palsy on the affected side. Inner ear infections can interfere with the cat's sense of balance so the cat may circle and fall toward the affected side. Extreme damage from otitis may result in deafness.

Treatment depends on identifying and addressing the cause of the inflammation. Sedation or an ANESTHETIC may be needed to thoroughly examine a cat's sore ears. An instrument called an otoscope has a magnifying lens and light that makes it possible for the veterinarian to examine the horizontal and vertical ear canal to see if the eardrum is intact.

The nature of the discharge can then be evaluated, as well as the status of swelling or scarring of the ear canal. Foreign bodies may be visible during this examination as well. The veterinarian also collects a sample of the discharge and examines it under the microscope to see if bacteria, yeast, or ear mites are present.

The ears must be thoroughly cleaned and allowed to dry before any treatment can be effective, and general anesthesia may be required for the cleansing. The veterinarian should perform the initial cleansing to avoid further trauma to the ears. If the eardrum is ruptured, some ear cleaning solutions or medications can actually damage the middle ear, and make a bad situation even worse.

After the veterinarian's initial cleaning and flushing of the affected ears, owners can treat most cases at home (see ADMINISTERING OF MEDICATION). Topical antibiotic ointments and drops—sometimes paired with steroids to reduce itchiness and inflammation—are generally prescribed for bacterial infections. Medicine is usually administered twice a day for two weeks.

Yeast infections are treated with antifungal creams or drops twice daily for two weeks, then once a day for another week. If the infection is caused by more than one thing, an antifungal/antibacterial cream may be prescribed to address all issues.

Acute otitis usually resolves within two or three days with treatment. But chronic problems take much longer to cure. Up to six weeks of treatment may be necessary when the eardrum is punctured in order to prevent permanent damage to hearing or balance. Occasionally, the eardrum requires lancing to relieve the pressure of infection that has built up; the eardrum usually heals quickly thereafter.

When infections are deep inside the ear, drops and ointments may not reach the source, and surgery may be necessary to clean out these pockets of infection. Long-term oral antibiotics are given to fight the infection, along with steroids to address inflammation and prevent nerve involvement. Still, neurologic signs like head tilt, eye twitches, or circling may continue for the rest of the cat's life even after the infection is cured.

The best way to prevent otitis is to routinely check your cat's ears every week for parasites, and to keep them clean. Use a bit of baby oil or commercial ear cleaner on a cotton ball or cotton swab, and gently wipe clean the area you can see. Make ear maintenance a part of your cat's GROOMING regimen.

Ovariohysterectomy

O

See SPAYING.

Pain

Pain is extreme discomfort, usually in a specific part of the body, that is caused by illness or injury. Pain is a protective mechanism designed to prompt action that stops the sensation, which in turn prevents further damage to the body. For example, a burn stimulates the paw or tail to recoil, while the pain of a broken bone motivates resting of the area, which helps speed the healing.

Before pain can be treated, the underlying cause of the discomfort must be determined. Pain can result from any number of things, including ARTHRITIS, FRACTURES, PERITONITIS, PERIODONTAL DISEASE, or even a systemic disease like FELINE PANLEUKOPENIA VIRUS.

Common pain medications such as ASPIRIN *and Tylenol that people typically use to relieve pain are* POISON *to the cat.* When pain is due to inflammation, sometimes the veterinarian will prescribe steroid-type medications to make the cat feel more comfortable. If you suspect your cat is in pain, have the veterinarian examine him to determine the underlying cause.

SIGNS OF PAIN

Cats in pain don't act like themselves. Retiring cats become demanding; friendly cats tend to hide. It's hard to tell sometimes what your cat is trying to say. Be alert for these signs, and have the cat checked by your veterinarian:

1. Hides
2. Remains very still and quiet
3. Becomes vocal, meowing or crying
4. Acts agitated, can't get comfortable
5. Pants or drools
6. Refuses food
7. Flinches, hisses, or strikes out when touched in tender place
8. Trembles
9. Limps or carries paw
10. Assumes hunched posture
11. Squints eyes or has watering eyes

p

Pancreatitis

Pancreatitis is the inflammation of the pancreas, an organ situated near the liver that provides digestive enzymes and insulin. While the condition is common in dogs, it's relatively rare in cats.

The cause is unknown, but probably a number of factors are involved. OBESITY, sudden high levels of dietary fat (such as trimmings from your roast beef), trauma, and certain drugs are thought to contribute to the condition. TOXOPLASMOSIS, FELINE INFECTIOUS PERITONITIS, and FELINE PANLEUKOPENIA VIRUS have been associated with pancreatitis in cats.

Damaged cells of the pancreas release abnormal amounts of enzymes that, instead of digesting food, break down the fat in nearby tissues. This can spill toxins into the bloodstream, cause bleeding, and send the cat into shock and possibly kill it.

There is no definitive way to diagnose pancreatitis in the sick cat. Signs of pancreatitis in cats are so vague and nonspecific that often the condition isn't diagnosed until the cat's body is examined after death. Signs may include VOMITING, fever, or ANOREXIA.

Panleukopenia

See FELINE PANLEUKOPENIA VIRUS.

Parasites

See EAR MITES, COCCIDIOSIS, CUTEREBRA, FLEAS, GIARDIA, HAEMOBAR-TONELLOSIS, HEARTWORM DISEASE, HOOKWORMS, LICE, LUNGWORMS, MANGE, ROUNDWORMS, TAPEWORMS, and TICKS.

p

Periodontal Disease

Periodontal disease refers to disorders that affect the TEETH and gums. Seventy percent of cats develop gum disease by age three, and all cats are at risk for dental problems. As the cat ages, the risk becomes greater, because periodontal disease slowly worsens over time.

PERIODONTAL DISEASE

SYMPTOMS

Bad breath, yellow to brown debris on teeth, red swollen gums that easily bleed, loose teeth, receding gums, reluctance to eat

HOME CARE

None

VET CARE

Anesthetize cat to clean and/or extract decayed teeth, sometimes antibiotics are required

PREVENTION

Clean cat's teeth regularly (weekly), avoid feeding exclusively soft diets

P

Food that sticks to the surface of the cat's teeth as he eats is the perfect environment for bacterial growth. As the bacteria grow, a couple of things happen. A soft material called plaque accumulates and sticks to the tooth surface. Left unchecked, the plaque turns to a chalklike material that mineralizes and forms hard deposits called calculus or tartar. Tartar is a buildup of yellow to brown crusty material on the teeth. This increase in bacterial activity in the mouth can produce BAD BREATH, which is an early warning sign of dental disease.

Enzymes released by the bacteria attack the surrounding tissue, causing inflammation. Called GINGIVITIS, this inflammation of the gums is another early sign of periodontal disease. The gums at the tooth line will appear red and swollen, and tissue will be tender and may bleed easily.

The cat's IMMUNE SYSTEM attempts to fight the bacteria, but instead causes even more inflammation and tissue destruction. The gums begin to recede from the teeth, and bone destruction loosens them until teeth simply fall out. Loose teeth or exposed roots are signs of gum recession due to chronic infection.

According to the American Veterinary Dental Society, 28 percent of cats will suffer from a unique type of tooth decay called a cervical cavity, or neck lesion. The decay tends to form between the root and the crown at the neck of the tooth where the gum line begins. These cavities are often hard to detect since they're usually hidden beneath swollen gum tissue. X-RAYS may be necessary to find neck lesions and determine the tooth involvement.

The initial entry hole is often tiny, but the cavity may have eaten away almost the entire inside of the tooth, leaving nothing but a fragile hollow shell. Researchers are trying to discover what causes these cavities. They theorize that diet, an immune disorder or virus, or even the environment may have something to do with the development of neck lesions in cats.

Mouth infections are not only painful, but they also impact the cat's overall health. Chewing literally pumps the bacteria into the cat's bloodstream, which in turn spreads infection throughout the body. Periodontal disease has the potential to damage lungs, heart, liver, and/or kidneys, and can cause either sudden disease or a slow, progressive deterioration that shortens the cat's life.

Today, veterinary dentistry is a growing specialty. Depending on the extent of the problems, a veterinary dentist can provide many of the same services available to people, including teeth cleaning, fillings, crowns, root canals, and even orthodontia work.

To treat periodontal disease, a thorough cleaning is required. Animal patients must undergo general anesthesia for this procedure because tartar must be scaled from the teeth even below the tender gum line. An ultrasonic cleaner removes the deposits, then the veterinarian polishes the teeth to smooth out irregularities in the enamel that collect plaque. A fluoride treatment to help protect the teeth completes the cleaning.

When infection is present, antibiotics are prescribed. Feline cavities are difficult to fill because they leave teeth so fragile that often the tartar is all that holds them in place. Usually, decayed teeth are extracted. But simply removing the painful tooth often so relieves the cat that he almost immediately begins acting like a kitten again.

Periodontal disease in your cat can be prevented by routine dental hygiene. How quickly plaque and tartar develop is influenced by a number of things, particularly food. The raw diets that cats in the wild eat tend to keep teeth clean; tearing through fur, skin, and raw flesh naturally abrades the teeth. The processed foods that provide pet cats with complete and balanced nutrition often fall short on adequate dental abrasion.

Food textures and the chemicals in the ration do, however, influence the effect food has on the teeth and in the mouth. Wet foods tend to stay in the oral cavity longer because they stick to the tooth surface more readily than dry foods. The detergent action of crunching kibble helps clean tooth surfaces above the gum line, which means dry foods are beneficial for pet dental health.

However, dry food alone does not prevent problems from occurring. Veterinary dentists estimate that eating dry food helps at best about 10 percent. Cats typically do not chew food a great deal, so the detergent action has less impact than when a person eats an apple. Also, most feline dental problems occur at or below the gum line, not on the crown of the tooth where the kibble makes contact. All things being equal, some cats are simply more prone to dental problems than others. Inherited tendencies, the strength of the immune system, and even the structure of the mouth help determine how much plaque and tartar develop.

Research is under way to develop commercial pet foods that better address dental concerns. Added fiber that promotes the detergent action of eating is being investigated, as are special chemicals added to food that help prevent plaque and calculus from attaching to teeth.

Veterinary dentists recommend that cats have their teeth professionally cleaned as routine prevention just as often as people have their teeth professionally cleaned. Once or twice a year for cats younger than five years of age is recommended, but more frequent cleanings are beneficial as the cat ages. By feeding a dry rather than wet food, and cleaning the cat's teeth at home, the frequency of professional cleanings can be reduced. Some lucky cats may require professional cleaning only two or three times during their lifetime.

Ideally, as an owner, you should brush your cat's teeth as frequently as your own—after each meal. Two to three times a week is often adequate, though, and once a week is better than nothing.

Toothbrushes and pastes designed for cats are available from veterinarians and specialty pet stores. *Never use human products.* Our toothbrushes generally are too large and stiff for a cat's tender mouth.

Also, the levels of fluoride in human toothpaste are excessive for cats, and may potentially result in kidney damage when the cat swallows the toothpaste. Cats aren't able to spit, and swallowing human toothpaste can also upset their stomachs.

Special feline toothbrushes are typically smaller with softer bristles than those designed for people. Pet toothpastes don't foam, and come in malt or chicken flavors that most cats relish.

Introduce cats to dental care one step at a time, and make it a part of normal interaction. While petting your cat, progress from rubbing and scratching his cheeks and chin (which most cats love!) to stroking his lips and handling his mouth for short periods. Reward him with a play session or a healthy treat. From there, try rubbing the cat's teeth and gums with one finger. Don't force the cat's mouth wide open—simply slip your finger through the lips into the cheek. Try flavoring your finger with the feline toothpaste.

Then progress to using a soft cloth wrapped around your finger. Spread the paste on the cloth, and massage your cat's teeth and gums as long as he allows. Be satisfied if you complete one side, and don't force the cat beyond his tolerance level; you can always finish the rest at the next session.

You then may want to try a finger toothbrush for cats that slips over your finger and has tiny rubber bristles. A feline toothbrush is the next step, but the cloth or finger brush are more than adequate and may be tolerated more readily by the cat because they are an extension of you. Dental rinses with antibacterial properties that help prevent plaque buildup, promote healing, and control bad breath are also available.

Kittens often tolerate brushing well, but all cats and especially adults will probably need coaxing. Don't expect success the first time you attempt to clean your cat's teeth. You'll need patience to get your cat to accept the procedure, but don't give up; the rewards may extend your cat's life.

Peritonitis

Peritonitis is an inflammation and sometimes infection of the abdominal cavity. It should not be confused with FELINE INFECTIOUS PERITONITIS, which is caused by a virus.

Peritonitis results from a contamination of the abdominal area. This usually is caused by perforation of an abdominal organ like the stomach, intestines, or uterus. This can happen due to infections like PYOMETRA, or from SWALLOWED OBJECTS that puncture or cut the organ.

The cat experiences abdominal pain, and assumes a hunched posture to protect the stomach area or a stiff-legged gait when walking, or he may refuse to move at all. High fever is common, as is a loss of appetite and depression. Sometimes the abdomen swells.

PERITONITIS

SYMPTOMS

Extreme abdominal pain, hunching posture, stiff-legged walk or refusal to move, anorexia, depression, fever, swollen abdomen

HOME CARE

None

VET CARE

Emergency surgery to clean out infection and repair damage, antimicrobial therapy to fight infection

PREVENTION

Keep swallowable objects away from the cat

Prognosis for cats suffering from peritonitis is not good, and the survival rate is poor. Treatment includes supportive care and massive antimicrobial therapy to fight infection and to stabilize the cat. Surgery is necessary to repair the damage and flush out the infection. Preventing your cat from swallowing dangerous objects will avoid the potential hazard of peritonitis.

Plague

Plague is a deadly bacterial disease historically associated with humans and wild rodents. Plague is considered a disease of antiquity, but despite advances in modern medicine that make cures possible, pockets of the disease still exist. Today we know that plague not only affects traditional victims but also causes disease in cats.

Epidemics so vast they were called pandemics began in the Mediterranean centuries ago. The pandemic of A.D. 541 killed 40 million people before it was through. Plague was named "the black death" when it returned during the fourteenth century; at that time it killed 25 million people in Europe alone. China suffered an outbreak in 1855; around that same time, Dr. Alexandre Yersin from the Institut Pasteur of France identified the bacterial organism that caused the disease, and named it *Yersinia pestis*.

Plague is a disease of rodents and FLEAS; historically, rats were the main reservoir for disease. Today, in the United States, ground-living rodents like prairie dogs and ground squirrels are the primary reservoirs. According to the Centers for Disease Control, the states of New Mexico, Arizona, Colorado, and California account for about 90 percent of reported plague cases, with more than half occurring in New Mexico. Plague has also been reported in Texas, Montana, Wyoming, and Utah. On average, ten to fifteen cases of human plague are reported each year in the United States, with ten to thirty yearly cases of plague in cats reported in New Mexico.

Rodents that become infected may get sick, resulting in massive die-offs of the population. Other times, the organism causes no health problems, and the rodents are simply carriers. But as fleas feed on the

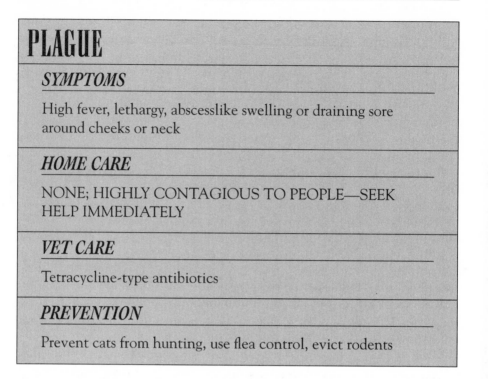

PLAGUE

SYMPTOMS

High fever, lethargy, abscesslike swelling or draining sore around cheeks or neck

HOME CARE

NONE; HIGHLY CONTAGIOUS TO PEOPLE—SEEK HELP IMMEDIATELY

VET CARE

Tetracycline-type antibiotics

PREVENTION

Prevent cats from hunting, use flea control, evict rodents

infected animal, they swallow the organism in such massive quantities that the bacteria literally block the flea's gut. The flea regurgitates and actually injects the organisms into new hosts with subsequent feedings.

Human infection usually results from bites of infected rodent fleas (which are different from the fleas that typically affect cats). Although plague fleas prefer the rat, squirrel, or prairie dog, they'll make do with an available dog, cat, or human, if necessary.

Pets allowed outdoors in endemic regions, particularly those who hunt, are at highest risk. Dogs rarely get sick the way cats do, but any roaming pet can become infested with infected rodent fleas and bring them home, where they can potentially infect people.

Cats commonly contract plague by eating infected animals. Prevalence appears to be cyclic in wild rodent populations, and spills over accordingly into cat and human populations. Plague can occur all year long, but the incidence seems to rise during the summer months of flea season.

Signs vary between bubonic, pneumonic, and systemic forms of the disease; each form involves a different part of the body. High fever and lethargy are the earliest signs in all three forms, but are often overlooked.

Cats typically suffer from *bubonic plague*, which incubates only two to six days. Lymph nodes that filter the organism from the BLOOD are infected first, and become swollen by the second or third day after exposure. The painful swelling, typically in the groin area or armpits for people, is the "bubo" that gives this disease its name.

Cats usually develop a bubo beneath the chin on one side or the other. The feline bubo looks like a typical ABSCESS, particularly when it ruptures and drains highly infectious material.

Extreme caution is necessary when handling or treating cats with plague to prevent humans from catching the disease. Use gloves or wrap your cat in a towel before transporting her to the hospital. Alert the veterinarian of your suspicions so appropriate precautions may be taken.

Septicemic plague is much less common in cats. It circulates throughout the blood and causes a more generalized illness. *Pneumonic plague* is the deadliest and most contagious form, and infects the lungs. Incubation takes only two to three days, and signs are similar to PNEUMONIA. The pneumonic form is spread by inhaling infective droplets spread through coughing. Thankfully, this form of plague is rare in cats, for it is virtually always fatal.

Plague is most often diagnosed from clinical signs, but blood tests sent to specialized laboratories for analysis confirm the disease. Because plague is a human health risk (see ZOONOSIS), suspect cases are required to be reported to public health officials.

Untreated or extremely late treatment of bubonic plague has a 50 percent mortality rate; untreated systemic plague has a 70 to 90 percent mortality rate; and pneumonic plague is 100 percent fatal when left untreated. But plague can be cured when caught in time. The organism is susceptible to antibiotics such as tetracycline, which may also be used as a preventive for cats and/or people who may have been exposed to plague.

Prevention involves avoiding exposure by confining cats indoors, using flea control, and evicting rodents that may be reservoirs of the disease. Avoid total rodent extermination, or you'll end up with fleas with nothing to bite but you. Instead, clean out brush and wood piles, barns, and sheds, and make them inhospitable to flea-carrying varmints.

Play

Play, in terms of the feline, refers to behaviors in cats perceived by humans to be recreational in nature. Historically, many experts have theorized that play activities in KITTENS is instinctive behavior designed to hone adult hunting skills necessary for life in the wild. It follows that the domestic cat, as an adult, would continue play behaviors as a replacement for frustrated hunting activities.

However, some experts aren't convinced this is true, since many wild animals continue to play even as adults. In fact, even domestic cats that regularly hunt continue to indulge in play behavior. In any event, play is great fun for cats, whether kitten or adult.

Play behavior can be divided into three categories: locomotory, social, and object. Locomotory play involves running, jumping, rolling, and climbing. Such activities may involve two or more cats, but kittens often engage in this type of play all by themselves. Social play is inter-

Kittens often jump, run, roll, and climb. *(Photo credit: Ralston Purina Company)*

Two felines engage in object play. (*Photo credit: Lillian Zahrt*)

active, and may include wrestling and biting, pouncing, episodes of play-fighting, and even games of tag. Object play is just that—the kitten or cat plays with some interesting object such as a ball or feather.

Kittens begin social play as early as four weeks of age. The intensity escalates, then peaks between nine and fourteen weeks of age, and declines as the cat matures. Adult cats may enjoy playing with kittens, and in fact introducing a youngster into the household may give a stick-in-the-mud adult cat a new lease on life. Social play isn't as common between adult cats, though, probably because unless they know each other very well, the play easily escalates into real fights. However, in multicat homes, adult cats may wrestle, play-stalk each other, or engage in other forms of social play. Cats who know each other are able to COMMUNICATE their intention to play; they read the cues and understand it's a game.

Object play is often carried into adulthood. Cats enjoy pawing, stalking, biting, and "capturing" objects, and seem to react as though they are dealing with something alive. Some cats, particularly kittens, engage in object play with objects that are invisible to the owner.

Play behavior can be an expression of emotion or of an individual cat's personality, and styles vary somewhat across breeds. Abyssinian and Rex breeds are athletic cats who tend to enjoy games of chase, Siamese like to fetch, Turkish Vans are fascinated by water, and Persians are sedate and tend to play more quietly.

Commercial fishing pole–style toys that prompt the cat to stalk, pounce, and leap are one of the best interactive cat games available. But toys don't need to be expensive to be successful. A peacock feather is popular with cats, as is an empty paper (*not* plastic) bag in which to hide. A Ping-Pong ball or a crumpled piece of aluminum foil tossed into the bathtub provides lots of fun. Take care that the toys you choose for your cat are safe. Feathers and string toys or anything that can be swallowed should only be used when you can supervise to prevent your cat from swallowing an inappropriate object (see SWALLOWED OBJECTS).

Joint play serves to reinforce social bonds among group members. And because an owner is perceived by the cat to be almost a surrogate-mother figure, playing with your cat brings you closer together. In fact, play is often a particularly effective therapeutic tool in cats with health or behavior problems.

Interactive play encourages a tubby tabby to exercise and stimulates healthy weight loss in OBESE cats. Aggressive cats may benefit from play, for it allows them to release their energy in a more productive way. And play can boost the confidence of a shy cat, distract the fearful cat, and help relieve STRESS.

Pneumonia

Pneumonia is an inflammation or infection of the lungs, and can be caused by virus, bacteria, or parasites. Occasionally, pneumonia develops as a result of aspiration, which means something that should have been swallowed was instead inhaled into the lungs. Aspiration of vomit may occur while the cat is under the influence of an ANESTHETIC or suffers a seizure. Administering liquid medications incorrectly may also cause aspiration.

Most commonly, pneumonia affects very young kittens as a result of UPPER RESPIRATORY INFECTION. Mortality rate can be as high as

PNEUMONIA

SYMPTOMS

High fever, rapid or strained breathing, wheezing, blue-tinged gums, coughing

HOME CARE

SEE VETERINARIAN ASAP; humidifier (or breathing in a steamy bathroom) helps relieve breathing difficulty

VET CARE

Antibiotics, supportive care

PREVENTION

Vaccinate for upper respiratory infection

50 percent in these instances. Old cats, those suffering poor nutrition, and cats with suppressed IMMUNE SYSTEMS are also at higher risk for pneumonia.

Signs generally include a high fever with rapid or strained breathing. Cats that aren't able to get enough oxygen may have blue-colored gums. Coughing helps clear the lungs, but cats with pneumonia may make bubbly wheezing sounds when they breathe. Humidifying the air may help ease the breathing until veterinary attention is available. Diagnosis is based on examination of the lung secretions and chest X-rays.

Pneumonia requires prompt veterinary intervention, so get your cat to a hospital as soon as possible. Treatment usually consists of antibiotic therapy.

P

Poison

Poison as it applies to cats refers to any substance that, through chemical reaction, impairs, injures, or kills the cat. *Poisoning is a life-threatening emergency that should be addressed immediately by a veterinarian.* The sooner the cat is treated, the better are his chances of survival.

If you suspect your cat has been poisoned, call your animal emergency center immediately and provide them with as much information as possible, then rush the cat to the hospital. When the veterinarian knows the kind of poison involved (check the label), how much was ingested, the time elapsed from exposure, and the symptoms the cat is showing, better preparations can be made for your cat's swift treatment upon arrival. Take the package with you to help identify the poison, and if the cat has vomited, bring a sample.

Signs of poisoning vary depending on the chemical agent, the amount of exposure, and the individual cat. Treatment and/or antidote is often specific to the poison involved as well. It is aimed at getting rid of or neutralizing the poison, and may involve supportive care of the cat to combat SHOCK and systemic signs. Treatment for a specific poison attempts to do one or a combination of the following: decontamination, neutralization, and dilution/absorption. However, the wrong treatment may cause more harm than good, which is why your veterinarian should address poisonings.

If the cat is unconscious or experiencing seizures, first aid will not help; however, certain home treatments may in some instances improve the cat's chances for survival, particularly if immediate veterinary help is unavailable.

In any event, do not attempt to give home medications by mouth unless the cat is fully conscious and remains in complete control of his body. Attempting to administer oral treatments to an unconscious cat risks aspiration of the medication into the lungs, and possible suffocation.

In general, with contact poisons on the skin surface, treatment usually begins by flushing with plain water to decontaminate the cat. Wash or rinse the entire cat (for whole-body poisoning) or the affected area

POISONOUS PLANTS

TOXIN	SIGNS/SYMPTOMS	TREATMENT
APPLE SEEDS, APRICOT PITS, CHERRY PITS, HYDRANGEA, PEACH PITS	difficulty breathing, muscle tremors, convulsion, death	SEE VETERINARIAN ASAP: These contain cyanide, which acts to suffocate the cat. A chemical antidote administered by the veterinarian is required to save the cat's life.
AZALEA	salivation, vomiting and diarrhea, muscle weakness, seizures, coma, and death	Administer lots of water to wash out the stomach, along with activated charcoal to absorb toxin, then see your veterinarian.
BELLADONNA, DATURA, HENBANE, JESSAMINE, JIMPSON WEED	dry mucous membranes, excessive thirst, rapid heartbeat, dilated pupils; can lead to coma or convulsions, and death	SEE VETERINARIAN ASAP: Supportive care along with chemical antidotes are required if the cat is to survive.
BIRD OF PARADISE, BOX THORN, CROWN OF THORNS, DAPHNE, ENGLISH IVY, HONEYSUCKLE, IRIS, SNOW-ON-THE-MOUNTAIN	intestinal irritation with nausea and vomiting; cat exhibits stomach pain and suffers diarrhea immediately upon ingestion	Induce vomiting; administer lots of water to dilute toxin, or several tablespoons of milk to coat the stomach; give activated charcoal to help absorb the poison; SEE VETERINARIAN ASAP.
BLACK LOCUST, CASTOR BEAN, ROSARY PEA	signs can be delayed up to 24 hours after ingestion, then abdominal pain, bloody diarrhea, and vomiting; cats may suffer fever or act depressed; signs can progress to coma, seizures, and death	HIGHLY POISONOUS: Eating a single pea or bean can kill a cat. Induce vomiting, then SEE VETERINARIAN IMMEDIATELY.
CALADIUM, DIEFFENBACHIA (DUMB CANE), JACK-IN-THE-PULPIT, PHILODENDRON (HEART-LEAF AND SPLIT-LEAF), SKUNK CABBAGE	irritation of the mouth, tongue, and throat; increased salivation, with possible ulcers and swelling that may interfere with breathing	DO NOT INDUCE VOMITING; offer water or milk to cleanse the cat's oral cavity; rarely fatal; see veterinarian if breathing becomes difficult.

p

TOXIN	SIGNS/SYMPTOMS	TREATMENT
CHINABERRY, MARIJUANA, MORNING GLORY, PERIWINKLE	bizarre or odd behavior, trembling, convulsions	Induce vomiting and get to the veterinarian.
CREEPING FIG, CHRYSANTHEMUM, WEEPING FIG	contact rash affecting the skin surrounding and inside of the mouth	Wash area with cool water to soothe rash, see veterinarian.
DAFFODIL, TULIP, WISTERIA (especially the bulbs)	gastric irritation, violent vomiting, possible depression, death in severe cases	Induce vomiting; administer lots of water to dilute toxin or several tablespoons of milk to coat the stomach; give activated charcoal to help absorb the poison; see a veterinarian ASAP.
ENGLISH HOLLY, EUROPEAN HOLLY	abdominal pain, vomiting and diarrhea when two or more berries are eaten; death is reported rarely	SEE VETERINARIAN ASAP: Supportive care is necessary to treat the digitalislike toxin.
FOXGLOVE, LARKSPUR, LILY OF THE VALLEY, MONKSHOOD, OLEANDER	slowed heartbeat (these plants contain digitalis) followed by severe abdominal pain and vomiting; finally, signs of agitation are exhibited, followed shortly by coma and death	SEE VETERINARIAN ASAP: A plant's toxicity can stop your cat's heart.
GOLDEN CHAIN, INDIAN TOBACCO, MESCAL BEAN, POISON HEMLOCK, TOBACCO	salivation, incoordination, muscle twitches, rapid heartbeat; breathing becomes labored and the cat can collapse in minutes to hours following ingestion	SEE VETERINARIAN ASAP: These plants contain nicotine and require a chemical antidote to save the cat.
JERUSALEM CHERRY, POTATO (GREEN PARTS AND EYES)	signs may not appear until 18 to 24 hours following ingestion; then the cat exhibits a painful abdomen, bloody diarrhea, vomiting, and dry mouth; severe cases may proceed to tremors, paralysis, and cardiac arrest	DO NOT INDUCE VOMITING as this may further damage the gastrointestinal tract; IMMEDIATE VETERINARY ATTENTION is imperative.
MOTHER-IN-LAW PLANT	vomiting, salivation, mouth irritation, diarrhea, occasionally staggering or collapse	DO NOT INDUCE VOMITING; offer water or milk to cleanse the cat's oral cavity; rarely fatal; see veterinarian if cat loses coordination or collapses.

p

TOXIN	*SIGNS/SYMPTOMS*	*TREATMENT*
POINSETTIA	irritates mucous membranes of mouth, may cause excessive salivation or vomiting but not death	Offer water or milk to cleanse the cat's oral cavity; consult your veterinarian.
RHUBARB (upper stem and leaves)	vomiting, excessive salivation, abdominal pain, staggers followed by convulsions	Induce vomiting, then get your cat to the veterinarian. (Without treatment, the toxin causes extensive damage to the cat's kidneys.)
YEW (American Yew, English Yew, Japanese Yew, etc.)	irregular heartbeat, dilation of the pupils, shivering, nausea, and/or abdominal pain; death often occurs without warning signs	SEE VETERINARIAN ASAP; induce vomiting if possible.

OTHER POISONS

TOXIN	*SIGNS/SYMPTOMS*	*TREATMENT*
ACID POISONS (bleach)	when swallowed, drooling, pawing at mouth, painful abdomen; when spilled on skin, vocalizations, signs of distress, rolling, licking area	DO NOT INDUCE VOMITING! flush the area of skin contact with plain water for at least 10 minutes; if substance was swallowed, administer 2 teaspoons of milk of magnesia, then SEE VETERINARIAN ASAP.
ALKALINE POISONS (drain cleaner)	when swallowed, drooling, pawing at mouth, painful abdomen; when spilled on skin, vocalizations, signs of distress, rolling, licking area	DO NOT INDUCE VOMITING! flush the area of skin contact with plain water for at least 10 minutes; if substance was swallowed, administer 6 tablespoons of half water and half lemon juice or half water and half vinegar to neutralize, then SEE VETERINARIAN ASAP.
ANTIFREEZE (ETHYLENE GLYCOL)	drunken behavior, excessive thirst, increased urination, diarrhea, vomiting, convulsions, loss of appetite, panting	EMERGENCY! SEE VETERINARIAN ASAP. If ingested in last 2 hours, induce vomiting and/or administer activated charcoal; veterinary treatment administers 100 proof alcohol.

p

TOXIN	SIGNS/SYMPTOMS	TREATMENT
CHOCOLATE	drooling, vomiting and/or diarrhea, excessive urination, hyperactivity, muscle tremors, seizures, coma	EMERGENCY! SEE VETERINARIAN ASAP. If ingested in last 2 hours, induce vomiting.
COAL-TAR POISONING (phenol disinfectants like Lysol, treated wood, tar paper, heavy oil)	depression, weakness, incoordination, coma, death	SEE VETERINARIAN ASAP. Lysol is absorbed through skin; wash cat immediately if exposed.
FLEA PRODUCTS (ORGANO-PHOSPHATES, CARBAMATES, AND CHLORINATED HYDROCARBONS)	signs may be delayed due to skin absorption of toxin; a variety of signs possible, including: apprehension, muscle twitches, shivering, seizures, drooling, diarrhea, hyperactivity or depression	Wash cat as soon as you realize poisoning has occurred, even if several hours have passed and no signs are yet seen; SEE VETERINARIAN ASAP.
MEDICATIONS, ASPIRIN OVERDOSE	loss of appetite, drooling, dehydration, hyperactivity or depression, blood in vomit and/or diarrhea, drunken behavior	EMERGENCY! SEEK VETERINARIAN ASAP. If ingested in last 2 hours, induce vomiting.
MEDICATIONS, OTHER	various signs dependent upon toxic agent	induce vomiting if ingested within last 2 hours; SEE VETERINARIAN ASAP.
MEDICATIONS, TYLENOL	difficulty breathing, blue-tinged gums, collapse	EMERGENCY! SEE VETERINARIAN ASAP. If ingested in last 2 hours, induce vomiting.
PEST BAITS, ANTICOAGULANT TYPES (warfarin, pindone, Dcon, Mouse Prufe II, Harvoc, Talan)	bleeding in stool and/or urine or from nose, ears, and beneath the skin and gums	EMERGENCY! Induce vomiting if ingested within past 2 hours; SEE VETERINARIAN ASAP; blood transfusions and treatment with intravenous vitamin K is a specific antidote.
PEST BAITS, ARSENIC (slug/snail bait, ant poisons, weed killers, insecticides)	thirst, vomiting, staggering, drooling, abdominal pain and cramps, diarrhea, paralysis	EMERGENCY! Induce vomiting if poisoning occurred within last 2 hours, then SEE VETERINARIAN ASAP; a specific antidote is available.
PEST BAITS, BROMETHALIN (Assault and Vengeance rodenticides)	muscle tremors, staggering gait, high fever, stupor, agitation, seizures	EMERGENCY! Induce vomiting if ingested within past 2 hours; SEE VETERINARIAN ASAP.

P

TOXIN	*SIGNS/SYMPTOMS*	*TREATMENT*
PEST BAITS, CHOLECALCIFEROL (Rampage, vitamin D$_3$)	vomiting, diarrhea, seizures, heart/kidney failure	EMERGENCY! Induce vomiting if ingested within past 2 hours; SEE VETERINARIAN ASAP.
PEST BAITS, METALDEHYDE (rat, snail, and slug bait)	drooling, incoordination, excitability, muscle tremors, progressive weakness	EMERGENCY! Induce vomiting if ingested within past 2 hours; SEE VETERINARIAN ASAP.
PEST BAITS, PHOSPHORUS (rat and roach poisons, matches and matchboxes)	vomiting, diarrhea, garlic breath; sometimes a symptom-free period, then return of signs with painful abdomen, seizures, and coma	EMERGENCY! Induce vomiting if ingested within past 2 hours; SEE VETERINARIAN ASAP.
PEST BAITS, SODIUM FLUOROACETATE (rat poison)	vomiting, agitation, straining to defecate/urinate, seizures, staggering gait, collapse	EMERGENCY! Induce vomiting if ingested within past 2 hours; SEE VETERINARIAN ASAP; a specific antidote is available.
PEST BAITS, STRYCHNINE (rat, mouse, mole, coyote poison)	agitation, apprehension, excitement, seizures prompted by noises like clapping hands, drooling, muscle spasms, chewing, collapse	EMERGENCY! SEEK VETERINARY HELP ASAP. Cover cat with towel to prevent stimulation of further seizures; if poisoned within 2 hours, induce vomiting.
PEST BAITS, ZINC PHOSPHIDE (rat poison)	depression, difficulty breathing, weakness, seizures, vomiting (with blood), coma	EMERGENCY! Induce vomiting if ingested within past 2 hours; SEE VETERINARIAN ASAP.
SNAKE BITE	restlessness, drooling, panting, weakness, diarrhea, collapse, sometimes convulsions, paralysis, or coma	EMERGENCY! SEE VETERINARIAN IMMEDIATELY. If help is more than 30 minutes away, apply tight bandage between bite and cat's heart and loosen for 5 minutes once an hour; keep cat quiet until help is available. *Don't wash bite, don't cut bites to suction out poison, and don't apply ice to bites*—all could increase venom absorption and/or damage tissue further.
TOAD POISONING	slobbering or drooling, pawing at mouth, sometimes convulsions, blindness, or even death	Flush cat's mouth with plain water for at least 10 minutes, and induce vomiting; SEE VETERINARIAN ASAP.

p

for at least ten minutes. Cats exposed to natural gas, smoke, or carbon monoxide should be exposed to fresh air as soon as possible.

If the poison was swallowed within the past two hours, VOMITING may help get rid of as much toxin as possible. However, vomiting is not appropriate for caustic poisons, like drain cleaner or bleach, which can do as much damage coming back up as they did going down. And DO NOT USE SYRUP OF IPECAC to induce vomiting; it can be toxic for pets. Instead, one tablespoon of 3 percent household hydrogen peroxide that foams when squirted to the back of the tongue may induce vomiting within about five minutes. However, cats are notoriously difficult to make vomit, even for veterinarians; you may try a second dose if the first one fails, but stop there and get the cat to the veterinarian.

For caustic poisons like drain cleaner or bleach, DO NOT INDUCE VOMITING; not only will the poison burn on its way back up, but retching could cause the already damaged stomach to rupture. A *half and half solution of lemon juice and water or vinegar and water helps neutralize the effects of caustic alkaline poisons such as drain cleaner.* Give the cat a total of about six tablespoons of the liquid (water/lemon juice or water/vinegar). Acids like bleach can be neutralized by giving the cat about two teaspoons of milk of magnesia.

Encouraging the cat to drink lots of water or milk helps dilute the poison as well. Milk also helps coat and soothe the injured stomach, and may prevent certain poisons from being absorbed. Activated charcoal also helps absorb toxin. It's available as tablets or a powder that's mixed with water.

Here is specific advice on how to identify and handle some of the most common poison types (and please also note the poison treatment charts on pages 313–317):

Poisonous Flea Treatments: The most common poison affecting cats involves owner misapplication of insecticides, especially flea products (see FLEAS). Toxicities often result from using dog flea products on cats, or misreading label applications and using too much of the substance. Some so-called natural products containing citrus oil ingredients like citronella can be poisonous to cats.

A wide variety of behavior changes can develop, from subtle to obvious. Cats poisoned with flea products may simply act lethargic, or drool a lot with bouts of vomiting and DIARRHEA. Shivering, incoordination, or a staggering gait may be seen.

Usually the exposure is dermal, meaning the cat absorbs the toxin through the skin when the dip, spray, or shampoo is applied. Signs may be delayed for several hours after exposure. However, as soon as you realize what has happened, decontaminate the cat by giving him another bath in plain lukewarm water, whether your cat is showing symptoms or not. See a veterinarian to be sure follow-up care is provided.

Home Medications: The second most common feline poisoning involves the misuse of medications, especially human pain relievers like Tylenol, ASPIRIN, ibuprofen, and neproxen sodium (Aleve). The cat metabolizes these drugs more slowly than people do, which means smaller doses remain in the cat's system for much longer periods. Giving a five-pound cat a single five-grain aspirin tablet is like a human taking thirty tablets. One extra-strength Tylenol can kill a ten-pound cat. Signs of aspirin toxicity include excitability or depression, vomiting, diarrhea, and incoordination. Tylenol acts primarily on the blood and can interfere with oxygen transportation, so cats turn blue (look at their gums) and have difficulty breathing.

Cats may also get into other medication and inadvertently overdose. The signs and treatments depend on the type of medication and how much was taken. Induce vomiting or give activated charcoal, then get the cat to the veterinarian.

Houseplants: A number of plants contain toxins that are harmful to pets. These substances may be limited to certain parts of the plant, such as the leaves, bulb, or seed, or may be throughout the plant. Contact with the plant delivers the toxin in some cases, but the most dangerous contact requires chewing or swallowing. And while cats typically don't chew and eat plants nearly as often as dogs do, a cat may shred the plant with his claws, and then become poisoned when he licks and cleans himself.

The symptoms of poisoning can be as varied as the number of plants involved. Signs range from localized contact irritations and rashes; to systemic poisonings that result in drooling, vomiting, and diarrhea; to hallucinations, convulsions, and even death. In addition, individual cats appear to have varied tolerances for certain toxins; what causes severe mouth irritations in one cat may be eaten without problems by another. Therapy is aimed at counteracting or preventing the effects of the poison. Depending on the individual plant, the toxin may be addressed either by flushing the area of irritation, inducing vomiting, or diluting or neutralizing of the poison.

Household Products: Cats may suffer toxicities from cleaning agents like bleach, drain cleaner, or phenol preparations like Lysol disinfectant or coal-tar products. Usually, poisoning occurs when the product is splashed on the cat, or the cat walks through a spill. Flush the area with lukewarm water to remove the toxin from the skin, and get the cat to a veterinarian. Other common household poisons that cats may willingly eat or drink are ANTIFREEZE and CHOCOLATE.

Pest Poisons: Cats that catch small game may be exposed if they eat a rodent that's ingested poison. Strychnine can result in seizures, arsenic can kill before signs develop (the cat's breath may smell like garlic), and anticoagulants such as warfarin result in BLEEDING from the rectum, nose, and even the skin. Induce vomiting immediately if you see the cat swallow the poison, then get the cat to a veterinarian, who administers specific antidotes for each.

If you are unable to reach a veterinarian, call the National Animal Poison Control Center (NAPCC) located at the University of Illinois College of Veterinary Medicine. They can walk you through emergency home remedies appropriate to your circumstance. Consultations can be charged to a credit card by calling 1-800-548-2423 or to a phone bill at 1-900-680-0000, or you can visit their web site at http://napcc-hp.cvm.uiuc.edu.

Polydactyl

See CLAWS.

Porcupine Quills

Outdoor cats may inadvertently encounter a porcupine—with devastating results. The porcupine's needlelike quills, up to four inches long, are barbed and designed to penetrate flesh and continue moving inward. Dogs seem more prone to injury than the more cautious cat. When an animal is stuck with quills, the quills typically will be in the face or open mouth.

The quills are very painful and can cause even the most tractable cat to lose control, roll with pain, and strike out at anything within reach trying to relieve the pain. Accessible quills can be removed at home, using needle-nose pliers to grasp the quill near the skin. However, the barbs can break off and continue to travel into the body, causing further pain and possibly infection, and many small quills may be hidden by fur and missed. In almost every case, it's better to have your veterinarian remove the quills after anesthetizing the cat. Usually, each wound is also treated with a disinfectant, like peroxide or betadine.

The only way to prevent your cat from encountering an irate porcupine is to keep her indoors and/or supervise all her outside adventures.

PORCUPINE QUILLS

SYMPTOMS

Needlelike barbs protruding from body, particularly face or mouth, crying with pain, rolling, pawing of injured area

HOME CARE

If quill is accessible, grasp with needle-nose pliers close to skin, pull straight out, disinfect each wound; vet care usually required

VET CARE

Anesthetize cat, remove quills, swab each wound with disinfectant like peroxide or betadine

PREVENTION

Keep cat indoors and/or supervise outdoor excursions

P

Predatory Behavior

See HUNTING and PLAY.

Pregnancy

See REPRODUCTION.

Pulse

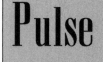

The pulse is the rhythmic speed at which the heart pumps blood. Each cat's pulse rate is different, but the normal range for an adult cat is 160 to 240 pulses each minute. Young kittens have a pulse rate of 200 to 300 beats per minute.

The pulse should be strong and regular. A fast pulse may indicate anything from excitement to blood loss, infection, or heart disease; a slow pulse may indicate illness.

You can determine your cat's pulse by counting the number of beats in a minute. With your cat standing, place the flat of your fingers on his side above the ribs directly behind his left front elbow. The pulse can also be felt by pressing your fingers firmly against the inside of your cat's thigh, where the leg attaches to the body.

Purring

Purring refers to the rumbling sound produced by cats and kittens. It is found in wild cat species as well as in pet cats. The true purpose of purring isn't known, but it is thought to be a form of communication. The purr of a QUEEN may signal her presence to newborn kittens, and when the babies begin purring as early as two days old, they may be telling their mother that they are warm, safe, and fed.

Experts believe purring in adult cats may be a carryover of kittenish behavior, and point to the KNEADING behavior that often accompanies it. Cats purr only when in the presence of another cat or person, and some behaviorists believe the purr may communicate submission. While we tend to think of purring as a sign of contentment, cats often use deeper, louder purrs when they are in pain or upset, and may even purr as they die, perhaps in an effort to comfort themselves.

Exactly how cats produce the purr remains a mystery. Some experts theorize that structures in the cat's throat, called vestibular folds or false vocal chords, make the sound by rubbing together as air passes through when the cat inhales and exhales. Another theory purports that purring is caused by a rapid contraction and relaxation of the muscles surrounding the voice box and diaphragm, which in turn produces a turbulent air flow through the trachea.

Yet a third explanation points to a turbulent flow of blood through a large vein in the cat's chest, again caused by diaphragmatic muscle contractions; the resulting vibrations are transmitted through the windpipe to the sinus cavities, which amplify the sound. This last theory seems supported by cats who have lost their "voices" due to injury, and can no longer vocalize meows but are still able to purr.

p

Pyometra

Pyometra is an infection of the uterus. This is a life-threatening condition that must be addressed by a veterinarian as an emergency.

High levels of the hormones estrogen or progesterone over a long period of time can result in pyometra. An intact QUEEN over five years of age who infrequently or never produces kittens is at the highest risk. Therefore, queens who are not in a professional breeding program should be spayed.

Signs most commonly develop about a month after the cat goes out of heat. Symptoms include loss of appetite, lethargy, increased thirst and urination, and a swollen abdomen. There may be a cream- to pink-

PYOMETRA

SYMPTOMS

Loss of appetite, lethargy, increased thirst and urination, swollen abdomen, sometimes a cream to pinky brown discharge from vagina

HOME CARE

None—EMERGENCY! SEE VETERINARIAN ASAP

VET CARE

Spay surgery removes infected uterus, antibiotic therapy

PREVENTION

Spay cats that aren't to be regularly bred

or brown-colored discharge from the vagina. Diagnosis is based on the above signs, and confirmed with an X-RAY or ULTRASOUND. The treatment of choice is SPAYING the cat to remove the infected reproductive organs and prevent the condition from recurring.

p

Quarantine

Quarantine, as it applies to felines, refers to the isolation of cats that are ill or suspected to be ill in order to prevent the potential spread of disease or pests to healthy pets or people. New cats should be evaluated and treated appropriately by a veterinarian prior to or very shortly after ADOPTION. But even with a clean bill of health, quarantine is a prudent choice whenever a new cat or kitten is to be introduced into a home that already has pets.

It's obvious that a new cat or kitten showing signs of disease should be isolated from healthy animals. However, a cat can appear healthy and expose resident pets to disease before showing signs of illness himself. The amount of time between the cat being exposed to disease and then developing symptoms of illness is referred to as the incubation period. The length of time varies depending on the causative agent, with the incubation period for some viral diseases like rabies being months or even years. It is for this reason that countries like the United Kingdom and states like Hawaii impose a quarantine of up to six months on pets imported into these areas.

Usually, though, a cat incubating a highly contagious disease becomes sick within two to three weeks of exposure. Quarantine the new cat for a minimum of two weeks (a month is better) to reduce risk of exposure for your other pets. If the new cat does not become ill during the quarantine period, he can then be integrated into the household.

Prepare a special area—a bedroom or enclosed porch—and furnish it with all the kitty necessities. The new cat and your resident pets should have no direct contact—not even sniffing noses through the screen. Use a disinfectant to keep the quarantine area and new cat accoutrements clean. One of the best and most economical disinfectants is Clorox at a dilution of one cup bleach to two gallons of water. Don't forget to disinfect yourself after interacting with the new cat to prevent you from carrying something nasty out of the room on your shoes or hands, and infecting your other pets.

Queen

The term *queen* suggests royalty, and so is highly appropriate when used to speak of cats. The title is bestowed upon females of breeding age. It more specifically may refer to those female cats that produce kittens.

Quick

See CLAWS and GROOMING, Clipping Your Cat's Nails.

Rabies

The rabies virus belongs to the family *Rhabdoviridae* and causes a viral disease that attacks the brain. Rabies affects all mammals, including dogs, cats, and people. Once the typical neurological signs appear, the disease is always fatal and victims suffer an agonizing death. However, after the first vaccine was developed by Louis Pasteur in 1884, rabies became preventable.

Rabies has been recognized for centuries and has been found nearly everywhere in the world. Today, a few places—for example, Hawaii and Great Britain—have eliminated the disease through enforcement of strict QUARANTINE requirements.

However, rabies continues to be a presence in wild animal populations, and can appear in any species. Different strains of the virus affect specific kinds of animals, and there is a regional incidence associated with rabies. Animals most often associated with the disease include raccoons in the northeastern United States (New York, Connecticut, New Jersey, Maryland, and spreading), coyotes in Texas and the Southwest, foxes in Alaska, and skunks in Kansas. Bats are also often associated with rabies.

There is a spillover from wild animal disease into domestic populations. Pets allowed to roam outdoors are at the greatest risk for contracting rabies, because they are most likely to encounter a rabid animal and become exposed.

RABIES

SYMPTOMS

Refusal to eat or drink, hiding, depression, drooling, throat paralysis and inability to swallow—or vicious, violent behavior, excessive vocalizing, spooky eyes, wobbly rear legs

HOME CARE

None—EXTREMELY CONTAGIOUS TO PEOPLE

VET CARE

None—EUTHANASIA; test brain tissue to confirm diagnosis

PREVENTION

Vaccinate cat, prevent contact with wild animals

Currently, the incidence of rabies is much higher in pet cats than in pet dogs, probably because only about 4 percent of owned cats in the United States receive VACCINATIONS for rabies compared with about 40 percent of owned dogs. Close association with at-risk pets places owners at risk as well.

Rabies is spread by direct contact with an infected animal, usually through a bite that introduces virus-laden saliva into the wound. Following the bite, the virus multiplies in the tissue, then travels through the nerves to the spinal cord and on to the brain. The time it takes from the bite to the development of symptoms varies from days to years. Signs appear once the virus reaches the brain, and in most cases, this incubation period happens within three to eight weeks of the bite. From the brain, the virus spreads to other tissues, like the salivary glands.

All infected animals exhibit behavior changes. Typically, the infected cat stops eating and drinking, and hides. The disease then progresses to one of two forms: paralytic or dumb rabies, and furious rabies.

In the dumb form cats act extremely depressed and sick, and then experience paralysis of the throat and jaw muscles. Such cats drool excessively and can't swallow, and may appear to have something stuck in their throat. They are insensitive to pain. Cats with dumb rabies typically become comatose and die within three to ten days of initial signs.

Cats more commonly exhibit the furious form, and become extremely vicious and violent. They may roam for miles, attacking real and imaginary objects in their path. These cats fear nothing, not even natural enemies, and often chew or swallow foreign objects. Such cats tend to exhibit a blank, spooky, or anxious look. They vocalize a great deal, and owners of stricken cats have also described a wobbly or collapsing gait that affects the rear legs. Progressive paralysis results in death within four to seven days after onset of these signs.

There is no cure for rabies; once signs appear, the animal or person will die. Therefore, all pets should be protected with a rabies vaccination. Even indoor cats are at risk; a rabid animal could enter the house through a pet door, chimney, or open window and infect the pet, or an indoor cat can be exposed when he escapes outside. Because of the human health risk (see ZOONOSIS), some states require by law rabies vaccination of cats and dogs.

Rabies diagnosis requires microscopic examination of the brain tissue of the suspect animal, which cannot be done while the animal is alive. Wild animals that attack humans or pets should be euthanized immediately, and the brain examined for evidence of rabies. If your cat is bitten by a wild animal that cannot be tested for the disease, the cat should be considered exposed to rabies.

The rules regarding rabies exposure in pets vary from state to state. It's believed that animals are infectious only shortly before and during the time they show symptoms. If a biting animal was infective at the time of the bite, it usually exhibits signs of rabies within a ten-day period, which is the recommended period of quarantine in such cases.

But as the handling of potentially infected animals poses such a high human risk, it's usually recommended that unvaccinated dogs and cats exposed to rabies be euthanized and their brains examined for the disease. Depending on individual county and state laws, it's possible that exposed pets may be allowed to live under stringent quarantine for six months and, if no signs develop, vaccinated prior to release. Recommendations for pets current on rabies vaccination that are exposed to the disease include immediate revaccination, and strict owner control/observation for no less than forty-five days.

Avoid exposure for your cats and yourself by keeping cats indoors and providing them with proper protective vaccinations. Contact with wild animals exhibiting abnormal behavior, including STRAY or FERAL cats, puts you and your pet at risk. If you or your pet is bitten by such an animal, seek immediate medical evaluation.

Several states are conducting vaccination programs designed to immunize populations of wild animals to create "immune barriers" to slow or prevent the spread of the disease. Typically, vaccine-laced bait that the animal eats is seeded in rabies-prone areas.

The rabies virus can be killed by simple household detergents and soaps. Thoroughly wash bite wounds with soap and hot water as a first aid, then consult a doctor immediately. Also, there is a postexposure vaccine available for humans that is virtually 100 percent effective when administered within the right period of time.

Reading Food Labels

Pet foods are subject to national, state, and local regulations, including compliance with the Food and Drug Administration (FDA), the Federal Trade Commission (FTC), the U.S. Department of Agriculture (USDA), and State Feed Control Laws developed by the Association of American Feed Control Officials (AAFCO). These regulations cover everything from what goes into the food to how it's distributed, sold, and even labeled. Reading and understanding food labels allows cat owners to choose the best product for their cat's needs.

All pet foods must disclose on their labels a guaranteed analysis, a list of ingredients, and a statement and validation of adequacy. Research continues to refine the definition of exactly what the cat's nutritional needs are. The most recent feline nutrient profiles were determined by a panel of feline nutrition experts from the FDA, academia, and industry, and were adopted as the industry standard by AAFCO in 1992. Reputable cat-food manufacturers follow the AAFCO nutrient profiles or nutritional standards based on other research to formulate their foods.

The principal display panel of the label identifies the product by specifying the brand and product name. It states the total amount of food in the package, and may include a nutritional claim. Finally, the words *cat food* or a similar designation must appear prominently on the label.

But even such food names are regulated. Flavors are allowed to be identified in the name only if there's enough for the cat to actually recognize that flavor. Meat, poultry, or fish must make up at least 25 percent of a product for that ingredient to become part of the product name. A modifier, like beef "cakes," or liver "dinner," may also be used—for example, a food called Kitty-Tom's Fish Dinner indicates that fish makes up at least 25 percent of the product. The same name *without* the modifier means the food contains at least 95 percent of that ingredient—for example, Kitty-Tom's Chicken Cat Food indicates that chicken comprises at least 95 percent of the product. "All" or "100 percent" in the product name means the product contains only the named ingredient, with only water, preservatives, flavorings, vitamins, and minerals added.

The information panel includes the guaranteed analysis statement, which lists the minimum levels of crude protein and crude fat, and maximum levels of crude fiber and moisture in the product. "Crude" refers to the amount measured by specific laboratory analysis, not the amount that can be used by the cat.

If the nutritional claim is not on the display panel, it's on the information panel. Cat-food manufacturers may label their products "complete and balanced" only if they meet the AAFCO standards, which must be validated by testing the food in one of two ways:

1. By laboratory chemical analysis or calculation of nutritional values. Products tested in this manner state that "(name of product) is formulated to meet the nutritional levels established by the AAFCO Cat Food Nutrient Profiles for (whatever life stage)."

   However, with this validation, the food is not actually fed to cats to prove it's beneficial to their bodies. Calculation does not determine or ensure digestibility or palatability, and it is a less expensive way for the manufacturer to meet the requirements.

2. Feeding trials that are done to show the food actually benefits the cat. The labels of products tested in this way will say that

"animal feeding tests using AAFCO procedures substantiate that (name of product) provides complete and balanced nutrition for (whatever life stage)."

Feeding trials are time-consuming and expensive, but they are the only way to truly determine the nutritional completeness of a given food. *The best foods for your cats are complete and balanced diets validated through feeding trials that determine palatability and whether the nutrients are actually usable by the cat's body.*

If the food does not say it is complete and balanced, choose another product. So-called gourmet canned foods are often not complete and balanced and contain single-protein-source ingredients; they are intended to be used as supplements to a complete and balanced food and shouldn't be fed exclusively.

Reputable pet-food manufacturers conduct long-term feeding trials to assure nutritional adequacy. These tests may cover growth, adult maintenance, or reproduction stages.

Reproduction tests show the diet is able to maintain the QUEEN through gestation and lactation, and the kittens until about six weeks of age. Growth tests begin with kittens at weaning, and run for about ten weeks to see if the diet will support normal growth. Adult maintenance tests last at least six months, with cats that are at least one year old. An "all life stages" claim is supported by testing the same cat(s) through all stages of reproduction and growth.

Pet-food manufacturers also conduct short-term tests to measure palatability and digestibility of diets. Palatability determines how good the food tastes to the cat by offering the feline choices of food. Digestibility is the difference between what is eaten and what comes out in the feces. Input and output levels are measured to determine how the animal's body is able to use the food.

Labels may also provide a statement of caloric content of the food. Calorie refers to the measure of energy that can be acquired from eating a given food. Labeling calorie content isn't required (except in "lite" diets), but when it appears it must be stated as "kilocalories per Kg of food." Usually it's also stated as "calories per cup of food" or "per can unit."

Dry rations generally contain 1,400 to 2,000 metabolized kilocalories per pound of diet (3,080 to 4,400 Kcal/Kg); semimoist have

1,200 to 1,350 metabolized kilocalories per pound of diet (2,640 to 2,970 Kcal/Kg); and canned rations provide only 375 to 950 metabolized kilocalories per pound of diet (825 to 2,090 Kcal/Kg). Therefore, cats must eat more of a canned food than of a dry diet to obtain the same energy requirements.

The average adult cat requires about 35 kilocalories per pound of body weight each day. Kittens, pregnant or nursing queens, and cats under STRESS have much higher requirements; inactive cats, less. Feeding guidelines are on the label only as a starting point for the amount to feed your cat.

The food label must also include a list of all ingredients used in the food. The ingredients must be listed in decreasing order of the amount present by weight. Therefore, ingredients listed first are used in the greatest amounts; those listed last, in the smallest.

Although ingredient quality can vary from excellent to mediocre, manufacturers aren't allowed to cite the quality of their ingredients.

In general, the ingredient list should have:

1. *One or more protein sources,* listed as one of the first several ingredients;
2. *Carbohydrate source,* such as cereals;
3. *Fat source;* and
4. *Large numbers of trace minerals and vitamin supplements,* which will be toward the bottom of the list.

Water content varies depending on the form of food: dry foods contain 6 to 10 percent moisture; soft-moist foods, 23 to 40 percent moisture; and canned foods, 68 to 78 percent moisture.

Any questions concerning a cat-food product should be directed to the manufacturer or distributor, whose name and address are required to be stated on the label.

The quality of a cat food isn't easy to determine, and the label will not tell you everything about the food. Feeding trials and quality ingredients cost more, which means that more expensive foods tend to offer better nutrition than cheap foods. The reputation of the manufacturer and the manufacturer's history in nutritional research are important when judging the quality of a food. But even a quality diet is worthless if the cat refuses to eat it. Smell, texture, and taste decide whether or not the food will be eaten—and the best judge of such palatability is your cat.

Reproduction

Reproduction refers to the process by which animals create offspring. The age at which a cat becomes sexually mature and able to reproduce varies depending on the cat's health, when he or she was born, and even the breed. Male cats typically reach puberty by nine months of age, and females between seven and twelve months. However, this varies a great deal from cat to cat, with some males not reaching sexual maturity before sixteen months of age. Female cats may experience their first breeding cycle, called estrus or heat, as early as four months of age. But some breeds—for example, Persians—mature later and may not experience their first estrus until they're nearly two years old. Still, the reproductive life of a cat is quite long, with both males and females often able to produce offspring well into their teens. Females are able to produce litters of two to six kittens two or three times a year.

During an estrus cycle, a female becomes sexually receptive to the male and breeding takes place. Again, the length of estrus is quite individual, but on average lasts five to eight days. This receptive period is followed by a "resting" period of three to fourteen days, when the cat is no longer receptive to breeding. Feline estrus occurs seasonally during specific times of the year, and is influenced by the amount of daylight. In the Northern Hemisphere, the feline breeding season generally is February through October. Cats that do not become pregnant continuously cycle in and out of heat during this time.

The period of estrus or heat is distinctive in cats, with felines showing mostly behavioral signs. The cycle begins with one to two days of proestrus, during which time a female becomes more vocal, treads with her hind feet, and becomes excessively affectionate toward people and other cats of both sexes. With full estrus, she howls her readiness for a mate for minutes at a time, rolls about on the floor, and spends most of her time with her bottom in the air and tail held to one side. Male cats are alerted to her receptivity by her behavior and distinctive odor. They mark territory by spraying smelly urine that announces their status as breeding males (see MARKING), defend that territory from other male cats in loud and often violent fights, and breed with the female felines.

Breeding nearly always concludes with pregnancy. Sadly, the births of unwanted, unplanned kittens usually results in the untimely death of those kittens because there are not enough good homes to go around. Thus, the vast majority of pet cats should be surgically sterilized by NEUTERING males and SPAYING females. This removes the reproductive organs and prevents accidental breeding.

Cat breeding involves much more than simply putting two attractive cats together. Feline matchmaking is a science, and the proper selection of cat parents requires a comprehensive knowledge of both feline health and genetics, as well as sufficient resources to defray the cost involved. Planned breeding should be undertaken only by experienced professional breeders.

Before planned breeding, both the male and the female cat should be in optimal health. Medication, worming, and vaccination should be avoided during pregnancy, and therefore must be addressed prior to breeding if possible. This not only protects the health of the QUEEN but also helps protect her kittens during and for a period after birth.

The female signals her readiness to mate by assuming the lordosis position; she crouches before the male cat, bottom in the air, and gives a distinctive cry that stimulates him to mount. He cautiously approaches her from one side, gently grasps the skin of her neck in his teeth, then straddles her as he treads with his rear feet. This prompts the female to arch her back, raising her rump and moving her tail to one side. Once the position is correct, the male begins thrusting, and ejaculates as soon as insertion takes place. Spines on the cat's penis stimulate the release of eggs from the ovaries when the male cat withdraws from the female's vagina.

As he withdraws, the female reacts with a cry or scream, and immediately rolls away from him. She may attack if he doesn't get out of her way quickly enough. The female typically engages in five to ten minutes of rolling, stretching, and licking of her genitals following mating. A single breeding may last up to ten minutes, or be as short as thirty seconds. Another breeding may follow immediately or several hours later. A single pair of cats may breed twenty or more times during the female's receptive period. It's also possible for a single litter to be fathered by more than one male. Ovulation usually occurs within thirty hours of breeding.

Gestation, the length of time between conception and birth, varies somewhat from cat to cat and from breed to breed. Feline pregnancy lasts from sixty-three to sixty-nine days, although Siamese cats typically carry their babies for seventy-one days.

Two to three weeks following conception, the first signs of pregnancy appear when the cat's nipples swell and change from light to rosy pink. Between day seventeen and twenty-five, a veterinarian can detect individual kittens by palpating, or feeling, the pregnant cat's abdomen. The mother cat's tummy won't noticeably thicken until about the fifth or sixth week of pregnancy.

Appropriate nutrition is particularly important for the pregnant cat if the unborn kittens are to mature correctly. Food intake typically increases during this time, but overfeeding and excessive weight gain should be avoided. Provide a high-quality commercial reproduction ration, like an energy-dense kitten food, as recommended by your veterinarian. FOOD SUPPLEMENTS are rarely required.

About two weeks before the birth of her kittens, the queen begins seeking an appropriate place to nest with her babies. A dry, warm, secluded area is preferred. Provide an easily cleaned nesting box for the prospective mother, but be prepared for her to make her own choices, like the sofa or the linen closet. During this time, queens typically rearrange the chosen spot—adjusting linens in the laundry basket or unmaking the bed—in an effort to create an appropriate nest.

Mammary glands begin to develop further a few days prior to queening, or giving birth. The fur on the breasts and genital region of longhaired mothers should be clipped in advance of the birth. During the first stage of labor, which lasts up to six hours, rectal temperature drops from the normal of 100 to 101.5 degrees to 98 or 99 degrees. During this time the queen pants and purrs and seeks an appropriate nest. Once the queen is settled in her nest, leave her alone; disturbing her may stop the labor. Healthy cats rarely have difficulty delivering kittens.

The second stage of labor usually lasts only ten to thirty minutes, and rarely longer than ninety minutes. A vaginal discharge signals imminent birth. Involuntary contractions begin, and soon the queen is fully involved and bearing down to deliver. If the first kitten isn't born within an hour following these strong contractions, take the mother to a veterinarian. Normally, a dark green-gray bubble, which is the placental sac containing the first kitten, begins to emerge from the vagina; it should be fully passed within thirty minutes. Normal kitten presentation can be either tail or face first.

After a kitten is born, the queen cleans herself and consumes the placenta that follows the birth of each kitten, and bites through the umbilical cord. She licks her baby to clean it and to stimulate breathing. The queen may nurse the firstborn for a time before the next kitten's birth. Kittens are usually born fifteen to thirty minutes apart.

A veterinarian's assistance should be sought if no kittens appear after ninety minutes of labor, or if labor stops before all the kittens are born. After the birth, seek veterinary help if the mother appears restless or feverish, ignores her kittens, or if there's BLEEDING or a colored, white, or foul-smelling discharge from the vulva.

The queen doesn't leave her newborns for twenty-four to forty-eight hours following the birth. During this time, she cleans and nurses them. The first milk, called colostrum, provides the kittens with important nutrients and protective antibodies (see IMMUNE SYSTEM). The

A mother and her offspring. (*Photo credit: Ralston Purina Company*)

mother licks their anal region to stimulate the newborns to eliminate, and then consumes their feces and urine.

A newborn kitten should actively squirm and cry. Kittens that feel cold to the touch and move or cry only weakly may be stimulated by massaging them with a dry, warm towel. Kittens that fail to breathe need immediate help. Wrap the baby in a dry, warm cloth and cup him in both hands, keeping his head secure as you swing him downward. This may help clear fluid from his lungs. When the baby begins breathing, give him back to the mother.

If for any reason the queen is unable to feed her babies, supplemental feeding may be necessary. Newborn kittens require feeding every two hours with an appropriate queen's milk replacer (see MILK, AS FOOD).

Nursing continues for up to eight weeks, and during this time the queen also protects and teaches her babies how to be cats. Depending on the time of year, estrus begins again a week or so following weaning.

Respiration

Respiration is defined as breathing. Cats on average breathe at a rate of twenty to thirty respirations each minute—about twice as fast as people. The cat's respiratory system includes the nasal passages of the NOSE, the throat, voice box, windpipe, bronchial tubes, and lungs.

Bronchial tubes are designed in a series of progressively smaller branches, like a tree. They culminate in tiny air sacs within the lung where blood and oxygen exchange occurs. The diaphragm and other muscles of the chest pump air in and out of the lungs.

Normal breathing is even and unhurried. Changes in the respiration rate or breathing sounds can be an indication of a number of feline illnesses and should be addressed by a veterinarian.

An UPPER RESPIRATORY INFECTION can cause obstruction of air passages and result in noisy breathing. Slowed respiration may indicate the presence of POISON. Increased respiration, or panting, typically occurs

RESPIRATORY DISTRESS

SYMPTOMS

Gasping, panting, slowed breathing; pale or blue color to lips, gums, or tongue; loss of consciousness

HOME CARE

Remove blockage from mouth (if present) and/or artificial respiration; SEE VETERINARIAN ASAP

VET CARE

Address the underlying cause, possibly oxygen therapy

PREVENTION

Prevent poisoning, electrical shock, or other traumas that can cause breathing problems

after exertion and is a way for the cat to cool off. But prolonged labored panting can be a sign of heatstroke (see HYPERTHERMIA).

Wheezing is the sound air makes when forced through narrowed or constricted breathing tubes. This sound is typical of cats suffering from ASTHMA, but may also indicate cancerous growths in the airways.

Pain due to rib FRACTURE, ELECTRICAL SHOCK, or other conditions causes the cat to breathe in shallow, quick breaths to keep from moving too much. Fluid in the chest, called pleural effusion, also results in shallow breathing.

Cats rarely cough, and when they do it's usually a sign of a problem. Coughing may be the cat's attempt to clear swallowed hair or even a SWALLOWED OBJECT from his throat. It can also be an indication of bronchitis or HEARTWORM DISEASE.

Restraint

Restraint, as it applies to cats, involves restricting feline movement for the purpose of medication or transportation, while preventing injury to the cat or the person handling the cat. Any cat that is in PAIN or frightened may become violent and cause injury to himself or the person attempting to help him. The amount of restraint necessary depends on the individual circumstances, the competence of the cat handler, and the personality of the cat.

As a general rule, cats resent being forced to do anything. Restrict the cat only as much and as long as necessary to accomplish what needs to be done. Gentle, sure, and firm movements are how you should best handle your cat.

Never swoop down on your cat without warning. Sudden or rough handling tends to frighten cats. Prepare in advance, gathering all necessary equipment and medication ahead of time so that you know what you're doing and are not rushed.

Your goal is to avoid the cat's teeth and claws. Two people are advisable when administering medication—one restrains while the other attends the cat. Use one hand to firmly grasp the loose skin at the back of the cat's neck, called the scruff, and use the other hand to enclose both of the cat's hind legs above the hock. Then gently stretch the cat out on his side and have the other party administer the medication.

For those owners who may be required to restrain and medicate a cat all by themselves, simply grasping the cat's scruff and gently pressing him flat to the table with one hand may, depending on the cat, be all that's needed while you medicate with the other hand.

Commercial mesh cat bags or feline muzzles that cover the mouth and eyes are also helpful for immobilizing a cat for treatment. Unfortunately, it may be just as difficult to get the cat into the bag or muzzle as it is to perform the actual treatment. And the more you fuss with a cat, the more agitated and difficult to handle he usually becomes.

One of the simplest and best ways to restrain a cat is simply to wrap him in a blanket or large towel while leaving the treatment area on his body uncovered. Drop the fabric over the cat, covering his entire body, and wrap him up. Be sure to allow him breathing space. Many times, the cat calms down and stops struggling once his movement is restricted. The cat can then be carried or placed in a high-sided box or carrier for transportation.

Ringworm

Ringworm is not a worm; it is a fungal infection of growing hair, dry skin, and, sometimes, the nails. There are many types, but about 95 percent of feline ringworm cases are caused by *Microsporum canis*, hereafter designated as *M. canis*. The condition also affects dogs and people (see ZOONOSIS).

Ringworm is a kind of biological contact dermatitis in which skin inflammation is caused by a substance produced by the fungus. The inflammation makes the skin inhospitable for the fungus, so it moves on to greener pastures. In people, the fungus grows outward, away from the initial central inflammation in ever-widening rings, leaving the center to heal. The name "ringworm" comes from the ringlike lesions typically seen in human cases.

In cats, sores also grow outward from the infection, but rarely produce the ring pattern found in people. Ringworm in cats can look like a variety of other feline skin diseases, but hair loss is the most usual sign. Bald patches may develop in only one area, affect several spots, or cover the entire body. Ringworm is the most common cause of hair loss in kittens.

The fungus, called a dermatophyte, lives only on hairs that are actively growing. Infected hairs eventually break off rather than fall out, leaving a stubby appearance to the coat. Mild to severe scaling or crusty sores typically develop, with varying degrees of itchiness.

Cats are usually infected by coming in contact with infected hair, but ringworm can also be spread by contact with contaminated grooming equipment or from the environment. Contaminated hairs that are shed into the environment can remain infective for months, and provide a reservoir for reinfection of recovering cats.

RINGWORM

SYMPTOMS

Hair loss, skin inflammation

HOME CARE

After veterinary diagnosis, miconazole preparations or lime sulfur dips; environmental treatment by thorough vacuuming and cleaning surfaces daily with bleach and water solutions

VET CARE

Culture hairs to diagnose, prescribe antifungal medication (griseofulvin) or possibly use ringworm vaccination therapy to treat skin disease

PREVENTION

Avoid contact with contagious pets, thoroughly clean infected environment

All cats can get ringworm, and the length of haircoat has nothing to do with the risk. Both longhaired and shorthaired cats are equally affected. However, the most common victims are immune-compromised, young, and debilitated pets. Puppies and kittens are affected most frequently. Some cats carry the organism without showing signs themselves, and spread ringworm to other cats and pets. If one pet in the household is diagnosed, all should be treated whether they are showing signs or not.

Ringworm in cats is diagnosed by identifying the fungus. The veterinarian may use a Wood's Lamp to screen suspect cases; about half of M. canis cases will "glow" when exposed to its ultraviolet light. More cases are identified using a culture test that grows the ringworm fungus. A sample of debris brushed from the cat's skin and fur is placed in a special medium designed to grow certain ringworm species. It may take up to three weeks before the test shows a positive result.

During treatment, infective animals should be kept in QUARANTINE from those not showing symptoms. Otherwise healthy cats tend to self-cure in sixty to a hundred days; treatment depends on the severity of the disease and the people at risk for exposure. People who are immune compromised, very young, or very old are at highest risk.

Shaving ringworm-infected cats to aid treatment is no longer routinely recommended, and may cause lesions to worsen. Recent studies also show that human products like athlete's foot preparations don't work. Neither do topical bleach solutions, captan, or ketoconazole shampoos.

Topical preparations of miconazole are helpful, but medicating the lesion before diagnosis may interfere with proper diagnosis. Lime sulfur dip (LymDyp) is extremely effective for treating feline ringworm but smells like rotten eggs; the cat must wear an Elizabethan collar until dry to prevent possible reactions to ingestion. Treat only after your veterinarian diagnoses the condition, and follow his or her recommendation.

An oral drug called griseofulvin (Fulvicin) is also effective in treating feline ringworm. After ingestion, the drug is incorporated into the growing hair where it slows the growth of the fungus. Pills are usually given for four to eight weeks, and should be continued two weeks beyond disappearance of symptoms.

However, griseofulvin may cause birth defects when given to pregnant cats, and a small number of cats show drug reactions ranging from a temporary loss of appetite to bone marrow suppression. There's no way to predict which cats will be adversely affected, and veterinarians watch for warning signs in order to prevent problems. A drug called itraconazole is another option for cats sensitive to griseofulvin. A relatively new vaccine is also available that is currently being used to treat cats that already have skin disease caused by M. canis infection.

Ringworm fungus can live in the environment for well over a year, and can continuously reinfect cats. For that reason, the infected environment must also be treated; however, fungal spores are difficult to eliminate. Studies indicate that common disinfectants like chlorhexidine and water are not effective. Concentrated bleach or one percent formalin (a formaldehyde solution) have been shown to be effective, but neither is very practical in a home environment.

Daily cleaning of all surfaces using a diluted bleach solution (one part bleach to ten parts water), along with thorough vacuuming, is the most effective and practical environmental treatment for most cat owners. Dispose of the vacuum bag by sealing it in a plastic garbage sack and removing it from the house.

Rodent Ulcer

See EOSINOPHILIC GRANULOMA COMPLEX.

Roundworms

The roundworm (an ascaridoid nematode) is an intestinal parasite found in almost all kittens. The species *Toxocara cati* most commonly affects cats; they are often passed in the stool or vomited, and look like masses of spaghetti.

Kittens usually acquire roundworms from nursing the mother cat's milk. Cats also contract the parasite by swallowing infective larvae found in the environment, or by eating an infected host like a mouse.

The larvae travel from the cat's stomach into the bloodstream, and on to the lungs. From there, they migrate into the windpipe and may cause the cat to cough. After again being swallowed, the parasites mature into one- to three-inch-long adults that live in the intestines. Mature worms mate and lay eggs, which pass with the stool. These eggs develop into infective larvae, completing the cycle.

Roundworms are rarely life-threatening, but massive infestations may result in intestinal damage or, rarely, bowel obstruction. More typically, they interfere with digestion. Affected animals often have a pot-bellied appearance, a dull coat, diarrhea, or mucus in the stool. Seeing the worms coiled in the feces or vomit is diagnostic, but usually diagnosis is made when the veterinarian identifies eggs during microscopic examination of a stool sample.

Liquid oral medication given in two doses two weeks apart is the

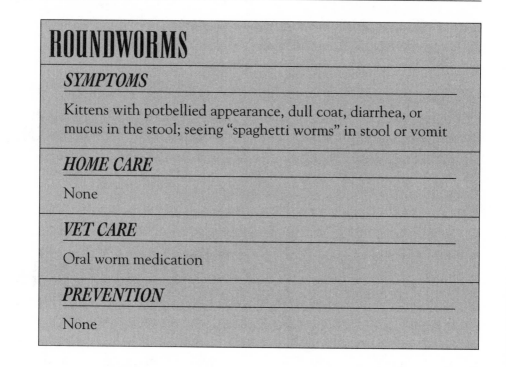

ROUNDWORMS

SYMPTOMS

Kittens with potbellied appearance, dull coat, diarrhea, or mucus in the stool; seeing "spaghetti worms" in stool or vomit

HOME CARE

None

VET CARE

Oral worm medication

PREVENTION

None

standard treatment for roundworms. Pyrantel, fenbendazole, and febantel are all quite effective, and are considered safe enough to use in three- to four-week-old kittens.

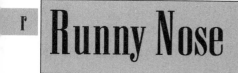

Runny Nose

See NOSE and UPPER RESPIRATORY INFECTIONS.

Salmonella

Salmonella is a kind of bacteria that is found naturally in the environment and in most animals. It can cause a variety of illnesses from diarrheal disease to life-threatening illness. Cats almost never become sick from salmonella; those that do are usually kittens, or adults stressed by other illness, and signs include DIARRHEA, fever, VOMITING, loss of appetite, depression, and "hunching" from abdominal pain. However, many healthy cats carry the bacteria without becoming ill, and they may intermittently shed the bacteria in their feces. This is important, because people can become infected with salmonella as well.

Cats contract the bacteria most commonly by eating food contaminated with infected bird or rodent droppings, or eating raw or undercooked meat. The condition is diagnosed from signs of illness, and from finding the bacteria in the feces, blood, or tissues of the affected cat. When ENTERITIS is the primary problem, treatment usually consists of fluid therapy. Antibiotic therapy is rarely used, because it may encourage the development of antibiotic-resistant strains of the bacteria.

To protect your cat from contracting salmonella, keep the cat indoors. Cats that eat rodents or other wildlife are at much greater risk. Keep the LITTER BOX clean and dispose of fecal material promptly. Don't feed your cat undercooked or raw meat or table scraps. And to protect yourself, always wash your hands after cleaning the litter box. When your cat is ill, wash your hands often after handling the cat, and

SALMONELLA

SYMPTOMS

Diarrhea

HOME CARE

None

VET CARE

Fluid therapy

PREVENTION

Don't feed raw/undercooked meats, prevent cat from eating wildlife

use dilute chlorine bleach and water to disinfect surfaces the cat frequents and any toys and food or water dishes.

Scent

See NOSE.

Scratching

Scratching, as it applies to cats, refers to scraping or scoring objects with the CLAWS. Cats use both front and rear claws to scratch them-

Cats score objects with their claws. *(Photo credit: Betsy Stowe)*

selves in response to skin irritation or as a part of GROOMING. They use front claws to scratch objects. Animal behaviorists believe cats scratch objects primarily as a function of COMMUNICATION; scratching leaves scent behind on the object, as well as visible marks, and both communicate that the cat has been there. It also conditions claws and tones muscles.

Scratching is normal cat behavior. Typically, the cat stretches forward as far as he can reach, extends his claws, and repeatedly draws them through or against the object's surface, back toward himself. This leaves visible scores on hard objects, and shreds or tatters softer materials. Scratching can become a destructive behavior when inappropriate objects in the home, such as the piano or sofa, are the cat's target.

Because scratching is innate, it's nearly impossible to prevent. In many cases, however, the behavior can be modified and redirected to more appropriate scratching surfaces. It is more difficult, though, to alter established habits than to prevent them from developing in the first place.

Probably the best approach is to offer the cat a scratching alternative while making forbidden objects less attractive. Cover forbidden horizontal surfaces with cat-repellent materials like heavy plastic runners, nub side up. For vertical objects, such as drapes or upholstered furniture backs, try plastic shelf paper that has adhesive on both sides. The plastic surface is a turnoff, and the sticky surface is singularly distasteful to the cat.

A variety of commercial scratching posts are available that give the cat adequate scratching opportunities. Cats are attracted to specific structures, surface textures, and locations. Observe your cat and take into account his past targets to determine his scratching tastes.

Most cats prefer scratching vertical objects, but some like horizontal surfaces. Whatever the choice, it must be tall enough or long enough to accommodate the cat's full-length stretch, and so stable it does not slide about the floor or tip over when the cat assaults it. Cats tend to prefer flat surfaces with corners that can also be scratched, rather than round posts without edges.

Texture preference varies from cat to cat, and is critical in determining whether the cat will scratch the item or not. Since one purpose of scratching is to leave visible marks, cats seem to prefer easily shredded material like loosely woven cloth coverings. This may be why cats snub posts with nubby, tightly woven fabric that catches claws, and instead return time and again to the sofa back.

The covering on a well-scratched post shouldn't be changed too often. Leaving the tattered material in place will keep a cat returning for more. If your cat is choosing a table leg or door frame, a harder scratching post surface such as tree bark may be more appropriate for your pet. Many cats like sisal coverings. And some commercial posts provide two or more surface types that satisfy both grooming and marking urges.

Prime scratching times are after meals and naps, and some cats use scratching as a greeting ritual. Cats can often be enticed to scratch posts located near food bowls, a favorite sleeping area, or a doorway. Because scratching marks are visual signals meant to be seen, the cat prefers to scratch in high-traffic areas and will ignore a commercial scratching post that's hidden away in a back room.

When redirecting scratch behavior, situate the replacement object directly in front of the damaged area on the forbidden item. You can gradually move the new scratching object to a more convenient location once the cat has switched his scratching allegiance.

For some cats, making the forbidden object distasteful by aversive training, such as with a water squirt, while providing an irresistible new alternative is enough to reduce or totally eliminate destructive scratching behavior. Other times, the cat needs encouragement to do the right thing.

However, cats dislike being forced to do anything, so carrying your pet to the object and physically rubbing his paws on it may not sit well with him. The most important and basic principle regarding cat training is this simple rule: *Let the cat think it's his idea.*

Rubbing catnip over the new post entices some cats. Other times, draw a cat's attention with a string or feather, drag it right up to and upon the scratching object, and let him sink in his claws when he captures the toy. Initially tipping a vertical post on its side and enticing the cat to climb aboard may get the message across when he feels the texture beneath his paws. The sound and sight of you scratching the surface with your own nails may also entice the cat to scratch. Reward spontaneous scratching with praise and petting.

Eliminate or reduce inappropriate scratching by remote correction techniques. Some behaviorists advocate the use of water squirted from a distance or a tossed soft toy that startles the cat out of the action. When this is done correctly, the cat doesn't connect the owner to the event, but associates a wet tail with scratching the inappropriate object.

Use voice reprimands with care; some cats do stop scratching when an owner shames them, but this could result in the cat waiting until you're not watching to sneak-scratch the preferred yet inappropriate object. Physical punishment rarely if ever works, and instead can make the cat fearful of you, and further STRESS him when his natural urges to scratch are thwarted.

Products like soft plastic nail coverings are an option for some hardcase cats. They are designed to attach to claws with a nontoxic adhesive. The plastic nail covers help reduce the damage claws otherwise inflict.

If you have tried everything and your cat still indulges in destructive behavior, consult with your veterinarian about surgically DECLAWING the cat. Although far from an ideal solution, declawing is preferable to getting rid of the cat.

S

Season

See REPRODUCTION.

Sexing

Determining a cat's gender is called sexing the cat, and is generally easily done in adult felines. Young kittens may be more difficult to identify, particularly longhaired varieties where fur tends to hide the clues.

To sex the kitten, simply lift the tail. By about eight to ten weeks of age, males should have visible testicles. Even before this, the genitals of male and female kittens are quite different upon examination. The male's urethra and rectum configuration resemble a colon (the urethral opening is round), while the female's looks more like an upside-down exclamation mark (the urethral opening is a slit).

S Shedding

Shedding is the normal loss of hair that occurs when new hair pushes the loose, old hairs out. The amount of the cat's exposure to artificial light or daylight—not the temperature—determines how much and when a cat will shed her coat.

The more exposure a cat has to light, the greater the amount she will shed. Indoor cats often shed year-round, while outdoor cats living in the northeastern United States typically shed seasonally for many weeks when daylight increases during late spring.

A cat's fur grows between one-quarter to one-third of an inch each day, with the most activity occurring in the summer and the least in the winter. This growth rate is not continuous, though. Hair grows in cycles, beginning with a period of rapid growth in the spring, followed by slower growth, and then ending in a resting stage. Mature hairs loosen in the follicles during this winter resting phase. In the spring, another cycle of hair growth begins, and new hair pushes the old out, resulting in shedding.

Cat hair is more easily pulled out during the winter resting period. During this time period, any episode of fright or stress may result in a sudden shed. That's because these emotions activate specialized muscles found along the cat's back and tail that are attached to the hair and cause it to stand on end when the cat is agitated. When the hair is already loose, these muscles literally pull the hair out.

The cat's hair grows and is shed in an irregular pattern. As the thick, woolly undercoat falls out, the cat may look moth-eaten. To help prevent skin problems and HAIRBALLS, groom the cat regularly, paying particular attention during shedding season (see GROOMING).

Shock

Shock is the collapse of the circulatory system. Shock usually results from trauma associated with burns, crushing injuries, or profound dehydration. Common causes of shock include trauma from being hit by cars or falling (see HIGH-RISE SYNDROME), HYPERTHERMIA, severe VOMITING or DIARRHEA, DEHYDRATION, and excessive BLEEDING.

Due to a decrease in blood volume or a collapse of the blood vessels, the heart can't adequately move the blood, and the tissues of the body become starved for oxygen. The body attempts to compensate by shutting down normal blood flow to nonvital areas. But as the organs become more and more oxygen-starved, they start to fail. This creates a vicious cycle that intensifies the shock. Left untreated, the cat will die.

Signs of shock include mental depression or loss of consciousness, a drop in temperature until the body feels cold to the touch, weakness, shivering, pale gums, shallow rapid breathing, and a faint but rapid

S

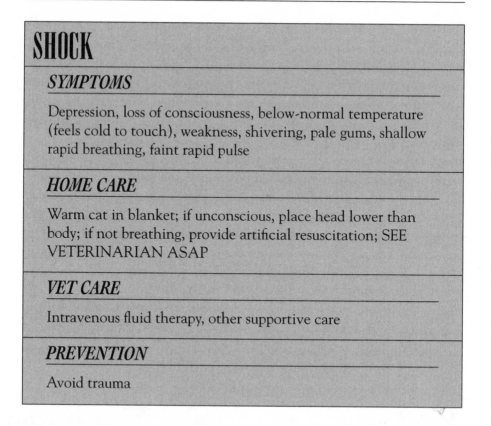

SHOCK

SYMPTOMS

Depression, loss of consciousness, below-normal temperature (feels cold to touch), weakness, shivering, pale gums, shallow rapid breathing, faint rapid pulse

HOME CARE

Warm cat in blanket; if unconscious, place head lower than body; if not breathing, provide artificial resuscitation; SEE VETERINARIAN ASAP

VET CARE

Intravenous fluid therapy, other supportive care

PREVENTION

Avoid trauma

PULSE greater than 240 beats per minute. Cases of shock must be treated as soon as possible by the veterinarian.

First aid includes keeping the cat warm by wrapping him in a blanket. If he's conscious, let him assume the most comfortable position. Speak calmly to soothe him. When he is unconscious, keep his head lower than his body to improve circulation to the brain. Check that he is breathing, and pull his tongue clear of the mouth to keep the airway open.

If he's not breathing or has no heartbeat, begin artificial respiration or CARDIOPULMONARY RESUSCITATION. Stabilize apparent FRACTURES, address bleeding with pressure, and then get the cat to the veterinarian as soon as possible. The ideal treatment is efficiently and quickly rehydrating the cat using intravenous fluids.

Skin

The skin is the largest organ in the body, and in cats it is much thinner than in most other animals. Skin acts as a protective barrier that insulates the cat's body from extremes of temperature and prevents the escape of moisture and the invasion of foreign agents like toxins or bacteria. The outer layer, called the epidermis, contains the pigment that screens the body from the harmful rays of the sun and gives the cat his distinctive color. The second layer, called the dermis, contains the nerve tissues and SWEAT GLANDS. The dermis supports the hair follicles that generate the root of each hair, and are adjacent to a pressure-sensitive pad that responds to TOUCH.

The furless paw pads and nose leather are the most sensitive surface areas of the cat's body. Therefore, the cat typically uses paw taps to test an object's relative safety.

The NOSE and muzzle area also are particularly sensitive to TEMPERATURE, able to detect variations of only a degree or two. Newborn KITTENS use this ability to seek warmth, using their heat-seeking muzzles to find their mother or siblings.

Skunk Encounters

S

Cats that are allowed outdoors may encounter wildlife of the smelly kind: skunks. When bothered by a curious feline, the skunk does what comes naturally, and sprays its own brand of defense on the offending cat.

The only thing you can do to get rid of the odor is bathe the skunked cat. It may take several sudsings and rinsings to be effective, but persevere. Your cat's normal pet shampoo will work, but there are more effective treatments available.

Pet stores often offer commercial products that help neutralize

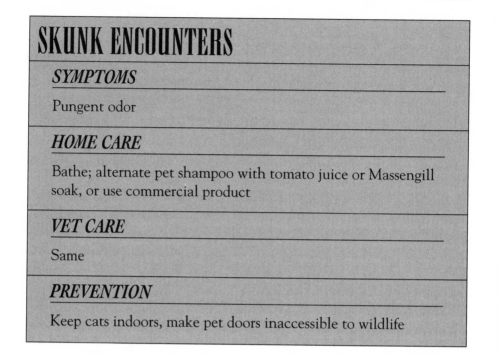

SKUNK ENCOUNTERS

SYMPTOMS

Pungent odor

HOME CARE

Bathe; alternate pet shampoo with tomato juice or Massengill soak, or use commercial product

VET CARE

Same

PREVENTION

Keep cats indoors, make pet doors inaccessible to wildlife

skunk odor. A home remedy that seems quite effective is tomato juice; wash the cat first with pet shampoo, towel him dry, then douse him with the juice and let it soak as long as the cat stands still. Then rinse him off and suds him again with the regular shampoo. Alternate the tomato juice soak with the shampoo bath until he's less pungent.

Some groomers recommend using Massengill brand douche as an odor-absorbing soak. Mix two ounces of the douche to a gallon of water, pour over the washed cat, and let soak for at least fifteen minutes. Then bathe with normal shampoo once more.

You can avoid the problem by preventing skunk encounters. Keep your cat indoors, or supervise outdoor excursions. If you want to have a pet door, provide those doors that only allow your cat access so that varmints don't come into your home.

S

Sleep

Cats spend two-thirds of their life, sixteen hours or more each day, sleeping. That's more than any other mammal, except for the opossum and some bats.

We don't know why cats sleep so much, but one theory is that predators that have few natural enemies can afford to sleep for longer periods of time. Others hypothesize that the need for sleep increases in direct proportion to the amount of energy required. Being a predator, the cat has extraordinary energy needs for hunting.

The sleep activity of cats, like that of people and many other mammals, is characterized by two patterns of brain activity. This activity has been measured experimentally with an electroencephalograph (EEG), a special instrument that records waves or pulses of activity on a graph.

When awake, the cat's brain broadcasts little, bunched-together, irregular peaks. The brain activity of the dozing cat, though, produces long, irregular waves called slow-wave sleep, which usually last fifteen to thirty minutes total. As he dozes, a cat generally lies with his head raised and paws tucked beneath him. Sometimes he actually sleeps sitting up, in which case his muscles stiffen to hold him upright. This way he's ready to spring into action should it be necessary.

When the feline moves from light to deeper sleep, his body relaxes; he stretches out, and rolls onto his side. His brain patterns also change; they become smaller and closer together—in fact, quite similar to waking patterns. However, the cat is fully relaxed and very difficult to awaken during this deep sleep, which is referred to by experts as "rapid sleep" because of the quick movement of the brain waves. This phase typically lasts only about five minutes, then the cat returns to slow-wave sleep, and thereafter alternates between the two until he wakes up. Rather than alternating types of sleep, kittens fall directly into deep rapid sleep until they are about a month old. Cat dreams are born during this rapid sleep.

The cat's senses continue to record sounds and scents during up to 70 percent of sleep. This allows a cat to awaken at the drop of a hat— or the squeak of a mouse.

S

More leisurely awakenings, however, are followed by a nearly ritualistic program of blinking, yawning, and stretching. First the forelegs, then the back, and finally the rear legs, each in turn, are flexed. Most cats then spend a few minutes getting their fur back in proper shape by GROOMING themselves.

Unlike humans, who sleep long hours at a stretch and usually at night, cats typically take short and long naps throughout the day. Individual sleeping habits vary, but very old and very young cats sleep more than healthy adults, and sleep time tends to increase on cold or rainy days. Conversely, when love is in the air, cats may sleep less in the pursuit of romance.

Cats tend to adapt to the people in their lives, sleeping when the owner is gone and spending awake time with you when you are home. Like their ancestors, cats are most active at daybreak and sundown.

Smoke Inhalation

See ARTIFICIAL RESPIRATION.

Socialization

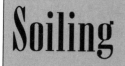

See KITTEN.

Soiling

Soiling refers to inappropriate elimination. Cats are normally fastidious in their bathroom habits, and refusing to use the litter box generally can be linked to some underlying cause. Urinating or defecating outside the litter box can be a sign of health problems like CYSTITIS, DIABETES MELLITUS, KIDNEY DISEASE, or LOWER URINARY TRACT DISEASE. Cats may lose litter box training because they physically can't control their bowels or urinary bladder, or because pain from a medical condition is associated with the litter box. So check with your veterinarian to rule out a medical cause.

Soiling is often confused with territorial MARKING, which is a dominance display usually of intact male cats. A change in the cat's normal routine, such as the addition of a pet, moving to a new home, or a change in the owner's work schedule, may prompt marking behavior in cats who are under STRESS and trying to bring their world back under control.

Cats also may snub their toilet if the litter material, the box itself, the location of the box, or its hygiene is not satisfactory. The cat's bathroom must be as attractive to the cat as possible, or bathroom habits will become hit or miss at best (see LITTER and LITTER BOX).

Cats do not like to eliminate in the same area where they eat. Strong-smelling deodorants used around the box or incorporated in the litter itself may cause cats to find another place. Remember, the cat's sense of smell is infinitely more sensitive than our own. A smelly toilet is the quickest way to train a cat to ignore proper bathroom behavior. Avoid ammonia-containing cleaners, which tend to intensify the smell of urine.

Any change in the placement of the toilet, or of the type of litter itself, can turn off the cat. Also, some cats require privacy when they use the bathroom, so placing the box in a high-traffic area may prompt deposits in more creative, hidden locations.

Be sure to thoroughly clean soiled areas of carpet with a commercial product designed for that purpose. If the scent is not eliminated, the cat may return to the scene of the crime and repeat the offense.

You may need to temporarily confine the cat if the soiling continues. Unless ill, a cat will not soil the area where he sleeps, so placing him in a very small room or cage with the litter box should prompt him to do the right thing. Once he's regularly filling the box, you can gradually increase house privileges. When dealing with more than one cat, or a small cat in a large area, more than one litter box can be helpful.

Spaying

Spaying is an ovariohysterectomy, a surgical procedure that removes the female cat's reproductive organs. Spaying prevents the births of unwanted kittens and eliminates or reduces the chances of health problems like PYOMETRA and obnoxious heat behavior. Sexually intact female felines also have seven times the risk of mammary CANCER than those that are spayed.

Cats should be spayed before reaching sexual maturity in order to reap the greatest health and behavior rewards. Individual cats and breeds mature at different rates—even the time of year influences the timing—but many cats are able to reproduce by the age of six months or even younger. The American Veterinary Medical Association (AVMA) currently recommends that female felines be spayed at four months of age.

Veterinarians prefer to perform the surgery when the cat is not in heat, because during estrus the reproductive organs engorge with blood, which slightly increases the risk of BLEEDING. But during breeding season it may be hard to avoid estrus, and postponement can result in unwanted kittens. If the cat is already bred, the procedure can still be done, but pregnancy slightly increases the cost and surgical risk. Surgery is also more complicated when the cat is nursing kittens. Consult with your veterinarian to determine the best schedule for your cat.

Surgery is performed while the cat is under a general ANESTHETIC. Most practitioners prefer that the cat abstain from eating or drinking for a period prior to surgery to avoid the risk of inhaling vomit while asleep. Tell the veterinarian if your cat eats something before the surgery, so that appropriate precautions can be taken.

Both injectable and inhalant anesthetics may be used, alone or in combination, and many practices offer preanesthetic blood work to help determine which anesthetic is best for your cat. Spaying a female cat is major abdominal surgery, and is a longer procedure than castrating a male cat. Inhalant anesthetics are usually used. Gas anesthesia is administered either through a mask that fits over the cat's face, or through an endotracheal tube inserted into the cat's mouth and down

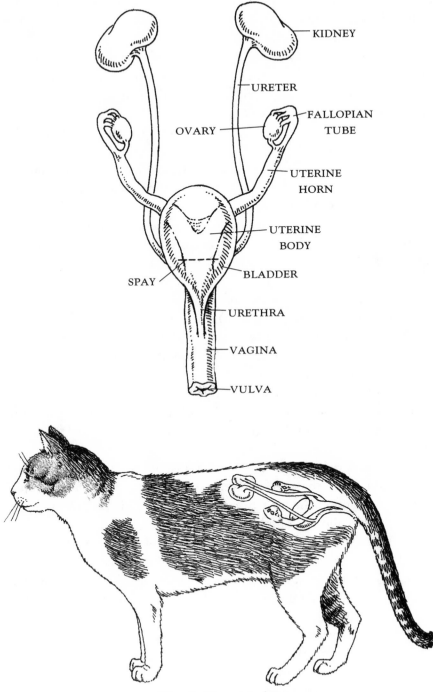

Female Urogenital Tract

the throat and into the lungs. The dosage for an inhalant anesthetic can be adjusted during surgery, and the cat awakens quickly after the anesthesia is stopped.

The sleeping cat is positioned on her back, usually on a towel or heating pad to keep her warm during the surgery. The sleeping cat's stomach is then shaved and disinfected with antiseptic soap solutions. Depending on the individual case, respiratory and cardiac monitors, or even EKG machines, may be used to monitor the cat during the procedure.

A small slit in a sterile drape is positioned over the cat's tummy. The surgery is performed through this opening in the drape, which helps keep the surgical field sterile.

An inch-long incision is made in the skin of the cat's shaved abdomen, usually just below the belly button and along the midline. A scalpel cuts through surface skin, a thin layer of fat, and then the abdominal wall. Special instruments hold the incision open so the surgeon can see into the cat's abdomen.

The cat's uterus is shaped like a Y with an ovary attached to the top of each "horn." An ovarian artery, vein, and nerve are attached to each ovary. The spay hook—a long, smooth metal instrument—is inserted into the abdomen to retrieve the uterus.

Each ovary is secured with stainless-steel hemoclips or an absorbable suture material to prevent bleeding, then is cut free in turn. The stumps containing the artery, vein, and nerve fall back into the abdomen.

Next the uterus is ligated, or tied off, just ahead of the cervix, then cut free just beyond the tie. The uterus and ovaries are discarded. Once the surgeon inspects the area to ensure that there is no bleeding, the uterine stump is allowed to fall back into the abdomen.

The incision is stitched closed in three layers. Internal stitches are often absorbable material that the cat's body eventually dissolves, or they may be metal suture material or even staples. The last layer, the surface skin, is stitched using tiny individual loops that are separately knotted. A routine spay is completed in fifteen to twenty-five minutes.

Recovery time varies depending on the anesthetic used. Cats are moved from the surgery table to a recovery area where they're kept warm and monitored as they wake up. The drugs may cause the cat to appear a bit drunk for a time. Sometimes the cat is kept overnight, while other times the cat is up and ready to go home within a few hours.

Most cats don't bother their stitches, but you should monitor the area to be sure your cat isn't the exception. Try to keep your cat's calisthenics to a minimum for a couple of days following the procedure. Stitches are removed in a week to ten days following the surgery, and outdoor cats should remain inside until after the stitches are out.

Complications are rare, and usually a bit of inflammation at the incision site is the worst that happens. Bleeding or swelling of the incision line, loss of appetite for more than twenty-four hours, or prolonged listlessness should be addressed by the veterinarian.

Spraying

See MARKING.

Steatitis

See YELLOW FAT DISEASE.

Stomatitis

Stomatitis is an inflammation and/or infection of the mouth. The condition can lead to dental problems like PERIODONTAL DISEASE. Stomatitis is often associated with infections of FELINE IMMUNODEFICIENCY VIRUS.

Stray

A stray is a once-owned cat separated from his home who must fend for himself. Stray cats exhibit a wide range of behaviors. Those treated well by owners in the past often seek human companionship. When there is a history of mistreatment or if the cat is injured, ill, or emotionally traumatized, extreme shyness is usually the norm.

Cats become strays when they are somehow parted from their owners. Perhaps an indoor cat accidentally slips outside and is chased far from home by a dog. Other times, an outdoor cat may learn he's fed by

Strays can make excellent pets, but approach the animal with care. (*Photo credit: Amy D. Shojai*)

FINDING YOUR LOST CAT OR THE STRAY'S OWNER

1. Monitor local lost-and-found advertisements for not less than a month
2. Contact area shelters and give them a description of the cat
3. Take area shelters a photo of the cat
4. Distribute posters around the neighborhood (with or without photo)
5. Check veterinary offices, pet stores, the post office, and community bulletin boards for lost-and-found notices; leave your own notice

several homeowners when he wanders his rural territory making his "rounds." Because cats are strongly attuned to place and territory, when owners move to a new home, the cat may attempt to return to his old stomping grounds and become lost (see NAVIGATION).

Strays are even more tragically created when an unwanted cat is simply abandoned to make his own way. Most stray cats are adults, primarily because they no longer possess the kittenish appeal that makes them more desirable to some. Generally, kittens are more closely watched and thus prevented from straying. If they are abandoned to the street, kittens rarely survive long enough to establish themselves as strays.

Even adult cats that have lived a sheltered life often will not survive for long on their own; they tend to have an even shorter life span on the street than FERAL cats. Strays are at high risk for disease, injury from other animals, and lethal encounters with traffic.

According to a 1996 national survey by the American Animal Hospital Association, about 25 percent of pet cats in the United States are found animals. These are strays or more rarely ferals that people adopt off the streets.

In fact, stray cats can and do make excellent pets. However, those that experienced mistreatment at human hands will not react in the same way as cats that have had strong positive relationships with previous owners. They may exhibit AGGRESSION, ALOOFNESS, or even fearful behavior.

If you have come into contact with a stray, before anything else, try to establish if the cat is a former pet or a wild feline. Feral animals require special handling (for information, contact Alley Cat Allies; see "Animal Welfare and Information Services" in Appendix C, "Resources").

Then, before actually catching the cat, decide your course of action once he's contained. Your options include relinquishing him to a shelter, temporarily holding him until you find his old owner or a new one, or adopting the cat yourself.

Shelters are warehouses for unwanted pets, and they strive to help animals the best way they can. When the stray is wearing IDENTIFICATION, the animal will be held while every effort is made to find the owner. Cats without identification are kept only a day or two, and if not adopted are put to sleep. Four cats in five meet this fate and are euthanized. It's a sad fact, but a quick end is infinitely preferable to a short life and prolonged death on the street.

The other options mean taking responsibility for the stray's life yourself, and require you to bring the cat into your home (see QUARANTINE).

Friendly strays that beg for your attention are obviously the easiest to help, but remember that you don't know this cat, so protect yourself. Wear long sleeves and padded gloves when handling any strange cat, and use a pet carrier to temporarily contain him before transporting him to the veterinarian for a health evaluation. Strays that are ill or injured will need special veterinary attention.

A recently lost pet is usually friendly and healthy. Tags on the collar, tattoos, microchip technology, or other identification techniques help reunite these pets with their lost owners, but it can take time and diligence to be successful. For more advice, see the chart "Finding Your Lost Cat or the Stray's Owner."

To find a new owner for the stray, advertise the cat's availability, sing his praises, describe his looks and affectionate nature, and remind everyone that he's a healthy neutered animal. Ask friends for the names of people who may want a cat.

Don't give the cat to just anyone. After rescuing a stray, you want a responsible, loving home for your adoptee, so don't hesitate to ask questions. Chances are you will fall in love with the stray before a new owner can be found, and will decide to keep the cat yourself (see ADOPTION).

If you already have pets and decide to adopt a stray, you must address your resident animals' health and feelings by providing safe quarantine and a proper INTRODUCTION.

Stress

Stress refers to an emotional condition that results in physical or mental tension that affects one's health. The most common cause of stress in cats is a change in the environment.

Moving to a new home; introduction of a new family member, whether a pet, baby, or spouse; or conversely, the loss of a close family member, often results in stress. Even a change in an owner's work schedule, a STRAY cat in the neighborhood, changing the carpet, or switching brands of cat FOOD or LITTER may cause stress to some cats. Felines in overcrowded conditions or with compromised health are also subject to stress-related behaviors.

One of the most common manifestations of stress is an increase in territorial MARKING and inappropriate elimination. Cats may become more demanding of attention, exhibit extremes of rubbing against owners and objects, and spray urine on and/or scratch objects to emphasize territorial boundaries. Sometimes stress will result in AGGRESSION toward other pets or the owner.

Insecure felines may react to stress by withdrawing. The affectionate cat suddenly ignores the owner, snubbing friendly overtures. Other times, the cat simply hides.

The best way to address stress in cats is to remove the cause, if it can be identified. In addition, PLAY therapy may help by giving aggressive cats an outlet and building the shy cat's self-confidence. Interactive games are best, such as fishing pole–style toys. A great deal of gentle enticement may be necessary to engage the withdrawn cat into a game, so be patient.

A small percentage of cats try to relieve their stress by licking

S

themselves excessively. Overgrooming behaviors are seen most often in the Siamese, Burmese, Himalayan, and Abyssinian breeds.

While GROOMING is a normal response that seems to help cats calm themselves, a few cats take the behavior to an extreme. They may worry an isolated area and cause an ongoing sore, usually on one leg, the belly, or flank. This condition is called psychogenic dermatitis.

More often, cats simply lick, nibble, and scratch themselves until the hair begins to break off in single or multiple areas of hair loss. Called psychogenic alopecia, this condition generally results in a line or stripe down the back of very short stubbled hair; the skin beneath appears perfectly normal. Removing the cause of the stress is a good first step in these cases, but psychogenic skin conditions usually result from behaviors that have become habit. Veterinary diagnosis followed by drug therapy and/or a feline behaviorist's intervention is probably necessary to break the cycle (see Appendix C, "Resources").

Stud Tail

Also referred to as tail gland hyperplasia, stud tail is a relatively uncommon condition affecting skin glands in the cat's tail. It's most common in sexually active Persian, Siamese, and Rex male cats, or "stud" animals, but can affect intact or neutered male or female cats as well.

A group of modified sebaceous glands found along the top of the tail base where it joins the body are collectively called the preen gland, or supracaudal organ. These glands produce a semifluid substance called sebum that is composed of fat and other components. Sebum covers the haircoat to give the fur a protective luster. Stud tail results when these glands overproduce sebum.

Signs include blackheads in the skin and a waxy black to yellowish debris at the base of the tail that clutters the fur. The hair looks greasy and may become matted and fall out. Occasionally, a secondary infection of the hair follicles may result in painful itching.

Treatment is simply keeping the area clean. A tar and sulfa shampoo formulated for cats is appropriate, but a nonmedicated grooming shampoo for pets may work as well.

STUD TAIL

SYMPTOMS

Skin at root of tail has blackheads, pimples, and/or waxy debris; oily fur, hair loss; sometimes itchy

HOME CARE

Wash tail twice daily with grooming shampoo or veterinary-approved tar and sulfa shampoo; apply benzoyl peroxide ointments like Oxy 2.5

VET CARE

If area is red and inflamed, antibiotics may be required

PREVENTION

Keep area clean, rub in cornstarch or baby powder to absorb and dry oil

Wash the area twice a day. Simply drape the cat's tail into the sink—you don't have to get the whole cat wet—but be sure to thoroughly rinse all the soap out. In between, rub baby powder or cornstarch into the affected fur to absorb the oily material.

Some veterinarians recommend judicial use of benzoyl peroxide–containing ointments to dry the area. Avoid anything stronger than a 5 percent solution. If the area is very red or appears infected, or the area is itchy, see the veterinarian for appropriate treatment.

S

Sunburn

Sunburn, or solar dermatitis, is an inflammation of the skin that results from overexposure to the sun. Cats are intrepid sunbathers, but thinly furred and light-colored cats are at risk for painful burns, just like fair-skinned owners. Pets living in particularly sunny regions, or in the mountains at higher elevations, tend to burn more quickly.

White cats with blue eyes, and those with white faces and ears, are at highest risk because of their lack of protective pigment in the hair and skin. The tips of the ears, nose, eyelids, and lips are commonly affected.

Initial signs are redness that progresses to hair loss, crustiness, itching, and even curling of the edges of the ears. Typically, the problem goes away as the weather turns cooler, then returns once again during the hot summer months. Not only is sunburn uncomfortable for the cat, it can also lead to disfiguring loss of the ear tips, or dangerous sun-induced CANCER.

Thinly furred and light-colored pets are at risk for painful sunburns. (*Photo credit: Amy D. Shojai*)

S

SUNBURN

SYMPTOMS

Redness or crusting of ear tips or nose, or curling of ear tips; hair loss; itchiness

HOME CARE

Apply cool, damp cloth; mist burns with water; or apply moisturizing cream like nonmedicated Vaseline, aloe vera, or jojoba several times a day

VET CARE

Topical steroid preparations, sometimes amputation of damaged skin

PREVENTION

Keep cats inside during prime sunburn hours, especially white or light-colored cats; draw blinds indoors; apply SPF 15 or higher-rated sunscreen to ears and nose of at-risk cats

Prevent sunburn by keeping the cat inside. If the cat must go out, avoid the most dangerous hours of the day—from ten A.M. to four P.M. Topical sunscreens containing PABA and a high sun protector factor (SPF) of 15 or more should be applied before sun exposure. Pet or play with the cat until the lotion is completely absorbed to keep him from licking it off.

To treat the burn, veterinarians may prescribe steroid creams or pills to control the inflammation. A cool, damp cloth or a moisturizing cream containing aloe vera or jojoba applied two or three times a day will help cool the burn.

Swallowed Objects

Cats, like babies and young children, tend to put objects in their mouths. Anything that is small enough can be swallowed by the cat.

Whole toys or parts of toys, jewelry, and coins are often swallowed. String-type material—the most common culprit—also causes the worst damage. String, thread with or without needles, yarn, fishing hooks and lines, and tinsel from Christmas trees hold particular risk for cats. Christmas trees are tempting to cats who are fascinated by the dangling, dancing ornaments. But breakable items, the hooks they are hung with, and even the needles from the tree cause problems when they are swallowed.

SWALLOWED OBJECTS

SYMPTOMS

Pawing at mouth, choking or gagging, vomiting, diarrhea, swollen stomach

HOME CARE

If possible, remove small objects caught in mouth; DON'T PULL STRING ITEMS, which risks killing the cat

VET CARE

Diagnostic X-rays, often surgery to remove object

PREVENTION

Supervise play with toys, keep swallowable objects out of reach

S

When the swallowed object is small enough, it may pass through the digestive system and be deposited in the LITTER BOX without causing the cat any problem. But objects, even tiny ones, can lodge in the intestinal tract and cause severe complications.

The symptoms vary depending on the location of the blockage. Extreme caution must be used when investigating cases of swallowed objects, because typically the cat will be greatly distressed and may bite an inquisitive owner who tries to open his mouth. It can be even more dangerous for the cat when the owner tries to remove the object. *Items like string should never be pulled, because often they are hooked to a needle or fishhook and attached to tissue farther down the digestive tract.* The veterinarian should evaluate and address the problem of swallowed objects.

Objects caught in the throat prompt a variety of signs, including pawing at the mouth when objects catch between the teeth or stick to the palate. Cats may also retch or gag, and possibly cough. An object caught in the stomach or intestines causes VOMITING, which may come and go for days or weeks if the blockage is not complete and food can pass around it.

Complete blockage is a medical emergency that results in sudden, constant vomiting. Cats refuse to eat, and any water they swallow is immediately thrown up. The stomach becomes bloated and painful.

Swallowed string is particularly deadly because of the way the intestines move. In up to half the cases of swallowed string, the end of the material wraps around the base of the cat's tongue while the rest goes down the throat. The body attempts to pass the string through the intestinal tract using muscle contractions called peristalsis that move through the entire length of the intestine to help push the contents through. But when the string is stopped at one end, the intestine literally "gathers" itself like fabric on a thread, resulting in a kind of accordion formation. This causes sudden severe vomiting and DIARRHEA, and rapid DEHYDRATION.

The veterinarian must determine exactly what to do in this circumstance. Pulling at the visible string can cut the intestines, which can kill the cat. Sometimes, cutting the thread from its anchor will allow the material to then be passed through the body without further problems. But other times, surgery is necessary to remove the obstruction.

Blockage that is ongoing may result in irreparable damage that can kill the cat. Sharp objects may slice or puncture, resulting in perforation of the bowel, and obstruction may interfere with blood flow to the organs and cause bowel tissue to die. PERITONITIS is the end result in either case, and usually kills the cat.

Symptoms generally are diagnostic, particularly if the owner has seen the cat swallow the item. But X-rays are also required not only to definitively identify the object but to determine the exact location and size of the blockage (see X-RAYS). Nonmetal objects won't be visible on routine radiographs, though, in which case barium helps clear things up.

Depending on the suspected location of the blockage, barium may be given to the cat either orally or as an enema. Barium is clearly visible in X-rays, and can provide a positive contrast that outlines the foreign object.

Once the object is pinpointed, surgery is necessary to clear the obstruction and repair the damage, if possible. Most cats recover, so long as the surgery is performed before peritonitis develops. When dead bowel syndrome is involved, the affected sections of tissue are removed and the living portions of bowel reattached; often, cats so treated have a good prognosis.

Preventing swallowed objects should be done at all cost. It is up to the owner to choose cat-safe toys (remove tiny pieces) and to supervise during play. Anything a child would put in his mouth is fair game for cats. Feather and string-type toys should only be used as interactive toys; the cat should not be allowed to play with them unsupervised.

Sweat Glands

Sweat glands are saclike structures in the skin that open to the air and secrete fluid. Cats have two kinds. The first type, called apocrine sweat glands, are found all over the body attached to most hair follicles, and aren't present in hairless areas. The largest are found in the cat's lips, face, scrotum, and upper surface of the tail. Apocrine sweat glands are coiled pockets that produce a milky, scented fluid that's released into the hair follicle and appear to influence sexual attraction.

The second type is the eccrine sweat glands, which are found only in the cat's foot pads. Eccrine glands appear to function in the same way as sweat glands in people. That is, high body temperatures, excitement, or stress prompts a release of fluid on the foot pad surface, which aids the cooling process by evaporation. That's why an excited or frightened cat may leave behind telltale damp paw prints.

Eccrine glands, however, are not nearly as efficient for cooling as are human sweat glands. Cats must rely on other means—like GROOMING—to cool themselves.

S

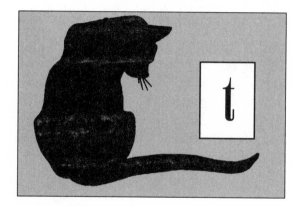

Tail

See COMMUNICATION.

Tapetum Lucidum

See EYES.

Tapeworms

Tapeworms (cestodes) are flat worms that look like ribbon or tape. They are the most common intestinal parasite affecting cats. There are several varieties, but *Dipylidium caninum* is seen most often in cats and dogs.

TAPEWORMS

SYMPTOMS

Ricelike debris or moving segments stuck to cat's anal area or in litter box

HOME CARE

None

VET CARE

Antitapeworm medication, either injection or pill

PREVENTION

Flea control

In order to infect a cat, the immature worm must spend developmental time inside an intermediary host. *Dipylidium caninum* is serviced by FLEAS. If the cat has fleas, statistically there is about a 45 percent chance the cat will also have tapeworms. Consequently, outdoor cats are at highest risk for tapeworms, and the incidence closely parallels flea season.

Flea larvae eat tapeworm eggs found in the environment, and the larval worm develops as the flea itself matures. Cats are so clean, they often groom away and swallow nearly half of all the fleas that parasitize them. In fact, cat owners may be surprised to see tapeworms, because they didn't realize their cat had a flea problem. But swallowing even one infective flea is enough to give the cat tapeworms.

Young tapeworms attach themselves to the wall of the small intestine using the hooks and suckers on their head end, which is called the scolex or holdfast. They then absorb nutrients through their body surface. Their body is made up of a chain of segments called proglottids that grow on the worms from the neck down. Adult worms continue to add segments as long as they live, and can reach two feet in length with hundreds of segments.

Both male and female reproductive organs are found in every segment, and when the segments are mature, eggs are produced. A single segment may contain up to two hundred eggs. The proglottids farthest away from the head are the most mature, and when fully "ripe" they break away and are passed in the cat's stool.

Proglottids can move independently, and they crawl about after leaving the cat's body. When they dry out, these segments look like grains of rice. Cats infested with tapeworms commonly have these segments stuck to the fur beneath their tail or surrounding the anal area. Owners may also see segments in the cat's stool in the litter box, or crawling about in the cat's favorite resting area. When the segments rupture because of dryness, they release eggs in packets into the cat's environment. The life cycle thus can be completed in two to four weeks.

Because egg-filled segments are passed sporadically, microscopic examination of the stool rarely diagnoses tapeworms. It's considered diagnostic to find the segments on the cat.

In most instances, tapeworms are more of a nasty nuisance than a medical problem. But left untreated, infestations can become massive and interfere with the cat's digestion and/or elimination. The worm's hooklike attachments can damage the intestinal wall. A large number of long worms may become suspended throughout the length of the intestinal tract, and in kittens this may cause blockage. DIARRHEA with mucus and occasionally blood may be seen as a result of tapeworm infestation. Ongoing infestation can cause a cat to have an UNTHRIFTY appearance and reduced energy.

Although flea tapeworms are by far the most common kind, cats also contract other kinds of tapeworms by eating wild animals like mice or rabbits. In addition, there is a human health risk associated with two species of tapeworms, and cats may potentially carry disease to people if they have eaten the host animal. *Echinococcus granulosus*, which has a sheep host, is found in Utah, California, Arizona, and New Mexico; *Echinococcus multilocularis*, which commonly affects foxes and rodents, is found in Alaska, the Dakotas, and surrounding north central states. Both cause deadly cyst growths in the liver and lungs of infected people. The Centers for Disease Control recommend that pets living in these areas, particularly those with access to host animals, be treated every month for tapeworms as a precaution.

Tapeworms are killed with a drug called Droncit (praziquantel), which can be given as a pill or injection. One dose is sufficient, unless the cat is under constant exposure for reinfection. Controlling fleas is the best way to prevent tapeworm infestation.

Tartar

See PERIODONTAL DISEASE.

Taste

See TONGUE.

Taurine

See CARDIOMYOPATHY and NUTRITION.

t

Teeth

Teeth are bony growths on the jaw found inside the mouth. Cats use them for capturing, killing, and preparing food, and as defensive tools. Almost without exception, kittens are born without teeth; by eight weeks of age, they will have twenty-six milk teeth, referred to as "deciduous teeth." An examination of the teeth can reveal a kitten's approximate age.

The twelve incisors, six on the top and six across the bottom that are located at the front of the mouth, are the first to appear at about two to three weeks of age. At four weeks, daggerlike canines appear next to the incisors, one on each side of the mouth, top and bottom. Between three and six weeks, the premolars grow behind the canines, three on the top and two on the bottom. The last deciduous premolar erupts by six to eight weeks of age. (Kittens don't have molars.)

Adult teeth replace the baby teeth beginning at about three to four months of age, when permanent incisors appear. The roots of baby

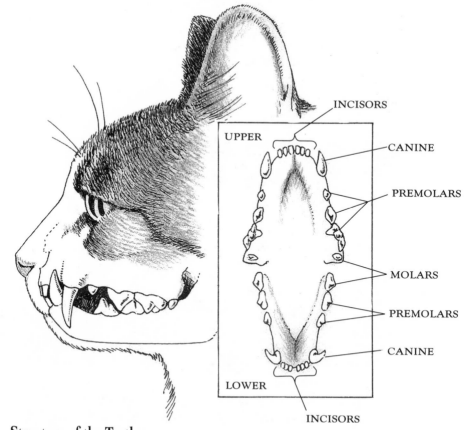

Structure of the Teeth

teeth are usually absorbed, so erupting adult teeth simply loosen and push out the baby teeth as they grow. The remaining permanent teeth make their appearance when the kitten is four to six months old. Permanent teeth replace baby ones tooth for tooth, and also add four molars, one on each side, both at the top and the bottom. Molars are sharp, triangular teeth located on the side toward the rear of the cat's jaw, and are the "carnassial" teeth characteristic of meat eaters. They work like scissors to shear flesh and crush bone. A total of thirty adult teeth are present in a feline by seven months of age.

If the deciduous teeth fail to fall out, the cat may appear to have a double set of teeth. These extra baby teeth should be removed to allow room for the permanent ones to come in. Otherwise, the teeth can be pushed out of alignment and cause possible problems with eating or dental hygiene. (See also PERIODONTAL DISEASE.)

Temperament

See AGGRESSION, ALOOFNESS, FEAR, and KITTEN.

Temperature

Temperature is the measure of body warmth. An adult cat's normal body temperature ranges from 100 to 102.5 degrees Fahrenheit, while a newborn kitten's temperature may be considerably lower (see KITTEN). An abnormal temperature is an indication of illness.

A temperature higher than normal is referred to as a fever, and can be a sign of infection related to a wide variety of illnesses, or of heatstroke (see HYPERTHERMIA). Those below normal can indicate SHOCK as a result of trauma, or loss of body heat due to extreme cold (see HY-POTHERMIA). Treatment depends on the underlying cause.

A rectal thermometer, either digital or bulb, is used to measure the cat's temperature. Cats may need to be restrained to have their temperature taken, particularly if they're not feeling well. The key is to be gentle but firm.

Shake down the thermometer until it registers about 96 degrees, and lubricate the tip using baby oil, mineral oil, or petroleum jelly. The cat should either stand or recline on his side for the procedure—whichever is more comfortable for the cat.

With one hand, gently grasp his tail and lift, then insert the lubricated tip of the thermometer about an inch into the anus with your other hand. Hold the thermometer in place for at least three minutes, then remove and wipe clean, and read the cat's temperature. Thoroughly clean the thermometer after each use with alcohol or a comparable disinfectant.

Territorial Behavior

See AGGRESSION, COMMUNICATION, DOMINANCE, and MARKING.

Tetanus

Also referred to as "lockjaw," this condition results from a bacterial neurotoxin. Almost all mammals are susceptible to tetanus, but the disease is considered rare in cats, which appear to have a high natural immunity.

The bacteria are found naturally in the intestinal tract of most animals but do not cause illness. However, soil is contaminated by infected cow or horse manure, and in most cases, the infectious agent is introduced into tissue through a deep puncture wound. Within two weeks,

TETANUS

SYMPTOMS

Muscle spasms especially in face and jaw, difficulty breathing

HOME CARE

None; EMERGENCY! SEE VETERINARIAN
IMMEDIATELY if you suspect your cat has tetanus

VET CARE

Tetanus antitoxin injection, antibiotics, fluid therapy, sedatives

PREVENTION

Keep cat indoors

signs of illness develop. The bacteria infect the central nervous system, causing severe muscle spasms particularly of the face and jaw, and interfere with blood circulation and respiration. The animal dies in about 80 percent of cases.

Veterinary treatment consists of tetanus antitoxin, antibiotics, fluid therapy to fight DEHYDRATION, and sedatives to control spasms. Recovery may take as long as six weeks. Prevent tetanus by reducing the opportunities for wounds. Keeping cats inside will virtually eliminate any chance for infection.

t

Ticks

Ticks are eight-legged bloodsucking skin parasites that are very common on dogs. They are found rather infrequently on cats, as felines have healthy GROOMING habits and keep their fur and skin clean. These

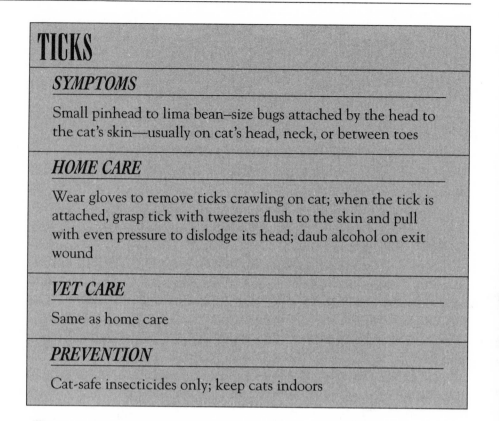

TICKS

SYMPTOMS

Small pinhead to lima bean–size bugs attached by the head to the cat's skin—usually on cat's head, neck, or between toes

HOME CARE

Wear gloves to remove ticks crawling on cat; when the tick is attached, grasp tick with tweezers flush to the skin and pull with even pressure to dislodge its head; daub alcohol on exit wound

VET CARE

Same as home care

PREVENTION

Cat-safe insecticides only; keep cats indoors

relatives of spiders are gray or brown, with oval-shaped leathery or hard flat bodies that balloon with blood as they feed. There are a wide variety of ticks, ranging from those the size of a pinhead to those as large as a lima bean when fully engorged.

Most ticks that affect cats spend 90 percent of their life cycle off the host. They usually have a three-host cycle, which means each stage of tick development feeds on a specific host. If the preferred host—a mouse or deer—isn't available, ticks will feed upon anything that's available, including cats, dogs, or people.

Tick eggs hatch into seed ticks, which are tiny six-legged larvae. The larvae crawl onto vegetation and climb aboard animals as they pass by. The larvae feed for several days, then drop off and molt into eight-legged nymphs, which again seek an appropriate host. After another blood meal, nymphs drop off and molt into adults. Adults must feed before they mate; after they find and drop off the host, the females lay one thousand to four thousand eggs. The entire sequence may take as long as two years.

Ticks are a concern not only because their bites can develop into infected sores, but also because massive infestation may result in ANE-MIA. Even more serious, ticks can carry and transmit a number of devastating illnesses that can affect cats and people.

However, the tick generally must feed for twelve to twenty-four hours before any organisms will be transmitted into the host. And although it's possible, people rarely get tick-borne diseases from their pets; you're much more likely to become infected from trimming vegetation like azaleas. Still, removing ticks from your pet with your bare hands can, in some instances, expose you to infection.

An infection that can affect your cat as a result of ticks is caused by *Cytauxzoon felis*, a protozoan parasite of the blood spread by ixodid ticks. Cytauxzoonosis is considered a rare condition, and is currently found most commonly in the wooded areas of the southern United States. The natural host appears to be wild cats—bobcats and lynx—where it usually causes no problems. But in domestic cats, infection quickly causes a fatal disease. The organism attacks red blood cells. Signs include loss of appetite, depression, fever, labored breathing, and DEHYDRATION or anemia. Diagnosis is made by examining a blood sample microscopically. Currently, there's no treatment; cats usually die within a week of infection. Infected cats do not transmit the disease to people or to other cats.

For people and dogs, Lyme disease is a blood-borne illness caused by the bacterium *Borrelia burgdorferi*. It's transmitted by the tiny deer tick, *Ixodes scapularis* (previously referred to as *Ixodes dammini*), found most commonly in the northeastern, north central, and Pacific coast states. People and dogs are often affected with devastating signs, but cats rarely show signs of illness and experts can't agree as to whether cats can be infected. The most common sign in dogs is lameness. People typically suffer an initial red circular rash surrounding the tick bite, followed by a variety of signs including weakness, fatigue, chills, and arthritislike joint pain. Left untreated, signs may disappear only to recur months to years later, with ever-worsening symptoms and possibly permanent damage. Antibiotic therapy during early stages of the disease is usually quite effective in eliminating the organism. (For more information, call the Lyme Disease National Hotline at 1-800-886-LYME.)

Rocky Mountain Spotted Fever is an infectious disease caused by the microorganism *Rickettsia rickettsii*. It's transmitted by *Dermacentor andersoni*, the Rocky Mountain wood tick, and by *Dermacentor varia-*

bilis, the American dog tick, both found throughout the western and northwestern United States and Canada. Cats don't get sick from this disease, but an infective tick hitchhiking on the cat could potentially expose the owner. Signs don't develop until several days after the bite. Early symptoms include fever up to 105 degrees, chills, headache, and muscle pain. About five days later, a spotted rash appears first on the backs of the hands, then spreads to cover the whole body. Early treatment with antibiotics is usually effective, but without treatment, the condition can be fatal.

Preventing ticks on your cats is the best way to avoid illness for you and your pets. Cats allowed outside are at the highest risk for ticks, so the best prevention is to keep them indoors.

Some flea preventive preparations are also effective against ticks. *However, many preventive preparations designed to address ticks in dogs can be deadly for your cat, so be extremely careful about using them.* Check with your veterinarian first. If your cat is allowed outside, inspect him each time he comes inside and remove ticks before they have a chance to attach themselves and transmit disease.

When removing ticks from your pets, wear gloves. Ticks are usually found on the head, back of the neck, or between the cat's toes where a cat can't easily groom them away. If the head of the tick is buried, use tweezers to grasp the tick right at the skin level, and firmly pull straight out.

Tom

The term *tom* refers to male cats of breeding age (see REPRODUCTION). It more specifically may refer to intact male cats capable of producing kittens.

Tongue

The tongue is a long, narrow, highly mobile organ rooted in the floor of the mouth. In cats, the tongue acts as a tool for GROOMING, EATING, and drinking, and contains the sensory organs responsible for taste.

Rows of horny, backward-hooked projections called papillae populate the center of the cat's tongue. These serve as rasps when licking food, a sponge to collect water, and a comb when self-grooming. Newborn kittens have only a single row of papillae rimming the tongue, which helps them grasp a nipple while nursing.

Feline taste buds are on the edges of the tongue and inside the mouth and lips. Cats detect sour in all areas, bitter at the back of the tongue, and salt only on the tip or front of the tongue. Cats can detect sweet, but unlike dogs, cats rarely respond to or seek out sweet tastes. When they do, sweet flavors can get them in trouble (see ANTIFREEZE and CHOCOLATE). Odors tend to be the determining factor in what a cat likes to eat, but taste plays a role as well, particularly in differentiating meaty flavors.

Touch

t

Touch refers to contact with the skin, which contains a multitude of temperature- and pressure-sensitive nerve endings.

Touch helps protect the cat from injury. The furless paw pad—one of the most sensitive areas of the cat's body—is used to test an object's relative safety. However, direct contact with the skin is not necessary for the cat to detect another's touch; merely brushing the tips of the cat's fur triggers a response. This is because the follicles (from which each hair grows) are adjacent to pressure-sensitive pads. And WHISKERS have the most sensitive nerve endings of all the fur.

Touch is also a pleasurable sensation, and is one of the first things the cat experiences as a newborn when he is washed by his mother. Stroking parallels the sensation a cat feels when he grooms himself. Touch also provides an emotional link between the cat and other creatures, and may be important in feline COMMUNICATION.

Cats crave warmth and are devoted sun worshipers. In fact, cats can tolerate temperatures as high as 126 degrees Fahrenheit before feeling discomfort. This insensitivity to high temperatures may result in the cat's tail becoming singed or even burned before registering pain, particularly in cats who enjoy sleeping close to the fireplace.

Toxoplasmosis

Toxoplasmosis is a disease caused by the single-cell organism *Toxoplasma gondii*, a parasitic protozoan. Infection with toxoplasmosis in animals, including people, is quite common, but the infection rarely causes death. The parasite is harbored in our bodies without making us sick. Domestic and wild cats are the only animals in which toxoplasmosis can reproduce, and the chance of contracting toxoplasmosis from a well-cared-for pet cat is extremely low. The most common infection source for people in the United States is undercooked or raw meat, especially pork.

Cats become infected either by swallowing the infective stage of the protozoan from the environment, by eating infected animals, or by eating raw meat. The protozoans multiply in the wall of the small intestine and produce egglike oocysts. Infected cats are the only animals that pass on these immature forms of the organism, which are shed in the cat's stool.

Oocysts are passed in great numbers in the cat's feces for two to three weeks. However, once this stage is passed it's rare for the cat to ever again shed the eggs.

After two to five days, oocysts mature into infective forms of the organism. These organisms can survive in moist or shady soil or sand for many months. The disease is spread when an animal or a person swallows these infective organisms.

TOXOPLASMOSIS

SYMPTOMS

Signs are rare, sometimes transient lymph node enlargement

HOME CARE

None

VET CARE

Rarely needed

PREVENTION

Prevent cats from hunting, don't feed rare or raw meat, keep litter box clean

Once inside the bird, rodent, cat, or person, the protozoan continues to mature, causing pockets of disease throughout the body. If the victim survives this stage of the illness, the symptoms usually go away and the disease becomes dormant (although the protozoan remains in certain muscle tissues and even the brain).

Cats are diagnosed when a microscopic examination of their stool reveals oocysts, which means the cat is *at that time* capable of spreading disease. A blood test shows if the cat has ever been exposed. A positive test in an otherwise healthy cat means the cat is actively immune and an unlikely source of disease.

Cats rarely show signs of the disease. The IMMUNE SYSTEM of most cats interferes with the life cycle of the organism, so that toxoplasmosis in cats enters a dormant phase often for the remaining lifetime of the cat.

However, some cats' immune systems aren't able to stop the disease, particularly those infected with FELINE LEUKEMIA VIRUS or other immune-suppressing illlnesses. In these cases, toxoplasmosis affects the lungs, eyes, lymph nodes, and brain with symptoms of rapid breathing, loss of appetite, and lethargy. Often, PNEUMONIA develops. Antibiotics are available to address the infection and help prevent the shedding of infective eggs.

Healthy adult humans rarely get sick when infected. In fact, it's been estimated that half the people in the United States have been exposed but never developed symptoms. Like cats, infected people may have brief signs and then their immune system sends the organism into a dormant stage. The most common sign is swollen lymph glands. However, the disease can cause life-threatening illness in immune-suppressed people. In these cases, the person is either unable to fight off the initial infection or the dormant disease reemerges. Toxoplasmosis also may severely damage or kill unborn babies if the mother first contracts the disease while she's pregnant; such mothers rarely show any symptoms themselves. A blood test can determine whether a person has ever been exposed to the disease. A positive test before pregnancy means exposure has already taken place, and the fetus will be protected against infection.

Commonsense sanitation prevents the spread of the disease. Since several days are needed for the oocysts to become infective, simply cleaning the cat's LITTER BOX each day eliminates that route of infection. People in high-risk groups, such as pregnant women or those with compromised immune systems, should have someone else perform litter box duty.

To reduce risk even further, wash your hands after handling raw meat, and cook all meat, especially pork, thoroughly before eating it. Don't feed your cat undercooked or raw foods, and prevent the cat from hunting. Wear gloves while working in the garden to prevent contracting the disease from the soil. (See also ZOONOSIS.)

t

Training

Training is teaching. With cats, training most often refers to educating the cat to understand the differences between acceptable and unacceptable behavior.

Unlike dogs, cats rarely seem to enjoy learning simply to please their owner; they want to please themselves, too. Cats are highly intelligent animals, and most relish learning anything that piques their interest.

Physical punishment such as slapping or hitting with hands or objects has no place in training cats or any other animal. Such discipline won't even work on the cat, and shouting isn't particularly effective either. Cats that are punished in this way may learn to hide the inappropriate behavior while continuing to practice it in private. Shy cats may become traumatized introverts, while dominant cats turn into attack animals (see AGGRESSION). Plus, the cat learns to associate hands with pain rather than petting.

Negative reinforcement, which means correcting (not punishing!) inappropriate behavior, does have its place in cat training, but it must be used judiciously. Negative reinforcement at its best either interrupts or distracts the poor behavior, or makes the behavior unpleasant enough that the cat stops on his own. Squirting water at the cat from a distance, clapping your hands, shaking a tin can with coins, judiciously applying a hot-tasting or foul-smelling spray to the forbidden object(s), or tossing a toy toward the cat all work as corrections.

Say "no" with a firm voice during such corrections, and eventually the cat should learn to stop the behavior on the word alone. Some cats respond better to the owner hissing *"ssssst!"* at them as another cat might do to show displeasure. Be aware, though, that dwelling too much on the negatives may teach the cat that misbehavior is a great way to get your attention.

The best way to train a cat is through the use of positive reinforcement. That simply means rewarding the desired behavior. With dogs, verbal praise is often reward enough; cats tend to need a more tangible prize to motivate their interest, such as a tasty treat or a special toy or game. Make the training session a game to engage your cat's interest and keep it.

Professionals who train cats for the movies often use a handheld clicker in conjunction with other incentives like tiny treats. The clicking sound reinforces the good behavior by signaling the cat he's done something right. Only click the clicker and give the treat or toy when the cat does what's expected. Soon, he'll associate the behavior with the reward, and eventually may only need the clicker prompt to perform correctly.

Both negative and positive reinforcement work only when you

catch your cat in the act. Pets aren't able to relate what happened hours ago with the reward or correction taking place this minute. Cats live in the here and now, and to get your message across, your reaction must be immediate. Don't give treats indiscriminately if that's what you're using for training rewards. Using negative reinforcement to interrupt the behavior, followed by positive reinforcement, often works wonders.

Consistency is key. You can't be lenient one day and expect the cat to toe the line the next. That's confusing to the cat, and it's not fair to change the rules. (See also LITTER BOX and SCRATCHING.)

Traveling

It is the rare cat that is not required to travel from home sometime during her life. All cats need to make regular trips to the veterinarian; others may travel to a boarding facility or groomer. Show cats travel a great deal.

Cats should travel in the safety of a confined carrier, even for relatively short trips. Unless a cat is quite accustomed to the excitement, a trip can upset her digestion and temper, and result in messes or tantrums better handled in confined, easily cleaned spaces. Even a cat used to car rides may be startled suddenly by something out the window. This can potentially interfere with your driving and possibly cause an accident. Should a car accident happen, an unrestrained cat in the car becomes a projectile that may injure you, and most certainly will suffer severe trauma herself.

Commercial carriers, from elaborate to simple, are available for the comfort and safety of the cat. The best cat carriers are large enough for your adult cat without being cramped. For quick trips, cardboard pet totes available from pet-supply stores or the veterinarian's office are fine. But if you'll be making a long trip or plan on several outings, invest in a more substantial carrier.

Hard plastic carriers must be airline-approved if your cat is to be transported with the luggage. Sturdy airline carriers are usually box-shaped with a grille opening in one side or the top. Only a few animals at a time are allowed to be on airplanes as "carry-on" luggage, so call ahead and reserve space if this is your intention. Canvas bags or duffle-type carriers with zipper openings are popular for car transportation. When riding in the car, secure the carrier with a seat belt if possible. Situate carriers in back seats away from air bags, which can actually crush the carrier and injure the pet when deployed.

Traveling can be stressful for the cat that's not prepared. Plan trips ahead of time, and acclimate your cat to riding in the carrier. If possible, turn the cat carrier into a play area or even a bed for the cat, so a trip to the vet isn't the carrier's only association.

Toss a Ping-Pong ball into a hard carrier, leaving the door wide open, and invite the cat to play. Put a favorite toy or blanket inside to make a snug nest. And take the cat for short car rides from kittenhood on—making sure they don't end up at the veterinarian's office. Then, when you really need to get the cat into the carrier quickly, the mere sight of it won't make the cat run from the room.

In some cases, your veterinarian may prescribe a tranquilizer for your cat to reduce his STRESS level during trips—and consequently your own!

Treading

See KNEADING.

Tumors

See CANCER.

Tylenol

See POISON.

t

Ulcer

An ulcer is an open sore that is slow to heal and can result in tissue loss and sometimes infection. Cats may develop ulcers on their eyes as a result of injury or on the skin surface secondary to trauma or insect bites, or due to other problems like EOSINOPHILIC GRANULOMA COMPLEX. Any slow-to-heal sore requires veterinary attention.

Ultrasound

An ultrasound is a diagnostic tool that uses high-frequency sound waves to penetrate body tissue. The waves pass through or over areas of varying density. The echoreflection of these waves produces a two-dimensional image that offers the veterinarian an accurate picture of soft areas of the body not visible with X-RAYS.

Unthrifty

The term *unthrifty*, as it applies to felines, refers to a cat's general unhealthy appearance and, more specifically, to a poor coat condition. Rather than clean and shiny, and lying close to the body in soft layers, the fur of an unthrifty animal appears unkempt and may be tangled or matted. Coat condition varies from dry and brittle to sticky, oily, and greasy. An unthrifty appearance signals illness, because cats tend to neglect their own grooming when they don't feel well.

Upper Respiratory Infections (URI)

Upper respiratory disease complex is caused by a variety of viral and bacterial agents, alone or in combination, resulting in an illness similar to flu and colds in people. The cat's habit of being led by the nose makes him extremely susceptible to URI, because along with interesting smells, a cat also inhales viruses and bacteria.

The most common infectious respiratory diseases in cats are feline viral rhinotracheitis (FVR), also called the feline herpesvirus 1; feline calicivirus (FCV); and chlamydia (also called feline pneumonitis), caused by a primitive bacterium called *Chlamydia psittaci*. Rhino and calicivirus cause up to 80 percent of all feline upper respiratory infections.

The disease is spread primarily through direct contact between cats. Infectious agents are in the sick cat's saliva and nasal and eye discharges. Nose-to-nose greetings between cats; contact with contaminated cages, food bowls, or LITTER BOXES; and coughing or sneezing spread the infection. The virus can also be carried on human skin, and may be spread simply by petting one cat after another. Chlamydia and

UPPER RESPIRATORY INFECTIONS (URI)

SYMPTOMS

Sneezing, stuffy nose or nasal discharge, runny eyes, mouth or eye ulcers, anorexia

HOME CARE

Nursing care including humidifying air to help breathing, soaking away crusts with soft cloth and warm water to keep eyes and nose clean, nutritional support

VET CARE

Supportive care (same as home care), antibiotics, surgery in extreme cases

PREVENTION

Vaccinate cat to prevent infections, avoid crowding of cats, wean kittens early

rhino agents don't survive long outside the cat, but calicivirus can survive one to two weeks at room temperature in the environment.

URI most often affects cats living in crowded conditions where the cats give it back and forth to one another. These infections are particularly devastating to cats with compromised IMMUNE SYSTEMS suffering from FELINE LEUKEMIA VIRUS or FELINE IMMUNODEFICIENCY VIRUS. Some cats, though, may recover from URI yet continue to shed the virus and infect other healthy cats. STRESS may trigger a recurrence of disease in such cats.

In otherwise healthy adult cats, URI signs are often quite mild. Sneezing is the most common sign of rhino and calicivirus infections. Cats also typically develop a transient stuffy nose or watery eyes. Chlamydia infections occur less frequently, and signs include mild eye or nasal inflammation and sometimes small, raised blisters on the surface of the eye.

U

Other times, infections can become life threatening, particularly in very young kittens or older cats. The symptoms are the same, just more severe. Plugged noses depress the cat's appetite, and fasting further debilitates the cat. Calicivirus can produce painful ulcers in the nose and mouth that can also make the cat refuse to eat. These infections may progress into the lower respiratory tract and result in bronchial infection or even PNEUMONIA.

The overlap of symptoms makes it difficult to identify the specific disease a cat may be suffering, but unless the condition becomes chronic, identifying the specific virus or bacteria probably isn't important. When necessary, the agent can be identified with laboratory tests that include microscopic evaluations of mucous membrane tissue scrapings, blood tests, culture, and virus isolation techniques. Even then, a specific diagnosis may not be possible.

There is currently no effective systemic antiviral medication available. Cats suffering from URI are treated with supportive care that may include administering fluids and therapy that softens nasal and eye discharge. If secondary infections are a problem, antibiotics may help relieve the signs and shorten the course of the infection. Tetracycline is helpful with chlamydia infections, and medicated eyedrops and ointments help soothe and heal painful corneal ulcers.

Simple nursing care provided at home is the single most important therapy the cat receives. Good nutrition must be maintained if the cat is to recover, and an owner nearly always is more successful in coaxing a reluctant eater at home (see ANOREXIA).

Nasal and ocular secretions are sticky and can dry and crust, making the cat feel even worse and breathing more difficult. Cleaning the cat's nose and eyes is an important part of therapy. Use a soft cloth or cotton ball dampened with saline or warm water to gently soak crusts away. A humidifier will also help the cat breathe. If you don't have a humidifier, simply run hot water in the shower or bathtub, and have the cat spend time in the steamy bathroom to ease congestion.

Chronic infections of rhinotracheitis can actually invade and destroy tissue or bone within the nose, resulting in ever more frequent infections as well as compromising the cat's sense of smell. Even more rarely, these infections climb from the nose into the brain. Surgery that cleans out the infection may be an option in such extreme cases.

URI is more easily prevented than treated, and VACCINATIONS are the best choice to avoid feline upper respiratory diseases. Be aware, though, that cats may be exposed to URI before they receive vaccinations, and become latent carriers. Also, because there are many strains of calicivirus, a vaccine that protects against one may have no effect on another; most vaccines include two or more strains for broader cross-protection.

In addition to a good vaccination program, reduce crowding of cats to help prevent infection. Isolate new cats before introducing them to your pets to help prevent contagion (see QUARANTINE). And provide good ventilation to help reduce the incidence of aerosol infection caused by sneezing and coughing.

Because cats may appear healthy yet be carriers, some experts recommend that catteries wean kittens early, at four to five weeks. This may help prevent a QUEEN from transmitting the virus to her kittens during this critical period. The kittens are raised away from adults to break the line of transmission.

Uveitis

Uveitis is an inflammation of the iris, which is the colored portion of the EYE. It is a common condition in cats and may affect only one or both eyes.

Signs of uveitis are striking. The eye color changes, and the surface of the eye roughens. This is a painful condition for the cat, and he typically squints and has watering eyes. The pupil may become quite small, and the inflammation results in a softening of the entire eyeball. Cats suffering from uveitis show sensitivity to light, and they may suffer from spasms in the eyelid. Loss of vision is also a symptom.

The most common cause of uveitis is systemic disease such as FELINE LEUKEMIA VIRUS, FELINE INFECTIOUS PERITONITIS, FELINE IMMUNODEFICIENCY VIRUS, or TOXOPLASMOSIS. Injury to the eye may also result in iris inflammation.

Blood tests are done to determine if the cause is infectious. The treatment addresses the inflammation as well as the underlying cause. Steroids are often helpful for relieving the inflammation. Pills or injections, along with eye ointments and drops, are typically administered

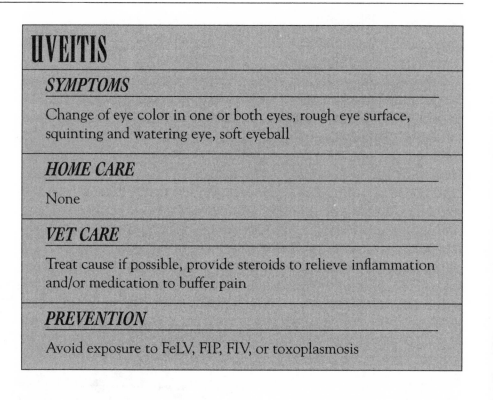

UVEITIS

SYMPTOMS

Change of eye color in one or both eyes, rough eye surface, squinting and watering eye, soft eyeball

HOME CARE

None

VET CARE

Treat cause if possible, provide steroids to relieve inflammation and/or medication to buffer pain

PREVENTION

Avoid exposure to FeLV, FIP, FIV, or toxoplasmosis

for two weeks. Eyedrops that contain atropine help the pupil to dilate and relieve the pain. Veterinary supervision is required to treat uveitis.

The best way to prevent the condition is to protect your cat from exposure to predisposing viruses, using appropriate vaccinations and other means.

U

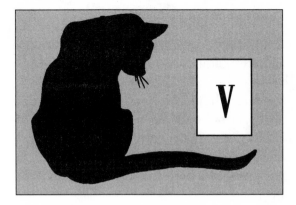

Vaccinations

Vaccinations are medical treatments, often injections, designed to stimulate the IMMUNE SYSTEM to mount a protective defense against disease. Vaccines literally program a cat's body to recognize disease-causing viruses and bacteria, and fight them off.

Vaccines stimulate immunity by exposing the cat to a non-disease-producing form of an infectious agent. This causes the immune system to produce protective cells and antibodies for a period of time. Acting like "smart bombs," these agents seek out and destroy dangerous pathogens hopefully before they are able to cause illness.

Your cat should be protected against those diseases for which she is at risk, and each cat's risk varies considerably depending on a number of factors. The less-than-robust immune system of very young and very old cats places them at high risk for disease. Free-roaming outdoor cats, particularly aggressive males who fight other cats, are also at higher risk for disease because of increased exposure. And cats in overcrowded conditions such as shelter or cattery environments, and show cats that travel a lot, have a higher exposure. Overcrowding and travel also increase the risk due to STRESS. Finally, the geographic location in which a cat lives influences risk for disease, because incidence for certain feline illnesses is much higher in some areas than in others. An "only" cat that is a healthy, exclusively indoor adult is probably at lowest risk for exposure to disease.

Because there are so many variables, a single vaccination program is not right for every cat. Your veterinarian will help you design the best protection for your particular pet.

Almost without exception a cat should be given vaccinations that protect against FELINE PANLEUKOPENIA VIRUS along with viral rhinotracheitis and calicivirus (which cause upper respiratory infections). These vaccinations are often given as a single three-in-one injection. In addition, vaccination against RABIES is imperative, and in some areas of the country required by law.

When a QUEEN with a healthy immune system gives birth, she passes her immunity on to her newborn KITTENS when they drink the first milk, called colostrum. This passive immunity in the kittens fades as their own immune system matures and takes over. However, the kitten's borrowed immunity also interferes with the effectiveness of vaccinations. The vaccines are perceived by the immune system to be foreign and are attacked and destroyed just as a virus would be. Consequently, a single vaccination given at six weeks of age may not protect kittens from becoming sick.

A kitten's immune system isn't fully developed until about six to eight weeks of age; the exact timing varies from kitten to kitten. In order to hit the window of protection when a mother's immunity has faded and the kitten's is finally mature, a series of vaccinations are given so that active immunity is provided just as maternal protection fades away.

Most vaccinations are administered by injection. Others, like those for calicivirus and rhinotracheitis, can be given as drops in the eyes or nose to stimulate local protection in those cells that first encounter these viruses. Maternal antibodies don't block this cell-mediated immunity, so such vaccinations can be given before six weeks of age if the kitten is at risk for exposure.

Schedules vary, but first vaccinations are typically given between six and nine weeks of age. Follow-up "booster" shots are given every three to four weeks thereafter until the kitten reaches twelve to sixteen weeks of age, when the rabies vaccination is first given. Vaccinations thereafter are repeated annually.

Other vaccinations are available that are useful for certain cats. Outdoor animals and those with multicat exposure may benefit from vaccinations against FELINE LEUKEMIA VIRUS. Before this vaccination, the cat should be tested to determine if he's already infected with the

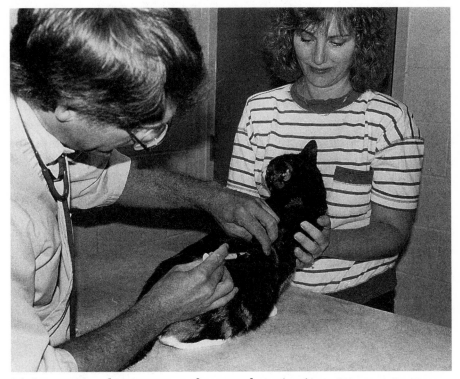

It's important to bring your cat for annual vaccinations. (*Photo credit: Fran Pennock Shaw*)

disease. If the test is negative, the first inoculation can be given as early as twelve weeks of age, with a second vaccination following in three weeks. Single cats kept strictly indoors, who are never exposed to other cats, are at extremely low risk for the disease and do not require routine vaccinations for FeLV.

Vaccinations for FELINE INFECTIOUS PERITONITIS are extremely controversial because the effectiveness of current preventives remains in question. Until the effectiveness of the vaccines is better validated, veterinary researchers are hesitant to advocate their use, and currently do not recommend routine vaccination.

Some vaccinations are designed to reduce or treat the symptoms of disease but not necessarily to prevent illness. A vaccine against *Microsporum canis*, the fungus that causes most cases of feline RINGWORM, does not prevent disease but appears to help relieve its symptoms. And a vaccine against chlamydia (see UPPER RESPIRATORY INFECTIONS) won't

V

prevent infection but will reduce signs of the disease if the cat does become sick.

No vaccine is 100 percent protective. Individual immune competence, exposure to disease, the strength of the virus or bacteria, and the type of vaccine all influence the effectiveness of a vaccine's protection.

Most feline vaccinations are of two types: modified live, or "killed." With the first type, vaccines can be modified so that their potential to cause disease is greatly reduced or eliminated, while retaining the ability to multiply inside the body the way a normal virus would. Because this more closely imitates a natural infection, the cat's immune system is better stimulated. Modified live vaccines also overcome maternal immunity more easily, and so provide a better and quicker protection for kittens than killed vaccines.

But with certain disease-causing agents like rabies and feline leukemia virus, it's not always possible to inactivate the virus enough to ensure that the vaccine won't cause the disease it is trying to prevent. Modified live vaccines may also cause problems in cats with suppressed immune systems, and can result in birth defects in unborn kittens when the vaccine is given to mother cats during pregnancy.

In these instances, killed vaccines offer a safer alternative. Killed vaccines have had the infectious portions inactivated or killed, so they stimulate immunity but do not cause disease. They are usually more expensive because they must also contain an additive called an adjuvant that stimulates the immune response. Also, while a modified live vaccine may be effective after only one dose, a series of two vaccinations is generally required when using killed vaccines to ensure the best protection.

Occasionally, a cat will suffer a reaction to the vaccination. The most serious is called an anaphylactic reaction, and will happen within ten to fifteen minutes after the vaccination. Signs vary from relatively minor problems, like facial swelling or hives, to severe problems with breathing, along with VOMITING, DIARRHEA, and collapse. These emergencies require immediate veterinary help.

The most common type of vaccination reaction is moderate lethargy or a slight fever for twenty-four hours or so after the treatment. These signs generally clear up without treatment. Local reactions may include tenderness or swelling at the injection site, but this also usually fades away in a few days. In rare cases, the bump develops into a tumor (see CANCER). If the swelling persists for more than a week, see the veterinarian.

Nobody really knows how long vaccination protection lasts, although studies have proven that the three-year rabies vaccination does in fact protect for that period of time at a minimum. We do know the protection time varies depending on the type of infectious agent that's being prevented, and the type of vaccine being used.

Immunity against viruses generally lasts longer than bacterial immunity, and some vaccinations, like the modified live vaccine for panleukopenia, provide virtually lifelong protection. But killed vaccines don't protect nearly as long as modified live, and local immunity in the nose or eyes doesn't last as long as systemic protection that includes the whole body. In fact, some vaccinations offer protection for less than a year.

Studies are being conducted to determine the actual duration of vaccination protection and the optimum revaccination schedule. Until then, revaccination is advocated *yearly*. Rely on your local veterinarian's recommendation to best protect your cat. He or she knows the disease incidence in your area, and your cat's individual situation.

Vision

See EYES.

Vitamins

See NUTRITION.

Vocalization

See COMMUNICATION and PURRING.

Vomeronasal Organ

See JACOBSON'S ORGANS.

Vomiting

Vomiting refers to stomach contents being forcefully expelled up the throat and out of the mouth by strong muscle contractions.

The process begins with salivation and repeated swallowing, and your cat may seek your attention during this time. Shortly thereafter, abrupt contractions of the stomach and abdomen begin; the cat extends his neck, opens his mouth, and makes a strained gagging sound as the stomach empties.

Gastric irritation is the most common cause of vomiting in cats. This is often due to swallowed hair resulting in HAIRBALLS, EATING GRASS or too much food, or simply eating too fast. Cold canned food prompts some cats to vomit.

Vomiting differs from regurgitation, which is a passive process that doesn't involve strong muscle contractions. Regurgitation happens minutes to hours after eating; the expelled material is undigested, and may even be tube-shaped, like the throat. Occasional regurgitation is quite common in cats, and probably isn't a cause for concern unless it interferes with NUTRITION. Chronic regurgitation is typically seen in

V

young cats, and as a result, growth is very slow. It can be caused by a birth defect that prevents the esophagus from properly coordinating the passage of food into the stomach.

Vomiting is probably not a cause for concern if it happens only once or twice and the cat acts normal before and after. Resting the cat's digestive tract by withholding food and water for twelve to twenty-four hours or so will usually resolve the gastric irritation.

But when vomiting fails to bring up the anticipated hairball, is not associated with eating, and/or the cat acts as if he feels bad before or after the event, vomiting may indicate serous illness.

Vomiting can be one sign of FELINE PANLEUKOPENIA VIRUS, HEART-WORMS, SWALLOWED OBJECTS, or LIVER or KIDNEY DISEASE. If there is blood in the vomit, if vomiting continues for more than twenty-four hours, or if other signs such as DIARRHEA accompany the vomiting, see your veterinarian.

In certain instances, when the cat has eaten something he shouldn't, vomiting should be induced by the owner or veterinarian (see POISON).

V

Weaning

See KITTEN and REPRODUCTION.

Whiskers

Whiskers are a type of specialized hair referred to as "vibrissae" or "sinus" hairs that are found on the cat's muzzle, eyebrows, sometimes the cheeks and chin, and the underside of the lower forelegs. Whiskers are very long and stiff, yet flexible, and serve a sensory function for the cat.

The hairs are seated deep in the SKIN, with the base of the hair surrounded by a forest of nerve endings. These nerves register the slightest vibration or contact with the hair. Whiskers are efficient antennae that detect everything from the measure of a narrow opening to shifts in the wind and barometric pressure. Whiskers also protect the cat's eyes from injury, providing a startle reflex that shuts the eyes if anything touches them.

Whiskers serve a sensory function for the cat. *(Photo credit: Ralston Purina Company)*

Wood's Lamp

See RINGWORM.

Wool Sucking

W

This behavior problem occurs most frequently in Siamese and Burmese cats and is seen almost exclusively in adult cats. The cat chews on cloth using the large molars at the side of his mouth. Loosely knitted or wo-

WOOL SUCKING

SYMPTOMS

Adult cat chewing or sucking on fabric, especially wool

HOME CARE

Offer fiber-enriched diet; supplement food with leafy lettuce, green beans, canned pumpkin

VET CARE

Same as home care

PREVENTION

Put target fabrics out of cat's reach; treat target items with cat repellent, like bitter apple

ven wool items are preferred, but other fabrics will be chewed when wool isn't available. Large holes can be made in sweaters, blankets, or other items within minutes. The behavior is erratic and unpredictable.

Wool sucking or chewing is not due to a nutritional deficiency, but is believed to be related to eating. The behavior can be prompted by withholding food and appears to abate when food or plants are made available. Experts believe wool sucking results from a craving for roughage or indigestible fiber.

A diet higher in fiber may help such cats. Try supplementing the diet with canned pumpkin, a leafy lettuce, crunchy green beans, or another vegetable source.

Some behaviorists recommend modifying the cat's behavior by treating a target item with something that smells or tastes bad to the cat. Commercial pet repellents are available, or use bitter apple. And keep tempting cloth objects out of reach.

W

Worms

See PARASITES.

W

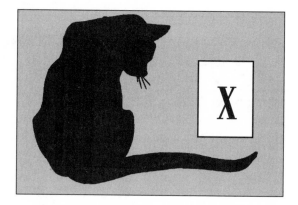

X-ray

X-rays, also referred to as radiographs, are a type of invisible wavelike electromagnetic radiation similar to but shorter than visible light. This

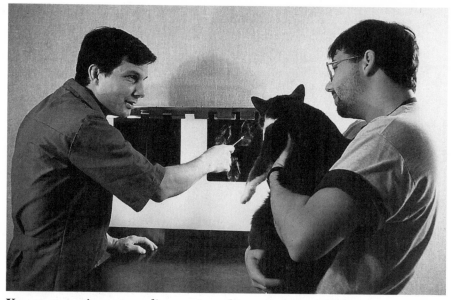

X-rays are an important diagnostic tool in veterinary medicine. (*Photo credit: Amy D. Shojai*)

specialized radiation is able to penetrate with varying success the different structures of the body, and leaves a record on photographic film.

Radiation that is able to penetrate all the way through the body results in a negative image on the film. The more waves that pass through, the darker the image; the fewer there are, the lighter the picture on the film.

Air allows the most penetration and these areas look black on the film. Fat is next and appears dark gray. Fluid or soft tissue will be recorded in varying degrees of medium to light gray. X-rays aren't able to penetrate extremely complex or dense portions of the body; bones, for example, will appear white on the film.

X-rays are an important diagnostic tool in both human and veterinary medicine. They make it possible to see broken bones, bladder stones, or swallowed objects, and allow the doctor to identify many conditions without the invasiveness of exploratory surgery. This enables the patient to receive a diagnosis and treatment that otherwise might come too late.

The radiation level in diagnostic X-rays is carefully regulated so that it won't cause health problems. When used therapeutically as a treatment for cancer, the intensity of the radiation is increased and targeted to specific areas (see CANCER).

X

Yellow Fat Disease (Steatitis)

Steatitis means an inflammation of fat. In cats, it refers specifically to a condition in which fat is changed into hard, painful deposits beneath the skin.

No one is certain what causes the condition. It's thought to occur as a result of excessive dietary fish oil fatty acids without adequate amounts of preservatives like vitamin E.

Historically, cats that became sick with this condition were fed diets primarily consisting of tuna. The strong flavor of this diet is highly addictive to cats, and many refuse to eat anything else once exposed to the flavor. Tuna fish is already low in vitamin E, and problems in canning processes used in the past resulted in a further breakdown of this vitamin. The resulting tuna diets were extremely deficient in vitamin E, and cats that ate them exclusively developed yellow fat disease.

When large amounts of unsaturated fatty acids are digested, compounds called reactive peroxides are produced. This oxidation process destroys vitamin E. The body tries to make up the vitamin E deficit by substituting other fatty acids like arachidonic acid, but this throws the fatty acid ratio out of balance and can result in fat disposition. Consequently, enzymes in the body react with the fat in a process called saponification; the fat is turned into hard, soaplike deposits beneath the skin. Typically, these deposits range in color from a dirty white to a dark

YELLOW FAT DISEASE (STEATITIS)

SYMPTOMS

Dull greasy fur, flaky skin, painful skin, stiff gait or refusal to move, lumpy or bumpy skin especially in groin area

HOME CARE

Feed complete and balanced diet; eliminate fish treats, especially tuna

VET CARE

High doses of vitamin E, steroids to reduce inflammation, antibiotics, sometimes surgical removal of infected area

PREVENTION

Feed complete and balanced diet

brownish mustard—which is how the condition came to be called yellow fat disease.

Steatitis is considered rare today, because the canning process has been improved and because commercial cat-food diets are much better. The condition is most often seen in pampered pets—typically young, overweight cats with finicky eating habits.

Changing a cat's diet regularly or offering highly palatable foods increases the odds of developing finicky feeding behaviors in your feline. Homemade diets and FOOD SUPPLEMENTS also raise the risk for the condition, particularly when cats are routinely fed treats or diets composed of tuna or fish.

The first signs of vitamin E deficiency are a dull, greasy haircoat and flaky skin. The fat deposits are painful, and cats typically are reluctant to be touched. They flinch when petted, and walk stiffly or refuse to move at all. Eventually, the cat stops eating, even refusing tuna.

Fat deposits may appear anywhere on the body, but most often are located in the groin area. The skin feels lumpy or bumpy. Diagnosis is

y

based on physical signs and a history of the cat's diet. A microscopic examination of a sample of affected tissue shows inflammation or changes in the structure of the fat.

Treatment consists of feeding the cat a complete and balanced diet, along with vitamin E supplementation. Oftentimes, 100 IU of vitamin E twice daily resolves the condition within a few weeks. Steroid therapy may help to relieve inflammation and make the cat more comfortable during recovery. Fat deposits that become infected require antibiotic treatment, and surgical removal of severely infected tissue may be necessary.

It's much easier to prevent the problem from ever occurring simply by feeding your feline an appropriate diet (see EATING, FOOD, and NUTRITION).

y

Zoonosis

A zoonosis is a disease that can be transmitted from an animal to a human under normal conditions. People are susceptible to a variety of viral and bacterial diseases, funguses, and parasitic disorders that more commonly afflict animals.

There are more than two hundred known zoonoses, but only a handful are associated with pets. Most problems are transient and easily treated, and the number of cases of transmission is relatively low. However, zoonoses should never be taken lightly, because a small percentage can cause debilitating illness or even death.

Without exception, the most common zoonotic diseases associated with cats can be avoided. Basic hygiene and other commonsense preventive measures will protect both you and your pet from illness. (See also CAT SCRATCH DISEASE, HOOKWORMS, PLAGUE, RABIES, RINGWORM, TAPEWORMS, TICKS, and TOXOPLASMOSIS.)

Appendix A

Cat Associations and Cat Breeds

CAT ASSOCIATIONS

A cat association is a national organization that registers cats, keeps records of their ancestry in pedigrees, publishes breed standards, sponsors cat shows, and determines who will judge them. Catteries are individual establishments that strive to produce the "ideal" cat of a given breed. These cats are then shown in contests sanctioned by the cat association in which that cat is registered. The goal is to determine which cat is closest to the breed standard of perfection.

Catteries often hold membership in local cat clubs, which in turn are members of one or more cat associations. There are a number of cat associations. Breed standards may vary from association to association, for not every cat association recognizes the same cat breeds. If you are interested in learning more about cat show opportunities for you and your cat, contact one or more of the following organizations.

American Association of Cat
Enthusiasts
P.O. Box 213
Pine Brook, NJ 07058
610-916-2079

American Cat Association
8101 Katherine Avenue
Panorama City, CA 91402
818-782-6080

American Cat Fanciers'
Association
P.O. Box 203
Point Lookout, MO 65726
417-334-5430

Canadian Cat Association
220 Advance Boulevard,
Suite 101
Brampton, ON L6T 4J5
Canada

Cat Fanciers' Association
1805 Atlantic Avenue
P.O. Box 1005
Manasquan, NJ 08736-0805
908-528-9797

Cat Fanciers' Federation
P.O. Box 661
Gratis, OH 45330
513-787-9009

The International Cat
Association
P.O. Box 2684
Harlingen, TX 78551
512-428-8046

National Cat Fanciers'
Association
20305 W. Burt Road
Brant, MI 48614

United Cat Federation
5510 Ptolemy Way
Mira Loma, CA 91752
714-685-7896

CAT BREEDS

Note: for unfamiliar feline terminology see BREED entry, pages 50–54.

ABYSSINIAN

The Abyssinian is a medium-size breed of cat first developed in England about 1868. Abys have distinctive agouti coloring that looks like wild rabbit fur; in fact, in the past they were called Bunny Cats. Each hair is ticked with two to three bands of color, giving the short, silky coat a wild look. Abys are accepted in different colors by various breed associations: ruddy, red (sorrel), blue, fawn, lilac, cream. The green- or gold-eyed Abyssinian is a regal, fine-boned yet muscular cat that seems to be always on tiptoe.

Curiosity and avid interest describe the typical Aby. This cat won't sit still long enough to make a good lap cat. Instead, his intelligence and athletic ability make him a mischievous cat who becomes easily bored without lots of attention. Abys love to climb, jump, and race, and may prefer perching on the tops of doors and scaling drapes to napping. They tolerate other cats but prefer to receive all the attention. Abys are wonderfully entertaining, extremely affectionate, in-your-face cats.

AMERICAN CURL

The American Curl is recognized for her distinctive ears that curl backward from the face. The breed is one of the newest and was founded by Shulamith, a stray black longhaired kitten with curled ears who was discovered in 1981. All true Curls of today are related to her. Because these cats are descended from an enormous gene pool of domestic cats, they are generally very hardy, healthy cats remarkably free of genetic defects.

Unlike the soft ears of most cats, the ear cartilage in Curls is firm like human ears. Kittens are born with straight ears that curl between two and ten days of age, then furl and unfurl until they reach their permanent shape—usually by six months. Some Curls actually end up with straight ears. Any coat color, pattern, or length is acceptable in this medium-size cat. Curls tend to be "people cats" who want to be in on everything. They retain a kittenish exuberance for life, and never seem to outgrow their delight in play. Curls enjoy being with other cats, as well as with children.

AMERICAN SHORTHAIR

The American Shorthair is the archetypical farm cat. This breed is a medium to large, strongly built cat that seems made for work. In the early 1900s, those interested in preserving these qualities began selectively breeding the finest examples, which they called Domestic Shorthairs. In 1966, the breed became known as the American Shorthair, and is distinct from the random-bred cat down the street that by chance may look similar.

American Shorthair cats come in a variety of coat colors and patterns. The fur is always short, thick, and hard in texture. They are loving cats, remarkably hardy and resistant to disease. These athletic felines have retained their hunting skills and enjoy being with other cats.

AMERICAN WIREHAIR

In 1966, a spontaneous mutation produced a kitten with a distinctive crimped coat of medium-length wiry fur. Unlike his littermates or either parent, Adam the barn kitten had a soft "Brillo-pad" coat and curly whiskers. He became the founding father of the American Wirehair breed, which is still considered a relatively rare cat.

Wires demand little grooming, are quiet, and tend to be the dominant force in any group of cats. These medium to large cats come in a variety of coat colors and patterns. They aren't terribly active, and may prefer to watch from a distance rather than be in the middle of things.

BALINESE

The Balinese is a lithe, long-bodied, blue-eyed cat with pointed coloring and a silky long coat. Unlike some other longhaired cats, the Balinese does not have a heavy double coat; the silky single coat lies close to the body. The most distinctive feature is a luxurious tail plume. American cat enthusiasts began promoting the Balinese as a new breed in the 1940s when Siamese cats gave birth to longhaired kittens. Coat length is the only difference between the short-haired Siamese and the Balinese.

The Balinese cat was named after the graceful dancers of Bali, as well as their Siamese heritage. Like the Siamese, the Balinese is a talkative cat that bonds closely with her people. These cats can be very energetic and demand much attention. Balinese are also said to be quite protective of their loved ones.

BENGAL

The Bengal is a hybrid cat produced by crossbreeding the Asian leopard cat with American Shorthairs. For years breeders wanted to create a domestic feline with the look of an exotic wild cat and the temperament of a lap cat. It wasn't until the 1980s that true success was achieved by breeding spotted tabby American Shorthairs with leopard cats. The Bengal has been recognized as a true breed by some registries only since 1991.

To ensure that Bengals remain a true domestic breed, cats must be several generations removed from their wild cousins. At least four generations of Bengal-to-Bengal breeding is required if that cat is to be shown.

This leopard look-alike comes in a variety of colors in either spots or a "marbling" coat pattern. Owners describe Bengals as doglike, in that they enjoy playing fetch and walking on a leash, and get along well with other pets and people. They demand to be the center of attention.

BIRMAN

The Birman is an ancient breed native to Burma, where for hundreds of years they were raised as temple cats. Imported to France in 1919, the breed was nearly lost during World War II; only one pair of Birman cats remained, and they founded the breed we know today. Birmans were recognized in the United States in 1967.

The Birman is a large, stocky, long-bodied, blue-eyed cat with easy-care, semilong fur that rarely mats. Birmans are born solid white; adult color develops over time. Predominantly white or cream fur on the body is misted with gold, and accented by dark masks (a dark contrasting color surrounding the eyes, and possibly encompassing the entire face) and legs usually in seal point (dark brown) or blue point (slate gray). The Birman's most distinctive feature is four white feet that look as if they were dipped in sugar.

Birmans are family cats that enjoy contact with children and other pets, and relish games of fetch. They are talkative yet soft-spoken cats with a low-slung, tigerlike gait, and always enjoy being petted.

BOMBAY

The Bombay is a medium-size cat with extremely short, close-fitting, jet-black fur and golden eyes. These "parlor panthers" were named for the city of Bombay because of their resemblance to the Indian black leopard.

Bombays are the result of breeding a black American Shorthair to a sable Burmese. In body type, the rounded head and muscular body make the Bombay similar to the Burmese, but the coat color, with its satinlike texture, make this cat different from any other.

The easy-care coat and gregarious personality make Bombays wonderful pets. Small and easily trained, these cats fetch naturally. They like lap-sitting and enjoy other cats and children.

BRITISH SHORTHAIR

The British Shorthair is to Great Britain what the American Shorthair is to the United States. These cats were found in the cities and farms all over the British Isles, and were prized as mousers. A British Shorthair cat was awarded the Best in Show prize at the very first organized cat show that took place in England in 1871.

British Shorthairs look similar to the American Shorthair but have a slightly rounder face and are known for their short, plush, weather-resistant coats. They come in a variety of colors, though for a time the blue (dark gray) variety was so popular it was referred to as a separate breed and called the British Blue.

These smiling cats are calm, congenial pets that are independent yet delight in children. They mature slowly, and fanciers consider them at their show peak at about five years of age.

BURMESE

The hybrid Burmese cat's ancestors probably originated in Burma. The founder of today's breed was a dark brown cat brought to San Francisco from Rangoon (now Yangon) in 1930, and bred to a Siamese. First registered in 1936, the Burmese of today is a medium-size, solid-boned cat surprisingly heavy for his size. The most popular color is sable brown, but recently other colors have become popular. The short coat requires minimal care.

Burms are animated cats that want to be in the middle of things. They leap great distances effortlessly and are equally at home in your lap or lounging on the tops of doors. They prefer being an only cat (more attention for them that way!), but do get along with other cats and pets.

CHARTREUX

The Chartreux is a shorthaired, thick-coated cat sporting dark blue-gray water-repellent fur. He has been described by some as a "potato on toothpicks" because of his solid body balanced on rather thin legs. This breed, which originated in France, has a sturdy, broad-shouldered bearlike look, with rather short, finely boned legs. The cat is known for his sweetly smiling face.

Chartreux enjoy playing fetch and often learn to come when their name is called. Rather quiet cats who prefer chirping to meowing, Chartreux cats thrive on attention and are loyal family members.

COLORPOINT SHORTHAIR

The Colorpoint Shorthair is essentially a Siamese cat with nontraditional point colors. These cats were developed from Siamese that were bred to British or American Shorthairs or Abyssinians. Today, some cat associations recognize Colorpoints simply as Siamese, while other associations register this cat as a separate breed.

Like the Siamese, the Colorpoint is a shorthaired foreign-type cat with blue eyes and a body color of white or off-white. The points come in solid colors of red or cream, lynx point in tabby patterns and colors, and tortie points of tortoiseshell colors. Colorpoints are loving cats that bond closely with all family members.

CORNISH REX

The Cornish Rex cat's unique look includes a greyhoundlike body with short curly fur that's missing a coarse top coat. The Cornish Rex first appeared in 1950 as a spontaneous mutation in Cornwall, England. The breed was developed by crossing these cats with Siamese, which defined the Cornish Rex's rangy, distinctive appearance.

These cats are very athletic and great climbers. Their wiry coat sheds less than some other breeds', which makes them easy-care cats. They get along well with other cats and people, including children, but their dainty structure precludes any roughhousing.

CYMRIC

Pronounced "kim-rick," this relatively new breed was recognized for show in the 1970s and was developed from the Manx cat. The Cymric is a Manx with long, silky fur.

Cymrics are medium-size, heavy-boned cats with a cobby body type, a rounded rump, and long hind legs. The coat length varies from one and a half to two and a half inches, and comes in most every color. Like the Manx, this breed has three degrees of taillessness: "rumpy" or no tail at all; "stumpy," with a tail one to five inches long; and "longie," with a complete tail. Cymrics are affectionate, active cats adept at jumping and climbing. Their personality is similar to the clownlike Manx, and they love being the center of attention.

DEVON REX

The Devon Rex breed appeared in 1960 when a curly-coated kitten was born to a feral cat living in Devonshire, England. The pixielike appearance of the Devon includes huge ears, an elfin face, large round eyes, and a hard, muscular body covered with soft wavy fur that resembles lamb's wool.

The Devon has a somewhat thinner coat than the curly-coated Cornish Rex, and while the Cornish has a Roman nose, the Devon has a definite stop or indentation to the nose. The Devon is an extremely active cat. People-oriented, he prefers lap-sitting to window-gazing.

EGYPTIAN MAU

This spotted, somewhat shorthaired cat is thought to be one of the oldest breeds, dating back to 1400 B.C. Ancient Egyptians revered the cat. Mau is the Egyptian word for both "cat" and "light." Spotted felines similar to today's Maus are depicted on the walls of Egyptian tombs.

These green-eyed cats are the only natural breed of domestic spotted cat. Their body is randomly spotted, with banding on the legs and tail. Coat colors are darker spots on lighter solid background, in either coppery brown, silver, or silver background with black spots.

The Mau is an athletic cat that has retained his wild ancestors' slinking cheetah gait. This breed needs much handling as a kitten to be properly socialized, as they tend to be reserved and fiercely independent. Maus prefer to be the only cat and are affectionate toward family members.

EXOTIC SHORTHAIR

This plush-coated, moderately shorthaired cat is a hybrid of the Persian and American Shorthair cat breeds. The Exotic Shorthair is a Persian in body type (cobby and solid, snub nose, round eyes) and temperament, but with a teddy-bear coat, and today is recognized as an independent breed.

Like Persians, this breed comes in a variety of coat colors and patterns. Quiet, undemanding, and exceedingly affectionate cats, Exotic Shorthairs are loyal companions who enjoy lap-sitting but don't bother their owners too much about it. They like interactive games as much as the next cat, but these laid-back kitties prefer quiet time with their owners to athletic endeavors.

HAVANA BROWN

This chocolate-colored shorthaired breed originated in England and is a medium-size cat with brilliant green eyes. Some say the name comes from the cat's color similarity to a Havana cigar, others to the Havana rabbit of the same color.

The Havana has a uniquely shaped muzzle unlike that of any other cat breed. Described alternately as a corncob or lightbulb stuck on the face, the Havana muzzle has a decided stop or indentation where the nose meets the eyes, similar to a dog's muzzle.

Havana Brown cats tend to be quiet, affectionate cats that enjoy the company of people and other pets. They like to be in the middle of things. Breeders describe their coats as easy-care. Havana Browns are said to be extremely fastidious and wash themselves and their companions frequently.

HIMALAYAN

This cat is recognized as a separate breed in some registries and as a color pattern of the Persian breed in others. It really makes no difference to the cat, whose striking features make her a standout whatever her designation.

The Himalayan was created by breeding Persians to Siamese cats to achieve Persian body type and coat with Siamese pointed coloring and eyes. Himalayans have the sweet laid-back temperament of the Persian, and get along well with other cats.

JAPANESE BOBTAIL

This natural breed has been a native of Japan for centuries but wasn't introduced to the United States until the late 1960s. The Japanese Bobtail is known for his corkscrew tail that fans into an attractive pouf on his rump. This distinctive tail is found nowhere else in the cat world.

The Japanese Bobtail is in no way related to the tailless Manx. The Bobtail is a shorthaired, sturdy cat and comes in all coat colors except pointed or the agouti coat of the Abyssinian. Preferred colors are combinations of white, black, and red.

Breeders describe these cats as active, soft-spoken yet talkative pets who enjoy games of fetch and are particularly good with children. Bobtails also accept other pets and dogs.

JAVANESE

The Javanese breed is virtually identical to the Colorpoint Short-hair cat, except for the coat length. The Javanese fur is longer and softer, and is described as a silk chiffon coat.

This dainty-appearing cat is extremely vocal, a characteristic inherited from Siamese ancestry. The baby-fine medium-length fur requires minimal grooming and rarely mats. Javanese are people cats who want to be in the middle of everything.

KORAT

This breed is a native of Thailand and boasts a distinctive silver blue coat and luminous green eyes that appear too large for the somewhat heart-shaped face. It may take up to four years for the eyes to develop their true adult color. The short fur lies close to the body, and each hair is blue, tipped with silver. Korats are medium-size muscular cats. They are relatively uncommon, even in Thailand.

The Korat is a quiet, gentle cat that dislikes loud or sudden noises. They are devoted to their special people, enjoy lap-sitting, and indulge in active play as well. They will accept other pets but tend to want their owner's exclusive attention.

MAINE COON

This breed appeared naturally and is a native American longhaired cat first recognized in Maine. The Maine Coon is one of the heaviest and largest breeds, with adult males reaching up to twenty pounds in weight.

Despite folklore to the contrary, the cat has no common ancestry with raccoons. More likely, the name arose because early cats sported tabby rings on their fluffy tails that looked similar to raccoon tails.

The Maine Coon's silky, shaggy coat comes in a variety of colors and patterns. The coat takes less care than other longhaired breeds, and will remain mat-free without a lot of grooming.

Coon cats are a muscular breed, often nicknamed Gentle Giants for their calm, kind natures. They are loyal, quiet cats who get along well with other pets and children.

MANX

The Manx cat is the definitive tailless cat. This is an old breed that has been popular for over a hundred years. Manx originated on the Isle of Man in the Irish Sea off the coast of England. Legend holds that tail-less cats swam ashore after a shipwreck and colonized the island, but nobody knows for sure how the cats came to arrive.

Manx can have varying degrees of taillessness: "rumpies" are completely tailless; "risers" have only a small bump where the tail should be; "stumpies" sport an abbreviated tail, either straight, kinked, or curled; and "longies" are Manx cats with full-length tails. Unfortunately, the gene that produces taillessness can also cause a variety of crippling spinal problems, which conscientious breeders are working to eliminate.

The Manx cat's short thick fur comes in a variety of colors and patterns. He is a medium-size cat with a round face and a short back that arches to a rounded rump and long back legs. Manx are wonderful companions, and are described by some as clownlike in behavior.

NORWEGIAN FOREST CAT

"Skogkatt" means "forest cat" and is the Norse name for this large, natural, longhaired beauty. The Norwegian Forest Cat is said to have accompanied the Vikings on their many voyages. To the uninitiated, he looks very similar to the Maine Coon, and in fact some speculate that he may be a forebear of the younger American breed. Fanciers point out that the Forest Cat has a boxier build, a more triangular face, and lower-set ears than the Maine Coon.

The Norwegian Forest Cat is a large, strongly built breed known for his impressive weather-resistant double coat. He comes in nearly all colors and coat patterns, except pointed, and has green to gold eyes. The breed does not fully mature until five years of age.

The extremely long outer guard hairs are silky to the touch, and the thick undercoat is cottony soft and thick. This undercoat is shed each spring. The long fur requires little maintenance beyond occasional combing, especially during shedding season. The Wegie is a gentle people cat who enjoys being a part of the family.

OCICAT

The Ocicat is a large, athletic, shorthaired cat covered with distinctive dark spots on a light background that make him look like the wild ocelot. The first Ocicat appeared in 1964 as the result of an experimental breeding arranged to produce Aby-point Siamese. Instead, a cream-colored cat with golden spots appeared, and the Ocicat was born. Today, Ocicats are seen in a rainbow of colors.

This man-made breed weds the allure of the exotic wild look with the predictable, lovable disposition of the pet cat. Ocicats are said to have a doglike devotion to their special people and make great family pets. They are quite easy to train and are not bashful with strangers. They don't like being left alone, though, and prefer to be in the middle of things. Ocicats get along well with other pets.

ORIENTAL LONGHAIR

The Oriental Longhair is a hybrid cat with ancestry that includes the Siamese, Colorpoint Shorthair, Oriental Shorthair, Balinese, and Javanese. Her body type and shape are very similar to all of these breeds.

The coat is long, fine, and very silky to the touch, but lies close to the body to give the cat a well-groomed, svelte appearance. The furred tail looks like a plume. Coat colors and patterns are virtually anything you can imagine. This relatively new breed is basically a longhaired Siamese that comes in all the colors of the rainbow (see SIAMESE).

ORIENTAL SHORTHAIR

This cat is essentially a Siamese cat wedded to the rainbow of coat colors and patterns found in the American Shorthair. Breeders have described the Oriental Shorthair as a Siamese in designer jeans.

Like the Siamese, this breed is a lithe, Oriental-type cat of medium size with a short, fine coat. Though delicate-boned and almost dainty in appearance, this strong muscular cat bursts with energy. Orientals become very attached to their people, and may prefer to be one-person pets.

PERSIAN

The Persian breed is arguably the most popular and recognizable breed of cat. These cats are said to be named for their country of origin, but their true beginnings may never be known. Persian cats have full long coats, and their short square bodies are the archetypical "cobby" type. They have distinctive, wide, flat faces with large round eyes.

Persians come in a variety of coat colors and patterns. The luxurious coat of the Persian cat has been developed to the point that only a protected indoor lifestyle is appropriate for this breed. Persians require a great deal of maintenance on an owner's part, including daily grooming and regular bathing.

Persians are quiet, serene cats who enjoy playing but are not boisterous. They prefer lap-sitting and posing for admiration, to climbing or leaping. These gentle, gorgeous cats make wonderful pets.

RAGDOLL

The Ragdoll came by her name for her tendency to go limp when held. This breed is a relatively new hybrid resulting from an accidental breeding of a seal-point Birman and white Persian, along with various other breeds.

The Ragdoll is the largest cat breed, with male cats tipping the scales at twenty pounds or more. Coat patterns are bicolor, colorpoint, or mitted (white feet). These longhaired, blue-eyed cats are also known for their extremely sweet, gentle nature.

RUSSIAN BLUE

His refined, graceful boning, emerald eyes, and sliver-tipped short blue fur make the Russian Blue a standout among cats. The breed arose in the Baltic area. He was at one time known as the Archangel Cat for his origination near the port of the same name on the White Sea.

Although historical accounts refer to the longhaired Archangel Cat, breeders had to re-create this variety. The new longhaired Russian Blue breed, called the Nebelung, is still being refined.

Russian Blue cats tend to be cautious with strangers and are slow to become acquainted. They are extremely agile cats who like to cram themselves into nooks and crannies, and never seem to outgrow their enjoyment of playing games. Because of their reserved personality, Russians are more suited to being only cats and do not do well in households with large numbers of other pets.

SCOTTISH FOLD

A Scottish Fold cat is named both for her country of origin and for her ears, which fold forward over the head. These distinctive ears give the cat a teddy-bear or owl-like appearance. The breed was developed from a folded-ear barn cat found in 1961 on a farm in Scotland.

The Fold is a medium-size cat with a rounded body and short, dense fur. Kittens are born with straight ears that begin to fold at about three to four months of age; some Folds have straight ears, but may nevertheless produce fold-eared kittens.

Breeding a straight-eared Fold to a fold-eared cat results in about 50 percent of the kittens in the litter having folded ears. Breeding a Fold to a Fold increases the numbers of fold-eared kittens, but it also increases the risk of crippling bone abnormalities, which breeders are trying to eliminate. Thick or poor mobility in the legs or tail indicates problems.

Scottish Folds come in nearly every coat color. Some need their ears cleaned often due to waxy buildup. They are sweet-tempered cats with quiet voices and ways. They tend to adjust well to multicat or multipet households and get along well with children.

SCOTTISH FOLD LONGHAIR

This breed is identical in every way to the shorthaired Scottish Fold except for its semilong fluffy coat. Some cat associations call this breed the Longhair Fold or the Highland Fold. They require almost daily grooming to keep the coat in shape.

SIAMESE

The Siamese is one of the oldest, best-known, and most popular of cat breeds in the world today. This is the native cat of what is today known as Thailand. The Siamese was treasured by royalty of ancient Siam and protected within their temple walls for at least two centuries.

The Siamese is a foreign-type, lithe, shorthaired cat with a triangular face, muscular tubular body, and intense blue eyes. He is best known for his "pointed" pattern, which consists of a lighter-colored body with solid contrasting-colored legs, ears, tail, and mask.

Siamese cats have a distinctive voice and are known to be talkative. They love to be part of a family. They are considered quite doglike because of their natural inclination to play fetch, follow their owners, and bond closely with people.

SINGAPURA

The Singapura is a native cat of Singapore. She was known as a Drain Cat because of her habit of sheltering in the city's sewers.

This is the smallest recognized cat breed. Adult Singapuras range in size from four to six pounds. The coat color is similar to the Abyssinian, but is much finer and very short, with only dark brown ticking on an ivory ground allowed. The eyes and ears are very large on this stocky but small cat.

The Singapura is a people cat who has never met a stranger. The word *curiosity* may have been invented to describe this friendly feline. The breed is still relatively uncommon in the United States, but growing in popularity.

SNOWSHOE

The Snowshoe is a relatively new breed developed during the 1970s by breeding a Siamese with a bicolor American Shorthair. The result was a medium-to-large muscular cat with the Siamese point patterns laced with white on the feet, nose, and tummy, and striking blue eyes.

The Snowshoe is a lap-sitter who prefers to be an only cat and have the owner's attention all to himself. Snowshoes are loving cats. They will accept other animals if they must, and enjoy children.

SOMALI

The Somali is identical to the Abyssinian cat except that she has long hair. The fur can be long and silky or thick and woolly, with variations in between.

These are medium-size, extremely active, athletic cats. They remind one of a fox because of their coloring, bushy tail, and full ruff. Like their Aby littermates, the Somali is an on-the-go cat who still enjoys a lap nap after a heady bout of chasing the dog.

SPHYNX

The Sphynx breed is an unusual cat because he has little or no fur. Such cats have appeared from time to time in the past, but efforts were not made to recognize them as a distinct breed until 1966, when a hairless kitten was born in Ontario, Canada. In 1980, two hairless stray female kittens found on the streets of Toronto were subsequently sent to Holland, where they founded the breed we know today.

The Sphynx is not truly bald. He has a peach-fuzz covering of fine down on his body and sometimes very short fur on his muzzle, tail, and feet. Sphynx cats come in any coat color or pattern. Early examples of the breed often had genetic problems that prevented them from fully developing healthy immune systems. Breeders are working to eliminate these problems.

The Sphynx requires frequent bathing to keep his skin clean and control the normal oils that are absorbed into the fur of other cats. The breed is more sensitive to extremes of temperature and has a body temperature a degree or so warmer than that of other cats.

Considered friendly, gregarious cats, Sphynx get along well with other animals. They have been described as part child, part monkey, and part dog for their innocent loving natures, athletic ability, and tendency to wag their tails when happy. The breed is considered quite rare.

TONKINESE

The Tonkinese is a hybrid cat developed by breeding the foreign-type Siamese with the stockier Burmese. The result is a medium-size pointed cat in mink colors with a body type somewhere between the two parent breeds. To the uninitiated, the Tonk may be confused with an old-style "apple-headed" Siamese. But his distinctive aqua- to turquoise-colored eyes make him stand out from any other breed.

In the Tonk you'll find a combination of the talkative, outgoing Siamese tempered with the gentle and affectionate Burmese nature. The result is an active, intelligent "people cat" who quickly learns how to open drawers and doors, and gets into all kinds of mischief. These energetic cats seem at home reclining on the tops of refrigerators or scaling even greater heights. Some breeders recommend getting two Tonks; that way, they'll entertain each other rather than get into trouble.

TURKISH ANGORA

The Turkish Angora is a centuries-old breed that originated in the area surrounding the city of Angora (now Ankara), Turkey. The breed is a slim, medium-size cat with medium-length silky or even wavy fur. Historically, these cats appeared in black, white, dark red, light fawn, mottled gray, and smoke colors. Today, we most commonly see this lovely breed in solid white.

The Turkish Angora is an intelligent, affectionate cat who enjoys petting and lap-sitting, and loves to play. She is also an opinionated cat, and may act stubborn when something isn't to her liking. The luxurious fur has no woolly undercoat, which makes the coat easy care and low maintenance.

TURKISH VAN

This ancient breed is a large, muscular cat that arose in the area that today encompasses Iran, Iraq, parts of the old Soviet Union, and eastern Turkey. Tradition holds that the cats come from the Lake Van region of ancient Armenia (now Turkey), hence their name. The term *van* refers to color markings on the head and tail with a white body.

The Van has semilong, easy-care fur that has a unique cashmerelike texture. The fur is waterproof, and these cats love the water—they are called swimming cats in their native region. The white body color is highlighted with markings typically set in a cap of color on the head and ears, the tail, and sometimes the back. A color mark on the shoulders is particularly prized and referred to as the "thumbprint of Allah." The Van is not common in the United States. Vans do not consider themselves pets, but equals and companions in the home. They have a doglike loyalty, love games of fetch, and do not give their affection lightly.

Symptoms at a Glance: The Quick Reference Guide for Home Diagnosis

The following correlates an alphabetical list of the common signs and symptoms of illness with the troubling condition(s) that each may indicate. To use the chart, look up one or more of the problem signs your cat may be suffering. Then read the corresponding entry topic to learn more about a given disease or condition. This will help you to identify what's troubling your cat and learn whether immediate veterinary care is necessary or a home remedy may suffice. Whenever possible, the appropriate home treatment is listed in the text entry so that, if possible, you can tend to your cat yourself.

However, this chart is only a *guide*. No book can ever replace the expertise of a veterinarian, who is in the best position to accurately diagnose and treat any troubling illness from which your cat may be suffering.

SIGNS AND SYMPTOMS	*DISEASE OR CONDITION*
aggression, toward people/other pets	dominance, fear, hyperesthesia syndrome, pain, rabies, stress
aggression, toward self (mutilation)	hyperesthesia syndrome

SIGNS AND SYMPTOMS	*DISEASE OR CONDITION*
appetite, increased	diabetes mellitus, hyperthyroidism
appetite, loss of (anorexia)	abscess, anemia, aspirin poisoning, cancer, cystitis, dehydration, enteritis, feline hepatic lipidosis and liver disease, FIV, feline panleukopenia, FIP, FeLV, fever, haemobartonellosis, hairballs, insect bites/stings, heart disease, kidney disease, LUTD, mastitis, pain, periodontal disease, peritonitis, pyometra, rabies, stomatitis, swallowed object, upper respiratory disease
blackheads/pimples, on chin and mouth	acne
blackheads/pimples, at tail root	stud tail
bleeding	cancer, poison, trauma
blood, in queen's milk	mastitis
blood, in stool	aspirin poisoning, coccidiosis, colitis, hookworms, other poison
blood, in urine	cancer, cystitis, LUTD
blood, in vomit	aspirin poisoning, other poison
bloody nose	head trauma (falls), hyperthermia
blindness	cataract, epilepsy, FIP, FeLV, glaucoma, taurine deficiency, trauma
breathing, choking/gagging	hairballs, swallowed objects
breathing, gasping, wheezing	asthma, cancer, heartworms, pneumonia
breathing, labored	cardiomyopathy, electrical shock, FIV, heartworms, insect bites/stings, lungworms, pneumonia, vaccine or drug reaction
breathing, panting	antifreeze poisoning, pneumonia, pain
breathing, rapid	anemia, eclampsia, pneumonia, shock

SIGNS AND SYMPTOMS	*DISEASE OR CONDITION*
breathing, stopped	drowning, electrical shock, hypothermia
bumps	abscess, cancer, cyst, plague, yellow fat disease, vaccination reaction
chewing, fabric	wool sucking
chewing/grinding teeth	seizure, rabies
choking/gagging	hairballs, swallowed objects
circling	head trauma, otitis
claws, nail bed sores	FeLV, FIV
claws, rapid growth	hyperthyroidism
coat condition, dry	giardia, roundworms, tapeworms, yellow fat disease
coat condition, oily	hyperthyroidism, stud tail, yellow fat disease
coat condition, ricelike debris	tapeworms
collapse	eclampsia, heartworms, insect bites/stings
constipation	cancer, hairballs, inflammatory bowel disease, mega colon
coughing	heartworms, lungworms, pneumonia
crying	dominance display, estrus, pain
depression	anemia, dehydration, fever, FeLV, feline panleukopenia, FIP, haemobartonellosis, kidney disease, peritonitis, rabies, shock, stress
diarrhea	antifreeze poisoning, changing diet, chocolate poisoning, coccidiosis, colitis, enteritis, feeding milk, feline panleukopenia, food allergy, giardia, hairballs, hookworms, hyperthermia, hyperthyroidism, liver disease, poisoning, roundworms, swallowed object

SIGNS AND SYMPTOMS	DISEASE OR CONDITION
drinking, difficulty/refusal	cancer, rabies
drinking, increased thirst	antifreeze poisoning, cystitis, diabetes mellitus, hyperthyroidism, kidney disease, LUTD, pyometra
drooling	aspirin poisoning, chocolate poisoning, eclampsia, foreign body, hyperthermia, insect bites/stings, pain, periodontal disease, poisoning, rabies, stomatitis
drunk, incoordination	antifreeze poisoning, aspirin poisoning, eclampsia, head trauma (high-rise syndrome), insect bites/stings, otitis, poisoning
ears, dark crumbly debris	ear mites
ears, discharge and/or odor	otitis
ears, red or raw	allergy, otitis
eyes, change of color	uveitis
eyes, cloudy	cataract, glaucoma
eyes, dilated	glaucoma
eyes, discharge/runny	FeLV, pain, upper respiratory infection
eyes, glazed/staring	hyperthermia, rabies
eyes, hard	glaucoma
eyes, pawing at	glaucoma, otitis, pain, uveitis
eyes, rough surface	uveitis
eyes, soft	uveitis
eyes, sores/ulcers	upper respiratory infection
eyes, squinting	glaucoma, otitis, pain, ulcer, uveitis
eyes, swelling	glaucoma

SIGNS AND SYMPTOMS	*DISEASE OR CONDITION*
flinching	pain, fear
hair loss	eosinophilic granuloma complex, fleas, hyperthyroidism, mange, psychogenic alopecia, ringworm, shedding, stress, stud tail
head tilt	head trauma, otitis
hiding	fear, pain, stress
hissing	aggression, dominance, fear, pain, stress
hunching (painful abdomen)	cystitis, feline panleukopenia, peritonitis, swallowed object, trauma
hyperactivity	aspirin poisoning, chocolate poisoning, hyperthyroidism
itching, all over	inhalant allergy, lice, mange
itching, of back and tail	fleas
itching, of chin	acne
itching, of ears	ear mites, otitis
itching, of face, mouth, head, and neck	food allergy, mange
itching, localized	insect bites/stings
itching, self-mutilation, esp. tail	hyperesthesia syndrome
lethargy	abscess, cancer, cardiomyopathy, cystitis, fever fleas, heartworms, hookworms, hypothermia, liver disease, LUTD, plague
licking, coat or skin	abscess, allergy, fleas, insect bites/stings, lice, mange, ringworm
licking, genitals	anal gland problems, constipation, cystitis, labor, LUTD
limping, lameness	abscess, arthritis, cancer, fracture

SIGNS AND SYMPTOMS	DISEASE OR CONDITION
loss of consciousness	asthma, chocolate poisoning, drowning, electrical shock, hyperthermia, hypothermia, shock, trauma
lumps	abscess, cancer, plague, vaccination reaction, yellow fat disease
milk, yellow/blood streaked	mastitis
mouth, blue-tinged tongue/gums	pneumonia, respiratory distress, Tylenol poisoning
mouth, bright red gums	carbon monoxide poisoning, gingivitis, hyperthermia, hyperthyroidism
mouth, brown tongue	kidney disease
mouth, burns	caustic poison, electrical shock
mouth, dry/tacky gums	dehydration, kidney disease
mouth, jaw paralysis	abscess, fracture, rabies
mouth, loose teeth	gingivitis, periodontal disease, trauma
mouth, pale	anemia, eclampsia, fleas, haemobartonellosis, hookworms, shock, trauma
mouth, pawing at	swallowed object
mouth, sores/ulcers	FIV, kidney disease, stomatitis, upper respiratory infection
mouth, stringy saliva	dehydration
mouth, swollen/bleeding	gingivitis, insect bites/stings, periodontal disease, trauma
mouth, yellow/brown tooth debris	periodontal disease
muscle tremors	chocolate poisoning, dehydration, eclampsia, hyperesthesia syndrome

SIGNS AND SYMPTOMS	*DISEASE OR CONDITION*
nose, bloody	cancer, hyperthermia, poisoning, shock, trauma
nose, discharge/runny	FeLV, upper respiratory infection
odor, anal area	anal glands, flatulence, poor grooming
odor, ammonia breath	kidney disease
odor, ammonia urine	cystitis, LUTD
odor, bad breath	periodontal disease
odor, of body	cancer, mange
odor, from ears	otitis, cancer
odor, mousy	mange
pacing	eclampsia
paddling, with feet	dreaming, seizure (epilepsy)
pale: ears, nose, toes, tail tip	frostbite
pale: lips, tongue, gums	anemia, eclampsia, fleas, haemobartonellosis, hookworms, shock, trauma
pulse, too fast	anemia, hyperthermia, shock
pulse, too slow	hypothermia, poison
rolling (female cats)	estrus, play invitation
rolling (male cats)	play invitation
scooting (on bottom)	anal gland problems, tapeworms
seizures	antifreeze poisoning, chocolate poisoning, electrical shock, epilepsy, hyperesthesia syndrome, low blood sugar (diabetes), kidney disease, liver disease, poisoning
shivering	hypothermia, shock
skin, loss of elasticity	dehydration, kidney disease

SIGNS AND SYMPTOMS	*DISEASE OR CONDITION*
skin, lumpy/bumpy	cancer, insect bites/stings, vaccination reaction, yellow fat disease
skin, painful	abscess, ulcer, yellow fat disease
skin, pepperlike debris esp. at tail	fleas
skin, red and peeling ears, toes, nose	frostbite, sunburn
skin, red and sores	mange, ringworm
skin, scabby	fleas, lice, miliary dermatitis, ringworm
skin, scaly	lice, mange, yellow fat disease
skin, thickened, esp. around eyes and ears	mange, sunburn
skin, waxy debris at tail root	stud tail
skin, yellow crusting	mange
skin, yellow tinge (jaundice)	haemobartonellosis, liver disease
sleeping too much	anemia, obesity
sneezing	upper respiratory infection
sores, draining	abscess, cuterebra plague
sores, slow healing	cancer, ulcer
stiffness, of joints	arthritis, cancer
stiffness, rear limb paralysis/pain	cardiomyopathy, rabies
stiffness, walking	eclampsia, pain, peritonitis, yellow fat disease
swelling, of abdomen (no pain)	FIP, giardia, obesity, pregnancy, roundworms
swelling, of abdomen (painful)	constipation, hairballs, LUTD (blockage), peritonitis, pyometra, swallowed object

SIGNS AND SYMPTOMS	*DISEASE OR CONDITION*
swelling, of breast	cancer, mastitis
swelling, of ear flap	hematoma
swelling, of ear tips, nose, tail, or toes	frostbite
swelling, of face/head	abscess, insect bites/stings, tight collar, trauma
swelling, of lymph nodes	FIV, plague, toxoplasmosis
swelling, of skin	abscess, acne, cuterebra, fracture, insect bites/stings, plague
temperature, too cold	anemia, antifreeze poisoning, dehydration, hypothermia, kidney disease, shock
temperature, fever	abscess, eclampsia, feline panleukopenia, FIP, FIV, haemobartonellosis, hyperthermia, mastitis, peritonitis, plague, pneumonia
urination, blocked	LUTD
urination, excessive	chocolate poisoning, diabetes mellitus, hyperthyroidism, kidney disease, pyometra
urination, frequent/small amounts	cystitis, LUTD
urination, in odd places	cystitis, LUTD, stress
urination, straining	cancer, cystitis, LUTD
urination, with blood	cancer, cystitis, LUTD, poison
vaginal discharge	imminent birth, pyometra
vomiting	antifreeze poisoning, aspirin poisoning, changing diet, chocolate poisoning, enteritis, feeding milk, food allergy, feline panleukopenia, FIV, hairballs, heartworms, hyperthermia, hyperthyroidism, inflammatory bowel disease, liver disease, roundworms, swallowed object, overeating

SIGNS AND SYMPTOMS	DISEASE OR CONDITION
weakness	anemia, cardiomyopathy, haemobartonellosis, hyperthermia, kidney disease, shock
weight, unable to maintain	giardia, poor nutrition, tapeworms
weight gain	diabetes mellitus, obesity
weight loss	anemia, cancer, diabetes mellitus, diarrhea, FeLV, FIV, FIP, heartworms, hyperthyroidism, kidney disease, liver disease, malnutrition, stomatitis

Appendix C

Resources

ANIMAL WELFARE AND INFORMATION SOURCES

Alley Cat Allies
P.O. Box 397
Mount Rainier, MD 20712
(feral cats)

American Humane
Association
Animal Protection Division
63 Inverness Drive East
Englewood, CO 80112-5117
303-792-9900

American Society for the
Prevention of Cruelty to
Animals
424 East 92 Street
New York, NY 10128
212-876-7700

Cat Fancy Magazine
P.O. Box 6050
Mission Viejo, CA 92690

CATS Magazine
P.O. Box 1790
Peoria, IL 61656

Delta Society
P.O. Box 1080
Renton, WA 98057-9906
(human/animal interaction)
206-226-7357

Friends of Animals
777 Post Road, Suite 205
Darien, CT 06820
(low-cost neutering)
800-631-2212

I Love Cats Magazine
950 Third Avenue,
16th Floor
New York, NY 10022-2705

National Animal Control
Association
P.O. Box 480851
Kansas City, MO 64148-0851

National Animal Interest
Alliance
P.O. Box 66579
Portland, OR 97290-6579
503-761-1139

PetLife Magazine
1227 W. Magnolia Avenue
Fort Worth, TX 76104

Pets for Patient Progress
P.O. Box 143
Crystal Lake, IL 60039-9143
815-455-0990

Pets for People
314-982-3028

POWARS (Pet Owners with
AIDS/ARC Resource Service)
1674 Broadway, Suite 7A
New York, NY 10019
212-246-6307

Tree House Animal
Foundation
1212 West Carmen Avenue
Chicago, IL 60640-2999
312-784-5488

PET SERVICES

American Boarding Kennels
Association
4575 Galley Road,
Suite 400 A
Colorado Springs, CO 80915
719-591-1113

Animal Blood Bank
P.O. Box 1118
Dixon, CA 95620
800-243-5759

AVID
3179 Hamner Avenue
Norco, CA 91760
800-336-2843
(microchip identification)

Eastern Vet. Blood Bank
2138-B Generals Highway
Annapolis, MD 21401
800-949-3822

Hemopet (blood bank)
17672A Cowan Avenue,
Suite 300
Irvine, CA 92714
714-252-8455

HomeAgain Companion
Animal Retrieval System
1095 Morris Avenue
P.O. Box 3182
Union, NJ 07083-1982
(microchip identification)

IdentIchip
8776 E. Shea Boulevard,
Suite B3A-323
Scottsdale, AZ 85260
602-661-1748
(microchip identification)

InfoPet Information Systems
415 W. Travelers Terrace
Burnsville, MN 55337
800-463-6738
(microchip identification)

Pet Loss Support Hot Line
University of California at
Davis
916-752-4200

Pet Loss Support Hot Line
University of Florida at
Gainesville
904-392-4700, ext. 4080

Pet Sitters International
referrals
800-268-SITS

Tattoo-A-Pet
800-TATTOOS
Once enrolled in program,
this hotline is free

VETERINARY RESOURCES

American Animal Hospital
Association
P.O. Box 150899
Denver, CO 80215-0899
800-883-6305

American Association of
Feline Practitioners
Kristi Thomson, Exec.
Director
7007 Wyoming N.W.,
Suite E3
Albuquerque, NM 87109

American Holistic
Veterinary Association
2214 Old Emmorton Road
Bel Air, MD 21015

American Veterinary
Chiropractic Association
P.O. Box 249
Port Byron, IL 61275

American Veterinary
Medical Association
1931 N. Meacham Road,
Suite 100
Schaumburg, IL 60173-0805

American Veterinary Society
of Animal Behaviorists
Dr. Wayne Hunthausen,
President
4820 Rainbow Boulevard
Westwood, KS 66205
Westwood Animal Clinic
913-362-2512

Animal Behavior Society
John C. Wright, Ph.D., Chair
Board of Professional
Certification
Psychology Department
Mercer University
Macon, GA 31207

Association of American
Veterinary Medical Colleges
1101 Vermont Avenue N.W.,
Suite 710
Washington, DC 20005-3521

The International Veterinary
Acupuncture Society
Box 142, The Mail Station
1750-1 30th Street
Boulder, CO 80301

FELINE RESEARCH FOUNDATIONS

American Veterinary
Medical Association
1931 N. Meacham Road,
Suite 100
Schaumburg, IL 60173-0805

Morris Animal Foundation
45 Inverness Drive East
Englewood, CO 80112-5480

Winn Feline Foundation for
Cat Health
1805 Atlantic Avenue
P.O. Box 1005
Manasquan, NJ 08736-1005

Grateful thanks to the following breeders/owners who allowed their cats to be photographed during the Ozark Cat Fanciers 24th Annual Cat Show in Fort Worth, TX.

Abyssinian, "Wil-O-Glen's Exeter of Zapzkatz"
Owned by: Marsha Zapp Ammons

American Curl, "Celticurl's Sinead O'Curler"
Owned by: Karen O'Brien

American Shorthair, "Rushmore"
Owned by: Margaret Jordan

Balinese, "KLM's Purrchance to Dream"
Owned by: KLM Willison

Birman, "Birjanji Sundance Kid"
Owned by: Jan & Jim Rogers

Bombay, "Charlicats Joanne Thompson"
Owned by: Charlie & Mary Lynn Farmer

Burmese, "Kel-Lin Blazer Girl of Charlicats"
Owned by: Charlie & Mary Lynn Farmer

Colorpoint Shorthair, "CJKATZ Vienna of Colla Voce"
Owned by: R. & Cyndi Wagner/ H. Woodward

Cornish Rex, "Kelty's Saizen"
Owned by: Cynthia Rigoni/Deborah Helm

Devon Rex, "Loganderry's Truffles of Dilettante"
Owned by: Wendy Renner/Gerri Logan

Exotic Shorthair, "Lion House Jacklynn of Kizzmitt"
Owned by: S. Fraser/Larry Rhoades/ Debra Greak

Persian/Himalayan, "Jordan's Fancy"
Owned by: Jennifer Renshaw

Japanese Bobtail, "Wyndchymes Scottie"
Owned by: Karen Bishop/Lynn Search

Korat, "Skookumchuck's Silver Belle"
Owned by: Mary Rollans/ L.P. Hrynkiw

Maine Coon, "Noogats Fooey-Poucet"
Owned by: Suzanne & Tom Shambaugh

Manx, "Cottori Juliet"
Owned by: Paul & Becky Cotter

Norwegian Forest Cat, "Wegiekatt
Flekke of Fig"
Owned by: Nancy Eckert/Connie
Nodland

Ocicat, "Jadanevada Texass Trouble"
Owned by: Janet Comory-Park

Oriental Longhair, "Casadecano's
Prince of KLM"
Owned by: Pat Decano/KLM
Willison

Oriental Shorthair, "Skan Amethyst
of Felitan"
Owned by: Richard & Barbara Levitan

Russian Blue, "Tsar Blu's Ziggy
Tsardust"
Owned by: Donna J. Fuller

Scottish Fold, "Lirkanes Timmins"
Owned by: Bruce & Sue Thompson

Scottish Fold LH, "Hautechat's
Marmalade of Dustyroad"
Owned by: Jeff Janzen/Judy Zinn

Siamese, "Cyndicat's Krista Bleu"
Owned by: Cynthia & Larry Trevino

Somali, "Foxykats Msheeyish
Limoonee"
Owned by: Kathy D. Black

Tonkinese, "Kinukatz Angelica"
Owned by: Tom & Louisa Buford

Turkish Angora, "Calypso Cove
Sharif of CJKATZ"
Owned by: Rob & Cyndi Wagner

Index

ABOUT THE AUTHOR

AMY D. SHOJAI is a nationally known authority on pet care and behavior who began her career as a veterinary technician. She is the author of ten books about dogs and cats, and more than 250 articles and columns that have appeared in national magazines and on the Internet. She is also a spokesperson for Purina™ brand cat foods.

Ms. Shojai has written widely in the pet field on training, behavior, health care, and the human/companion animal bond. She is the founder and president of the International Cat Writers' Association and a member of the Dog Writers' Association of America, and has won numerous awards for her books and articles.

Ms. Shojai frequently speaks to groups on a variety of pet-related issues, and has often been interviewed on national radio and television in connection with her work. She lives with her husband, Mahmoud, at Rosemont, their thirteen-acre "spread" located in Sherman, Texas, which they share with assorted critters. She most recently adopted a three-month-old stray chocolate-point kitten, Serendipity, who has carefully reviewed and approved this manuscript.

A FREE GIFT FOR YOU AND YOUR CAT

Send for your valuable collection of coupons and special offers, compliments of the Purina® Cat Chow® brand cat food family of products.

Complete this certificate and send to:

Purina® Cat Care
P.O. Box 14129
Mascoutah, IL 62224-4129

MAIL-IN CERTIFICATE | **EXPIRATION DATE: 9/30/2000**

NAME_____

ADDRESS_____
(NO P.O. BOXES ACCEPTED)

CITY_____ STATE_____

ZIP (required)_____

How many cats do you own? _____

What brand do you normally buy? _____

Check here if you would NOT like to be added to our mailing list and would NOT be interested in receiving possible future promotional offers. _____

Good only in USA, APOs and FPOs. Void where prohibited, restricted. Allow 6–8 weeks for shipment. Limit one per individual or address. Group requests void. One request per envelope. Copies of certificate not acceptable. Sale, purchase, assignment or other transfer prohibited. Fraudulent submission could result in prosecution under Federal mail fraud statutes.

Offer expires 9/30/2000 or good while supplies last.

Printed in U.S.A.   006